# *Options*

## Trading Strategies
## That Work

# William F. Eng

**KOGAN PAGE**

Kogan Page Limited
120 Pentonville Road
London N1 9JN
England


Published in the United States by
Dearborn Financial Publishing, Inc.
520 North Dearborn St.
Chicago, IL 60610-4354
USA


First published in 1992

©1992 by William F. Eng

**British Library Cataloguing in Publication Data**

A CIP record for this book is available from the British Library.

ISBN 0-7494-0919-3


Printed in the United States of America

# Dedication

This is dedicated to my father, Frank.
I am forever indebted to him on his 70th birthday.

# TABLE OF CONTENTS

# PREFACE

I have often wondered why most traders who are successful in trading are so often failures at outside projects. We read about what happened to traders such as Joseph Cutten, a renowned speculator of the 1900s who also invested in outside ventures. And Jesse Livermore, the great "Cotton King," who made millions trading, lost millions investing in real estate and finally ended it all by shooting himself in the head.

More recently, we have read about lawsuits between Peter Steidlmayer and a former partner (as acrimonious a parting as we shall ever see). And even former trading wunderkind Richard Dennis has failed in real estate and other think tank ventures. Why do these traders have such difficulty relating to the world outside of trading?

The answer rests with the peculiar environment in which traders find themselves. Traders perceive the real world differently. In their own fantasy trading world, they are confronted with situations that constantly require decision-making skills.

Excellent traders have honed such skills to a very fine point. They can assess and size up a trading situation and decide whether they should go long, go short or stay out of the markets entirely. However, most traders are terrible at managing people. Yet these are the skills that are required for success in the real world.

As a trader, I have encountered similar "people" problems in the handling of my book projects. I knew that these projects had to be completed within a certain time frame, so I evaluated my pool of talented writers, collaborators and contributors. I thought that all I had to do was to guide the projects along, as I would a profitable position. Here, I was wrong—in the real world much more guidance is needed to complete any project.

When my first book, *The Technical Analysis of Stocks, Options and Futures: Advanced Trading Techniques,* was published to rave reviews, it was a memorable month—my first son was also born. That book represented an encapsulation of 20 years' experience. My son, on the other hand, represented a future. In that month, I found my life going backward and forward in the same moment of time.

My second book, *Trading Rules: Strategies for Success,* was published in 1990 and again received very favorable reviews by industry peers. As my son approached the second year of his life, I was confronted with the dilemma of trying to be a good father or a good writer. I chose to spend as much time as I could with my son. As a result, my third book, *Options: Trading Strategies That Work,* is more than two years late.

For those readers who have been waiting for this volume for the last several years, I wish to express my deepest thanks for your patience and apologies for the tardiness. For those who have never read any of my works, I welcome you to a world of useful information, successful trading strategies and my sincere efforts to educate.

This book is intended to give readers the guidance necessary to be successful in the real world of trading. Many of the strategies employed in this book, when used consistently over a long period of time, will result in considerably better-than-average gains.

I would like to thank the 13 contributors to this first of a three-volume set: Robert Bonwell, David L. Caplan, Gary Dufield, Ronald J. Frost, John Gfeller, Jerry Kopf, Jon Najarian, Jerry Putnam, Keith Schap, Dr. Van K. Tharp, Steve Toan, Jim Yates and finally, Leonard S. Yates.

# CONTRIBUTORS

**Robert Bonwell**

Robert Bonwell has worked for Prudential Securities in Charleston, West Virginia, since 1963, where he is now senior vice president of investments. Most of his business involves covered call option writing and hedging portfolios for primarily conservative clients. Bonwell is one of only 11 top-ranked brokers in the entire company who has been a member of the Chairman's Council every year since its inception 13 years ago. He has been selling options for 23 of his 25 years in the business, long before the listed option exchanges started.

In 1989, Bonwell finished second in the U.S. Investing and Trading Championship options division with a nearly 70 percent gain. In addition to providing exceptional returns, he has built his business by prospecting off the beaten path, especially smaller towns, and looking for ways to add service. With options trading, he says, it's best to keep one thought in mind: "Think of every account like you would your grandmother."

Bonwell is a 1958 graduate of Virginia Tech and served in the U.S. Air Force from 1958 to 1962. He is married and lives in Charleston; his daughter graduated from the University of Alabama and his son attends Marshall University in Huntington, West Virginia. He enjoys snow skiing and water sports and was West Virginia's state chess champion for two years.

**David L. Caplan**

David L. Caplan is an options trader, trading adviser, writer and broker who has specialized in options since 1982. His firm, Opportunities in Options Inc., is located in Malibu, California, and helps clients structure options strategies that reduce trading risks and increase profits through mathematical probability.

Caplan has published his monthly newsletter, *Opportunities in Options*, since 1984 and is the author of *The Professional Option Trader's Manual*. His latest book is entitled *Using Options to Obtain a Trading Edge Over the Markets*.

Caplan has written many articles on option strategies for business and investment publications such as *Futures, Barron's* and *Intermarket*. He has also appeared on national business television programs and is a frequent speaker at investment seminars and conferences.

### Gary Dufield

Gary Dufield became a commodity broker in Dallas, Texas, in 1976 and has pursued his career in Chicago since 1980. He has worked for several firms, including Gerstenberg and Weinberg Bros., Clayton, Stotler & Company, and London Investment Trust. He currently works with colleagues in their own introducing brokerage firm at the Chicago Mercantile Exchange.

Dufield's philosophy has always been to develop trading approaches for his clients that he would use for his own account. This includes being in the market in order to catch the big moves, holding a trend, keeping costs and commissions low and reducing losses with self-hedging systems—especially if they can make money on market backfilling and corrections.

Dufield majored in journalism at Southern Illinois University, after living around the United States and abroad in an Air Force family.

### Ronald J. Frost

For 19 years, Ronald J. Frost was a vice president of the Chicago Mercantile Exchange. The CME became known as the creative marketing exchange because of his many innovations. He was responsible for marketing many new futures and options contracts and for introducing the International Monetary Market and the Index and Options Market to the world.

Frost organized the exchange's public relations department. He later headed the education and marketing departments and coordinated the exchange's award-winning advertising programs. He developed the first seminar programs and was responsible for 150 seminars and speeches per year.

As a writer, Frost developed more than 30 brochures and a book titled *Trading Tactics*. In 1989, Probus Publishing released his book *Options on Futures: A Hands-On Workbook of Market-Proven Trading Strategies.*

Frost supervised the development of the first software program for marketing CME options and an extensive compilation of basis numbers for the livestock and lumber markets. He also developed a pocket computer for options, *The Options Maven*, which calculates implied volatilities, deltas, gammas, thetas and vegas.

Currently, Frost has his own firm, The Frost Marketing Group, Inc., and is registered as a commodity trading advisor. He consults with exchanges, brokers, brokerage firms and does sales training seminars and motivational speeches. Naturally, he trades futures and options.

### John Gfeller

John Gfeller is an options and futures strategist with a major Swiss bank in Geneva. He counsels institutional clients and acts as a broker agent with direct floor access on the IMM, CBOT, PHLX and LIFFE. Gfeller was an independent trader in California from 1984 to 1987, where he developed and implemented trading systems. He received his training as a stockbroker with Bache Canada beginning in 1982.

Gfeller has been a top-ten options category finalist eight times in the U.S. Investing and Trading Championships (results reported in *Barron's, Investor's Business Daily, Futures* and *Stocks & Commodities*).

Gfeller graduated from Reed College in Portland, Oregon, in 1980 with a degree in history and literature and is fluent in several languages.

Gfeller is single and lives in St. Sulpice, Switzerland.

### Jerry Kopf

Jerry Kopf has been a member of the Chicago Board Options Exchange since 1974, where he was a market maker in Boeing, Skyline, Monsanto, Burlington Northern and Citicorp from 1974 to 1979. Kopf currently leases his membership while running the firm of Benjamin and Jerold, a deep discount options and stock brokerage, with his partner Ben Stevens.

Kopf founded Blue Page Publishing in 1985 and publishes the bimonthly *OEX Blue Page*, a stock and index option newsletter that stresses strategies, tactics and execution finesse for options traders. He also updates two options hotlines and holds seminars for traders.

Originally from New York, Kopf graduated from the State University of New York at Buffalo. He lives with his wife and three sons north of Chicago.

# Jon Najarian

Jon Najarian received his bachelor's degree from Gustavus Adolphus College in St. Peter, Minnesota. After being a linebacker for the Chicago Bears, he began his trading career as an arbitrage clerk for the New York Stock Exchange specialist firm Haupt, Andrews, Freeman and Hug.

Najarian has worked as an independent market maker at the Chicago Board Options Exchange for nine years. In 1983, he became a partner in the Chicago options trading firm of LETCO. In 1989, he formed his own firm, Mercury Trading Ltd., a designated primary market maker firm at the CBOE and a Cincinnati Stock Exchange specialist. Frequently featured on CNBC/FNN's "The Option Report," Najarian analyzes the markets and fields questions from the public. He also gives options trading strategy seminars for CBOE to banks and brokerage institutions and works with these firms on training their representatives. An active member of the CBOE, Najarian serves on the marketing and floor officials committees and as instructor at the Options Institute, the exchange's educational arm.

# Jerry Putnam

Jerry Putnam and Steve Toan have 25 years' combined experience in the brokerage business. Both are currently employed by Prudential Securities in Chicago, where they manage corporate and individual accounts with $100,000 minimum equity.

Putnam is a senior vice president who services institutional and individual clients on both an advisory and discretionary basis. He has over ten years' experience in the options brokerage business. He was senior vice president with PaineWebber, vice president at Jeffries & Company and vice president at Walsh Greenwood. He is a graduate of the University of Pennsylvania.

# Keith Schap

Keith Schap is currently the senior editor for *Futures* magazine in Chicago, Illinois. In this capacity he is directly on the pulse of the leading-edge trading and portfolio management strategies.

Among his many responsibilities at the leading industry magazine, Mr. Schap is in charge of the following columns: Markets and Commercial Tactics, Chartviews and Trader Profiles. His articles focus on risk management, portfolio tactics and commercial strategies; he applies option knowledge to duration and convexity analyses, portfolio yield enhancements and synthetic asset allocations.

Schap comes to this project with impeccable outside writing credentials. He has both an MA and a PhD from Indiana University in English literature. He received his BA from North Central College, also in English. From 1969 to 1980, he taught English at Vassar College and Purdue University. From 1980 to 1988 he free-lanced articles on many different matters: artificial intelligence, biotechnology, chemical engineering, construction, factory process simulation, machine tool building, medical technology and robotics. He coauthored a book with Jeff McKinzie on bond basis trading in 1988.

### Van K. Tharp

Van Tharp is an internationally known research psychologist and efficiency expert who has helped thousands of traders and investors make money in the markets. For more than 20 years he has studied how stress affects human performance and is an expert in the Neurolinguistic Programming techniques of duplicating success. Tharp is the leading authority on developing peak performance in the financial industry.

Tharp developed his theories by working with some of the best traders in the world, and clients frequently double or triple their profits after consulting with him. He founded his company, Investment Psychology Consulting, in 1983.

Tharp has completed a five-volume, four-cassette course on the psychology of investing and has written numerous articles for the major financial publications. He also conducts seminars and workshops and appears on various media around the country.

Tharp received a PhD from the University of Oklahoma in 1975.

### Steve Toan

Steve Toan and Jerry Putnam have 25 years' combined experience in the brokerage business. Both are currently employed by Prudential Securities in Chicago, where they manage corporate and individual accounts with $100,000 minimum equity.

Toan is first vice president of investments. He has been in the brokerage business since 1975 and active in listed options since they were introduced at the Chicago Board Options Exchange. He is a former senior vice president of Bear Stearns, vice president of Jeffries & Company and vice president of Oppenheimer & Co. Toan is a graduate of Southern Illinois University at Carbondale, Illinois.

### Jim Yates

James W. Yates is president of DYR Associates, an investment research firm providing risk management data to the professional investment community. The DYR daily and weekly reports are read by more than 10,000 brokers at more than 30 firms. In addition, the Institutional Option Writers Index is used by a number of investment management firms as a gauge of option-writing performance.

Jim also helped develop and is a consultant to the CBOE Options Institute. In that capacity he has taught more than 4,000 investment professionals. Readers in the United States can see Jim discuss the options market as a regular guest on CNBC/FNN.

In 1987, Jim wrote *The Option Strategy Spectrum*. This book was based on the poster of the same name developed for the Options Institute. In addition, Jim is a contributor to *Options: Essential Concepts and Trading Strategies*, published by Business One–Irwin.

Jim, who is a native of Raleigh, North Carolina, is an alumnus of North Carolina State University. A veteran of 23 years in the securities business, he was a founding partner of The Options Group, an options consulting and research firm.

### Leonard S. Yates

Leonard S. Yates, an active options trader for many years, is the founder and president of OptionVue Systems International, Inc., of Vernon Hills, Illinois. Since 1983, the company has been developing investment software for professional money managers, traders and serious private investors, focusing entirely on options.

Yates has also studied corporate finance and financial models and has made important contributions in the field of options pricing models. The most notable is the "Yates Adjustment" to the popular Black-Scholes model as applied to American-style puts. By accounting for the possibility of early exercise, this model has the advantages of both speed and accuracy, which are mutually exclusive qualities in other models.

Yates worked for six years as a software engineer at IBM and for two years at Tandem Computers. He holds a degree in electrical engineering from Purdue University, where he graduated with top honors.

# CHAPTER 1

# The Gold in Options

*BY ROBERT BONWELL*

**Editor's Note:**

Robert Bonwell is a successful stockbroker in his own right. His approach, as illustrated in this chapter, is a happy medium of two apparently opposite goals: maximizing commissions and maximizing returns to clients.

It has always amazed me to see that most brokers will never stop and think that in order for them to get what they want, their clients must get what they want. The clients want returns on investments and safety of capital. The brokers want commission dollars.

Unlike most brokers, this author creates a happy medium. He applies a simple approach initially: covered writes of existing stocks in a client's portfolio. From this point, the author then will sell a particular stock only when his firm recommends liquidation; otherwise he maintains such a position and generates commission dollars on covered writes.

At times, when the conditions are right, he will sell the options premium when chances are good that they will never be exercised.

The approach is simple—no detailed thinking or strategy involved. The editor knows this strategy will work for two reasons: First, the person who executes this approach must be dedicated to the goal of cranking out the returns, day in and day out; and second, the spreading of such minimal risk over a large portfolio of underlying stocks should mitigate catastrophic market risk.

Here's a strategy that will increase the rate of return to client portfolios handsomely.

As this author is a broker with Prudential Securities, we have been requested to note for the reader that the strategy illustrated here is solely of the contributing author and does not represent Prudential Securities' investment approaches.

How many of you have walked down the sidewalk, seen a nickel, dime or quarter and failed to pick it up? Chances are that you have even reached down to pick up a penny; I know I have. How would you like to pick up $5, $10 or $20 each month on many stocks in your portfolio? You can do it quite easily.

I have read literally thousands of publications on how to make money in the stock market during the 25 years I have been in the investment business. The average investor finds it difficult to read these publications and apply the ideas since they are technically oriented. In this short chapter, I am going to show you one very simple area that can enhance the returns of your portfolio dramatically, with no additional risks. Since the world of options trading is arcane, I will limit my use of terms to only the simplest. Keep in mind that this is but one small step in an overall investment program.

## OPTION BUYERS ARE MOSTLY LOSERS

Most people, when they hear the word *option*, immediately think of speculation. This may be true in many instances, but there are also ways you can utilize options in your portfolio in an ultraconservative investment strategy.

Many different approaches can be taken in using options. You can use options to protect your portfolio on the downside. You can initiate certain option strategies to carry a profit from one year to the next. You can even initiate, quite legally, certain strategies to create losses in a particular taxable year. Other areas become even more complicated. There are bull spreads, bear spreads, butterfly spreads and strip and strap options, all of which entail the use of call and put options. Trying to cover all these strategies here would be impractical, so we will be studying one small but very lucrative part of the option strategy spectrum: covered writes.

Many people who have been exposed to options have lost a big percentage of their investment simply because they were buyers of options. Statistics show us that 85 percent of option buyers lose 100 percent of their investment. To put it bluntly, the options they purchased expired worthless. The 15 percent of the time that the options buyers made money does not mean that the options sellers lost money. It simply means that the sellers may have given up the additional gain on the security if they elected not to sell the options.

Let's give one brief example. You have a stock trading at $27 on which you elect to sell a two-month call option based on a price of $30. The premium that you receive for this option is $50. Sure enough, on option expiration date the stock is trading at a price of $32 and is called away from you at a price of $30. Obviously, the option buyer who paid $50 for the option has a profit on the transaction. However, the option seller *also* made an additional $3 on the capital appreciation of his or her shares. Therefore, it is important to remember that even when the options buyer does make money on a transaction, the option seller also makes additional money when the option is written out of the money.

## THEREFORE, SELLERS ARE BASIC WINNERS

The converse of the above is also true: 85 percent of all options sellers make money 100 percent of the time. The other 15 percent of the options buyers make the money; the other 15 percent of the options sellers lose the money.

Now I will show you how to substantially increase the yield on your stock portfolio with virtually no effort on your part, through the use of stock options in a simple strategy.

Let's determine how much more income from your portfolio you can obtain by implementing my strategy. Before this can be done, you first must look at the asset value of the common stocks in your portfolio. Next, look at the total income from that portfolio.

Chances are good that your portfolio has a composite yield in the area of 4 to 5 percent per year. If you have a $100,000 portfolio and are receiving $5,000 per year in dividends, all we have to do is take in an extra $400 per month (or $4,800 per year) to double your dividends to between $9,800 and $10,000. If the average price of stocks in your portfolio were $25 per share, you would have 4,000 shares of stock; if we could take each of those 4,000 shares and increase the return an additional $1.25 per share a year we would have an additional $416 per month ($1.25 × 4,000 = 5,000; $5,000 ÷ 12 months in a year = $416 per month).

Even if we only got an extra $6.25 per 100 shares of stock that you owned (instead of the $12.50 per 100 shares in the above example), this would still result in an extra $250 per month to you.

Keep in mind that in these examples I am talking about the smallest units of trading (call and put options that are traded on major exchanges deal in 100-share units of stock); there will be options written at higher prices, greater than $6.25 per 100 shares of stock. In fact, some will be

**Figure 1.1**   Disney Options Series for 4/10/90

| Option & NY Close | Strike Price | Calls–Last Apr | May | Jul | Puts–Last Apr | May | Jul |
|---|---|---|---|---|---|---|---|
| D W G | 10 | 7/8 | 1½ | r | 3/16 | r | r |
| 10⅝ | 12½ | 3/16 | 9/16 | 1⅛ | 1¾ | r | 2½ |
| 10⅝ | 15 | 1/16 | s | ½ | r | s | r |
| Dexter | 20 | r | 1⅝ | r | r | r | r |
| 21 | 22½ | 1/16 | r | ¾ | r | r | r |
| 21 | 25 | r | r | 5/16 | r | r | r |
| Dig Eq | 65 | r | s | r | 1/16 | s | r |
| 80 | 70 | 10½ | s | r | ⅛ | s | 1⅜ |
| 80 | 75 | 5½ | 6¾ | 8 | 9/16 | 1½ | 2⅝ |
| 80 | 80 | 2 | 3¾ | 6 | 2 | 3⅜ | 4½ |
| 80 | 85 | 9/16 | 1¾ | 3⅝ | 5¼ | 6 | r |
| 80 | 90 | 3/16 | ¾ | 2¼ | r | r | r |
| 80 | 95 | 1/16 | s | 1¼ | r | s | r |
| Disney | 100 | 14½ | s | r | ⅛ | s | r |
| 113¾ | 105 | r | r | 13⅛ | 3/16 | 1 | 2 |
| 113¾ | 110 | 4½ | 6⅞ | 10 | ⅝ | 2 | 3¼ |
| 113¾ | 115 | 1⅜ | 3⅜ | 6⅜ | 2⅜ | r | r |
| 113¾ | 120 | ¼ | 1⅝ | 4¼ | r | 6¾ | 8 |
| 113¾ | 125 | ⅛ | 13/16 | 2⅝ | r | 10¼ | 11½ |
| 113¾ | 130 | 1/16 | s | 1⅞ | r | s | r |
| 113¾ | 135 | r | s | 1 | r | s | r |
| du Pnt | 35 | r | 3¾ | 4⅜ | 1/16 | r | 11/16 |
| 38½ | 36⅝ | 2⅛ | s | r | r | s | 15/16 |
| 38½ | 38⅜ | ¾ | s | 2 1/16 | 9/16 | s | r |
| 38½ | 40 | ⅛ | ½ | 1¼ | 1⅝ | 2⅛ | 2½ |
| 38½ | 41⅝ | 1/16 | s | ¾ | r | s | 3¾ |
| 38½ | 43⅜ | 1/16 | s | 5/16 | r | s | r |
| FHLM | 60 | r · | s | r | r | s | 1½ |
| 66⅝ | 65 | 2½ | 3⅜ | r | ¾ | r | 3¼ |
| 66⅝ | 70 | ⅛ | 1½ | 3⅛ | 4 | r | r |
| 66⅝ | 75 | 1/16 | r | r | r | r | r |
| FleetN | 17½ | s | r | r | s | ⅝ | r |
| 19⅝ | 20 | ⅜ | 1 | 1½ | 9/16 | 1⅜ | 2 |

written at substantially higher prices. Here we will use only low-priced options.

The one small problem, however, concerns the professionals who can aid you in executing my strategy. As I will explain later, chances are that neither your current broker nor banker will show you how to make these simple transactions in your portfolio. To understand how to play the game, then, we certainly must know how to read the program.

## HOW TO READ THE WALT DISNEY OPTION STOCK OPTIONS TABLE

Figure 1.1 shows an exact replica of the Walt Disney option series as it appeared in *The Wall Street Journal* on April 10, 1990. Please note the format carefully, especially if you have not read these tables before. Walt Disney call and put options for 100 shares of stock with three expiration dates (April, May and July) and eight exercise prices (100, 105, 110, 115, 120, 125, 130 and 135) are shown.

Figure 1.2 explains each symbol in the table. The name of the stock is identified by the number 1. Number 2 identifies the strike price, the price at which we would sell stock. Number 3 identifies the exchange on which the options are traded. Number 4 shows the expiration months of the options (April options expire on April 20, 1990, May options expire on May 18, 1990, July options expire on July 20, 1990). Numbers 5 and 6 show call and put series, respectively. Number 7 shows the closing price of the underlying stock, in this case $113.75. The letter *r* shows that that particular option series did not trade this day. The letter *s* shows that no option is available for trading in this series.

Number 10 shows the option price. Recall that each option represents 100 shares of stock. A price of $1 for the option means the option costs $100 ($1 per stock times 100 shares, or $100). From the chart, we have the following information:

Disney Apr 120 calls at $1/4$ or $25.00
Disney Apr 125 calls at $1/8$ or $12.50
Disney May 125 calls at $13/16$ or $81.25
Disney Jul 130 calls at $1 7/8$ or $187.50
Disney Apr 105 puts at $3/16$ or $18.75
Disney Apr 110 puts at $5/8$ or $62.50
Disney May 110 puts at 2 or $200.00

I encourage you to pick out several stocks of your own and follow them on a daily basis so you can get used to reading the price changes on the different call option series. You will find it easy after reading the tables for several weeks. See the explanation of symbols for Chrysler quotations in Figure 1.3.

When you are looking in the newspaper to find the option prices on your securities, be careful. Remember that the options trade on different exchanges. Also remember that every option does not trade in the same series of months. Therefore, look carefully at the option headings, and do not confuse the puts with the calls.

## SQUEEZING ADDITIONAL RETURNS FROM THE PROGRAM

Many strategies are risky and will result in losses. But other strategies are considered very conservative, and from these I use one that is like dropping money into your account every month with very little effort. This strategy is to write (sell) call options against stocks in your portfolio.

We'll make this even more conservative by using only covered call options with a very short time to expiration. The calls we deal in must also be out of the money. In other words, we will find and sell options that have fewer chances of being exercised.

**Figure 1.2**  Explanation of Symbols

| | | Apr | May | Jul | Apr | May | Jul |
|---|---|---|---|---|---|---|---|
| Disney | 100 | $14^1/_2$ | s | r | $^1/_8$ | s | r |
| $113^3/_4$ | 105 | r | r | $13^1/_8$ | $^3/_{16}$ | 1 | 2 |
| $113^3/_4$ | 110 | $4^1/_2$ | $6^7/_8$ | 10 | $^5/_8$ | 2 | $3^1/_4$ |
| $113^3/_4$ | 115 | $1^3/_8$ | $3^3/_8$ | $6^3/_8$ | $2^3/_8$ | r | r |
| $113^3/_4$ | 120 | $^1/_4$ | $1^5/_8$ | $4^1/_4$ | r | $6^3/_4$ | 8 |
| $113^3/_4$ | 125 | $^1/_8$ | $^{13}/_{16}$ | $2^5/_8$ | r | $10^1/_4$ | $11^1/_2$ |
| $113^3/_4$ | 130 | $^1/_{16}$ | s | $1^7/_8$ | r | s | r |
| $113^3/_4$ | 135 | r | s | 1 | r | s | r |

The headers above are: AMERICAN / CALLS (Apr, May, Jul) and PUTS (Apr, May, Jul). Circled reference numbers 1–10 point to various parts of the figure.

1. Name of stock
2. Strike price, or price at which we would sell the stock
3. Exchange where option is traded
4. Month in which price is based
5. Call series
6. Put series
7. Closing price of the stock the prior day
8. Not traded (r)
9. No option available (s)
10. Option price 1 = $100 per 100 shares
    (all quotes are per 100 shares)

**EXAMPLES**

Disney Apr 120 call = $^1/_4$ or $25.00
Disney Apr 125 call = $^1/_8$ or $12.50
Disney May 125 call = $^{13}/_{16}$ or $81.25
Disney Jul 130 call = $1^7/_8$ or $187.50
Disney Apr 105 put = $^3/_{16}$ or $18.75
Disney Apr 110 put = $^5/_8$ or $62.50
Disney May 110 put = 2 or $200.00

Prices as of close on 4-9-90
April options expire 4-20-90
May options expire 5-18-90
July options expire 7-20-90

For an option to be trading at a low price, the following conditions must exist. First, the option probably has a very short time left before it expires. Since the buyer of the option would have little time for the option to become profitable, he or she is willing to pay only a small price

**Figure 1.3**  Explanation of Symbols for Chrysler

| | | Jan | Feb | Apr | Jan | Feb | Apr |
|---|---|---|---|---|---|---|---|
| | | CHICAGO BOARD | | | | | |
| | | CALLS | | | PUTS | | |
| Chryslr | 20 | $7^1/4$ | $7^1/2$ | $7^3/8$ | r | r | $^1/16$ |
| $27^1/8$ | $22^1/2$ | $4^5/8$ | $5^1/4$ | $5^1/8$ | r | r | $^3/16$ |
| $27^1/8$ | 25 | $2^1/8$ | $2^7/16$ | $3^1/8$ | r | $^1/4$ | $^3/4$ |
| $27^1/8$ | 30 | $^1/16$ | $^1/4$ | $13/16$ | r | r | $3^1/4$ |
| $27^1/8$ | 35 | r | s | $^1/8$ | r | s | r |

1. Name of stock
2. Strike price or price at which we would sell the stock
3. Exchange where option is traded
4. Month in which price is based
5. Call series
6. Put series
7. Closing price of the stock the prior day
8. Not traded (r)
9. No option available (s)
10. Option price $^1/8$ = $12.50 per 100 shares
    (all quotes are per 100 shares)

**EXAMPLES**

Chrysler Jan 30 call = $^1/16$ or $6.25
Chrysler Feb 30 call = $^1/4$ or $25.00
Chrysler Apr 30 call = $13/16$ or $81.25
Chrysler Feb 25 put = $^1/4$ or $25.00

Prices as of close on 1-12-89

for the option. Second, the stock price is far from the strike price of the option. Therefore, the out-of-the-money strike price option reflects lower price volatility.

**One Example of a Covered Write**

For example, if the price of the stock were $26 and a call option with a strike price of $30 was expiring in three weeks, the stock price must move up 15.86 percent (15.86% of $26 = $4.12; $4.12 + 26 = $30.125) within three weeks in order to cause the call option buyer to consider exercising the call.

Keep in mind that an option that is in the money by at least ¹/₈ of a point ($12.50) will most likely be exercised. Let's assume the buyer paid $1 for the option three weeks ago and now can recover only ¹/₈ if he or she were to sell it. Someone will usually exercise this option on the last day simply to recover ¹/₈ of a point. There is another situation where the call expires with the stock slightly below the strike price of the call. In this case, exercises of such options have occurred. In other words, the call price is $30 and the stock closes on option expiration date at $29⁷/₈ (or ¹/₈ of a point below the $30 strike); it is possible that this stock can be called from the seller of the call.

In most cases, an option this far away with only several weeks to go would have a very small market value. There is an outside chance, however, that the value could be higher due to takeover rumors or other events that might result in a rapid price appreciation of the stock. Do not sell the option if you think your security has a chance of reaching an option price within the time period remaining on the option and you do not want to sell your stock.

*The whole idea is to sell your securities eventually at a price at which you would have sold them without an option writing program in place.*

## A Second Example of a Covered Write

Here is another example. Let's assume a stock is trading at $26 and you give your broker or banker an order to sell your stock at $28. Wouldn't it be a good idea to sell options based on a price of $30 as long as someone were willing to pay you money for these options? With the stock currently priced at $26 your limit order to sell at $28 or $28¹/₂ probably would not be executed in two or three weeks. Therefore, the logic of selling an option based on a price of $30, which can currently be executed, would have to be overwhelmingly in your favor.

If you are happy to sell a stock at a specified limit that is above its current price, you should be ecstatic about selling a short-term option with a higher strike price than your limit order. In this particular example, you planned to sell the stock at a limit of $28 when the stock was at $26. With four weeks to go before expiration in the options series, you decide to sell call options with a $30 strike on 1,000 shares of stocks that you own. The market price of the calls is ¹/₈ of a point. At ¹/₈, which is $12.50 per option (100 shares per option times $0.125 cents per share), or, in this case, ten times that, since you are selling 10 options of 100 shares each (that's 1,000 shares), you will receive $125 for your call option sales. Chances are good that you would not have sold your stock within four weeks at your higher limit price; if you had done so, you would have picked up $2 capital gains per share. So by electing to sell the option you have brought $125 into your account.

With a week to go before expiration of your option, good news comes out on your stock. It trades up to a price of $29, which is higher than your original targeted sales price. At this point, you could sell your stock and buy back your option. With only a week to go, chances are that you could still repurchase your option at $1/8$ of a point.

If the news was such that there was a chance the stock could move *substantially* higher within the week to expiration, the option could be trading a bit higher. However, the important point to remember is that once you sold the $30 call option, current market conditions changed, "forcing" you to sell your stock at a price higher than your original target. This was done at no additional risk to your portfolio. It is not absolutely necessary to repurchase the option after having sold out the stock; however, this would result in your position being uncovered, which is a very dangerous strategy.

An uncovered option means you have sold an option without having an underlying long position in the stock. This is, by far, the most dangerous type of strategy and should never be used by income-oriented or conservative accounts. If you decided to have your security sold at your price of $29, but not to cover or buy back your option, you are assuming the risk of having it called in the last week before expiration.

This is what can possibly happen with an uncovered call position created by lifting one side of the covered write strategy. The next day or at any time before the expiration of your call option, you are horrified to see that a takeover offer for your stock has been announced at a price of $42. You are glued to the telephone with your broker or banker waiting for your stock to open. It finally opens at a price of $39. Now when the stock is called away from you within the next week, you are obligated to go out and buy the stock at the current market price (remember that you have already sold the stock out at $29), which may be $39 or even higher, and deliver the stock at $30, because you owe someone stock at $30 from the uncovered call position. This amounts to a nice loss of nine to ten points per share, or $9,000 to $10,000 on 1,000 shares. This happened because the option was not bought back when the stock was sold at $29.

While the above is an extreme case, this is the kind of risk you would assume if you did not repurchase your option. Remember that you would not have written the option in the first place if you thought there was going to be a takeover of your stock. Also, and most importantly, you decided to sell the stock at $28 after deciding that there was not going to be a takeover. Again, and I cannot emphasize this point enough, you should be very careful in selling an option on a security when the news justifies the possibility of a dramatic upward movement in the price of the stock. The odds of this happening are remote but possible. If you decide to sell your stock before the option expiration, you must buy back your option at the same time to close out the covered write strategy. If you have sold a $30 option at a $1/8$ or $3/16$ when the stock was at $26 and the stock is now trading at $28$3/4$ with one week to go before expiration, chances are very good the option has now dropped to a price of zero to $1/16$. Therefore, in both cases we should have a profit: a profit on the capital gain from the upward stock movement from $26 to $28$3/4$, and a profit on the deterioration of the call premium from $1/8$ or $3/16$ to $1/16$.

## A Third Example of a Covered Write

Suppose you own a security that is trading at $25, and the highest price for the stock during the year has been $28$1/2$. There is a call option on your security that expires in the next four weeks and is trading at $1/16$ or $1/8$. In fact, if it is a low beta stock (a stock with low price movements), the option is probably offered at $1/16$, with no bid. Remember that $1/16$ in options jargon means $1/16$ of $100 per option. In other words, for each 100 shares the maximum you could hope to obtain in this case would be $6.25 or, if you had 1,000 shares, $62.50 gross. Since the stock had been as high as $28$1/2$, there is a good chance that when it was in this price top a large number of call options could have been sold (written) with a $30 strike price.

In fact, there might well be a large open interest in this particular option series, which would reflect interest for this stock at around the $30 level. If you have a diversified portfolio and a number of your stocks were substantially below available option strike prices, the chances would be high that large numbers of options were traded and are still outstanding (the open interest) from transactions that took place at the higher prices. Your broker, from the quotes in the financial pages of the newspapers, can tell you the open interest for the particular option series in question. The larger the open interest, the better your chance of selling the option.

Why in the world is someone going to pay $1/16$ or $1/8$ to buy your options and give you this additional $62.50 or $125 on 1,000 shares of stock?

There are two possibilities. The first is that someone has sold this option in the past for maybe $1 or $3/4$ and has since seen the stock decline to $25; or perhaps this person sold a six-month option when the stock was at $25 and got $1/2$, $5/8$ or more. In any case, the person decides to sell the stock before the option expires. He or she also does not want to assume the risk of leaving the option uncovered (see previous section on the hazards of uncovered call options). It is always possible that some extraordinary news could come through on this security and force the price to skyrocket through the $30 area. In any case, the seller of the stock does not wish to assume this risk and decides that the repurchase of this option at a lower price is a great bargain. Therefore, he or she must go in and buy the option at $1/16$ or $1/8$.

The second type of potential buyer who will give you $62.50 per 1,000 shares is created by laws. In certain situations, some people are actually forced to go in and repurchase their option once they sell their stock from a covered write strategy. Certain types of fiduciary accounts are legally prohibited from selling an uncovered option. Again, an uncovered option is one that is sold without owning the underlying stock. Let's say that a bank trust department decides to sell 1,000 shares of ABC stock and had written options five or six months ago. Since they are not allowed to have an uncovered option, they must go into the open market and repurchase the option at the going price, which again would be $1/16$ or $1/8$.

## WHAT DOES THIS COVERED WRITE STRATEGY MEAN TO YOU?

Here we have the chance to get some of those 5-dollar, 10-dollar and 20-dollar bills that are just lying on the ground. You may think that there is nothing exciting about $1/8$ of a point on 100 shares of stock, but let's make a few calculations. An extra $1/8$ point on a share of stock per month is $150 per year on 100 shares. An extra $1.50 per year on a $25 stock, or an extra $150 return on $2,500, or 100 shares, is an additional 6 percent return per year.

All of a sudden, instead of getting a yield of 5 percent from the original dividend return on the outright stock hold, you are getting a composite yield of at least 11 percent. Once again, remember that we are only selling a call option on a stock at a price at which we would be willing to sell the stock, all within a certain period of time. Therefore, if the stock is trading at $17, you sell a call option with a strike price of $20, and if the stock is called, your return for that month is more than 15 percent. You pick up $3 on the stock appreciation, which is the difference of the call-away price of $20 and the price of your stock at $17, and whatever you received when you sold the option. One wonders if anyone reading this would not be happy with a 15 percent monthly return on any stock they owned; a lower return of 5 to 10 percent wouldn't be bad either.

## FINDING THE RIGHT PERSONNEL TO EXECUTE THIS STRATEGY

It is easy to see that if you have 20 stocks, you may decide to enter limit orders on 16 or 17 of those stocks. The three or four remaining ones that you may elect not to sell outright are the ones that are trading very close to the original purchase price, have a potential tax problem or have takeover possibilities.

Let's suppose we decide to enter limit orders on 17 of your securities in a market that is trending downward. As luck would have it, we are only able to execute several sales of call options at our limits. Within the next four or five days, our broker or banker lowers the limits of the call options. We are talking about the potential for 30 different orders (cancellation of 15 old orders and replacement with 15 new orders) in a very short period of time. Obviously, the broker or banker is spending quite a bit of time writing these low-priced options in order to squeeze that extra $400 to $500 from your portfolio each month.

Most of these small transactions will be processed at a loss by your broker or banker. Be aware that the cost of commissions as a percentage of profits will seem high because of the expense of processing low-priced options. Executions done through your banker will probably be a bit more expensive than through a discount broker, or even in some cases through a full-service broker, since most bankers will receive a percentage of each commission or charge you a service fee.

In addition, most people are unaware that full-service brokerage firms have substantially lower commissions on small transactions than discount firms. This is probably the only area in commission costs where the full-service broker is lower than the discount broker; discount firms have relatively high minimum transaction fees on the smallest trades, not wanting small, unprofitable trades to execute. A full-service broker, on the other hand, processes losing transactions with the expectation that future profitable transactions will make up for the losers; they feel an obligation to perform this service for the client.

Also, the full-service broker is compensated by the firm at the lowest possible rate. Since covered write strategies require constant monitoring, the services of a full-service broker willing to implement such a program are a relative bargain.

Once you start selling the options in your portfolio through your broker or banker, you will find that your discussions get shorter regarding which options to sell. As you become more familiar and more comfortable with this strategy, it will become quite easy for you to run through 25 or 30 stocks in just two or three minutes. Some of you will find your broker or banker reluctant to enter into this type of options writing program where so much additional time will be required. The solution to this is quite simple—you find a broker who will execute such orders.

Bankers, however, have one additional step to perform in executing options for clients: They are required to deliver an option escrow letter for each option sold. Most people are surprised to learn that the portfolios they hold in a bank trust department can also use covered call writing techniques unless this is expressly forbidden for a particular trust. I have never seen a trust that specifically forbade the use of covered call options on listed option exchanges. Again, the bottom line is whether or not it is in the client's best interest.

### Actual Examples of the Covered Write Strategy

Now let's give some actual examples of short-term options that have been sold. You will note on the chart in Figure 1.4 a number of transactions that were executed during March 1990. Out of the many options that were written during this month, some of the shorter-term, smaller-priced options have been isolated for this chapter. Again, keep in mind that the low-priced option strategy is but one part of an overall investment program.

I have broken down the chart so that you can see not only gross proceeds, but the closing price of the stock on the date the option was sold. Also noted are the number of trade days to expiration of the option, the percentage move required to reach the strike price and several actual confirmations of the noted trades in the chart. See Figure 1.5 for random examples of actual trades executed.

Remember, the whole idea is to sell options at the point where you are completely comfortable that the option will not be called. If you have a stock trading at $29 and there are rumors going around about a potential takeover, you are not going to write an option at $30 if you don't want to lose the stock through an exercise. In this particular case, you may elect to wait until the stock moves through the price of $30 and the options exchange adds a new option series of $35. Then you may start all over again with your strategy based on selling the option at a price of $35.

It is very simple. There should be a point in your mind each month at which you would feel comfortable entering an order to sell the call option, even if it is for only $1/16$. You might even consider your active stock trading at $29 as a call option selling candidate if you only had two or three days to go before expiration of the option. This strategy is good with low-priced options and results in little risk of losing your stock. If you do lose your stock, it could only be for one reason: a substantial move in a very short period of time. The sale of higher-priced options involves other strategies.

## AN ISSUE OF TIMING THE EXECUTION OF THE STRATEGY

When is the best time to enter options orders? I like to go through each stock in my accounts during the first week of trading of a new options series. How the market is trending will determine the prices at which I suggest the options be written. For example, if the market is trending on the downside and you are writing short-term options, you are usually better off writing the option as soon as possible. Remember we are only talking about a four-week or five-week period of time. If a stock is trading at $27, the premium of the $30 call will disappear quite rapidly.

Let's take a stock trading at $27, where the call option is bid $3/16$, ask $1/4$. In a market trending to the downside, I will usually enter at the ask price for a few days. If the order is not executed, then I will lower the limit figure. If the market is trending upward and the last price on Friday's expiration is $3/16$ or $1/4$, I will usually enter an order at a limit price that is $1/16$ or $1/8$ higher and change to the lower price within a week if not executed. Note that none of these orders is classified as discretionary, since I have talked about a price with a limit to be changed within a specified period of time. This eliminates the need for additional conversations with busy clients.

As you start reading the options tables, especially if you have a large portfolio, it will not be long before you will be writing options that have more time to expiration. Let's take a stock that is trading at $26, where your target is $28 1/2$, and you have been writing the options with a $30 strike price with less than four weeks of life left. The stock suddenly moves to $28, the option expires, and the two-month option is trading for $1, or $100 for 100 shares of stock. You may elect to forgo selling the stock at 28 1/2 and bring in $1,000 on your 1,000 shares for a two-month period of time. Obviously you do not have to sell only the lowest-priced options, but this is the specific area being covered in this chapter.

## KEEPING THE LONG-TERM GOAL IN SIGHT

Over the years, I have made it a point to find out what total return would satisfy my clients. By total return I am talking about appreciation and income. I have found that very few people will give a percentage much higher than the current certificate of deposit rates. You might mentally think to yourself right now, "What percentage would I be completely satisfied with on my portfolio?" Let's say your answer is 14 percent. Let's assume you have a security selling at $16 and there is a call option with a strike price $17 1/2$. We arrive at a strategy to sell this option each month at $1/8$, receiving an extra 9 percent on your security. If the stock is yielding 5 percent based on the dividend payout, you are getting a composite return of 14 percent on your money by selling an option at $1/8$. If you can condition yourself to making an additional 9 percent through this strategy, you certainly have an attractive situation going, even if the stock never moves.

**Figure 1.4**   Examples of Short-Term Options

## January Option Series

| Trade Date | Option Description | Trade Price | Net Proceeds | Comm. | Closing Stock Price | Trade Days to Expiration | % Move Required to Strike Price |
|---|---|---|---|---|---|---|---|
| 1-04 | Sell 50 calls GE Jan 50 | $1/16$ | 292.04 | 18.84 | $44^{3}/_{4}$ | 12 | 11.73% |
| 1-04 | Sell 8 calls BLS Jan 45 | $1/16$ | 44.82 | 3.57 | $39^{3}/_{8}$ | 12 | 14.29% |
| 1-04 | Sell 3 calls F Jan 55 | $1/8$ | 31.31 | 4.58 | $51^{1}/_{8}$ | 12 | 7.58% |
| 1-04 | Sell 2 calls GS Jan 40 | $1/8$ | 19.89 | 3.50 | $34^{1}/_{2}$ | 12 | 15.94% |
| 1-04 | Sell 30 calls FEXC Jan $17^{1}/_{2}$ | $1/16$ | 174.23 | 11.66 | $13^{1}/_{2}$ | 12 | 29.63% |
| 1-04 | Sell 100 calls LOW Jan $22^{1}/_{2}$ | $1/8$ | 1,099.00 | 149.35 | $21^{1}/_{4}$ | 12 | 5.88% |
| 1-05 | Sell 6 calls PEP Jan 45 | $1/16$ | 28.17 | 7.72 | $39^{3}/_{4}$ | 11 | 13.21% |
| 1-05 | Sell 20 calls WEN Jan $7^{1}/_{2}$ | $1/16$ | 107.33 | 16.06 | 6 | 11 | 25.00% |
| 1-06 | Sell 16 calls GNN Jan 45 | $1/8$ | 173.67 | 24.72 | $40^{1}/_{4}$ | 10 | 11.80% |
| 1-06 | Sell 50 calls PEP Jan 45 | $1/16$ | 258.13 | 52.75 | $39^{1}/_{2}$ | 10 | 13.92% |
| 1-06 | Sell 50 calls MOB Jan 50 | $1/16$ | 273.20 | 37.68 | 46 | 10 | 8.70% |
| 1-10 | Sell 10 calls GS Jan 40 | $1/16$ | 59.14 | 1.75 | 34 | 8 | 17.65% |
| 1-11 | Sell 3 calls PEP Jan 45 | $1/16$ | 12.81 | 4.33 | $39^{3}/_{8}$ | 7 | 14.29% |
| 1-12 | Sell 48 calls GP Jan 40 | $1/16$ | 262.15 | 36.24 | $37^{1}/_{4}$ | 6 | 7.38% |
| 1-12 | Sell 20 calls LOW Jan $22^{1}/_{2}$ | $1/16$ | 99.30 | 24.09 | $20^{7}/_{8}$ | 6 | 7.78% |
| 1-13 | Sell 5 calls OXY Jan 30 | $1/16$ | 28.70 | .94 | $26^{1}/_{4}$ | 5 | 14.29% |
| 1-13 | Sell 25 calls GRA Jan 30 | $1/8$ | 274.50 | 36.38 | 28 | 5 | 7.14% |
| 1-17 | Sell 10 calls X Jan 35 | $1/16$ | 56.52 | 4.37 | $32^{1}/_{4}$ | 3 | 8.53% |
| 1-19 | Sell 2 calls JNJ Jan 90 | $1/16$ | 7.46 | 3.43 | 86 | 1 | 4.65% |

**Figure 1.4**  (Continued)

## February Option Series

| Trade Date | Option Description | Trade Price | Net Proceeds | Comm. | Closing Stock Price | Trade Days to Expiration | % Move Required to Strike Price |
|---|---|---|---|---|---|---|---|
| 1-20 | Sell 18 calls MYL Feb 10 | $1/8$ | 186.32 | 37.07 | $8^3/4$ | 20 | 14.28 |
| 1-23 | Sell 6 calls OXY Feb 30 | $3/16$ | 100.80 | 10.09 | $27^3/8$ | 19 | 9.59 |
| 1-23 | Sell 4 calls EK Feb 50 | $1/4$ | 81.00 | 17.39 | $46^1/8$ | 19 | 8.40 |
| 1-24 | Sell 25 calls G Feb 35 | $1/8$ | 274.50 | 36.38 | $30^3/8$ | 18 | 15.23 |
| 1-25 | Sell 12 calls BA Feb 65 | $1/4$ | 257.62 | 40.77 | $61^1/8$ | 17 | 6.34 |
| 1-25 | Sell 7 calls AMI Feb $17^1/2$ | $1/4$ | 146.80 | 26.59 | 17 | 17 | 2.94 |
| 1-25 | Sell 23 calls T Feb 35 | $1/16$ | 123.88 | 18.26 | $30^7/8$ | 17 | 13.26 |
| 1-25 | Sell 5 calls G Feb 35 | $1/8$ | 51.47 | 9.42 | 30 | 17 | 16.67 |
| 1-26 | Sell 5 calls GE Feb 50 | $1/8$ | 57.52 | 3.37 | $46^7/8$ | 16 | 6.67 |
| 1-26 | Sell 10 calls UPJ Feb 35 | $1/16$ | 59.14 | 1.75 | $29^7/8$ | 16 | 17.15 |
| 1-26 | Sell 5 calls NYN Feb 70 | $1/4$ | 108.32 | 15.07 | $68^3/4$ | 16 | 1.82 |
| 1-26 | Sell 12 calls T Feb 35 | $1/16$ | 63.18 | 10.21 | $30^7/8$ | 16 | 13.36 |
| 1-27 | Sell 50 calls GE Feb 50 | $1/4$ | 1,150.40 | 97.95 | $47^3/8$ | 15 | 5.54 |
| 1-27 | Sell 64 calls MOB Feb 50 | $3/16$ | 1,094.35 | 104.01 | $48^5/8$ | 15 | 2.83 |
| 1-27 | Sell 4 calls SBC Feb 45 | $1/4$ | 85.58 | 12.81 | $43^1/2$ | 15 | 3.45 |
| 2-01 | Sell 10 calls GS Feb 40 | $1/8$ | 117.33 | 6.06 | $35^5/8$ | 12 | 12.28 |
| 2-01 | Sell 50 calls NSM Feb 10 | $1/16$ | 292.04 | 18.84 | $8^5/8$ | 12 | 15.94 |
| 2-01 | Sell 8 calls NSM Feb 10 | $1/16$ | 38.41 | 9.98 | $8^5/8$ | 12 | 15.94 |
| 2-01 | Sell 5 calls NSM Feb 10 | $1/16$ | 28.70 | .94 | $8^5/8$ | 12 | 15.94 |
| 2-01 | Sell 5 calls OXY Feb 30 | $1/16$ | 24.93 | 4.71 | $27^1/2$ | 12 | 9.09 |

**Figure 1.4**   (Continued)

## February Option Series Continued

| Trade Date | Option Description | Trade Price | Net Proceeds | Comm. | Closing Stock Price | Trade Days to Expiration | % Move Required to Strike Price |
|---|---|---|---|---|---|---|---|
| 2-01 | Sell 8 calls FEXC Feb 15 | $1/4$ | 174.97 | 23.42 | $13^{1}/_{2}$ | 12 | 11.11 |
| 2-02 | Sell 10 calls FEXC Feb $17^{1}/_{2}$ | $1/8$ | 100.38 | 23.01 | $13^{5}/_{8}$ | 11 | 28.44 |
| 2-02 | Sell 11 calls FEXC Feb $17^{1}/_{2}$ | $1/8$ | 111.12 | 24.77 | $13^{5}/_{8}$ | 11 | 28.44 |
| 2-03 | Sell 15 calls G Feb 35 | $1/16$ | 89.66 | 2.48 | 31 | 10 | 12.90 |
| 2-03 | Sell 10 calls WEN Feb $7^{1}/_{2}$ | $1/16$ | 59.14 | 1.75 | $5^{7}/_{8}$ | 10 | 27.66 |
| 2-03 | Sell 50 calls G Feb 35 | $1/16$ | 292.04 | 18.84 | 31 | 10 | 12.90 |
| 2-03 | Sell 10 calls AXP Feb 35 | $1/16$ | 56.52 | 4.37 | $30^{1}/_{2}$ | 10 | 14.75 |
| 2-03 | Sell 10 calls BAC Feb $22^{1}/_{2}$ | $3/16$ | 156.49 | 29.40 | $20^{7}/_{8}$ | 10 | 7.78 |
| 2-06 | Sell 5 calls WY Feb 30 | $3/16$ | 79.02 | 13.12 | $27^{3}/_{8}$ | 9 | 9.59 |
| 2-06 | Sell 19 calls GNN Feb 45 | $3/16$ | 306.10 | 48.53 | $42^{7}/_{8}$ | 9 | 4.96 |
| 2-06 | Sell 14 calls KO Feb 50 | $3/16$ | 232.97 | 27.92 | $47^{1}/_{2}$ | 9 | 5.26 |
| 2-07 | Sell 5 calls BUD Feb 35 | $1/4$ | 118.01 | 5.38 | $34^{1}/_{2}$ | 8 | 1.45 |
| 2-09 | Sell 46 calls BMY Feb 50 | $1/8$ | 510.60 | 62.78 | $46^{5}/_{8}$ | 6 | 7.24 |
| 2-14 | Sell 4 calls PAC Feb 35 | $1/16$ | 22.61 | .78 | $33^{3}/_{4}$ | 3 | 3.70 |
| 2-14 | Sell 7 calls GRA Feb 30 | $1/16$ | 40.87 | 1.27 | $28^{1}/_{4}$ | 3 | 6.19 |
| 2-16 | Sell 20 calls WEN Feb $7^{1}/_{2}$ | $1/16$ | 120.18 | 3.21 | $6^{1}/_{2}$ | 1 | 15.38 |

**Figure 1.4**   (Continued)

## March and April Option Series

| Trade Date | Option Description | Trade Price | Net Proceeds | Closing Stock Price | Trade Days to Expiration | % Move Required to Strike Price |
|---|---|---|---|---|---|---|
| 3-01 | Sell 6 calls ACY Apr 55 | 75.00 | 390.10 | $50^{7}/_{8}$ | 36 | 8.11% |
| 3-01 | Sell 18 calls OXY Mar 30 | 6.25 | 107.97 | $28^{3}/_{8}$ | 11 | 5.73% |
| 3-01 | Sell 8 calls OXY Apr 30 | 31.25 | 213.36 | $28^{3}/_{8}$ | 36 | 5.73% |
| 3-01 | Sell 10 calls UK Apr 30 | 25.00 | 212.60 | $22^{1}/_{4}$ | 36 | 34.83% |
| 3-01 | Sell 4 calls UPJ Mar 40 | 25.00 | 96.56 | 36 | 11 | 11.11% |
| 3-02 | Sell 6 calls TX Apr 65 | 25.00 | 124.87 | $58^{7}/_{8}$ | 35 | 10.40% |
| 3-02 | Sell 18 calls C Mar 20 | 6.25 | 107.97 | $17^{1}/_{4}$ | 10 | 15.94% |
| 3-02 | Sell 40 calls FEXC Mar 5 | 6.25 | 190.46 | $3^{1}/_{8}$ | 10 | 60.00% |
| 3-05 | Sell 25 calls C Apr 20 | 18.75 | 405.85 | $17^{1}/_{2}$ | 34 | 14.29% |
| 3-06 | Sell 5 calls TX Apr 65 | 25.00 | 102.94 | 60 | 33 | 8.33% |
| 3-06 | Sell 5 calls TX Mar 65 | 6.25 | 28.70 | 60 | 8 | 8.33% |
| 3-06 | Sell 2 calls OXY Mar 30 | 6.25 | 10.43 | $28^{1}/_{8}$ | 8 | 6.67% |
| 3-06 | Sell 10 calls KR Apr 15 | 18.75 | 178.15 | 13 | 33 | 15.38% |
| 3-06 | Sell 10 calls CDA Mar 20 | 6.25 | 59.14 | 18 | 8 | 11.11% |
| 3-07 | Sell 8 calls MYG Mar 20 | 6.25 | 46.96 | $17^{3}/_{8}$ | 7 | 15.11% |
| 3-07 | Sell 30 calls EK Mar 45 | 6.25 | 181.23 | $39^{7}/_{8}$ | 7 | 12.85% |
| 3-07 | Sell 15 calls RBK Apr 20 | 37.50 | 496.17 | $18^{3}/_{4}$ | 32 | 6.67% |
| 3-07 | Sell 10 calls AL Mar $22^{1}/_{2}$ | 6.25 | 59.14 | 21 | 7 | 7.14% |
| 3-08 | Sell 3 calls ACY Mar 55 | 18.75 | 51.61 | $53^{3}/_{8}$ | 6 | 3.04% |
| 3-08 | Sell 2 calls MER Apr 25 | 25.00 | 47.21 | $22^{3}/_{8}$ | 31 | 11.73% |
| 3-08 | Sell 17 calls MYG Mar 20 | 6.25 | 101.87 | $17^{7}/_{8}$ | 6 | 11.89% |

**Figure 1.4**  (Continued)    March and April Option Series Continued

| 3-09 | Sell 4 calls GM Apr 50 | 37.50 | 131.01 | $46\frac{1}{4}$ | 30 | 8.11% |
|---|---|---|---|---|---|---|
| 3-12 | Sell 5 calls GT Mar 40 | 6.25 | 28.70 | $36\frac{3}{8}$ | 4 | 9.97% |
| 3-12 | Sell 3 calls X Apr 40 | 25.00 | 69.62 | $35\frac{3}{4}$ | 29 | 11.89% |
| 3-12 | Sell 100 calls JNJ Apr 60 | 37.50 | 3,489.68 | $55\frac{3}{8}$ | 29 | 8.35% |
| 3-13 | Sell 3 calls GM Mar 50 | 6.25 | 16.52 | $47\frac{1}{8}$ | 3 | 6.10% |
| 3-14 | Sell 3 calls CHV Mar 75 | 6.25 | 16.52 | 69 | 2 | 8.70% |
| 3-14 | Sell 2 calls AL Mar $22\frac{1}{2}$ | 6.25 | 9.75 | $21\frac{1}{2}$ | 2 | 4.65% |
| 3-15 | Sell 6 calls EK Apr 45 | 12.50 | 69.49 | $38\frac{1}{8}$ | 26 | 18.03% |
| 3-16 | Sell 2 calls IP Apr 55 | 56.25 | 104.90 | 52 | 25 | 5.77% |
| 3-19 | Sell 4 calls UK Apr 30 | 6.25 | 22.61 | $22\frac{3}{8}$ | 24 | 34.08% |
| 3-21 | Sell 12 calls GM Apr 50 | 50.00 | 529.10 | $46\frac{7}{8}$ | 22 | 6.67% |
| 3-21 | Sell 5 calls XON Apr 50 | 18.75 | 83.39 | $46\frac{1}{4}$ | 22 | 8.11% |
| 3-21 | Sell 6 calls S Apr 45 | 12.50 | 65.58 | $39\frac{7}{8}$ | 22 | 12.85% |
| 3-21 | Sell 3 calls MYG Apr $22\frac{1}{2}$ | 6.25 | 16.52 | 17 | 22 | 32.35% |
| 3-21 | Sell 3 calls UK Apr 30 | 6.25 | 16.52 | $22\frac{3}{8}$ | 22 | 34.08% |
| 3-21 | Sell 55 calls BUD Apr 40 | 12.50 | 585.30 | $36\frac{5}{8}$ | 22 | 9.22% |
| 3-21 | Sell 4 calls X Apr 40 | 12.50 | 47.26 | $35\frac{5}{8}$ | 22 | 12.28% |
| 3-22 | Sell 3 calls EK Apr 45 | 18.75 | 43.14 | $38\frac{1}{2}$ | 21 | 16.88% |
| 3-22 | Sell 1 call IBM Apr 115 | 25.00 | 22.48 | $106\frac{1}{2}$ | 21 | 7.98% |
| 3-23 | Sell 2 calls EK Apr 45 | 12.50 | 22.69 | $38\frac{3}{8}$ | 20 | 17.26% |
| 3-26 | Sell 8 calls OXY Apr 30 | 6.25 | 46.96 | $27\frac{3}{8}$ | 19 | 9.59% |
| 3-27 | Sell 2 calls LLY Apr 70 | 18.75 | 34.95 | $64\frac{7}{8}$ | 18 | 7.90% |
| 3-27 | Sell 2 calls MMM Apr 90 | 25.00 | 47.21 | $84\frac{5}{8}$ | 18 | 6.35% |
| 3-28 | Sell 2 calls GE Apr 70 | 18.75 | 34.95 | $64\frac{7}{8}$ | 17 | 7.90% |
| 3-29 | Sell 2 calls TOS Apr 25 | 25.00 | 47.21 | $22\frac{1}{8}$ | 16 | 12.99% |

**Figure 1.5**   Examples of Actual Trades Executed

| Client Confirmation | | | | | Prudential-Bache Securities | | |
| --- | --- | --- | --- | --- | --- | --- | --- |

Prudential-Bache Securities Inc. 100 Gold Street, New York, N.Y. 10292 Tel. (212) 791-1000

| Type | Trade Date | You Bought | You Sold | Description | Price | % Mkt | Code Class |
| --- | --- | --- | --- | --- | --- | --- | --- |
| 2 | 010489 | | 8 | CALL 100 BELLSOUTH CORP    JAN 45<br>PREFERENTIAL COMMISSION RATE<br>OPEN CUST   COVERED | 1/16 | 2 | 1 |

| Amount | Interest | State Tax | Commission | Exch. Fee | Postage/Ins. | Misc. Tax/Fee | Net Amount | Due Date |
| --- | --- | --- | --- | --- | --- | --- | --- | --- |
| 50.00 | | | 3.57 | .01 | | 1.60 | 44.82 | 010589 |

For Prudential-Bache Securities Inc. Use Only

Account Number  012   Acct. Exec.

Trf 25S   Code ABC   0798609A21   Cusip/Security No.   8900492874012   Trade Identification

Payment for securities purchased and delivery of securities sold must be received by Prudential-Bache Securities Inc. on or before the due date (as noted above) as prescribed by the regulations of the New York Stock Exchange. Inc.

If an odd lot differential has been included in the price of this trade, that fact is noted above. The amount of the differential is available upon request.

Please return payment (and/or securities) together with remittance copy by due date to the Prudential-Bache office which services your account.

All Checks Are To Be Made Payable To: **Prudential-Bache.**

CS-175

**We Welcome This Opportunity To Serve You**
Please See Reverse Side For Explanations

Credit And Transfer Copy

| Client Confirmation | | | | | Prudential-Bache Securities | | |
| --- | --- | --- | --- | --- | --- | --- | --- |

Prudential-Bache Securities Inc. 100 Gold Street, New York, N.Y. 10292 Tel. (212) 791-1000

| Type | Trade Date | You Bought | You Sold | Description | Price | % Mkt | Code Class |
| --- | --- | --- | --- | --- | --- | --- | --- |
| 2 | 010489 | | 2 | CALL 100 GILLETTE COMPANY    JAN 40<br>PREFERENTIAL COMMISSION RATE<br>OPEN CUST   COVERED | 1/8 | 2 | 1 |

| Amount | Interest | State Tax | Commission | Exch. Fee | Postage/Ins. | Misc. Tax/Fee | Net Amount | Due Date |
| --- | --- | --- | --- | --- | --- | --- | --- | --- |
| 25.00 | | | 3.50 | .01 | | 1.60 | 19.89 | 010589 |

For Prudential-Bache Securities Inc. Use Only

Account Number  012   Acct. Exec.

Trf 25S   Code ABC   3757669A2H   Cusip/Security No.   8900492587014   Trade Identification

Payment for securities purchased and delivery of securities sold must be received by Prudential-Bache Securities Inc. on or before the due date (as noted above) as prescribed by the regulations of the New York Stock Exchange. Inc.

If an odd lot differential has been included in the price of this trade, that fact is noted above. The amount of the differential is available upon request.

Please return payment (and/or securities) together with remittance copy by due date to the Prudential-Bache office which services your account.

All Checks Are To Be Made Payable To: **Prudential-Bache.**

CS-124

**We Welcome This Opportunity To Serve You**
Please See Reverse Side For Explanations

Credit And Transfer Copy

Source: Reprinted with permission from Prudential Securities.

If this stock remains completely unchanged for the year, we have gone from a 5 percent return to a 14 percent return. Let's say that the stock moves up to $17 from $16; the $17 1/2 option is no longer going to be trading at 1/16 or 1/8, but may well be trading at 3/16 or 1/4. At this point, we may decide not to write the $17 1/2 strike price option for fear the stock will move higher than the strike price; we would be forced to buy the option back at a higher price. So we decide to wait a bit to see if the stock will move above $17 1/2, because once it does, the exchange will add call options with a $20 strike price. Sure enough, within several weeks the stock moves to $17 3/4, and a $20 strike price call is added. (The $20 puts are also added, but we are not doing anything with this type of option.) We decide to sell the $20 call option.

At this point we may be averaging 1/8 to 3/16 instead of 1/16 to 1/8 each month. Also, if we decide to go out an additional month, we may get 1/4 or 5/16. These are not large amounts, but ten options at 1/8 is $125; ten options at 3/16 is $187.50; and ten at 1/4 is $150. All of a sudden, we have opportunities to pick up $125, $187.50 and $250. Why aren't we doing it? Remember, at this point we are only talking about the lower-priced options. Assume your target might be $20 on the stock to begin with, and at some point the stock might close off the month at $19 1/4. Then you might have the opportunity to sell a three-month option for maybe $1. You may decide to go for the larger premium. The point is, the decision is yours. If you set an overall target of 10 percent, 12 percent or 14 percent a year on your portfolio, it should become increasingly evident that you are likely to achieve these gains through the use of covered call options writing with little upward movement in the market.

## How To Start the Covered Write Program

What is the proper way to start an options writing program? Assume you have a $100,000 portfolio, which would typically have 10 to 15 different securities. While most people try to buy in round lots, chances are you have odd lots because of stock dividends, rights offerings, etc. If you took your portfolio to three different firms, you would get three different ideas on how to adjust your portfolio based on what that particular firm favors at that particular time. Brokers will typically look at your portfolio based on immediate transactions that place commission dollars in their pockets. My own feeling, over the years, is that no firm can tell you that a particular security should be bought or sold at a particular point in time. I am talking here about an overall portfolio, not about isolated cases where there are problems with a particular security you might own. The very security you are told to sell this month might come back in favor next month, and you might be told to buy it back.

Let's look at an alternate solution. First, we analyze each security based on what it means to the client. For example, most firms categorize stocks on the basis of a simple buy, sell or hold classification, whereas other firms will rate stocks based on a numeric scale from 5 (most attractive) down to 1 (least attractive), with 3 being neutral. Chances are that you have a diversified portfolio in which most of your securities rate in the neutral area, with several on the buy list of the firm and several on the sell list. The most important consideration is to show the client how to make additional money with his or her portfolio and how to put cash in the client's hands based on his or her specific investment objectives.

Let's say you have 175 shares of XYZ stock. The brokerage firm has a neutral recommendation for it. A portfolio review suggests these shares be replaced by another security that the firm favors. My approach has always been the opposite. Unless there is some obvious reason to sell the security, we would carefully review the stock to see why the stock had been bought in the first place. If you purchased the stock with income as the primary objective and you are receiving 5 percent in income, you could receive another 4 or 5 percent income on the stock simply by writing an option on it.

For example, if the stock is trading at $17, yielding 5 percent, and you can write an option averaging 1/2 points each six months, then you are taking in another 5 percent. We have taken a stock this firm does not favor and turned it into an income stock yielding 10 percent.

When the stock eventually hits $20, we will very happily sell it and switch into one that is favored by the particular firm. The new stock would be purchased because of the dividend and because we could sell options on it. We would go through the entire portfolio using this thought process. Instead of selling out any odd lots, we would add enough to make the holdings into round lots so that call options could be sold against them. In other words, virtually no changes would be made to the portfolio.

Think of your portfolio as a new car. We certainly aren't going to take it to the garage and get a tune-up. Therefore, I usually recommend only very minor changes for each new portfolio I receive. The idea is to start bringing in money to clients, not to have them pay out a lot of commissions. It is very easy and quite legitimate for brokers to recommend a number of changes based on the research recommendations of their firms. If one has additional funds to invest, then of course we would add new positions to the account. Wouldn't it be nice, for a change, if you walked into a brokerage office, and your broker gave you six recommendations that would result in a check being sent to you the next day for $1,000? Since the settlement on options is one business day, you have immediate use of these funds. Of course, you remain liable for the options until they expire.

Option income is classified as short-term capital gain, which is a tremendous advantage to the seller of the option. Most investors make the mistake of selling their good securities and taking profits, while holding their bad securities and hoping they will recover. An options writing program will force you to correct this bad habit. Let's say you have a $100,000 portfolio, and toward the end of the year you total up your options premiums and realize you've taken in $4,500. Since this is all short-term capital gain, it would be to your advantage to sell your worst-performing stocks in order to reduce your tax liability.

Another suggestion, as you get your options program going, is to stagger your options over different months. Obviously, most of these remarks have been addressed to the lower-premium option, where the risk of being assigned is very, very low. However, in most options programs, you would have different securities staggered in different months. For example, if you have all of your options expiring at one time, it would be entirely possible the market would be at a low point. Therefore, to average the market, you might stagger your portfolio three or four months or more, depending on your own investment objective. Of course, tax considerations always play an important part in selling an option.

An interesting benefit in selling nothing but the short-term option would be that if you were wrong you would have additional option months to sell and perhaps increase your profit. For example, say you own a stock at $26 and you sell a one-month option with a strike price of $30 at $\frac{1}{8}$. All of a sudden, with one week to go, the stock jumps to $31. The stock will probably be called away. You have but a week to decide if you want your shares called. Since you have written only the near-term options, you have at least two and maybe three other choices in this particular option: the near month, the middle month and the long-term month. With the stock trading at $31, your $30 option is probably trading at $1\frac{1}{4}$. Since the stock is trading at $31, there will now be an option with a strike price of $35. The middle-term option is probably trading at $1\frac{1}{4}$ or more, and the long-term option is probably trading at $1\frac{1}{2}$ or $1\frac{3}{4}$. In other words, we can buy back the $30 option (for a short-term loss), turn around and sell a $35 option, and end up with more money. Now our stock has to be called five points higher, or at a price of $35 instead of $30. Remember when we sold the option at $30 with the stock at $36? We had made up our minds we would be satisfied with a price of $30.

Situations can change, however. Maybe some extraordinary development in the company has caused the stock to take a dramatic move on the upside. We may reevaluate the security and decide we will go for an additional five points. We may even decide not to write the option at all, but to watch the price action of the stock very closely before deciding. Since we have written the option for a very short period of time, it is much easier to make an adjustment. You can usually buy back your old option, sell a new one, and actually end up with more money in your account.

## CONCLUDING REMARKS

There is no question that this isn't exactly the most exciting way to make money, but it works! Simply think of each of your securities as a slot machine sitting in a room. Once a month or so, we are going to walk into the room and pull the handle one time. We know one thing for sure—we will break even or win. The only thing we do not know is how much we are going to win. Once you start picking up these $50 and $100 bills that are lying on the ground every month, you will never stop.

In many cases, you will have substantial capital gains in a number of your securities. Therefore, you must be more careful in selling the options in a potential capital gains situation than in a security when you have a slight profit or loss. If you are hesitant about initiating this type of trade on your entire portfolio, start with one stock. If you have 20 stocks, start with two stocks. If you have 30 stocks, start with three stocks. As you write the options, note the commissions that are paid and the expiration dates, and be sure to follow the options on those particular stocks in the options tables. I assure you that after three or four months your three stocks will turn into six, and in a year your six stocks will turn into twelve. Before long, you will be writing options on practically your entire portfolio. Keep in mind that this low-priced strategy is simply a starting point to other types of options strategies.

Another misconception I have found over the years is that people think the option premium is held in escrow until the option is called or expires. This is not the case. In fact, as I mentioned before, since options settle in one day, you could sell an option on Thursday and pick up a check from your broker or banker before the weekend.

Good luck!

# CHAPTER 2

# In Search of the Obvious

*BY STEVE TOAN AND JERRY PUTNAM*

**Editor's Note:**

Steve Toan originally applied the approach explained in this chapter, but it was Jerry Putnam who actually articulated it for the editor to incorporate in this book.

Selling vertical bull or bear spreads is somewhat opposite the basic covered write strategies. This strategy is akin to selling stock short and buying a call to cover the risk of the short stock position. The two authors sell an in-the-money option and buy an out-of-the-money option to cover the risk. The difference between the strike price, less the premium received from the sales, is the maximum amount of risk; if the examples are based on $5 between strikes and the sales creates a $1.50 credit, then the maximum potential loss is the difference, or $3.50.

In this approach, the authors consider other areas of returns on investments. Any credit amount derived from selling the vertical bull or bear spreads is treated as a profit play due to the fact that interest is paid on this balance.

Any additional capital gains that can be derived from the underlying legging out of the spread is also factored into the returns equation. One strategy employed by these two authors is to take profits on the in-the-money options when those premiums erode to fractions of dollars and allow the other position, the long out-of-the-money option, to ride naked.

The time horizon to expect options sold to decay is 60 days or less of life left on the option.

Again, as in most of the strategies employed in this book, the consistent application of this approach over a large portfolio of equities results in considerably better-than-average gains.

As both authors are brokers with Prudential Securities, we have been requested to note for the reader that the strategy illustrated here is solely of the two contributing authors and does not represent Prudential Securities' investment approaches.

There are two fundamental truths in options trading. First, most people who speculate in the options markets lose money. Second, professional traders make money by taking advantage of those speculators. Floor traders have several advantages over individual investors, such as the ability to buy on the bid and to sell on the offer side of the market. They also get to see firsthand all the trades in the options in which they make markets.

Since most options expire worthless, the individuals or professional traders with the best chance to profit are those who can control risk while taking advantage of the fact that options are wasting assets. In this chapter we will show you how to control risk while selling option premiums that eventually become worthless.

## BUILDING A STRATEGY SELLING OPTIONS

Our method of managing money incorporates different ways that people perceive investing and reduces those perceptions to realities in the specific marketplace.

Our objective is to provide exceptional rates of constant return, while defining risk and maintaining good liquidity (typically 60-day time horizons). We take advantage of all statistical probabilities based on historic data and couple them with fundamental evaluations of the current marketplace.

We consider several aspects. The word *premium*, in the context of options strategy, means that you are paying a premium over and above the real value of the asset. Obviously, we all would like to receive a premium on any asset we had for sale, whether a car, a house, a painting or a stock.

Our first quest is to fundamentally and statistically evaluate risk of potentially profitable premium situations. Even with the advantage of receiving a good premium, we may be wrong in our assumptions, and we want to define our risks from inception.

Most conventional trades are based on assumptions of current value and subsequent market movement. For example, let's say the S&P 500 Stock Index is trading at 15 times earnings and XYZ Corp. is trading at only eight times earnings. If we assume that XYZ is growing at a constant rate, we see it as an undervalued situation, so the stock is a buy. An alternative approach is to use technical analysis to arrive at a value assessment. The method of determining value, however, is not as important as the discovery of an opportunity to reap a reward.

You are immediately at risk when you buy an investment. Theoretically, you are at risk for your entire investment. (In a short position, your risk is more.) Simply stated, you invest a dollar with the expectation of getting back the dollar plus a return on it. The return comes in the form of either income or capital appreciation. The investor's first concern is with the return of his or her principal and then the return on the investment. If there is no income, risk is increased and there is only one opportunity to make money: through capital appreciation.

Our method increases the potential for dramatic returns and takes advantage of options premiums and income. If you increase the opportunity for profit, you increase the potential for profit. Imagine how your potential to make money increases when, rather than taking a dollar out of your pocket and putting it into an investment that needs to grow on a timely basis, you sell something that is already overpriced, receive someone else's money and have those funds to use immediately! Consider also that what you have sold is a wasting asset and your risk is defined.

## THE GAME PLAN

First, we deposit funds in an account and receive interest on those funds. This deposit entitles us to create options positions—through the sale of options premiums—that create additional credits (cash). These additional funds go into the account and earn interest. We also define our risk on each transaction so we know our maximum exposure. We know the potential for each position at the time these positions are created. In short, we put up a dollar and we immediately receive more than a dollar's worth of positioning power. We even have a good chance of keeping the entire premium as well as getting our dollar back.

We receive income on the dollar plus the premium received. Our advantage is that we have potential for capital preservation. Our profit is based on the underlying asset appreciating in price, going down in price or staying the same. Compare this to conventional investing, which provides you with profit only when you make a purchase. Your value assumptions demand price assumptions.

How can this be? We put ourselves in a position where we make money if the asset stays the same or goes slightly up or down in value.

You notice our chapter is entitled "In Search of the Obvious"; the following are 15 things we've discovered, or history has shown us:

1.  Short-term rates always outperform inflation and are higher than S&P income returns.
2.  Most options purchased are losers.
3.  Most options written are not exercised.
4.  Historic returns in the stock market average about 10 percent per year, of which about half is income.
5.  Option premium is not factual or fundamental, but emotional.
6.  Value and market movement don't necessarily have anything to do with one another.
7.  Options are time-wasting assets.
8.  Stocks do better in declining-rate environments.
9.  Stocks do poorly in increasing-rate environments.
10. If someone gives you money with the hope of getting it back and you have the use of that money with no charge, your returns should be higher than if you used only your own money.
11. Everyone is wrong sometimes and most people have trouble admitting it.
12. Perception of risk and reality of risk are different.
13. Perception of performance and reality of performance are different.
14. Timing is everything.
15. Diversification is good.

We try to combine all these criteria in our approach. By increasing the opportunity to make money, we've increased the likelihood of making money. *We sell options spreads and take in cash with a maximum time horizon of less than 60 days.* Our returns are based on how much we keep of the credit received from the sale of spreads, on the interest rate on our original deposit and on the credits received. We know our maximum exposure or risk on each transaction as well as our maximum return. We have all the statistical applications on our side when we enter into a transaction, and we always have time on our side. Our goal is to achieve annual rates of return that consistently exceed 25 percent.

The following simple example shows how it works:

    Price of stock—$50
We can position either in puts:
    Price of put option with a $45 strike—$1—sell
    Price of put option with a $40 strike—$0.25—buy
    We obtain a $3/4$-point credit
or we can position in calls:
    Price of call option with a $55 strike—$1—sell
    Price of call option with a $60 strike—$0.25—buy
    We obtain a $3/4$-point credit

By selling both put and call spreads on the same underlying position, we are in a position to make money on both spreads, yet our potential loss at expiration is only on one side. If the stock closes between 45 and 50, we keep the premium from the sale of the put spread as well as the sale of the call spread. The same holds true if the stock is 55 to 50 at expiration—we keep both the put and call premium. You might say we have a total profit range of 45 to 55.

A close at expiration at any point in that ten-point range will allow the seller of these spreads to keep the entire premium. A stock close of $43\frac{1}{2}$ and $56\frac{1}{2}$ (not including commissions) will still yield a profit. The closing prices that would cause a loss are below $43\frac{1}{2}$ and above $56\frac{1}{2}$. Since you've purchased a put and call to hedge your put and call sale, you have defined your risk as to any other possible closing price.

As you can see, we have the ability to make a profit if the price of the underlying issue goes up less than $6\frac{1}{2}$ points or down less than $6\frac{1}{2}$ points. Most conventional investments allow you to profit only if you guess right on the direction of the issue: a price increase if you purchase the underlying issue or a price decrease if you're short the issue.

Another advantage to this strategy is that since all options eventually expire, we know there must be premium decay in the options prior to that expiration date. Therefore, we know our strategy has timing on our side. Remember, we are selling an option premium; that premium must move to zero on expiration date.

Figure 2.1, which shows the time value premium decay curve, will help illustrate our point. The vertical axis is price premium, while the horizontal axis is time movement from left to right. Through our strategy we are selling premium when it is in its most rapid point of decay.

This does not mean we cannot lose money. What it means is that we know we will get premium shrinkage over time. Studies show that the greatest premium erosion occurs during the last six weeks prior to expiration. The erosion increases dramatically in the two weeks prior to expiration. With other investments you have no way of knowing that you will get timely price movement.

Another advantage of this strategy is that your original funds earn interest at a higher rate of return than most conventional issues. Remember, you receive interest not only on the monies you deposited, but also on the monies that were created via the sale of option premium.

Theoretically, this strategy offers less total risk than conventional investing. If you invest $1, your risk is that entire dollar, or 100 percent. With this strategy you sell premium equal to about 15 percent of the underlying deposit. This means that if all your spread positions go against you, you would still retain 15 percent; your risk on this strategy is equal to only $0.85 on every dollar deposited.

**Figure 2.1**   Time Value Premium Decay of Options

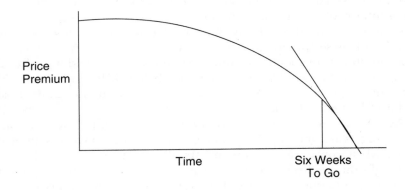

*What this strategy does not allow for is unlimited upside potential.* Figures 2.2 and 2.3 illustrate the limited risk/return characteristics of our strategy. The vertical axis is underlying stock price and the horizontal axis is profit/loss.

Selection of the individual positions is determined by myriad factors (value assessments). The structure allows us to receive and keep income while stacking the deck in our favor.

## THE MECHANICS OF THE PROGRAM

The following theoretical examples will demonstrate our simple yet well-thought-out program of executing vertical spreads.

### Part I: Buying the Vertical Put Spread

XYZ stock is $50. We sell a 60-day put on that same stock with a $45 strike price and at the same time purchase a $40 strike price put and receive in cash, say, $1 for the spread.

We break even if the underlying stock is at $44 or above on the expiration date (yet we have had the use of that dollar for 60 days earning interest). If the underlying stock is above $45 per share on expiration date, we keep the entire dollar.

**Figure 2.2**   Short Put Spread Risk/Reward

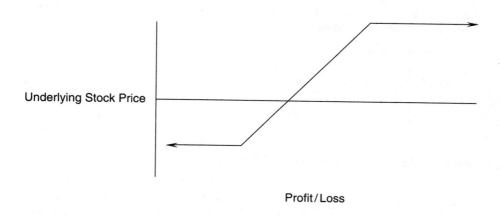

Underlying Stock Price

Profit / Loss

**Figure 2.3**   Short Call Spread Risk/Reward

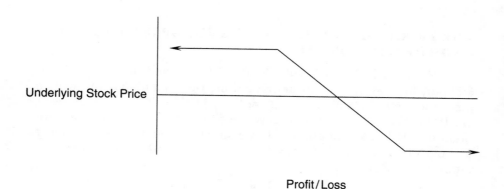

Underlying Stock Price

Profit / Loss

Since we sold a $45 put, the maximum potential loss is $4 per position, which is the difference between the put sale at $45 and the put purchase at $40, less the $1 credit received. In a straight equity purchase, your risk is the entire investment, $50.

Stock price 0—Potential loss $4
Stock price 44—Break even
Stock price 45—Profit $1
Stock price 50—Profit $1
Stock price 100—Profit $1

### Part II: Buying the Vertical Call Spread

XYZ stock is $50. We sell a $55 strike price call with 60 days to expiration and at the same time purchase a $60 call for a credit of $1.

If XYZ stock is at $55 or less, we keep the entire investment. If XYZ stock is at $56, we break even and have had the use of those funds. We have risk of $4 if the price of the stock at expiration is between $56 and $60. Above $60, the $60 call purchase protects us.

Stock price 0—Potential gain $1
Stock price 56—Break even
Stock price 55—Profit $1
Stock price 50—Profit $1
Stock price 100—Potential loss $4

## THE PROGRAM: COMBINING THE PUT SPREAD AND THE CALL SPREAD

XYZ stock is $50. We sell a 60-day $45 put and purchase a 60-day $40 put, for a $1 credit. At the same time, we sell a 60-day $55 call and purchase a 60-day $60 call for a credit of $1.

If the stock at expiration is between $45 and $55, we keep the entire premium. Below $43 or above $56, we have three points risk to either the $40 put or the $60 call. In any instance, we've had the use of the premium in all examples.

Stock price 0—Potential loss $3
Stock price 40—Potential loss $3
Stock price 45—Potential gain $2
Stock price 50—Potential gain $2
Stock price 55—Potential gain $2
Stock price 60—Potential loss $3
Stock price 100—Potential loss $3

**Figure 2.4**   What Is Required for This Strategy To Return a Composite $25,000 on $100,000 Invested per Annum

| Risk-Free Interest Rate | Interest per Year | Additional Amount Needed per Year | Additional Amount Needed per Month |
|---|---|---|---|
| 6% | $ 6,000 | $19,000 | $1,583 |
| 7% | 7,000 | 18,000 | 1,500 |
| 8% | 8,000 | 17,000 | 1,416 |
| 9% | 9,000 | 16,000 | 1,333 |
| 10% | 10,000 | 15,000 | 1,250 |
| 11% | 11,000 | 14,000 | 1,166 |
| 12% | 12,000 | 13,000 | 1,083 |
| 13% | 13,000 | 12,000 | 1,000 |
| 14% | 14,000 | 11,000 | 916 |
| 15% | $15,000 | $10,000 | $ 833 |

## OUR INVESTMENT RETURN OBJECTIVE

The most important variable in our investment program is interest rates. On this type of program we typically receive a premium of $15,000 per $100,000, 15 percent of the deposit to use for 30 to 60 days. To earn $25,000 per year on $100,000 (or 25 percent per annum), Figure 2.4 shows what is needed every year.

As you can see, we can give back most of the monthly premium received and still achieve our goal of 25 percent on an annual basis.

We figure our returns based on the following:

• The $100,000 deposit purchases a three-month T-bill and earns interest.
• The credits from the options program earn interest via money market.
• The premium received and retained would provide a capital gain.

The first factor, interest earned on $100,000, is independent of our strategy. The second factor, credits earned via money markets, and the third factor, premium gained, affect the amount of additional income that must be generated to provide a total 25 percent rate of return. This is the added value of the program.

Because of margin restrictions, your actual interest returns are slightly lower than actual cash purchases.

T-bill = $100,000
Sale of spreads = Credit
Price of stock at expiration determines profit or loss

## SUMMARY REMARKS

Remember that we are selling time-wasting assets and making assumptions about the directional range the underlying asset will take. If the asset moves in that direction, our return should be accelerated based upon the fact that we sold a time-wasting asset. So if everything is equal, timing will always be on our side. Again, we're looking for consistently high rates of return, and we are using historic data to achieve these rates. Remember, short-term interest rates are usually higher than dividend rates on the S&P. *We don't have to be right in a directional assumption to make money. All we have to do is not be really wrong.*

## SAMPLE PORTFOLIO STRATEGIES

The following are two sample portfolios from June 1, 1989, through August 18, 1989. They should give you an example of the type of activity and commission costs to expect in the program.

Our sample portfolios assume the following conditions:

- We are using $100,000 as the option spread portfolio.
- Risk-free interest rate is 9.35 percent over the life of the sample portfolios.
- We execute 20 put spreads every time we institute the program.
- The first portfolio ends with the July options expiration.
- The second portfolio ends with the August options expiration.

## FIRST PORTFOLIO STRATEGIES

*June 1, 1989:* First day of the program with 52 days to go.

| Stock | Price | Action |
|---|---|---|
| 1. Xerox Corporation (XRX) | 63³/₄ | Sell XRX Jul 60<br>Buy XRX Jul 55<br>Credit ³/₄ = $1,500 |
| 2. Northwest Airlines (NWA) | 108 | Sell NWA Jul 100<br>Buy NWA Jul 95<br>Credit ³/₄ = $1,500 |
| 3. Smith, Kline Beckman (SKB) | 61³/₈ | Sell SKB Jul 60<br>Buy SKB Jul 55<br>Credit ⁷/₈ = $1,750 |

| | | |
|---|---|---|
| 4. Phelps Dodge (PD) | 59½ | Sell PD Jul 55 Buy PD Jul 50 Credit ⅞ = $1,750 |
| 5. Compaq Computer (CPQ) | 97¾ | Sell CPQ Jul 90 Buy CPQ Jul 85 Credit ⅞ = $1,750 |
| 6. Time Life (TL) | 127 | Sell TL Jul 110 Buy TL Jul 105 Credit ¾ = $1,500 |
| 7. Federal National Mtg. (FNM) | 89⅝ | Sell FNM Jul 85 Buy FNM Jul 80 Credit 1¼ = $2,500 |
| 8. Missouri Pacific (MO) | 139 | Sell MO Jul 130 Buy MO Jul 125 Credit ⅝ = $1,250 |
| 9. Hilton Hotels (HLT) | 86¾ | Sell HLT Jul 75 Buy HLT Jul 70 Credit ⅝ = $1,250 |
| 10. Holiday Inns (HIA) | 48¼ | Sell HIA Jul 45 Buy HIA Jul 40 Credit 1¹/₁₆ = $2,125 |

After adding up all the credits received from instituting the put spreads, we find we have a total credit of $16,875. Interest earned on the $16,875 over the life of the program, 52 days, is $244.78 at 9.35 percent.

*Potential 52-day return:*
$1,332 interest on $100,000 at 9.35 percent for 52 days
16,875 credit received from put program
 225 interest on credits ($16,875 @ 9.35 for 52 days)
$18,432 , or 18.432% for 52 days ($18,432 ÷ $100,000)

If we factor in an approximate commission cost of $2,000 for the program, we find that we can still expect to net out $18,432–$2,000, or $16,432.

At this point of program inception, we don't know the cost to close out the positions and are hoping that the majority expire worthless. The investor can be assured that about 75 percent of all options purchased expire worthless and are never exercised.

### Adjusting and Modifying the First Sample Portfolio

We are now ready to adjust and modify the portfolio by considering all the opportunities that arise during the next 52 calendar days.

*June 9, 1989 Adjustment in Sample Spread Portfolio Dated June 1, 1989*
9 days into the program with 43 days to go.
We adjust original position #6:

| | | |
|---|---|---|
| 6. Time Life | 127 | Sell TL Jul 110 |
| (TL) | | Buy TL Jul 105 |
| | | Credit $3/4 = \$1,500$ |

By:
Repurchasing the TL 110 put and closing out position at $3/16$ credit, or approximately \$1,000 profit ($1/2$ credit should have been $3/16$).
We add position #11:

| | | |
|---|---|---|
| 11. Sea Container | 59⅞ | Sell SCR Jul 55 |
| (SCR) | | Buy SCR Jul 50 |
| | | Credit $1 = \$2,000$ |

Potential is increased by approximately \$1,100 after commission.

*June 15, 1989 Adjustment in Sample Spread Portfolio Dated June 9, 1989*
15 days into the program with 37 days to go.
We adjust original position #9:

| | | |
|---|---|---|
| 9. Hilton Hotels | 86¾ | Sell HLT Jul 75 |
| (HLT) | | Buy HLT Jul 70 |
| | | Credit $5/8 = \$1,250$ |

By:
Repurchasing HLT Jul 75–70 spread at $3/16$ credit, for approximately \$875 profit.
We add new position #12:

| | | |
|---|---|---|
| 12. White Motors | 36¼ | Sell WH Jul 35 |
| (WH) | | Buy WH Jul 30 |
| | | Credit $1 = \$2,000$ |

Potential is increased by approximately \$1,200 after commission.
Total increase to date is approximately \$3,300.

*June 19, 1989 Adjustment in Sample Spread Portfolio Dated June 1, 1989*
19 days into the program with 33 days to go.
We adjust original position #2:

| | | |
|---|---|---|
| 2. Northwest Airlines | 108 | Sell NWA Jul 100 |
| (NWA) | | Buy NWA Jul 95 |
| | | Credit $3/4 = \$1,500$ |

By:
Repurchasing the NWA 100–95 spread at ³/₁₆ credit, for approximately $1,125 profit.
We add new position #13:

| 13. Warner Comm. (WCI) | 59³/₈ | Sell WCI Jul 55 Buy WCI Jul 50 |
|---|---|---|
| | | Credit 1 = $2,000 |

Potential return is increased by approximately $1,225 after commission.
We adjust position #11 instituted on June 9:

| 11. Sea Container (SCR) | 59⁷/₈ | Sell SCR Jul 55 Buy SCR Jul 50 |
|---|---|---|
| | | Credit 1 = $2,000 |

By:
Repurchasing SCR Jul 55–50 spread at ³/₁₆ credit, for approximately $1,225 profit.
We add new position #14:

| 14. Time Life (TL) | 158³/₄ | Sell TL Jul 130 Buy TL Jul 125 |
|---|---|---|
| | | Credit 1 = $2,000 |

Potential is increased by approximately $1,100 after commission.
Let's take a look at our current account status:

1. Potential total return for 52 days now exceeds 22.5 percent prior to interest income and closing commissions.
2. Initial credits received at inception of program on June 1, 1989 totaled $16,875.
3. Current credits possible on existing portfolio are $17,250.
4. Capital gains booked are $5,225.
5. Thus, we have existing total potential of $22,475 prior to interest income and closing commissions.
6. Time remaining until July expiration is 33 days.

Two days later, we saw our capital gains increase to $7,150. Potential total return for 52 days now exceeds 23.5 percent prior to interest income and closing commissions. Initial credits received on June 1, 1989 total $16,875. Current credits possible on existing portfolio are now $18,200. Capital gains booked increase to $7,150. Existing total potential $23,350 prior to interest income and closing commissions. Time remaining until July expiration is 31 days.

*June 22, 1989 Adjustment in Sample Spread Portfolio Dated June 1, 1989*
22 days into the program with 30 days to go.
We adjust original position #10:

10. Holiday Inns                    48¹/₄          Sell HIA Jul 45
    (HIA)                                          Buy HIA Jul 40

                                                   Credit 1¹/₁₆ = $2,125

By:
Repurchasing the HIA Jul 45 at ¹/₈ credit, or approximately $1,925
profit.
We add new position #15:

15. United Airlines                 132¹/₄         Sell UAL Jul 125
    (UAL)                                          Buy UAL Jul 120

                                                   Credit ³/₄ = $1,500

Potential is increased by approximately $950 after commission.

*June 27, 1989 Adjustment in Sample Spread Portfolio Dated June 1, 1989*
27 days into the program with 25 days to go.
We adjust original position #3:

3. Smith, Kline Beckman            61 ³/₈          Sell SKB Jul 60
   (SKB)                                           Buy SKB Jul 55

                                                   Credit ⁷/₈ = $1,750

By:
Repurchasing SKB Jul 55 at ³/₁₆ credit, for approximately $1,325 profit.
We are not adding a new position to replace #3 at this time.
Current profits booked at $8,475. Maximum potential to expiration is
$22,975, or 22.975 percent prior to interest income.

*June 28, 1989 Adjustment in Sample Spread Portfolio Dated June 1, 1989*
28 days into the program with 24 days to go.
We adjust original position #8:

8. Missouri Pacific                  139           Sell MO Jul 130
   (MO)                                            Buy MO Jul 125

                                                   Credit ⁵/₈ = $1,250

By:
Repurchasing position MO Jul 130 at ³/₁₆ credit, for approximately
$825 profit.
We are not adding a new position at this time.
Current profits booked at $9,300. Maximum potential to expiration is
$22,550, or 22.55 percent prior to interest income.

*July 6, 1989 Adjustment in Sample Spread Portfolio Dated June 1, 1989*
36 days into the program with 16 days to go.
We adjust original position #7:

7. Federal National Mtg.           89⁵/₈          Sell FNM Jul 85
   (FNM)                                           Buy FNM Jul 80

                                                   Credit 1¹/₄ = $2,500

By:

Repurchasing FNM Jul 85 at $3/16$ credit, for approximately $2,100 profit.

We are not adding a new position to replace #7 at this time.

Current profits booked at $11,400. Maximum potential to expiration is $22,150, or 22.15 percent prior to interest income.

*July 10, 1989 Adjustment in Sample Spread Portfolio Dated June 1, 1989*

40 days into the program with 12 days to go.

We adjust original position #1:

| | | |
|---|---|---|
| 1. Xerox Corporation | $63^3/4$ | Sell XRX Jul 60 |
| (XRX) | | Buy XRX Jul 55 |
| | | Credit $3/4 = \$1,500$ |

By:

Repurchasing XRX Jul 60 at $3/16$ credit, for approximately $1,075 profit.

We adjust original position #15:

| | | |
|---|---|---|
| United Airlines | $132^1/4$ | Sell UAL Jul 125 |
| (UAL) | | Buy UAL Jul 120 |
| | | Credit $3/4 = \$1,500$ |

By:

Repurchasing UAL Jul 125 at $3/16$ credit, for approximately $1,075 profit.

No new positions entered.

Current profits booked at $13,550. Maximum potential to expiration is $23,175, or 23.1 percent prior to interest income.

*July 12, 1989 Adjustment in Sample Spread Portfolio Dated June 1, 1989*

42 days into the program with 10 days to go.

We adjust original position #10:

| | | |
|---|---|---|
| 10. Holiday Inns | $48^1/4$ | Sell HIA Jul 45 |
| (HIA) | | Buy HIA Jul 40 |
| | | Credit $1^1/16 = \$2,125$ |

By:

Repurchasing the HIA Jul 45 at $1/8$ credit, or approximately $1,925 profit.

We adjust original position #4:

| | | |
|---|---|---|
| 4. Phelps Dodge | $59^1/2$ | Sell PD Jul 55 |
| (PD) | | Buy PD Jul 50 |
| | | Credit $7/8 = \$1,750$ |

By:

Repurchasing PD Jul 55 at $3/16$ credit, for approximately $1,350 profit.

No new position added.
Current profits booked at $14,900. Maximum potential to expiration is $22,775, or 22.8 percent prior to interest income.

*July 14, 1989 Adjustment in Sample Spread Portfolio Dated June 1, 1989*
44 days into the program with 8 days to go.
We adjust original position #13:

| | | |
|---|---|---|
| 13. Warner Comm. | 59³/₈ | Sell WCI Jul 55 |
| (WCI) | | Buy WCI Jul 50 |
| | | Credit 1 = $2,000 |

By:
Repurchasing WCI Jul 55 at ¹/₈ credit, for approximately $1,825 profit.
No new position added.
Current profits booked at $16,725. Maximum potential $22,475, or 22.5 percent prior to interest income.

*July 17, 1989 Adjustment in Sample Spread Portfolio Dated June 1, 1989*
47 days into the program with 5 days to go.
We adjust original position #5:

| | | |
|---|---|---|
| 5. Compaq Computer | 97³/₄ | Sell CPQ Jul 90 |
| (CPQ) | | Buy CPQ Jul 85 |
| | | Credit ⁷/₈ = $1,750 |

By:
Repurchasing CPQ Jul 90 at ⁵/₁₆ credit, for approximately $775 profit.
We adjust original position #12:

| | | |
|---|---|---|
| 12. White Motors | 36¹/₄ | Sell WH Jul 35 |
| (WH) | | Buy WH Jul 30 |
| | | Credit 1 = $2,000 |

By:
Repurchasing WH Jul 35 at ³/₈ credit, for approximately $900 profit.
We adjust original position #6:

| | | |
|---|---|---|
| 6. Time Life | 127 | Sell TL Jul 110 |
| (TL) | | Buy TL Jul 105 |
| | | Credit ³/₄ = $1,500 |

By:
Repurchasing TL Jul 110 put at ¹/₄ credit, for approximately $1,550 profit.

We are now closing out these remaining positions based on the fact that the market has been up for eight days in a row, and the July expiration is Friday. Current profits booked at $19,950, or 19.5 percent prior to interest income.

Let's evaluate the results of this program of buying vertical put spreads only.

*July 18, 1989 Sample Portfolio Results Dated June 1, 1989*
We attained capital gains of $19,950. The interest income on $100,000 deposit of a three-month T-bill amounted to $1,102. The interest on credits received from the program was $178; the balance was approximately $17,000 at 8 percent. The total return on the program for 48 days was about $21,230.

On a comparative basis, the Dow Jones Industrial Average gained only 2.5 percent from June 1, 1989 to July 17, 1989. For the same time period, the S&P 500 gained only + 3.3 percent. The sample spread portfolio, however, gained at the rate of 21.2 percent after commission costs of $5,250.

## SECOND PORTFOLIO STRATEGIES

We now embark on a second portfolio with the same approach. Using our estimates and actual returns from the first portfolio, we now determine what we can expect if we constructed a similar portfolio to span from July 19, 1989 to close to the next expiration, August 17, 1989, or about 29 days.

*July 19, 1989:* First day of portfolio with 29 days to go.

| Stock | Price | Action |
|---|---|---|
| 1. Hilton Corporation (HLT) | $104^5/_8$ | Sell HLT Aug 100 Buy HLT Aug 95 Credit $1^1/_4 = \$2,500$ |
| 2. Warner Communications (WCI) | $65^5/_8$ | Sell WCI Aug 65 Buy WCI Aug 60 Credit $1^3/_8 = \$2,750$ |
| 3. Holiday Inns (HIA) | 58 | Sell HIA Aug 55 Buy HIA Aug 50 Credit $2 = \$4,000$ |
| 4. Du Pont (DD) | $113^5/_8$ | Sell DD Aug 110 Buy DD Aug 105 Credit $1 = \$2,000$ |
| 5. United Airlines (UAL) | $178^3/_4$ | Sell UAL Aug 155 Buy UAL Aug 150 Credit $^{15}/_{16} = \$1,875.50$ |

| | | |
|---|---|---|
| 6. White Motors (WH) | 35¼ | Sell WH Aug 35<br>Buy WH Aug 30<br>Credit 1 = $2,000 |
| 7. IBM (IBM) | 115¼ | Sell IBM Aug 110<br>Buy IBM Aug 105<br>Credit 9/16 = $1,125 |
| 8. Walt Disney (DIS) | 102 | Sell DIS Aug 100<br>Buy DIS Aug 95<br>Credit 1⅜ = $2,750 |
| 9. Smith, Kline Beckman (SKB) | 59⅝ | Sell SKB Aug 60<br>Buy SKB Aug 55<br>Credit 1 = $2,000 |
| 10. Digital Equipment (DEC) | 95⅛ | Sell DEC Aug 90<br>Buy DEC Aug 85<br>Credit ¾ = $1,500 |

After adding up all the credits received from instituting this second program, we find we have a total of $22,505.50 credit. Interest earned on $22,505.50 over the 30-day life of the program is $760.
*Potential 30-day return:*

> $760.00  interest on $100,000 at 9.25 percent for 30 days
> 22,505.50  credit received from put program
> <u>    171.00</u>  interest on credits (22,505.50 @ 9.25 for 30 days)
> $23,436.00  or 23.43 percent for 30 days ($23,436/$100,000)

Once again, we factor in an approximate commission cost of $4,000 for the program and find that we can still expect to net out $23,436 – $4,000, or $19,436.

## Adjusting and Modifying the Second Sample Portfolio

We are now ready to adjust and modify the portfolio by taking into consideration all the opportunities that arise during the next 30 calendar days.

*July 26, 1989 Adjustment in Sample Spread Portfolio Dated July 19, 1989*
8 days into the program with 22 days to go.

We adjust original position #2:

| 2. Warner Communications (WCI) | 65⁵/₈ | Sell WCI Aug 65 |
| | | Buy WCI Aug 60 |
| | | Credit 1³/₈ = $2,750 |

By:

Repurchasing WCI Aug 65 at ⁵/₁₆, for a $2,075 profit.
We add position #11:
11. Sell SCR Aug 65
    Buy SCR Aug 60
    Credit 1
Increase potential by $1,075
New potential: $20,757, or 20.6 percent

*July 28, 1989 Adjustment in Sample Spread Portfolio Dated July 19, 1989*
10 days into the program with 20 days left to go.
We adjust original position #9:

| 9. Smith, Kline Beckman (SKB) | 59⁵/₈ | Sell SKB Aug 60 |
| | | Buy SKB Aug 55 |
| | | Credit 1 = $2,000 |

By:

Repurchasing SKB Aug 60 put at ¹/₈ credit, for approximately $1,700 profit.
We adjust original position #3:

| 3. Holiday Inns (HIA) | 58 | Sell HIA Aug 55 |
| | | Buy HIA Aug 50 |
| | | Credit 2 = $4,000 |

By:

Repurchasing HIA Aug 55 at ³/₁₆ credit, for approximately $3,575 profit.
New potential: $20,032, or 20 percent

*August 2, 1989 Change in Model Spread Portfolio Dated July 19, 1989*
14 days into the program with 16 days left to go.
We adjust original position #8:

| 8. Walt Disney (DIS) | 102 | Sell DIS Aug 100 |
| | | Buy DIS Aug 95 |
| | | Credit 1³/₈ = $2,750 |

By:

Repurchasing DIS Aug 100 at ¹/₄ credit, for approximately $2,200 profit.
Current profits booked from July 19, 1989 to August 2, 1989: $9,550
Potential: $19,482, or 19.48 percent

August 8, 1989 Adjustment in Sample Spread Portfolio Dated July 19,1989
20 days into the program with 10 days to go.
We adjust original position #4:

| | | |
|---|---|---|
| 4. Du Pont | $113\frac{5}{8}$ | Sell DD Aug 110 |
| (DD) | | Buy DD Aug 105 |
| | | Credit 1 = \$2,000 |

By:
Repurchasing DD Aug 110 put at $\frac{3}{16}$ credit, for approximately \$1,575 profit.
We adjust original position #7:

| | | |
|---|---|---|
| 7. IBM | $115\frac{1}{4}$ | Sell IBM Aug 110 |
| (IBM) | | Buy IBM Aug 105 |
| | | Credit $\frac{9}{16}$ = \$1,125 |

By:
Repurchasing IBM Aug 110 put at $\frac{1}{8}$ credit, for approximately \$825 profit.
We adjust original position #10:

| | | |
|---|---|---|
| 10. Digital Equipment | $95\frac{1}{8}$ | Sell DEC Aug 90 |
| (DEC) | | Buy DEC Aug 85 |
| | | Credit $\frac{3}{4}$ = \$1,500 |

By:
Repurchasing DEC Aug 90 put for a \$1,200 profit.
Current profits booked from July 19, 1989 to August 8, 1989: \$13,150

*August 9, 1989 Adjustment in Sample Spread Portfolio Dated July 19, 1989*
21 days into the program with 9 days to go.
We adjust original position #5:

| | | |
|---|---|---|
| 5. United Airlines | $178\frac{3}{4}$ | Sell UAL Aug 155 |
| (UAL) | | Buy UAL Aug 150 |
| | | Credit $\frac{15}{16}$ = \$1,875.50 |

By:
Repurchasing UAL Aug 155 put at $\frac{1}{8}$ credit, for approximately \$1,575 profit.
Profits booked: \$14,725
Potential: \$18,175, or 18.5 percent

*August 11, 1989 Adjustment in Sample Spread Portfolio Dated July 19, 1989*
23 days into the program with 7 days to go.
We adjust original position #1:

| | | |
|---|---|---|
| 1. Hilton Corporation | $104\frac{5}{8}$ | Sell HLT Aug 100 |
| (HLT) | | Buy HLT Aug 95 |
| | | Credit $1\frac{1}{4}$ = \$2,500 |

By:
Repurchasing Hilton Aug 100 put at $5/16$ for a profit of $1,825
Profits booked: $16,550
Potential: $17,500, or 17.5 percent prior to interest

*August 17, 1989 Adjustment in Sample Spread Portfolio Dated July 19, 1989*
30 days into the program with zero days to go.
Original position of:

| 6. White Motors | 35¼ | Sell WH Aug 35 |
| | | Buy WH Aug 30 |
| | | Credit 1 = $2,000 |

We decide to close out this position by:
Repurchasing WH Aug 35 at 1—same price as sold.
Profit reduced: $200
Total profits booked: $17,925 prior to interest
17.925 percent for 29 days prior to interest income

On a comparative basis, the Dow Jones Industrial Average gained only 3.6 percent from July 19, 1989 through August 17, 1989. For the same time period, the S&P 500 gained only 2.6 percent. The sample spread portfolio, however, gained at the rate of 18.6 percent after commission costs of $4,000.

For the 78-day period from June 1, 1989 to August 17, 1989, the combined sample portfolios gained about 40 percent (21.2 percent from the first portfolio and 18.6 percent from the second portfolio).

In conclusion, it is evident that any investment strategy will not work all the time. However, the historic components of this strategy *have* worked over time. Remember, we are not making a prediction as to where the market or any individual issue is going, but only as to how the premium will react to the emotional assessments. As with all approaches, maximum performance is achieved through disciplined application of your strategy.

Good trading!

# CHAPTER 3

# Options Trading: The Best of the Blue Page

## BY JERRY KOPF

**Editor's Note:**

This chapter, provided for us by Jerry Kopf, is not a strategy chapter. Rather, like David Caplan's chapter, it contains useful tidbits from floor specialists and market makers and methods to trade certain spreads.

The author illustrates two options traders: one is methodic, another is haphazard. The methodic one is the one who brings home the bacon, so to speak. With a floor trader's background, Kopf brings an abundance of knowledge that will help in trade execution. His explanation of how to use the public limit order book, how to execute spreads without price skids, how to play the Christmas tree spread and other inside trading tips makes this chapter worthwhile reading. In effect, it is a summation of the best of the materials in Kopf's newsletter, *OEX Blue Page*.

To make best use of the information in this chapter, underline the salient strategies and tips that are immediately useable. Keep the other, less applicable techniques in the back of your mind. Somewhere along the way to market success, you will encounter a situation that will require pointers found in this chapter. Knowing that the needed information has been encountered before will help you in particularly stressful, unprofitable situations.

Dreams are stronger than reality. This adage is proven daily by lottery ticket buyers who buck odds of 12 million to one, hoping to win life's great jackpot. Warren Buffett, legendary Omaha investor and CEO of

Berkshire Hathaway, says, "The propensity to gamble is always increased by a large prize versus a small entry fee, no matter how poor the true odds."

Traders in stock options also make bets, but whereas lotto is a game of chance, options are a game of skill and experience. The key is that players can stack the odds in their favor. The rub, however, is that very skilled people such as doctors, TV production executives, computer software developers and national baking contest winners—many of whom earn six figures and are notable in their fields—manage to strike out as options players. They might as well be playing a game of chance!

What stops most public players from enjoying profitable expirations? Do they simply fail to learn the basics, e.g., types of orders, nuances of exercise and assignment, proven strategies? Are standard trading rules violated, or are poor money management skills the culprit? Perhaps psychological hang-ups trip them up: carelessness in not actually placing stop or contingent orders, inertia inflicted by back-to-back losses or stubbornness in being wed to a fault-laden strategy.

Rookie traders harbor dreams of glorious riches. They come in, thrash around (overtrade) and, in many cases, try to reinvent the wheel. In their search for the grail of options trading, they land in the sinkhole. Most get an expensive education.

Baseball's better pitchers lengthen their major league careers and make winning easier by adding a repertoire of three pitches to their fastball. Flexibility is the key. Successful options traders must also be flexible, since no one strategy fits all markets.

## A TALE OF TWO PLAYERS

Here are the stories of two investors who are both well along on the options learning curve. Both are determined to make it as at-home traders, but with more than ten expirations under their belts, results are still under par. Their shortcomings may seem familiar as we examine their styles and mind-sets. For the majority of players, persistence and a bit of coaching can correct most maladies. It's simply a matter of commitment.

### Mary the Homemaker

Mary is a 45-year-old homemaker from North Carolina who says that she gets a real kick out of trading options. She survived the crash of 1987 in reasonable shape. Since then, however, buying puts in an up market, especially without using stops, has cost her more than $10,000 of her $25,000 stake. Basically, she has been fighting the market.

While Mary knows that short positions are sometimes a necessary strategy, she admits to a phobia against using them. I reminded her that being a one-punch fighter in the options game curtails flexibility and short-circuits some very profitable opportunities. I also reminded her that the poor man's short sale is a credit spread that caps open-ended risk (and allows the premium seller to sleep at night). Mary says that she knows all this but does nothing. She plods along, interprets her charts and chases prices from the long side. Advice falls on deaf ears.

While Mary does poorly at options, she is a consistent winner at national baking contests. Her prizes in dollars and new kitchens prompted her accountant to suggest that she stick to her strength in baking and avoid her half-baked approach to options trading.

### Larry the Mechanic

Larry is a 40-year-old aircraft mechanic who dreams of chucking wrenches, engine wires and management's self-serving edicts and becoming a money manager. Two months ago, he made a concerted push to trade OEX options. He geared up with a real-time quote system and a fancy on-line charting package that Larry says is terrific. He also attended three options seminars and, to his credit, is dedicated to a fault. Larry's goal is to make $2,000 a month, but so far he is short of his goal.

Larry's Achilles' heel is his fixation with credit spreads. To the exclusion of all other strategies, he enters most expirations short calls, short puts or short strangles (combinations). His nemeses—gapping markets and trend days that cause the index to carry through to new highs or new lows—have zapped Larry with whopping losses.

I mentioned to Larry that short strangle players never enjoy participating in a big market move. They are always looking for nice, quiet expirations, which occur about 75 percent of the time. They win frequently, but profits are paltry compared to sums lost when gapping markets hit.

I suggested that Larry be flexible and sandwich in a debit spread between him and his short premium. Essentially, he would create a Christmas tree spread. Then, when a trend kicks in, just one phone call would cover all shorts. He will have effectively backed into a long position: the residue left after the shorts have been covered. Larry listens and agrees but, like Mary, does nothing. Ah, stubbornness!

## A COMPLETE APPROACH TO OPTIONS TRADING

Steady losses will force Mary and Larry to reckon with their faults because failure is a more compelling motivation for change than success. Sadly, they'll conclude that for them, trading OEX options is too slippery an endeavor, beyond their ability. Their temperaments and market understanding may be better suited to more comprehensible and deliberate-moving stock options such as IBM, Sears, Ford and Syntex.

Many investors have told me that, while stock options reward them handsomely, they get mauled in the whipsaw-inducing index. Bottom line: The allure of OEX options is powerful, but stock options bring home the bacon with greater consistency. Mary and Larry will learn what many other semiprofessional traders eventually learn when their desire exceeds their ability: Options trading (and futures trading) is the hardest way to make an easy buck.

Do successful traders simply have "the knack"? Is it talent, pluck or plain dumb luck? According to Peter Steidlmayer, legendary Chicago Board of Trade futures trader, about one in six floor traders is blessed with God-given talent. To them, trading is a piece of cake. Most public traders, however, spend their early learning months at home, experimenting in a vacuum. Sometimes they manage to reinvent proven strategies, and other times they concoct "new," convoluted strategies. Such research in a vacuum often leads to a rash of overtrading and lots of needless commissions.

There are winners, though, who play a knowledgeable game and have fun doing it. A growing minority of public players have gone around the track three or four times, paid their dues (in the form of losses) and acquired the winning habit. These investors never forget that options is a game of singles and doubles with an occasional home run. They have good money management skills and seldom strike out. These players are a highly disciplined lot and stick to their proven game plan; they rarely take shots.

The winners also come to the table relaxed and with deep pockets, but their wallets don't determine what's best to do. That would be counterproductive and surely an express ticket to mediocre performance. Winning players don't have a large "nut" (overhead expense) to cover each month. Usually, an income stream separate from their option activities supports them during flat months. Unlike Larry, they don't have to make a certain amount a month to survive.

### Option Shooters versus Spreaders

Options market timers and options relationship traders occupy major places in the spectrum of call and put investors. Timers, or "shooters," go for the home run by simply buying premium (i.e., going long a put or call). Relationship traders grind out small but consistent yardage by stacking probabilities in their favor. Because they are skilled at spreading and know beforehand what an option's price (theoretical value) should be, they capitalize on price discrepancies.

Market timers make subjective decisions based on:

- *News*. Monthly trade and employment figures, the producer price index and other external market data. A few years ago, when the M1 was in vogue, market timers keyed into Thursday afternoon's money supply figures.
- *Opinions*. From the forecasts of newsletter advisers to predictions of the "elves" on television's "Wall Street Week."
- *Feelings*. Intuition about whether the next 50-point Dow Jones Industrial Average move will be up or down. Money market timers use charts or other technical indicators that suggest future market direction. Recognize that charts or waves are subject to the ability of the interpreter to read them correctly; in actuality, a subjective market call.

Relationship players make objective decisions based on:

- *A numbers approach*. By knowing the precise mathematical relationship between options and their underlying cash instrument, relationship players often trade from a spread position. For example, the May 280, 285 call spread may be a bargain at a $3/4$ debit, fairly priced at a 2 debit and overvalued at a debit of $2^{1/4}$.
- *The hidden art of forecasting an option's implied volatility*. When traders accurately forecast volatility levels, they buy undervalued options and sell overvalued options. Relationship traders usually do large volume and have a small profit margin per trade.

In the perpetual tug of war between options shooters and options spreaders, the timers win many battles, but the value players win the war.

An options trader who buys premium but ignores implied volatility and avoids what-if price situations is, to use a metaphor, playing baseball with a football. Such timers would be best off trading futures, playing football with a football. Futures are a pure directional play on the market. They fluctuate with the underlying cash. Because they have to contend with less time decay and implied volatility, futures are a less complex trading vehicle. For players who are natural premium sellers, seeking a low-cost and truly leveraged tool, options are the trading vehicle of choice.

## OPTIONS + MATH

If the relationship approach is geared to spreading via a mathematical system, how can the average retail customer combine his or her opinion and theoretical value input to generate profits regularly?

The answer is that prior to establishing a position, he or she runs a price simulation. Chris Brecher, a Chicago Board Options Exchange (CBOE) trader who makes a market in IBM, routinely blends his opinion of what the market will do by first running a computer simulation of his intended position. This exercise allows him to peek into the future and avoid trades that may, with less scrutiny, look good.

For example, in early August of 1988, with about two and a half weeks to expiration and the S&P 100 Index (OEX) at 259, Brecher had a strong feeling the market would be reversing its 150-point rally and heading down. To capitalize on his belief, he shorted 150 Aug 265 calls at $1^{11}/_{16}$.

Brecher's decision was based on his opinion. In the event that he was wrong in his call and the market went against him, he measured his potential loss by doing a simple price simulation on a Schwarz-a-tron. Public traders can do similar price simulations and play "what if" with options software on personal computers.

First, Brecher jacked the price of the index up three points to 262. Then he chopped three days off the time to expiration. Three points up and three days hence, the simulation flashed that the theoretical value of the Aug 265 calls would be just slightly higher. Seeing this, Brecher recognized that given a mildly fluctuating market, the calls were fully priced. At 262, Brecher would suffer a very small paper loss, a risk he felt worth taking. "It's great," he says, "if I see the index can rise a few points against me and I can still make money. I like those kinds of odds."

Three points up and three days out is really arbitrary, according to Brecher. "I'm more likely to sell premium on a Thursday or a Friday because when you take three days off the time to expiration, the theoretical value of the options falls sharply." He keeps the volatility level constant in his simulations because he finds it difficult to predict volatility on a short-term basis. Would he still have sold the Aug 265 calls if the Aug 260 calls were overvalued? Brecher says that he takes a different tack from many traders who sell premium just because they are premium sellers or the Schwarz-a-tron says a call is overvalued. "I have an opinion first," he explains. "Then, when I sell premium, my style is to have some points of protection as a cushion. So I sell out-of-the-money calls rather than at-the-money calls."

Why not buy puts if you are negative on the market? For Brecher, puts are a hedge against the takeover stocks he is holding long. "This is an imperfect hedge," he admits, "but it gives me some protection. Psychologically, it lets me sleep better at night."

"I prefer to short calls rather than go long puts because I feel I have a wider margin for error. You see, in case I'm right but I'm early, there is a bigger range before the losses really start to mount up. When I am long puts, I must be almost exact in my timing of the buy and be right on the direction of the market or the time decay kills me. By shorting calls, I can be wrong on the direction of the market to a certain point and wrong on my timing to a certain point, and still make money."

Brecher let the Aug 265 calls expire worthless but, many times, if he sees the market reversing, he says he won't hesitate to repurchase them prior to expiration.

## EVERYTHING YOU EVER NEEDED TO KNOW ABOUT THE BOOK

How would you like to save $125 the next time you place an OEX order or trade options on Ford, IBM or other CBOE-listed options? Sound farfetched? Not if you understand how and when to use the public limit order book (the *book*) and manage to hone your order-placing skills.

The book is the public customer's best tool for getting a price edge because your limit order receives price priority. For example, while watching prices on your Quotrek (a hand-held quote receiver marketed by CNBC/FNN Signal) or other quote receiver, you notice the OEX Index May 290 calls are volleying between 4 and 4 1/8. You can easily place a market order and pay the 4 1/8 offer, but you see no reason to chase the price because the market is trading in a narrow range and is relatively quiet. Instead, you instruct your phone clerk to book your order and buy the May 290s at the bid price of 4. You hope the market will temporarily tick down a tad and a seller will hit your bid.

As soon as the OEX crowd's order book official receives your ticket, he files your order in the book. Two important events occur: First, the order is flashed on a large screen for all 300 market makers and floor traders to see; simultaneously, your 4 bid is broadcast around the world on every viewer's personal quote receiver. Pat Brigden, an experienced OEX options trader, says the process time for booking orders by the public is one to three minutes in quiet markets and five to seven minutes when busy.

The May 290 calls are indeed a very liquid option; more than 16,000 contracts are traded daily. Because of their superior liquidity, chances are a 4 bid already exists either in the crowd or in the book. If a bid for 50 lots is ahead in the book, your order is next in line and will be filled once the 50 lot is hit. It's a first-in, first-out system. If there is no public bid in the book and the 4 bid is a market maker's bid, your booked order, *no matter what size*, preempts the market maker's bid. The bottom line: *You* have order priority at 4. Before the May 290 calls can trade in the crowd at 4, your order in the book must be filled at 4.

*The book is the domain of the public and gives the customer a distinct advantage; market makers can buy and sell the book but cannot place their orders in the book.*

You must tell your phone clerk to book the order. Otherwise, it's likely that the floor broker in the crowd who handles your broker's order flow will hold the order in his deck and try to execute it himself. This is especially true if your price limit of 4 is within close range of where the 290s are trading, say ¹/₂ point higher, at 4¹/₂. But if your price limit is 2 and the 290s are trading at 4¹/₂, the floor broker will find it impractical to hold the order in his deck. Instead, he'll toss your order in the book.

Most floor brokers are very ethical. Sometimes, however, an order destined for the book is detoured and remains in the floor broker's deck. To be certain your order is actually booked, occasionally ask your phone clerk to do a spot check. In addition, get a status report by asking how many contracts are ahead. You'll find that it pays to keep the floor broker on his or her toes.

Suppose the market doesn't tick down for you to buy at your price limit. In fact, as soon as the order to buy ten May 290 calls is placed, the market upticks and the bid and offer for the May 290 calls jump to 4¹/₈ bid to 4¹/₄ offered, 4¹/₄ bid to 4³/₈ offered, 4³/₈ bid and so on. How smart is it to wait for a fill at 4 in the book with the market moving dramatically in the other direction?

Savvy traders recognize the possibility of an abrupt reversal and hedge their order. They buy half their total position at the 4¹/₈ offer to establish a beachhead. The remainder of their order is booked at 4. In the worst case, the market roars ahead and they participate with a partial position. In the best case, the market, as expected, downticks and they save $62.50 on the ten lot, or half the $125.

Many public customers are unaware that the book exists, let alone how to use it, because neither discount brokers nor major wirehouses advertise the benefits of booking public orders. When customers book an order, they bypass paying brokerage to the floor brokers between $0.50 and $1.50 per contract executed.

You have a choice of where to enter your orders: into the book or with a floor broker. If you feel you may need to change an order quickly once it is entered, skip the book and enter the order with a broker. A good phone clerk will put you on hold while your order is fished from the floor broker's deck and changed. This usually takes about two minutes.

The drawback to using the book is based on turnaround time. In a normal market, orders can be entered and changed quickly. In active markets, however, a considerable number of orders flow through the book and create bottlenecks. Once an order is booked, a straight cancel or cancel/replace (usually a change in price unit) can take 10 to 15 minutes. For active traders, this is an eternity.

What's the difference between RAES (Retail Automatic Execution System) and the book? RAES electronically executes up to ten-lot market orders and marketable limit orders. This means that with the market at 4–4$\frac{1}{8}$, a press of a button guarantees a 4$\frac{1}{8}$ fill for buyers and a 4 fill for sellers. RAES is used for speed. On the other hand, if price is paramount and a speedy fill isn't the issue, the book is the customer's broker of choice.

How can you tell how many contracts, if any, are ahead on the book? Call your phone clerk and ask for the book's bid and offer. The clerk will call the trading desk, which has the only quote machines that give the book's market. He or she may relay, "3$\frac{1}{2}$ bid, 4$\frac{1}{8}$ offer, 25 × 10." This means that 25 contracts are bid at 3$\frac{1}{2}$ and ten are for sale at 4$\frac{1}{8}$. If there is a 4 bid by a market maker, you'll preempt it with your public order if you book your bid at 4. In a quiet market, a good phone clerk will relay this quote to you in one to two minutes. Note that the book will show only the current bid/offer and size. It won't show, for example, if any contracts are 3$\frac{3}{8}$ bid or 2$\frac{7}{8}$ bid if the best bid in the book is 3$\frac{1}{2}$ and the best offer is 3.

The book was created by and is indigenous to the CBOE. All options traded on the CBOE use the book's system. Other options exchanges such as the Amex use a specialist system, which has a book that is open to traders. Only at the CBOE is the book the exclusive province of the public customer. The book will accept limit orders, GTC (good till canceled) limit orders and market orders, but not contingent orders, spread orders, stop orders or GTC stops.

Our subscribers tell us that they prefer CBOE markets to other exchanges. The spreads between the bid and ask are narrower, there is better liquidity and, of course, the book gives them the edge at their limit.

Is there any time when the book doesn't have order priority? Yes: When a floor broker is completing a spread order, he or she may touch the book on one side but may not buy or sell contracts placed on the book at that same price. For example, your 10 lot is a 4 bid in the book, and a 50 lot is traded at 4. If your phone clerk tells you you're not filled, a floor broker begins executing the spread by buying 50 lots at 4 in the crowd, touching the book on one side, then completes the spread by executing whatever is on the other side. This does occur at times—much to the chagrin of active traders.

## THE ALL-PURPOSE OPTION STRATEGY:
## THE CHRISTMAS TREE SPREAD

When a football team breaks from its huddle, the players set up at the line of scrimmage in a formation, usually the L or T formation. As the center snaps the ball, each player knows exactly what to do; there's no guesswork, no deciding at the line. Gaining a first and ten depends on how well each play is executed.

Investors who expect to profit from put and call strategies should apply this strict football discipline to options trading. The most versatile strategy is a type of spread known as the Christmas tree. It should be established monthly, about five weeks before expiration.

The Christmas tree offers the average retail trader a structured approach to trading options. Rather than taking shots willy-nilly, the Christmas tree forces a trader to be disciplined and mechanical in implementing a set strategy on a monthly basis.

The Christmas tree spread is a combination of a basic vertical spread and an out-of-the-money option, sold against the vertical spread. The long option is the spreader's anchor and should be at the money.

An example of a Christmas tree:

| *Vertical Spread* | and | *Short an Out-of-the-Money Option* |
|---|---|---|
| | | Short Dec 265 call @ $1^7/8$ |
| | | (delta -0.25) |
| Short Dec 260 call @ $3^1/2$ | | |
| (delta – 0.38) | | |
| Long Dec 255 call @ 6 | | |
| (delta + 0.54) | | |
| = Debit $2^1/2$ | | = Credit $1^7/8$ |

Overall result is a debit of 5/8 with a delta of –0.09.

### *Profit and profitability profile:*

A vertical spread is established with five points between strike prices (255 and 260). The maximum gain or loss can be five points. A $2^1/2$-point debit spread offers a maximum gain of $2^1/2$ and a maximum potential loss of $2^1/2$. Some spreaders use 10 OEX points and skip the middle strike price.

It is best to establish an at-the-money vertical spread with five weeks to expiration for about a 2 debit. Such a spread offers a reward of 3 while risking 2. At no time should more than a $2^1/2$ debit be paid. It is unwise to buy an investment in which the risk/reward is just 50/50, or the maximum potential loss exceeds the potential gain, e.g., debit of 3 or $3^1/2$.

In terms of probability, the Dec 255 calls have a delta of 0.54, while the Dec 260 calls have a delta of 0.38. The 255 calls will move 0.54 of a point if the underlying moves 1.00 point. As the underlying moves more, the delta of the 255 calls will increase until the calls become in the money, at which point the delta of the 255 calls becomes 1.00 because the calls will move point for point with the underlying. In this example, the two-point debit spread is skewed to the upside with a net delta of + 0.16.

The Christmas tree is completed by hedging (shorting) Dec 265 calls (−0.25 delta) against the debit spread. The result is to reduce the debit from $2^{1}/_{2}$ to $^{5}/_{8}$ ($2^{1}/_{2}$−$1^{7}/_{8}$), but in terms of deltas and net call contracts, it skews the total spread to the short side: The delta of the 265 call is −0.25; add it to the +0.16 from the vertical call spread, and you get a −0.09 delta.

*Worst case:*

If the market immediately goes berserk on the upside, this spread quickly shows a loss. Prior contingent stops—points to adjust—should be placed to avoid a major loss.

*Best case:*

This spread becomes a comfortable winner in a market that creeps up to the 265 level. The 265 shorts collapse from $1^{7}/_{8}$ to $^{1}/_{16}$, giving a gain of $1^{7}/_{8}$ − $^{1}/_{16}$, or 1.8125, while the debit spread returns a profit of $2^{1}/_{2}$ points (5 − $2^{1}/_{2}$). (See the example.)

*Poor situation:*

If the index thrusts down, the maximum potential loss, at expiration and with no adjustments, is $^{5}/_{8}$ of a point.

A call and put Christmas tree should not be done simultaneously because they both imply different price ranges. The essence of a Christmas tree spread is that it offers a cheaper ticket to a wide price distribution, e.g., long 255 calls, short 260 calls, short 265 calls indicate a profit profile at expiration between 255 and 267 (DJIA 2100 to 2175). If a spreader expects the index to trade in the 255 to 235 range (DJIA 2100 to 1940), a put Christmas tree is more appropriate.

For greater maneuverability, skip a strike between the long and the short of the put debit spread, e.g., long 255 puts, short 245 puts instead of shorting the 250 puts. The put Christmas tree is completed by selling one or two out-of-the-money puts against the debit spread, e.g., short one or two 235 puts. Take care to actually place stops contingent on the index trading at a specific lower level, e.g., 242. *Being net short put contracts is potentially a high-risk business if adjustment points are not predetermined and not adhered to.*

*Margin requirements:*

The fallout from October 19, 1987 forced brokerage firms to raise collateral requirements on naked short positions to a minimum of 10 percent of the index plus 100 percent of the current premium. In simple terms, $3,000 plus or minus $500 is needed to support one short contract. Since a hefty sum of approximately $30,000 is required for a 10 lot, capping the net short contract liability by converting the shorts into a credit spread reduces margin requirements by $2/3$, e.g., ten long 225 puts are bought against ten short 235 puts. Margin drops to \$10,000 from \$30,000. Call Christmas trees can be skewed to the short side, but profitability often depends on two factors:

1. the degree to which the spread is skewed (e.g., $2 \times 1 \times 2$ or $1 \times 1 \times 2$, or 2 (skip/strike) $\times 5$, etc.)
2. the exact price at which the options are adjusted

If a spreader forecasts a mildly fluctuating market with a slight downward bias, a call Christmas tree spread skewed to the short side $(1 \times 1 \times 2)$ would be more productive than establishing a put Christmas tree.

Regarding adjustments, no surefire formula exists. Generally, the more a spread is adjusted, the more the yield is tossed away. "Less is more" applies to options as well as architecture. In our own terms, profits come when the positions are allowed to "cook."

Should a spread be "legged" on? That is, should the longs and shorts be put on at two different times and not simultaneously? Or should the Christmas tree be done as a spread? Traders have a great temptation to try for better prices by legging on a Christmas tree. Legging occasionally works and $3/8$ of a point or more is corralled. When legging fails, the cost is $1/2$ point plus. The real bugaboo is when discipline lags and legging results in an unhedged position at day's end. By ignoring the standard Christmas tree formation in a trading range market, a spreader usually winds up a willy-nilly trader.

A compromise legging tactic is to establish half the total Christmas tree formation at current prices, e.g., long 12, short 12, short 12 and leg the remaining $12 \times 12 \times 12$. The spread may not be perfect, but a partial Christmas tree is preferable to an unhedged position.

When shorts dwindle to $1/16$ or $1/8$, should they be brought in? Absolutely! Even if there are just a few days remaining to expiration, get in the habit of booking a GTC order and close out the shorts. Paying $1/16$ to $1/4$ eliminates risk. Does it pay to be greedy and squeeze the last nickel? Routinely allowing shorts to expire worthless will find a distant expiration erupting into a very, very costly expiration.

Is it realistic to expect to collect on both the debit spread and the shorts? Some expirations are very cooperative. In a trading range market, both longs and shorts often deliver their maximum profit. But realistically, some expirations find the debit spread delivering all the profits. The shorts are just a break-even affair.

It is wise to monitor the spread daily. When a $1^{3/4}$-point to $2^{1/4}$-point profit is evident, unwind half the Christmas tree—as a spread—e.g., sell 12, buy 12, buy 12 and, worst case, put stops in on the outstanding spread positions $12 \times 12 \times 12$—where originally established.

## IF YOU ARE EXPECTING A VOLATILE MOVE:
## THE BACKSPREAD STRATEGY

Investors who expect a stock or the index to move dramatically *and* quickly should consider establishing a *backspread*. The technical name of a backspread is reverse ratio spread; it is also known as a volatility spread. Here's an example of how it could work: A trader would buy a larger number of higher strike calls and would simultaneously sell a smaller number of lower strike calls. The maximum upside profit potential for a call backspread is unlimited because more calls are long than short. The maximum downside profit potential for a call backspread is the initial credit received.

Surprisingly, public traders seldom use backspreads. They go long calls, they buy puts, they use ratio spreads, debit and credit spreads. But only once have I found a public trader who backspreads as a basic trading strategy.

"Basically, you can go broke just buying options and waiting for a surge or collapse in the market," according to CBOE market maker Dan Sheridan. A backspread done at the right time and with a 10 percent edge has fabulous potential.

A backspread is generally established for a credit. In fact, if it cannot be done for a credit, it usually is not worth doing. Why? If the premium paid for the long calls is too rich (a very high implied volatility reading will indicate this), a creeping market will cause them to wither more rapidly than the short calls. Creeping markets are anathema to backspreaders.

### Actual Use of a Backspread—Icahn's Bid for Texaco

When Texaco was selling for $47, Carl Icahn, the takeover impresario, bid $60 for the company. Most investors figured that if Icahn were successful, the stock would zoom to $60 or beyond. If he lost the proxy battle, the stock could very well collapse.

If an investor bought the Jul 55 calls at $1^3/_{16}$, and Icahn were subsequently successful, the calls would have traded at $5 or better, a 423 percent gain. But if Icahn lost (which he did), Texaco would fall and the Jul 55 calls would tumble to $^1/_4$ (which they did), a 79 percent loss.

Even when absolutely sure, simply buying calls—taking a shot—is an all-or-none gamble. An alternative would be to establish a backspread. It would corral a handsome profit if Icahn were victorious, but an investor would still emerge a small winner should he fail. For example, consider the following hedged strategy:

Long the Jul 55 calls at $1^3/_{16}$, while shorting the Jul 50 calls at $3^1/_8$. Ratio: 2 × 1 for a $^3/_4$ credit ($1^3/_{16} × 2 = 2^3/_8 - 3^1/_8 = {}^3/_4$). (The reverse of a backspread is a ratio spread: long the 50s, short the 55s, 1 × 2, $^3/_4$ debit.)

### Parameter for gains:

Computer plots show that by July 1, two weeks later, this backspread would begin to turn a profit at $57. Since the total position is net long calls, the maximum potential gain is unlimited. If, on the other hand, Texaco fell to 47$^1/_2$ or less, a maximum credit of $^3/_4$ would be netted.

### Worst case:

Maximum loss from a slow creep up. This spread will turn into a loser, given no adjustments and a slow creep to the strike price of the long calls at 55. At that point, the Jul 55 calls would be worthless, a loss of 1$^3/_{16}$ × 2, while the short Jul 50 calls would trade at $5, an additional loss of 1$^7/_8$.

### Question:

If Texaco's calls are backspread and Texaco surges, large profits result. Yet a fall under the lower strike price of 50 results in only the $^3/_4$ credit. How can an investor make a profit if Texaco plunges to 35 by expiration?

### Answer:

Backspread both the calls and the puts. Buy the Jul 40 puts and sell the Jul 45 puts, 2 × 1 for a credit. Should Texaco plunge under $35, profits will swell because the position is net long put contracts. If, by expiration, Texaco closes between 45 and 50, both the call and put credits would be netted. A maximum loss would occur if Texaco should trade at the lower strike price of 40 on expiration. Again assume there are no adjustments. The loss is mitigated, however, by the $^3/_4$ credit netted for the call backspread.

Is there an ideal time to establish a backspread? In terms of time to expiration, some market makers establish their backspreads six weeks before expiration. Expiration-type backspreads are established two days prior to expiration. One market maker warned us "not to be long premium two weeks prior to expiration." That's when time decay of out-of-the-money options really gathers strength.

In terms of volatility and stock price movement, the ideal time to backspread is when implied volatility is about to expand *and* a very sharp, extended move occurs in the market. Recognize that a sharp, extended move causes volatilities to balloon.

In terms of pure market timing, use a backspread when you have a strong feeling a tremendous move is in store but you're not sure whether it will be up or down.

What is the worst time to be backspread? Right after a huge market move such as the October 1987 crash. Implied volatilities jumped from 18 to more than 100, and option premiums were in the stratosphere. This is the time you absolutely don't want to be net long premium. In fact, you would want to be a premium seller.

Investors may have also taken a cue from social scientists and statisticians who use a concept called "regression to the mean." This concept explains why extraordinary events like the 1987 crash tend to be followed by more ordinary events. In other words, things get back to normal. In terms of regression to the mean, the worst time to backspread is right after a tremendous market surge or major collapse.

Another benefit of backspreads is that margins or costs are lower because there are no uncovered options. A backspread is, in essence, a credit spread with more options added to the long position. For example, returning to Texaco:

Long 10 Jul 55 calls at $1^1/_4$
Short 10 Jul 50 calls at $3^1/_4$
Ratio $1 \times 1$ for a 2 credit $(3^1/_4 - 1^1/_4 = 2)$

The total margin needed for this credit spread is $3,000. This sum is derived by subtracting the credit ($2 per share, or $2,000 in this example) from the spread between both strike prices (Jul 55 strike minus Jul 50 call). ($5-2=3$, or $3,000.)

To convert this credit spread to a backspread, just tack on additional long 55 calls. If we double our long position and buy ten more Jul 55 calls at $1^1/_4$, we pay another $1,250. $3,000 plus $1,250 = $4,250 in money needed to support a backspread $20 \times 10$. $3,000 is margin and $1,250 is the cost of buying the extra calls.

To reverse the position and establish a ratio spread of $10 \times 20$ we need a margin of $2,000 for the debit portion of the spread (you must pay the debit portion outright, just as with a long call or long put). To support the additional ten-lot short requires a *minimum* of $5,000 (10 percent of the stock), so a $10 \times 20$ ratio spread needs $7,000 in collateral to support the position. ($2,000 + $5,000 = $7,000.) This is the *minimum* margin, and it may grow.

What about the possibility of an early exercise? When a call backspread is established and a dramatic rise occurs, the short calls will trade deep in the money. If deep-in-the-money options trade at parity or below, the call buyer may choose to exercise the longs (you, the seller, are assigned). Your short position would be eliminated, and you would be left long the higher strike price calls. This may not be an altogether bad situation. It may force you to sell your longs at a nice profit, or you could stay long these calls, expecting even higher prices.

## USE PUT OPTION INSURANCE TO SKEW PAYOUTS

In 1987, IBM fetched a lofty price of $175 per share. In August 1989, IBM was trading at $115. At $115, IBM would seem a bargain, but technology firms suffer from intense competition and a shortened product cycle. Though such stocks are the darlings of yesteryear, bumpy earnings cause their prices to seesaw. In IBM's case, the bias has been downward.

Investors who bought IBM at $115 were possibly compelled by its cheap price. To reduce risk and supplement IBM's 4 percent dividend, they also sold call options against their long stock purchases.

Such a strategy is simple to buy (not to mention commission intensive): 100 shares of stock are bought, and a call option is simultaneously sold. In the process, extra income is eked out while the underlying stock's volatility is reduced. The fly in the ointment is the position's risk versus potential reward: Simply put, it's negative. Eventually, investors become undone when a sharp down move occurs.

Fault-laden strategies such as the buy-write and strangle selling have derailed many traders. The loser's graveyard is littered with players whose one common thread was a negative risk/reward ratio. Advocates of the buy-writes stress that quiet, nondirectional expirations result in raking in "free" premium income. Since these expirations occur most of the time, this extra income seduces newly minted writers into continuously redoing the strategy. For example, after Mobil Oil swallowed up Superior Oil in the early 1980s, it spent eight expirations at the $30 level. Habitual writers who sold the Aug, Nov, Feb and May 30 calls routinely collected extra income that improved the stock's 6 percent cash dividend.

## QUIETNESS VERSUS EXPLOSIVENESS

Most stocks, however, eventually break up or down from their trading range. Mobil did too. The breakout is often dramatic, with amplitude of 30 percent or more. When the move is up, it's bittersweet for buy-writers because they lose their Nabisco, Kraft, Time Life or Pillsbury at a strike price 20 to 50 points lower than the new, current price. In essence, buy-writers leave a lot of money on the table.

On the other hand, IBM buy-writers are stuck with a declining stock and a 15-point paper loss. The tiny profits from call options never compensate for the sizable losses in the underlying stock. Sometimes, these losses take years to recover.

A negative risk/reward strategy leads to a large number of low-profit transactions, but the few losses that occur are whoppers! On balance, total losses usually exceed total gains.

## ALTERNATIVE TO THE BUY-WRITE

The long stock/long put strategy skews a holder's position to a favorable risk/reward. An investor essentially "marries" a put option to a long stock position. Upside potential for the underlying stock is unlimited, while the put "insurance policy" protects against a stock price collapse. Using puts as an insurance policy is no guarantee of profits, but protection against a colossal loss. It's easy to make back $1,500 but psychologically almost impossible to recover $20,000. Review your past 20 trades—especially buy-writes and credit spreads. Check how much better off your profit picture would have been with a favorable risk/reward ratio.

For example, when IBM was at $96 and the company was buying back millions of shares along with streamlining its work force, it would seem the stock should rise. But from a risk/reward basis, 200 shares at $96 was still a $19,200 outlay, which for most investors is no small change. Buying two Jan 95 puts at $2, for a cost of $400, to protect a long position of 200 shares of IBM at $96, would have insured that if IBM traded at $85 by the third Friday in January, holders could put 200 shares of stock to the premium seller at $95. Instead of losing $2,200, the loss would be contained at $600. (Cost of put: $400 + 1 point loss on 200 shares.)

Seasoned put practitioners include the $400 put premium in their cost of doing business. They figure that if IBM was worth $96 per share, it certainly was worth $98 per share. In essence, the put purchase serves, for a five-week period, as a protection of a $19,200 asset from an unqualified decline—no mean feat, nevertheless. Some traders with a broader time frame may choose to pay a little more premium to buy puts that expire 90 days out (e.g., Apr 95 puts for $3\frac{3}{4}$).

## THE NEXT STEP

Remaining in a 1:1 ratio of stock to puts is a simple insurance hedge. But go a bit further than this hedge and a new opportunity arises. Buy 50 percent more than the original put purchase and this creates a hedged position *plus*. A dramatic move in IBM either way—under 92 or over 99—will deliver a substantial profit. The position now takes on the characteristics of a backspread, in which a small sum may be lost if quietness prevails, but a fabulous potential exists once a big directional move occurs.

These extra puts add to an investor's maneuverability. For example, if IBM drops briefly to 93, the extra put(s) can be sold for a profit without disturbing the original put insurance hedge. In fact, investors can custom-make a put hedge to gear it to their own forecast, wallet size, threshold of pain or desire for reward.

The downside to such a seemingly terrific strategy is that you can become "insurance-poor." Long premium in a quiet market is generally a losing proposition. Do it automatically across the board and it will dent your wallet. You've got to pick and choose and, as in all successful endeavors, put your own spin on the ball. Marrying puts to a 6 percent-yielding Ford at $49 is sometimes as smart as buying puts on high-tech Apple Computer at $45, which pays less than 1 percent. Ford fell to $41\frac{1}{2}$, while Apple fell to $33\frac{1}{3}$ in one month.

For example, long stock/long put strategies are far more capital-intensive than doing put credit spreads. One hundred shares of IBM at $96 per share cost $9,600. On 50 percent margin, $4,800 cash plus interest to carry the $4,800 debit balance is required. Add the price of the long puts and the costs increase. A 1 × 1 put credit spread done for a $1\frac{1}{2}$ credit requires only $350. Do it 10 × 10 and only $3,500 is needed. Witness the trade-off: *negative risk/reward but much leverage. Positive risk/reward but large capital outlay*.

Take this example of getting more options for $400. It takes $400 to buy two Jan 95 puts. The Jan 90 puts are cheaper to buy. If the price is $\frac{1}{2}$, then eight puts will cost $400 and four puts will cost $200. Success depends on the degree to which the put hedge is skewed. Note that, while premium expenditures drop, break-even points are stretched considerably. Shrewd put hedgers sometimes buy a quantity of the 95s *and* some 90s.

Experienced traders whose forecast for IBM has a downward bias may instead short it at $96 and simultaneously buy the 100 or 95 calls for protection. Short sellers are obligated to pay the dividend on the borrowed stock. In IBM's case, that's a hefty $1.12 per quarter, per share.

What is the best time to use this strategy? Generally, if you wait for the stock to make an extreme move one way and then pull the trigger, your put hedge may be done at advantageous prices. A quick bounce will allow you to peel off some stock at higher prices and pay for a chunk of your long puts.

Carefully watch the implied volatility levels of the options you buy: If an option is theoretically valued at 2 but sells at $4\frac{1}{2}$, it's way overpriced. The stock may go your way, but this fully priced put won't serve as a hedge with an edge. Your break-even points will really widen because you've overpaid for the put in the first place.

Puts and stop loss orders can both be used to protect a position, but puts are preferred for the simple reason that unexpected bad news may cause a stock to gap down; stops offer absolutely no gap protection.

## MOBIL REDUX

After two years of sitting on a trading range around 30, Mobil broke out on the upside and in two months settled in the 40 to 44 range. All the call premiums earned from the buy-write strategy pale compared to the missed opportunity of the 10 to 14 points Mobil made during its two-month move. In conclusion, the only thing that buy-writes can add to your portfolio is might-have-beens, which won't keep you warm on cold winter nights.

## BUYING AND SELLING: TWO-STEP WITH A STOP TACTIC

Good options traders promptly jump on a developing trend, but the cost of buying a wasting asset too early saddles the buyer with a temporary paper loss. Later, when the forecast proves correct and the calls climb sharply, the benefit of scaling down (when the calls traded lower) becomes evident.

Some floor traders are reluctant to average down because they abide by the maxim "Never average a loss." That may be a good rule for market makers; in a bind, they can spread off calls or puts with other options.

Most retail customers, however, are market timers. Their initial buy price depends on where in the intraday trading range they got filled. Most often, they have paid up and chased the price of a call or put. For these customers, averaging down, just once—with a stop below—has some real tactical benefits.

Like professional traders, the average retail customer is often right and often early. One fundamental tactic used to avoid nonrecoverable losses (a major hit) is to predetermine risk in dollars on a per-trade basis, e.g., $500, $1,000, $2,000. In this way, you won't drop half your stake due to one bad trade. "Never, never allow yourself to take a major hit," says CBOE market maker Ernie Naiditch. "A trader can afford to take a lot of small losses as long as he always makes the corrections necessary to be on the right side when the big move comes."

## SPREADING RISK

Let's assume a beginning trader has $15,000 to risk in an options trading account. There may be $30,000 or $300,000 in stocks and bonds in the same account. These assets may be used as collateral to support various options positions, but only $15,000 is earmarked for options activity and subject to loss. If this at-risk stake is lost, options trading ceases.

## PREDETERMINING RISK

A potential dollar downside of $1,500 is assumed for each position taken. The odds are remote that ten losses in a row or ten profits in a row will occur. So the possibility of risking and losing $15,000 in quick order—a nonrecoverable loss—is slim.

## EXAMPLE OF SCALE-DOWN BUYING

The Oct 250 calls are trading at $5 and Mr. Public thinks they are a good buy. A six-lot position is established at $5 for an outlay of $3,000. That's the total dollar risk.

Sure enough, an intraday market squall crushes these calls to 4, at which point Mr. Public scales down and doubles his position. He is now long twelve lots with an average price of $4^{1/2}$. His total dollar risk now becomes $5,400.

Since Mr. Public is not in the business of risking $5,400, or 1/3 of his risk capital, on one trade, he places a stop at $3^{1/4}$. His total dollar risk is $1^{1/4} \times 12$, or $1,500. In lieu of placing a price stop ($3^{1/4}$), a stop can be placed contingent on the index trading at a particular level. For example, if OEX trades at $254.50, the floor broker will execute the sell order on the calls. This is called a contingent order.

Worst case: After scaling down at 4, the calls keep falling. The stop at $3^{1/4}$ triggers a market order. He gets filled at $3^{1/8}$. The calls then trade a shade lower to $3, turn on a dime and rally to $10. Loss: $1,500 plus commissions. Feeling: miserable!

Being prematurely stopped out is a hazard of using stops, but stops must be lived with! Buying a call at $4^{1/2}$ and watching it expire worthless in the hope the underlying index rallies is a direct route to tapping out.

Another scenario: Mr. Public doesn't average down. Instead he buys his whole position—a twelve lot at $5, for an outlay of $6,000.

The problem of shooting the works at one price is that it leaves no cash reserve and, in terms of human nature, little willpower to scale down when prices edge down. A two-point stop (on a drop from 5 to 3) would cause Mr. Public to suffer a $2,400 loss plus commissions. This is considerably more than the $1,500 dollar risk limit originally established for each trade.

Best case: After Mr. Public scaled down once at $4, the calls rally to $10. With an average price of $4^{1/2}$, Mr. Public has a $5^{1/2}$-point profit. That's $6,600 plus commissions.

Next best case: Mr. Public's original buy at $5 was right on target; the calls immediately travel to $10. While he doesn't get an opportunity to scale down, his profit is 5 points on a six lot or $3,000. Not too shabby.

Where does scale-up selling enter the picture? As soon as calls bought at 5 start trading in the $5^{1}/_{2}$ to 6 zone, immediately book a limit order to sell half the position at $6 and put a trailing stop on the remainder at $5^{1}/_{4}$. The value of this tactic is to lock up some profit and protect the remainder of this paper profit from loss.

You could also immediately place a trailing stop at $5^{1}/_{4}$ for the total twelve lot position. As calls climb, raise the trailing stop. Eventually, the calls will reverse their climb and the position will be stopped out—on the way down. But you won't wind up taking a loss after you've had this nice paper profit.

A few comments about profits. A trading adage, "Never allow a paper profit to turn into a loss," can be executed effortlessly with trailing stops. The trailing stop is your protection from turning profits into losses.

Why not just sell this entire position when the calls rise from 6 to 7? It's human nature to cash in all your chips for a quick $2,000 profit in a very short time. But if you do cash in your total position the first point up, you'll have no "bullets" left to sell if the option reaches 10 or higher. And you will never make a big score.

*You can't hit only singles in the options game because the losses manage to nullify the singles. It's the big hit, the double, triple and home run—even with half your initial position—that leaves you comfortably on the plus side.* Please remember that when you apply this scaling tactic.

When is the best time to enter a scale-down buy or scale-up sell? Believe it or not, some investors have trouble lifting their phones to average a position. Perhaps they have a change of heart. Perhaps they feel good money is following bad money. Not so! Set your parameters and place your second order *immediately after* the first order is filled. Get mechanical about it!

# CHAPTER 4

# Getting a "Trading Edge" over the Markets

*BY DAVID L. CAPLAN*

**Editor's Note:**

David Caplan presents a series of minor strategies when applying options to the task of making profits. This chapter is less singular in strategy than in tidbits of valuable information.

If this chapter can be summarized adequately, this is how the editor would do it: "It's a chapter which tells the readers about all the little 'gotchas' in the options game. These little 'gotchas' by themselves won't take the trader out of the options game, but they will add up to large debilitating losses which will take the trader out."

Throughout this chapter, the author points out the difficulties with using options and where the reader can encounter traps. He doesn't mince words when he lists the misconceptions about options trading. As a nice balance to pointing out the flaws with which most traders use options, he also lists ten ways to use options effectively. This is somewhat akin to being slapped and then immediately being rewarded—no different than what the market does to us.

The author emphasizes the point that how we feel about the underlying market is how we should design our options plays. If we feel that a stock is to go up, we should design bullish options strategies. Even knowing whether or not the stock will go up volatilely or in a slow meandering fashion is reflected in different strategies. Our author points out that the quality of the upmove is important in designing the right options strategy.

This chapter contains lots of good information that the reader can implement immediately. The reader, however, should be warned that perfection with little details will make him a detailed trader. Attention to how these little details add up to make a larger trading strategy will make the detailed trader a very successful trader.

## INTRODUCTION

Options can be one of the most powerful weapons in a trader's arsenal, but they are one of today's most overlooked and misused opportunities. Less than 10 percent of traders have integrated options as a regular part of their strategy, and even these traders use them improperly most of the time. Usually traders will buy a call or sell a put option if they are bullish on a market, or buy a put or sell a call if they are bearish, with the expectation that they will profit if the market moves in the predicted direction. This doesn't always work because time of expiration, volatility, delta and time decay all come into play and affect the premium value. First, you must understand the mechanics of trading and be able to use the quirks in options behavior and pricing to your benefit.

We will focus on actual hands-on trading techniques to help you determine when to use which options, whether to buy or sell, which strike price and expiration to use, how to recognize options trading opportunities and much more. In this way, we will improve on the many books on options trading that give little more than definitions, descriptions of the markets and complicated mathematical formulas for calculating premiums, volatility, etc.

## FOUR OF THE MOST COMMON MISTAKES MADE BY OPTIONS PLAYERS

I've concluded that beginning options traders commonly make these four mistakes:

1. overemphasis of the limited-risk aspect of options purchases
2. selling options without a game plan
3. implementing arbitrage or spread plays too soon
4. overtrading

First, most traders have been introduced to options by purchasing an option based on an analysis or feeling that the underlying market was about to move in a certain direction. In deciding which option to purchase, little regard was paid to the month or strike price. The emphasis was placed on the limited risk of the option purchase and on buying options as cheaply as possible to keep potential losses at a minimum.

Then, one of four things invariably happened:

- The market moved dramatically, almost vertically in their favor, allowing these traders to reap huge profits. Although I have heard such stories, I have never seen this happen to anyone I know personally.
- The market moved adversely to their positions and they lost money. The traders at least felt vindicated that they were smart enough to choose options instead of the underlying futures or stocks, thereby limiting their risk to only the purchased options.
- The market remained neutral, and although an underlying position would not have lost money, the options lost all their value.
- The market moved in their favor, but not quickly enough to alleviate the loss of the time value of their options. They were right in their market prediction but lost money anyway. This is probably the worst event that can happen to a trader.

Unfortunately, the last three scenarios occur more than 90 percent of the time.

A second problem occurs after traders learn how to profit from selling options but without sticking to a plan. This can work for awhile, but eventually they get caught in front of severely trending markets such as we have seen recently in currencies and stock indexes. Although the odds are in their favor for profiting on a particular trade, the times they get caught in a severely trending market will cause losses that can be devastating to their accounts.

A third mistake occurs when traders attempt to do arbitrage or complex spreads with options. After reading many books about the opportunities for substantial profits with low risk in arbitrage strategies, these traders decide to profit from the small disparities in price that often arise between the S&P 500 and New York Futures Exchange options, or Swiss franc and Japanese yen options or different months of bond options. They also attempt complex spreads such as butterflies and conversions to lock in small profits.

These traders soon learn that although these strategies sound great, they are almost impossible to execute off the floor. They would be competing with floor traders and large companies with immense resources, huge volume and lower trading costs, not to mention faster execution. They would have the same chance of profiting at arbitrage as they would beating John McEnroe in tennis; they may be great country club players, but these are world-class pros who always win.

Finally, there's a danger of overtrading when you don't take breaks from trading to relax and recharge your batteries. Traders are very reluctant to get away from the markets and miss potential opportunities, but long stretches of trading can be extremely draining and cause traders to act like brainwashed prisoners of war. They are ready to abandon all their old trading plans and follow any system that promises profit. This is when it would be much more beneficial to take time out to examine and learn from previous errors. Don't worry: With more than 30 markets now having options, each containing three months of option expirations, ten or more strike prices and all configurations from bullish to bearish, there will always be enough profitable opportunities to keep the most nimble traders busy. But if you're fatigued, you may fail to recognize obvious opportunities.

## SOME POPULAR MISCONCEPTIONS ABOUT OPTIONS TRADING

Certain misconceptions advanced by many books and brokers are also responsible for significant losses by many traders. Let's look at four of these oft-heard but money-draining ideas:

1. *"If you buy an option and the market goes in your favor, you will always profit."* Wrong, wrong, wrong. When you purchase an option, you pay not only for its intrinsic (actual) value, but for its time value. This means that each day you hold an option, the time value must drop somewhat. The market must move in your favor enough to offset this decay in time value premium. And in most cases, unless you cash the option out at an opportune time, it must continue to move in your favor. Buying options is like swimming upstream; unless you move very fast, you'll be swept away. (See Figure 4.1.)

   In the beginning of 1991, the S&P 500 advanced more than 3,000 points in four months (a gain of $15,000 per futures contract). Some call options eroded in price during this period. Even more distressing, a not-so-well-priced call option, available to many investors because of its "reasonable" price, *lost* value even as the market made new, all-time highs. These situations are not uncommon.

2. *"There is big money to be made selling overvalued options."* This is another one of those good news/bad news situations. The good news is that about 80 percent of the time this statement is correct. The bad news is that the other 20 percent of the time can cost you far in excess of all the profits you've made. This is because when selling options your profits are limited strictly to the premium you receive, but your risk is not. Over time, all markets will make giant, unexpected moves. Over the last several years, I've seen moves in silver equal to $20,000 in a futures contract in one hour; 5,000-point moves ($25,000) in the S&P in one day; moves in bonds of 10 points ($10,000) overnight. Getting caught in one of these moves without a trading plan can wipe out years of profits.

**Figure 4.1**   TOP: Price Chart of S&P 500 from Jan. 1, 1991 to May 31, 1991. BOTTOM: Price Chart of S&P 500 Call with $390 Strike Price for the Same Period.

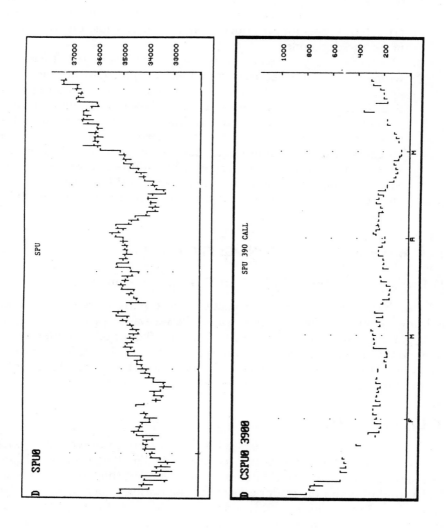

Source: Reprinted with permission from FutureSource.

It is like slowly walking upstairs (building profits) and then jumping out the window (losing it all at once).

3. *"Computer programs can tell you how to trade options—which ones to buy and sell, and which strategy to use."* There is no question that computers are useful in trading options, but the state of the art is not developed enough to analyze all the factors that go into options trading. Computers should be used to help evaluate strategies, crunch numbers and produce "what-if" scenarios, but you must make the decisions.

4. *"Trading is a zero-sum game,"* implying that for every loser there is a winner. This often-abused statement is quoted over and over again. The truth of the matter is that there are many more losers than winners. This is because the trader bears all the hidden costs of trading: the brokers, exchanges and their employees, regulatory agencies, computers, publications, etc. An average of 15 to 20 cents of each trading dollar pays for expenses, so that every year we must profit by this amount just to break even. Even Las Vegas casinos give their customers better odds! This is not an easy task, and it is another reason to choose only the very best plays.

## TEN WAYS TO USE OPTIONS EFFECTIVELY

### 1. Use an Option Instead of a Stop To Protect a Contract.

Purchasing an option for protection will greatly reduce the risk of holding a contract. This is a significantly better way to protect a position than placing a stop in the market, which could be hit on a sudden reaction close to the low of the entire move. The cost of the option is a very small price to pay for the protection, considering the potential for profit on the futures contract.

### 2. Use Covered Option Writing.

This strategy is initiated by selling an out-of-the-money call (put) option against a long (short) futures position. The best time to initiate this strategy is when a market is at a very oversold (put) or overbought (call) condition and the trader expects consolidation to occur. The trader receives premium (additional income) from the sale of the option and is still in a position to profit if the market continues to trend in his or her favor.

In June 1987, after the S&P 500 had been in a four-year uptrend, out-of-the-money calls were becoming very overvalued. I recommended that my clients hedge their futures and cash positions by selling out-of-the-money calls. Over the next several months, the S&P 500 continued to trend higher and the futures position became much more profitable.

The calls sold were also profitable, however, because the decay in their time value outweighed the move in the underlying futures contract. This is a safe, conservative strategy for all traders to consider. It also requires no additional margin other than that already used for the futures position.

### 3. Protect a Futures Position by Combining the Purchase of a Put with the Sale of a Call.

This strategy simply combines numbers one and two above and is highly recommended almost any time a position is at a substantial profit. You will have total downside protection with the potential for additional profit, all at little or no premium cost. This is because the premium for purchasing the puts is paid for by selling the call.

### 4. Buy a Low-Priced Option When a Contract is about To Expire.

In the last several weeks prior to expiration, you can purchase options with little time value remaining. For example, an at-the-money gold option with about two weeks to trade can be purchased for about $200. If you were to predict a gold move correctly, you would make only $200 less than you could have made with a futures contract. But you have limited your losses to $200 if the market moves against you overnight or on the weekend.

### 5. Use Options in Volatile Markets.

You may have strong feelings that a market is about to make an explosive move, but the risk involved in taking a net futures position is too great. You can still trade the market with limited risk by purchasing options or using options spreads.

### 6. Use Options To Profit from Trading Range Markets.

Markets are in a trading range more than 80 percent of the time, often making net traders frustrated and stopped out of positions. By using neutral options strategies, you can trade these markets, which actually provide some of the highest mathematical probabilities for success.

The total position isn't affected much as the market moves up and down. As the underlying futures price approaches the sold option's strike price, this loss is compensated by a gain on the other side. The continual loss of time value on both sides of the trade makes this strategy attractive anytime there is a neutral or nontrending market.

### 7. Use Options When You Need Lower Margin Requirements.

Reduced margins for many options strategies allow you to develop a diversified portfolio with less capital. Many options strategies require no margin at all. The premium you pay, often much less than a futures margin, is the maximum amount you can lose if the market moves adversely.

### 8. Find Higher Probability of Profit.

Positions using options premiums have higher probability of profit than futures positions: for example, ratio spreads constructed by purchasing fairly valued close-to-the-money options and selling overvalued out-of-the-money options when volatility is high.

### 9. Increase Risk/Reward Ratio.

By taking advantage of disparities in options premium by selling overvalued and/or buying undervalued options, you can initiate trades that have reduced risk but still significant profit potential.

### 10. Increase Trading Opportunities.

Circumstances such as lack of trend or high volatility provide opportunities in many markets for the options strategist that would be inadvisable for an outright position. The options strategist is the only trader that can trade flat, trendless markets profitably.

## EXPRESS YOUR EXACT FEELINGS ON A MARKET WITH PRECISE OPTIONS POSITIONS

Generally, you are limited to buying the market if you are bullish and selling it if you are bearish. You may adjust the quantity or stop loss points of your position based on your expectation of what the market might do, but this is the extent of your latitude.

Most traders look at options as a substitute for an outright bullish position, where you merely buy a call when you are bullish or a put if you are bearish. However, you can also use options strategies to express a more precise view on the market and initiate types of positions that are otherwise unavailable.

What would you do if you weren't sure exactly where the market was going but felt fairly sure it was going to maintain a certain range of prices in the near future? Suppose you felt the market had bottomed and you missed buying at its best prices: How could you buy this market at less than today's price or be absolutely guaranteed a profit? What if you were bullish but didn't want to lose if the market went slightly against you? And finally, what if you thought the market was going to move up slowly within a limited range and you wanted a position with a high probability of profit?

The following four positions are available to the knowledgeable options trader and add to the list of unique benefits of trading options.

### 1. How To Profit When You Don't Know Where the Market Is Going but Feel You Know Where It Isn't Going

There are two positions that can reflect your views in these instances: the synthetic futures position and the neutral options strategy.

In late 1985, the S&P had been in a bull market for almost two years but was languishing at the 170 to 180 level most of the year. At that time, I wasn't sure that a large rally would occur (even though it subsequently did); however, I was confident that the 170 level would hold. Therefore, with the market trading at about 180, I purchased a Dec S&P 195 call, sold the 170 put and received a credit (synthetic futures position). This meant that as long as the market stayed above 170 (my opinion), I would profit on the transaction. And if the market did rally strongly, I would not only have a call that didn't cost me anything but also the potential for unlimited profits above the 195 level.

At the beginning of 1988, bonds were trading at the 90 level, and it was my view that I would see a range in the next several months between 80 and 100. Option premium was also at historically high levels at that time, allowing us to sell 80 puts and 100 calls (neutral options position) for up to $1,000. Since these options would expire worthless in less than six months if bonds stayed within this large 20-point range, I would receive a return of almost 30 percent on margin (100 percent annualized) without having to predict market direction. (See Figure 4.2.)

### 2. How To Buy a Market at Less Than Today's Price

When silver plunged to near $4 an ounce in October 1990, some investors thought it was an excellent time to purchase silver, while others wanted to wait until it was at $3.80 or less. There was, in fact, a way to satisfy both views by purchasing silver at $3.75 and receiving a return that would be over 50 percent annually. Here's how:

In the middle of that October, when silver was trading at $4.15, you could sell a $3.75 Mar put option and receive a premium of $300. Since the margin required for this strategy was $1,200, this would produce a return of 25 percent (or 75 percent annually) if the contract was above $3.75 when this option expired. This is because no purchaser of a $3.75

**Figure 4.2**    Profit/Loss of Neutral Option Position

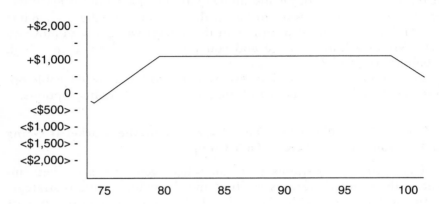

put would want to exercise this option, since he or she could sell silver at a higher price through the cash or futures markets. The $300 premium would be yours to keep when the silver option expired in four months, thereby producing a return of 75 percent per annum.

Once this put option expired, you could proceed to the next active trading month and initiate the strategy again. However, if silver fell to $3.75 or lower and the purchaser of the $3.75 put option exercised the put, you would owe silver at $3.75 per ounce less the $300 premium (or 6 cents per ounce) that you were paid for this put, an effective price of 75 cents per ounce. Since silver was trading above $4.15 when we initiated the strategy, we are effectively purchasing silver for almost 50 cents less than its previous price, a savings of more than 10 percent.

This strategy works similarly for any listed stock or commodity, but we must caution that this is for the long-term investor who wants to purchase the stock or commodity at a lower price. Why? Because if the market continues to move lower, you can experience losses (in the silver example above, below $3.69). Also, you will not be "in the market" if a large move begins to occur, although profits will be made if the market moves higher. Despite these two situations, however, the strategy is an excellent way to lower your ownership costs or obtain an excellent return in almost any market.

### 3. How To Trade a Bullish Market with No Risk of Loss if the Market Moves Lower (Against You)

In August 1987, silver was trading at between $7.50 and $8 after moving from $5.50 to almost $10 over the previous several months. At that time I was bullish, but since silver had been in a long-term down-trend, I felt that a position in futures or options was too risky. However, out-of-the-money silver calls had extremely high premiums (volatility), about twice that of closer-to-the-money calls. To take advantage of this disparity, I initiated ratio option spreads (buying a call, selling two higher calls) by selling two Dec silver $11.25 calls for each Dec silver $9 calls I purchased. I was able to receive a premium of $1,000 per position more for the two calls I sold than the one I purchased.

This position has no downside risk because all the silver options would be worthless if they expired with the price of silver under $9. In fact, I would profit by the amount of premium I had received—$1,000. But I was still able to participate in the upside move because I would make $50 for each cent by which silver exceeded the strike price of the options I purchased. (See Figure 4.3.)

In fact, these positions would be profitable through the $14 level of silver, a price that hadn't been realized since the early 1980s. The combination of all factors made this position an excellent one: no downside potential and profits available if the market continued to move up. The only risk at all is if the market price went beyond the strike price of the sold calls, since I was short two options for every one I purchased (I recommend closing out the entire position if this occurs). However, since the closest-to-the-money options would gain in value much more quickly than the out-of-the-money options, and the out-of-the-money options would deteriorate in time value more quickly, this position will continue to work in our favor in most instances.

## 4. How To Profit in a Slightly Bullish Market

In September 1989, bonds rallied to 100 and traded in a 94 to 98 range. My market view was long-term bullish; however, it looked like an intermediate top was in place that could last for several months. Therefore, I recommended buying the Mar bond 100 call and selling the 90 put and 104 call. By doing this, the price of the options I sold was paying for the calls I purchased. The position would not lose money unless bonds went below the 90 level. However, since there would be unlimited loss if this did occur, and it was my view in entering the trade that bonds would not go below the 94 level, I was using a close under 94 as my signal to exit the trade. This would have produced a loss of approximately $300. On the upside, my profit objective was $4,000, producing a position that had a risk/reward of 13.33 to 1. (See Figure 4.4.)

**Figure 4.3**    Profit/Loss of December Silver Ratio Spread

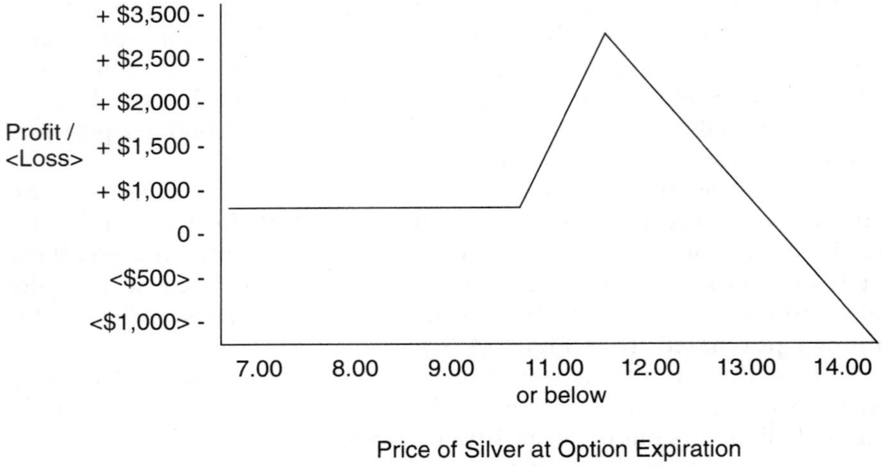

Price of Silver at Option Expiration

## CAN OPTION PUT AND CALL PRICES, RATIO OR VOLUME PREDICT MARKET DIRECTION?

Many market experts have attempted to determine whether or not options pricing and volume can be used to forecast imminent market movements. I have made the following conclusions:

### Changes in Options Premium Levels

Options premium levels are determined by the volatility in the particular market. Quite simply, if a market is not making significant moves in either direction, options premium should be low because buyers would not be willing to pay as much for an option with little expectation of value. Options sellers would also feel more comfortable selling in this type of market and be content with less premium than usual.

Conversely, in a very active market, options sellers will refuse to sell options without receiving a high premium, due to the unlimited risk of loss if the market moves against them. Options buyers would be willing to pay more because the options now have a higher probability of value.

The differences in options premium levels can be quite dramatic. For example, at the end of September 1989, with options premiums near historical low levels in silver, I could purchase the Mar silver 575 call, the closest-to-the-money option, for $650. This was only one strike price (25 cents) out of the money and had almost five months before expiration. However, in 1987 when silver rallied quickly from $6 to $8 and volatility

**Figure 4.4**   Profit/Loss Strategy for a Slightly Bullish Market

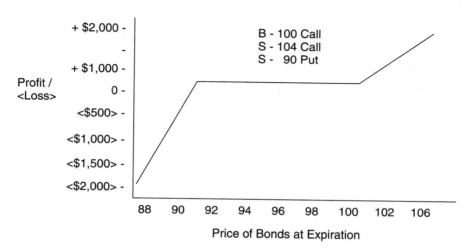

increased dramatically, I was able to sell $11.25 silver calls, options that were more than ten strike prices from the money ($3) for up to $2,000.

Rarely do changes in options premium levels occur in advance, making them indicators of what's likely to happen; they only mirror changes in the futures prices, flowing along with them. Even when they do lead the market action, the changes are very subtle. For example, prior to the 20-point break in bond prices from the 100 level in 1987, I noticed the premium on bond puts increasing around 20 percent, without any significant market action. Volatility was at that time close to historically low levels. This increase in volatility seemed to reflect the fact that large traders (professionals, hedgers, institutions) were entering the market, either speculatively or to hedge previously profitable positions. I felt that this increase in volatility was significant because bond options are much more liquid than any other option contract, and the typical bond option trader is a more sophisticated investor.

After trading options for the last nine years, I must say incidents like this are few, and the changes are usually so subtle that most traders will miss them.

### Changes in Put and Call Ratios or Volume

After studying changes in put and call ratios and volume of options traded over the last several years in many different options contracts, I have been unable to find any correlation that would help to accurately predict future price action. The reason is that options are still in their infancy and in the process of being discovered by many institutional traders. Many times the increase in volume in options contracts is tied simply to the fact that more traders are now beginning to use options. Another reason is that options can be used for so many purposes. A large trader who is bullish bonds may go into the market and purchase 1,000 bond calls to profit from the anticipated move. Another trader who is equally bullish bonds but who may be long futures or cash bonds may go into the market and sell 1,000 bond options just to hedge this position and lock in a specific rate of return. With so many trading objectives by those in the marketplace, there is usually no mathematical significance in the increase in volume or changes in put and call ratios.

## VOLATILITY

The significance of volatility is overlooked and underutilized by most options traders. This includes both the effect of volatility on the premium cost of the option when purchased and on future changes in volatility on the position.

Volatility is simply a mathematical computation of the magnitude of movement in an option, based on the activity in the underlying market. Volatility rises when the market makes a rapid move up or down, and in a quiet market, volatility will be low. These readings are compared to determine the historical volatility range, and whether current volatility is high or low.

### Using Options Volatility

There are two types of volatility: historical and implied. Historical volatility is calculated by using a past series of prices of an option. For example, a trader could use a 90-day, 30-day, 10-day, etc., price history to determine the option's historical volatility. Each set of calculations will result in a different figure for volatility and a different theoretical (fair) value for the option.

Implied volatility is calculated by using the most current options prices, commodity price level, time, expiration and interest rate. This provides a more accurate picture of an option's current volatility, as opposed to historical volatility's smoothing of past price action. I use implied volatility in my option pricing calculations and then compare the current numbers to past records of implied volatility to determine whether volatility is relatively high or low. (See Figure 4.5.)

When volatility is relatively low, you should look for options buying strategies because the market is likely to make a strong move; conversely, consider selling strategies when volatility is high, to take advantage of the relatively overvalued premiums.

**Figure 4.5**  Sample Volatility Composite Index

| | Two-Year Range | Six-Month Range | Feb | Mar | Apr | Volatility Trend | Ranking 1 = Low 10 = High |
|---|---|---|---|---|---|---|---|
| British Pound | 9.6 – 16.7 | 9.6 – 15.7 | 9.8 | 12.8 | 15.7 | UP | 9 |
| Cattle | 9.0 – 17.6 | 9.1 – 14.2 | 9.7 | 9.1 | 10.1 | DOWN | 2 |
| Corn | 14.5 – 28.6 | 15.4 – 28.6 | 19.8 | 21.2 | 20.8 | — | 5 |
| Copper | 20.0 – 41.8 | 20.0 – 34.2 | 27.5 | 24.5 | 20.0 | DOWN | 2 |
| Crude Oil | 24.6 – 98.2 | 29.4 – 98.2 | 63.7 | 32.4 | 30.2 | DOWN | 2 |
| Deutsche Mark | 9.2 – 16.7 | 9.2 – 15.2 | 10.6 | 12.9 | 15.2 | UP | 8 |
| Eurodollar | 10.4 – 28.8 | 10.4 – 21.2 | 19.9 | 14.7 | 12.8 | — | 3 |
| Gold | 13.4 – 34.3 | 13.4 – 34.3 | 18.1 | 14.9 | 13.4 | DOWN | 1 |
| Japanese Yen | 8.2 – 17.5 | 8.2 – 13.6 | 11.3 | 12.1 | 12.2 | — | 6 |
| S&P 500 | 15.3 – 33.8 | 15.3 – 31.8 | 18.2 | 16.7 | 15.3 | DOWN | 1 |
| Silver | 19.5 – 46.4 | 19.5 – 34.6 | 34.6 | 30.1 | 23.9 | — | 3 |
| Soybeans | 13.2 – 24.2 | 13.2 – 24.2 | 18.6 | 18.3 | 19.3 | — | 5 |
| Sugar | 22.7 – 36.4 | 25.0 – 35.8 | 22.7 | 25.0 | 32.6 | DOWN | 2 |
| Swiss Franc | 10.0 – 18.8 | 10.0 – 15.2 | 10.8 | 13.2 | 15.2 | UP | 9 |
| Treasury Bond | 8.5 – 16.3 | 8.5 – 14.2 | 10.1 | 9.2 | 9.1 | DOWN | 2 |

Volatility is an important factor in determining the price of an option; all options models depend heavily on the calculation of volatility in determining the fair market value of an option. What we are actually saying when we calculate volatility is that the odds are 67 percent or better that the market will hold within the calculated range for a period of one year.

For example, if gold is trading $500 per ounce and has a volatility of 20 percent, the probability is two to one that gold will hold a range of $400 to $600 (20 percent on either side of $500) for a one-year period. Based on this, options sellers can calculate the premium they would want to receive for selling various gold puts and calls, based on the probability that the strike price would be reached prior to the expiration of the option. If volatility is high, options sellers would determine that it is more likely that the option price could be reached, so they would ask a higher premium. If volatility is low, options sellers would determine that it is unlikely that the option would be exercised, so they would ask less for selling the option.

Changes in volatility affect the premium levels in options you are going to purchase as well as those you have already purchased or sold. A good example of this is the crude oil and S&P 500 option markets, where volatility has ranged from 20 percent to more than 100 percent. If you purchased an out-of-the-money option with volatility high, you would need a substantial price rise before that option would be profitable at expiration. The expense of the purchase price as well as time value would be working severely against you. However, with volatility at lower levels, this option would not only cost much less, but would require a smaller move for the positions to be profitable. This is because volatility is an additional factor working in your favor; volatility ordinarily increases when prices begin to rise, thereby increasing the option's premium.

Comparisons of volatility between different months and strike prices are often overlooked. I always use strike prices that are nearest to the money when I calculate volatility, because I consider this the most accurate representation of the actual volatility of the option contract. Premiums of out-of-the-money options can often be greatly distorted.

For example, in June 1987, silver ratio spreads provided a high probability of profit because the volatility for the out-of-the-money silver calls was double that of the at-the-money calls. This can lead to significant opportunities because volatility for all the strike prices tends to equalize when options approach expiration. In this case, I purchased the most fairly priced (near-the-money) calls and sold the most overvalued (out-of-the-money) calls. I could expect the options I sold to lose premium faster as the market moved in either direction. Even if the market were to move higher (except for a straight-up vertical move), this spread would have worked because the near-to-the-money options would have gained value more quickly than the already overpriced out-of-the-money options.

Another overlooked characteristic of options volatility is that when it drops, it does so gradually and then levels off. It can sometimes rise very sharply, however, driving option premium to extremely high levels. Although this is rare, such rapid rises can be very damaging to holders of short options positions. A recent example was the volatility increase in many markets at the beginning of the Gulf War. Oil volatility doubled, while other markets such as gold, bonds and currencies increased 20 percent or more. Even seemingly unrelated markets like cattle increased dramatically.

There are also intraday fluctuations in volatility and premium. Since implied volatility is based on the closing price of the option, intraday fluctuations in prices will often create options volatility that is much higher than volatility based on the closing price. These fluctuations almost always result in *higher* volatility; volatility rarely drops significantly during a trading day. A trader can find many opportunities by taking advantage of these intraday price swings and distortions in options valuation.

## How Options Volatility Can Predict Significant Market Moves

As discussed, I have found that a large move is highly probable when options volatility is low. It seems that when a contract is very quiet, traders "fall asleep" and don't expect anything to happen. Naturally, this is exactly when everything explodes! On the other hand, when the market has been very active (volatile) for a period of time, it is likely to maintain a trading range because most traders are already in the market.

Understanding this concept is much easier than using it in trading, however. Beginning options traders disregard volatility, only determining that a market is moving in a certain direction and purchasing an option that best fits their view of the market and risk exposure. These traders will lose 100 percent of the time when the market moves against their desired direction or remains neutral. They will also lose often even when the market does move in their direction, due to time decay of the value of the options premium.

Professional traders, on the other hand, will examine the volatility of the option contract and determine whether it's in the high, low or middle of its historical range. They will then examine a computer evaluation of what the different strike prices and months of options will do under various market conditions and not only choose the option that is the most likely to be profitable, but also determine whether this is an appropriate time to be purchasing options at all.

For example, call option purchases provided positions with an excellent risk/reward ratio in silver in 1987 and in the grains in 1988. The options had low volatility combined with reliable technical chart patterns that led us to believe that a breakout to the upside was strongly probable. (See Figure 4.6.)

The opposite picture was evident in the S&P 500 options. A trader who would have purchased any out-of-the-money options in the Dec S&P 500 would have lost money because the market had very high option volatility (premium) and a short time to expiration. All the out-of-the-money options, both puts and calls, lost value during this period. Therefore, it didn't matter whether you were bullish or bearish in this market: *All* options buyers were wrong, and all sellers were right.

Changes in volatility can also occur over short periods of time. Treasury bonds had decreased in volatility almost 50 percent in the beginning of 1987, reflecting a change in traders' views on the market move from volatility to stability. On the other hand, Swiss franc options decreased 30 percent in volatility in one day after a meeting of the European countries to reevaluate currency rates. Volatility on both puts and calls had increased dramatically the previous week, and when it was determined that no significant changes were going to occur as a result of the meeting, put and call options lost more than one-fourth of their value.

**Figure 4.6**    Weekly Charts of Corn and Silver Option Volatility,
Which Show a Corresponding Move of Volatility with
Prices. (Compare points marked by arrows.)

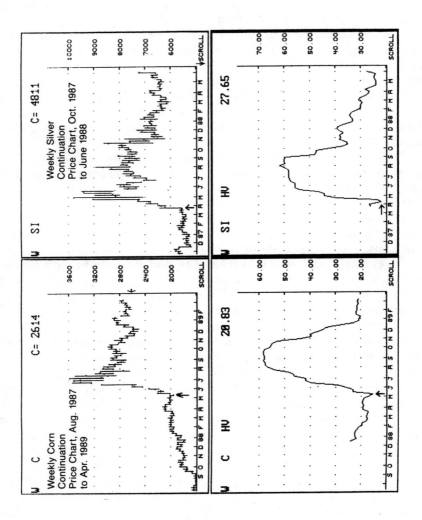

Source: Reprinted with permission from FutureSource.

## Using Trends in Options Volatility to Your Advantage

One of the first principles I learned when I started trading was that "the trend is your friend." I have found this to be one of the most important aspects of a trading plan. Attempts to fight the trend, guess tops or bottoms or trade the correction are probably the biggest causes of losses in the marketplace. I don't know of a single trader who hasn't done this at one time or another and who hasn't paid the price. Options offer the flexibility of using many types of strategies and designing a position to fit the market, not vice versa.

*Flow with these trends; don't struggle against them.*

Trends are important to options traders, not only in determining market direction, but also in determining if volatility is likely to move higher or lower. I have found that volatility trends similarly to price action. In fact, volatility trends are just as reliable and long-lasting as price trends. When volatility hits low levels and begins to turn up (or hits high levels and turns down), I find that volatility can continue to trend for several years. (See Figure 4.7.)

Volatility trends in options are extremely important in determining the type of trading strategies that are most likely to be successful.

At the beginning of 1988, options volatility in foreign currencies was extremely high, just coming off historically high levels on some of the foreign currency markets at the end of 1987. Similarly, options volatility was also near the high end of historical levels in the financial, Treasury bond and Eurodollar options markets. With volatility continually declining during 1988, you could sell options premium with high probabilities of profit. This is because the daily shrinkage of time value of options premium was accelerated by the decreasing volatility. In fact, there were many days during that period that options premium for both puts and calls moved lower. Obviously, this type of action was very beneficial for neutral options positions.

Similarly, the 1982–1984 period was excellent for options sellers. The markets had just come off large movements in metals, grains and other commodities, and traders believed these conditions would continue. In addition, options on futures were new, and disparity in pricing occurred more often.

One of my favorite positions during that time was ratio spreads because the out-of-the-money calls were overvalued in comparison to the closer-to-the-money calls. By using ratio spreads, I was able to take advantage of this comparative overvaluation.

In 1990, the markets were characterized by relatively low options premium. Options premium was also very low, relative to daily movements of some futures. For example, option volatility in the metals, grains and bonds was at the low end of historical levels. In the currencies,

**Figure 4.7**    Two-Year Historical Treasury Bond Options Volatility

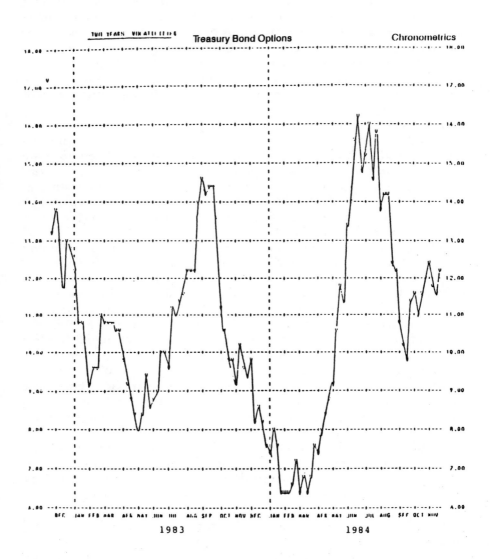

The above chart of Treasury bond option volatility shows a historical two-year low occurring in the first quarter of 1984. This corresponded to the end of a two-year bear market in Treasury bonds and the commencement of a major rally. Statistically, we find over 80 percent correlation between volatility changes and being able to predict market movement.

options volatility was neither high nor low historically, but was nevertheless extremely low in light of the large daily movement in the futures markets. Because of this lower volatility, the majority of my trades were options purchases with the objective of turning them into free trades.

## HOW TO BUY OPTIONS CORRECTLY

Indiscriminate purchasing of options is one of the biggest causes of trading losses because of time decay principles. A solid plan is essential.

The reason most often given to use options, according to books, advisers, brokers and the exchanges' own pamphlets, is the limited risk in purchasing them. They do provide the investor with limited risk, but only for a limited period of time. Options always expire at a definite time, and if "rolled" to a further expiration, a new premium must be paid. This means that if we are incorrect in our market judgment, we will lose our investment.

Unfortunately, this limited risk aspect of options can cause us to lose money even when our view of the markets is correct. There were many times during the last several years when traders who bought call options lost money even though the market virtually exploded in their favor. This type of loss is caused by purchasing the wrong option, or purchasing options at the wrong time. This is why options traders win and lose in the same percentages as other traders. Perhaps their only consolation is that they know, in advance, what they are going to lose. (This is about as comforting as knowing in advance when you are going to die.)

I recommend buying options under these three circumstances:

1. The option contains very little time value, by virtue of being either close to expiration or close to the money (for short-term moves only).
2. The volatility (premium cost) is relatively low.
3. The trader feels that a substantial market move is imminent.

In the following example, let's assume the trader feels a rally is going to occur in the bond market and therefore is interested in buying bond calls.

The trader must then make an appraisal of both the timing and the strength of the move. This does not have to be done with precision; he or she must only determine whether a move will occur in a week, a month, three or six months, etc., and whether the move will be gradual or sharp and immediate. This appraisal will greatly affect the month and strike price of the option we recommend purchasing. If the market were to make a sharp move, the nearest-to-expiration option will appreciate most quickly, but it will also lose its value most quickly unless this immediate move occurs.

**Figure 4.8**    The Disadvantage of Buying Farther-Out Options in a Bullish Move of the Underlying

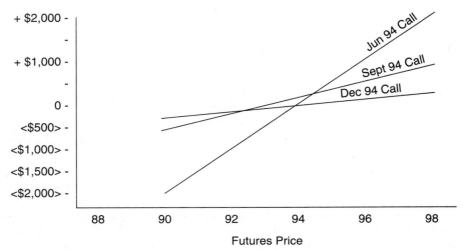

If the market makes a fast move higher, the close-to-expiration June option will gain the most.

For example, on May 4, 1990, the June bond contract was at 92–06, the September contract at 92–01 and the December contract at 92–26. The June contract will expire in three days, the September contract in three months and the December contract in six months. If we were to look at the 94 strike price (approximately two points out of the money), a move up of four points prior to expiration would cause the option to move from $250 to $2,000, a gain of eight to one, while the September and December options would merely double in value. If you had a very strong feeling the market was going to move quickly, you would have your greatest leverage using June options. (See Figure 4.8.)

The amount of risk you are willing to take is another consideration in purchasing an option. Although the risk is always limited to the amount of premium you pay for the option, and can be controlled by selling the option prior to expiration, generally the closer to the money and more expensive the option is, the more risk it will have.

Suppose we decide to purchase a 92 bond call in June, September and December 30 days prior to expiration, and one month later the market is unchanged. The June option will lose about $250, and the December option will lose $100. However, if the market were to move up four points, the June option would gain almost $4,000 in value, the September option about $2,600 and the December option about $2,000. On a move down of four points, the June call would lose $500, the September call $350 and the December call $250.

How do I balance the conflicting factors of trying to keep my risk low while increasing my leverage and applying sound money management principles? By using the following rules that I developed for buying options:

1. I never purchase an option with less than 60 days to expiration unless I expect a very quick, sharp move. I never risk more than $500 per option on this type of purchase, and I have a plan to either take profits at a preset level or to sell a higher-up option that will turn this into a free trade. This is to ensure that my profits don't waste away.
2. I purchase options with between three and six months to expiration.
3. The most difficult factor is determining which strike price to purchase; I use these two rules:
a. I never purchase an option more than three strike prices from the money. This is because farther-out-of-the-money options are unlikely to become profitable.
b. I look at the risk/reward of purchasing various options. For example, in deciding between the 92 and 94 September call, by comparing the actual cost of the two options I can determine that it would cost an extra $1,000 for the 92 call for an additional profit potential of only $1,000, a two-to-one risk/reward ratio. However, in deciding between the 94 or 96 Sep call, there is only a $500 difference between these two calls and therefore a four-to-one risk/reward ratio. I use four to one as my break point in determining which option to purchase: if the risk/reward is higher than four to one, I purchase the closer-to-the-money option; at four to one or less, I buy the farther-away-from-the-money option. This principle not only provides sound money management, but also improves my risk/reward ratio and normally allows the purchase of the most fairly valued option. Many times, as in the Treasury bond example above, the choice of options to purchase is a very close one, and either one could be correct. At other times, how-

ever, one option can cost only $25 or $50 more and give you an additional $2,000 or more profit potential. In that case, the higher-priced option is clearly the correct one to buy.

## HOW TO SELL OPTIONS CORRECTLY

Most public traders have stayed away from selling options, both from lack of understanding and the fear of potential unlimited loss. But professional traders frequently sell options as part of their strategies.

Statistical research in this area is very interesting. More than 90 percent of the public *purchases* options when speculating, and the public *loses* in option trading more than 90 percent of the time. Yet professional traders, the biggest *sellers* of option premium, *profit* most of the time because the mathematical odds favor the option *seller.*

As a wasting asset, options consist of time value premium. The longer an option has until expiration, the more value it should have. But the option will lose some of its time value each day, whether or not your assessment of the market is correct. In fact, the time decay of out-of-the-money options is so great that sometimes even a large move in favor of the buyer will not produce a profit.

## BASING YOUR OPTION BUYING DECISIONS ON YOUR VIEW OF THE MARKET

Some traders decide which options to buy according to the amount of money in their account or their broker's recommendation, neither of which is an effective method.

I recently had occasion to use these principles when I decided to purchase silver call options. I easily eliminated all but four options from consideration: The in-the-money ones provided too little leverage, the farther-out-of-the-money options were too speculative, and the far-from-expiration options were too illiquid. This left four possibilities: the Jul silver $4.25 and $4.50 calls, and the Sep silver $4.75 and $5.00 calls.

After several hours of analysis, however, I could find no reason to favor one of these options over the others. They were all well priced and provided excellent risk/reward. This prompted me to do a computer study of how these options would behave under various price and volatility changes, which allowed me to fine-tune my selection process.

My first choice before doing computer analysis would have been the Sep silver $5.00 call, which could have been purchased for about 8 cents ($400). I based this on both the low premium cost and the fact that even if the market moved to my stop-out point, I'd be able to hold this option for several weeks at a loss of not more than 3 cents ($150) per option.

What was distressing to me, however, was that if the market moved up 30 cents during this time period (a move of 8 percent of the contract value), this option would gain only about 5 cents ($250), not much of a reward for a fairly significant move in a short time.

On the opposite end of the spectrum was the Jul silver $4.25 call. This option would initially cost about $600 (50 percent more than the Sep $5.00 call). However, if the market moved to my stop point, this option would lose almost four times as much as the Mar $6 call, losing 2/3 of its value, or $400, in a three-week period. On the bright side, though, this option would gain 15 cents ($750) on a 30-cent move up.

I found the following general principles in comparing the four options:

1. Closer-to-expiration options will appreciate faster if the market moves in your favor; however, because of their time decay, they will lose much faster if the market remains stable or moves against you.
2. Deferred-month options will hold their value well in adverse conditions but will not appreciate as rapidly (barring a major move).
3. Closer-to-the-money options cost more but have a better chance to profit in normal market moves.
4. Farther-from-the-money options provide greater leverage but require a larger move to profit.

What this all means is that you must not only analyze market direction, but have a general idea on market timing and velocity of the move. If you feel the market is likely to make a major move within a short time period, the best option to buy would be close to expiration. Conversely, if you anticipate the market moving up slowly over a long period of time, look for deferred-month options. In major market moves, larger quantities of out-of-the-money options are a better choice, while in most normal moves, closer-to-the-money options are a better choice.

## HOW TIME AFFECTS OPTION PURCHASE DECISIONS

Many traders overlook the profit objective of the trade when purchasing options. Without a plan, you can watch an option quickly run up in value only to see your profit, even the entire premium, disappear. I use the following rules for sound money management to help prevent this.

### 1. Short-Term Moves

When purchasing an option for a short-term move, always sell half of your position if the price of the option doubles. This allows more flexibility and protection. When markets have a pullback or consolidation, the price of your option will plunge rapidly, especially one with a short time to expiration. By taking partial profits you not only protect yourself against loss, but will then be in a position to purchase additional options on a pullback without increasing your risk.

During the two weeks prior to expiration, severe moves can produce unbelievable returns in short time periods. For example, options on Treasury bonds can be purchased for leverage of more than 6,000 to one, providing returns of 1,000 percent or more in less than two weeks. I have seen cases where a low-priced option has risen more than $1,000 in a single day and I have often seen bond options rise ten times in value within two weeks of expiration. (See Figure 4.9.)

These examples are very exciting, but it isn't as easy as it looks. Let's examine the three hardest parts of the short-term trade: when to use it, which option to use and how to determine when to take profits and losses.

### When should this trade be initiated?

I don't recommend buying an option in the last several weeks of trading just because it is very low priced and provides substantial leverage. This will inevitably lead to losses. My trading plan allows me to trade only with the trend of the market, and then to obtain the most favorable entry point. If this opportunity falls within the last two weeks of trading and I feel an immediate move will occur, I buy the appropriate option. While purchasing options two or three strike prices out of the money may seem attractive, these options will not gain much in value unless the market makes a large move.

### Which option to buy?

In most cases, the best option to purchase for short-term moves is one that is at the money or just out of the money by one strike price. This option is more likely to gain in value if the market moves in my favor.

### When to take profits and losses?

Since I consider purchasing short-term options to be very speculative, I take profits on half my position if the options double in value, thereby giving me a free trade for the balance of the options. On the rest, I have no set rules, but I let the markets tell me when to take profits. Because options prices often spike up during big rallies or declines, I am always alert during these spikes to gain a favorable exit price.

## Longer-Term Moves

I have two rules for taking profits in longer-term option purchases:

1. Take profits if the option purchased goes into the money by more than two strike prices. I do this for money management and be-

**Figure 4.9** Graphic Comparison of the Underlying's Move versus the Option's Move

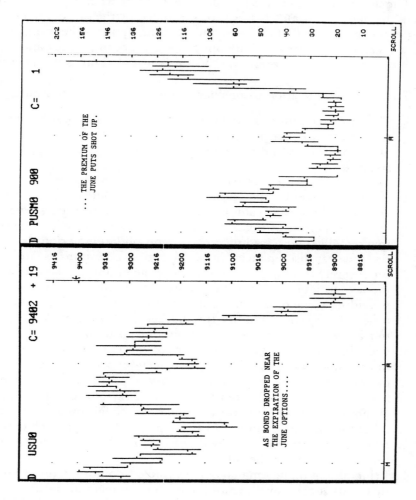

Source: Reprinted with permission from FutureSource.

cause the option otherwise becomes illiquid and difficult to trade. Also, at that point so much premium is built up in the option that it is cheaper (from a margin standpoint) to take a futures position.

2. Pick the strike price that corresponds with the resistance on the futures contract and put an order in to sell an option at the same price at which you purchased your original option. This turns the trade into a free trade.

## THE NEUTRAL OPTIONS STRATEGY

The neutral options strategy is one way to trade when you only know where the market is *not* likely to go. It is initiated by the sale of an out-of-the-money put and call of the same month of an option. The probability of profit can be high because both options are out of the money and both contain only time value premium. Value is lost by both options every day.

There are four factors to consider in the neutral options strategy:

1. The probable range of the futures contract underlying the option prior to the expiration of the option; also consider the long-term and short-term trend of the market, and contract and support resistance.
2. Comparison of the relative volatility level of the option; this is to determine whether the option contract has relatively high or low volatility (premium value). When high volatility occurs over an extended period of time, it is mathematically probable that the market will enter a trading range or consolidation period. In fact, the greatest discrepancies between option premiums occur during severely trending markets because the premium of out-of-the-money options can rise far in excess of their fair valuation, providing some of our best opportunities. On the other hand, in times of very low volatility the market is likely to make a large move, so I don't initiate neutral options positions.
3. Calculation (usually by computer) of the options that have the most disparity (overvaluation), to determine which combinations of options have the highest probability of profit (and least likelihood of loss) and the most favorable risk/reward ratio. Trade sheets are prepared that provide not only the fair option value for all of the options months and strike prices, but what each option or combination of options will do if the market moves in any direction anytime in the future.
4. Principles of money management. Since I do not attempt to predict market price or direction, management techniques are essential to succeed in these strategies. These principles include having enough margin available to maintain delta neutrality, adjusting a position up or down when the market moves strongly and trading only when the most significant opportunities are present.

I sell options during the 60 days prior to an option's expiration (especially the last 30 days) because the time value decay accelerates quite rapidly then. I also choose strike prices that are beyond the expected range of the contract, above substantial resistance and below strong support levels.

In addition to determining the expected range and resistance in a contract, I look at the risk/reward ratio in selling an option. For example, if an option can be sold that is $2,000 more out of the money with only $100 less premium received, the risk/reward ratio in this trade is increased by 20 to 1 by choosing the farther-out-of-the-money option.

My final rule is that I must receive at least $250 in premium to make the option sale advantageous, unless the option has less than 30 days to expiration. This makes the sale worthwhile, with commission costs and slippage; in fact, I generally like to receive $500 or more per option sold.

These positions should be closed out under any of the following conditions:

- The underlying future moves so that either option is within one strike price of being at the money.
- The loss on the position exceeds $500.
- Seventy-five percent of the potential premium is collected.

## THE FREE TRADE

The free trade is an options position that, when completed, is more commonly known as a vertical (bull or bear) spread. The difference is that in a vertical spread, both options are bought and sold at the same time, while in the free trade first an option is purchased, then the out-of-the-money option is sold. This setup makes a major difference in the risk/reward ratio of this position.

I do not usually recommend vertical spreads because I require that any trade initiated have a ten-to-one risk/reward ratio and/or a 75 percent probability of profit. Most vertical spreads have no better than a 50 percent probability of profit and a three-to-one risk/reward ratio (unless you sell an option that is almost worthless, which defeats the purpose of doing this position).

For example, being bullish the bonds in May 1990, I purchased the Sep 94 call at 42 points ($656) and assigned a risk level of $300 to this position. I would close it out if the position declined to 23 points, or $359. My objective was to sell a September bond 100 call on a rally, also at 42 points, for a profit objective of $6,000. This would provide a risk/reward ratio of 300/$6,000, or 20 to 1.

If I had considered a bull spread instead at that time, I could have purchased the 94 call for about 32 points ($500). This would have given me a risk/reward ratio of 500/$2,000, or four to one.

The other benefit of the free trade is that after it is completed, there is no margin or capacity necessary or potential loss. This accomplishes several objectives.

First, it keeps my account intact if the market turns against me. For example, after completing free trades in corn and soybeans in April and May 1990, I noted that the grain markets began to fall as quickly as they'd heated up. Even though most of my original call purchases were at a loss, free trade positions provided protection from loss.

Second, the protection inherent in the free trade gives me time to examine the position unemotionally, without the panic other traders may experience as their profitable positions begin to nosedive. I can wait for emotions to subside and the market to give me a better indication of its next move. I can then decide to hold my position and look for its full profit potential (while completely protected from loss), or I can cash out and take my existing profits.

Third, when the free trades are completed, I can turn my attention elsewhere because my capital is protected. I may find opportunities in other markets, or I can even take advantage of a pullback in the market in which I just completed the free trades to add more positions. This can now be accomplished without increasing my original risk because my first free trades are now risk-free. I find it difficult to closely monitor more than two or three net positions, especially in volatile markets. The free trade allows me to concentrate more fully on other situations.

The free trade also allows me to meet my objective of using options to get a trading edge over the markets: I am taking advantage of the increased volatility, which tends to overprice out-of-the-money options when markets start to trend, by selling out-of-the-money options at this more opportune time.

After the free trade is completed, three possible objectives are open to me:

1. I can hold my position until expiration and exercise my long option if it is in the money.
2. If the market has moved against me, I can allow both options to expire worthless.
3. I may decide at any time to close out my position and take profits.

Your decision must be determined through your trading plan and view of the market.

The only complaint I have heard about the free trade is that it limits potential gain by hedging with the sale of the out-of-the-money call. What other complaint could anyone have, since this is a risk-free position when completed, with no margin or monetary requirements? Yes, your profit is limited, but I feel this is more than offset by the no-loss aspect of the trade.

Furthermore, I can continue to add to this position in the farther-out months on the next pullback. In effect, I can keep building this position without increasing my initial risk, which can result in as much or more profit than just holding the original position.

## RATIO OPTION SPREAD

The ratio option spread is one of my favorite strategies. It allows me to profit without predicting the exact direction of the market, as well as to make maximum use of the overvaluation and disparity in price of the out-of-the-money options. The ratio option spread consists of buying an option that is close to the money and selling two options farther out of the money. It works particularly well in volatile markets, especially bullish ones, because then the far-out-of-the-money options become overpriced due to the traders' demands for cheap options.

An example of a ratio option spread would be purchasing one Apr gold 440 call for $2,400 while simultaneously selling two 500 calls at $1,350 each, for a $300 credit. This credit is very important in preventing losses if my prediction of market direction is wrong. This trade would be profitable if gold moved down below $440 or up over $110, for a range of probability of more than $550. If April gold expires at any dollar value from $440 to $0, both calls purchased and calls sold are worthless. I therefore lose the $2,400 paid for the 440 call but make $2,700 received for the two 500 calls, for a net profit of $300.

However, if the gold contract expires in the range between $440 and $500 (which is what I would be predicting in doing this spread), I am much more profitable. I still collect the $2,700 premium from selling the two 500 calls since they are expiring worthless, I still lose the $2,400 premium I paid for the 440 calls, but I make $100 for every $1 gold closes above $440.

Now, before everyone rushes out to put on this spread, let's look at the potential problem area. Ironically, the problem in the ratio option spread arises if the market does even better than predicted. Profits would diminish over the $500 level, until finally, at $560 per ounce, I begin to lose money! In effect, I would lose $100 for each $1 gold closes over $560 per ounce.

Because of this, I have a strict policy of risk management that requires closing out the position if the price of the contract rises above the strike price of the calls I sold. In the example above, it would require closing the position if gold closed over $500 per ounce. If this would happen quickly, say in one month after initiating, it would cause a loss. However, if I were able to hold the spread for three weeks or more, the decay of the premium for the short options should act to prevent any loss in this position even if I were forced to close it out.

The ratio option spread works so well because the two options sold contain only time value, which constantly decays each day as the option approaches maturity. In the example, the two 500 calls I sold will decay in value much more quickly than the 440 call because the 500 calls are much farther out of the money.

This is the real secret of the ratio option spread: being able to obtain extraordinarily high premiums for the out-of-the-money calls that I sell. The chart formation I'm interested in is always the same—a bullish market making an almost vertical move—since I am seeking to sell multiples of the farthest-out-of-the-money options at the highest possible premium.

For example, in 1990, with March copper trading at 115 after moving almost straight up from 60, I could buy one Mar copper 120 call and sell two Mar copper 140 calls, receiving a 100-point, or $250, credit. The 140 calls were the farthest-out-of-the-money calls available, and I could sell them at 700 points each. Being able to receive a large amount of premium provides not only more cash for my account, but significant protection if the market consolidates or turns around and heads lower.

In the March copper ratio spread, I was looking for a slow upward movement in the market, with March copper expiring at the 140 level. This would give me a 20-cent ($5,000) profit on the long call and no loss on the short calls because they would expire worthless. I would also collect my initial $250 credit.

The only problem is when March copper begins to exceed the 140 level. Since I would be short two options and only long one, I begin to lose 2 cents on the short options and gain only 1 cent on the long option for a loss of 1 cent ($250) for every penny copper moves over $1.40.

For this reason, I find it best to place mandatory stops on all ratio spreads at the level of my short calls; that is, if March copper were to exceed $1.40 at any time, I would recommend closing out the position. The amount of profit or loss would depend on the time at which copper reached this level; if it didn't reach it until the expiration of the option, I would have a profit on this spread.

The amount of time it takes for copper to exceed this level is important because the overvalued out-of-the-money calls will begin to lose their value quickly due to time decay as the contract nears expiration. However, the opposite will happen to the long 120 call if the market makes a slow move up. This call would be in the money and start to gain in value. In fact, during the last 60 days before expiration, with copper trading between 125 and 135, the option purchased could gain in value on many days, while the out-of-the-money calls that had been sold would lose value, thereby providing profit on both sides of the transaction.

## HEDGING WITH OPTIONS

Before options on futures were introduced in the 1980s, the futures market was commonly used for the hedging needed by farmers, producers, distributors and institutions to lock in costs and profits and limit potential losses. Options, however, brought more tools and flexibility for hedgers and enabled any trader of a stock or commodity to use options for hedging. Stock traders had the use of stock options to hedge as early as 1973. Following are the three most popular methods of hedging.

### 1. Purchasing a Put for Protection

Purchasing a put to protect a long position will provide absolute price protection if the market begins to decline. For example, assume that a trader has purchased a Jun S&P 500 contract at 335 and the market has now moved up to 365 and begins to consolidate. A trader with a long position and profits of $15,000 per contract could be very concerned that a severe correction is about to take place. Although a stop order could conceivably be used to protect his profits, a stop may not be sufficient if events occur overnight or if the market begins dropping rapidly. In addition, it can be frustrating if the trader finds himself stopped out of a good position that then takes off in his favor.

A better method would be to purchase an S&P 355 put. By using less than 10 percent of the profits of the trade (about $1,000 in this case), a put can be purchased that will provide absolute price protection below the 355 level. Profits of $10,000 can be locked in, and unlimited profits are still available if the market continues moving higher.

### 2. Selling Calls for Income

Using the example above, the trader may decide that the market is again consolidating after moving from 335 to 365, and wishes to add additional income to his account during the consolidation phase. To do this he would sell a 375 call and collect this premium for his account. This strategy will add substantial income to his account in a consolidating market on top of profits, whereas purchasing a put would be a drain on profits. The sale of calls, however, does not provide the substantial protection against a large break in the market that is offered by the put purchase.

### 3. "No-Loss, Cost-Free" Option Hedging

We have found that the best method of protecting positions is a combination of numbers one and two above, called the no-loss, cost-free strategy. In the old television quiz show called "Let's Make a Deal," contestants were usually given a prize, such as $1,000 worth of furniture or a vacation, which they could either keep or exchange for other prizes behind one of three doors. The new prizes ranged from booby prizes to expensive cars, boats, etc. The contestant was faced with the dilemma of whether to give up a sure thing for a potentially more valuable prize, with the risk of getting something worse.

This is the type of dilemma we must often face in the markets. For example, traders made enormous profits after crude oil exploded, but many worried they wouldn't be able to hold on to their profits. They needed to protect their capital in case the market dropped as fast as it had risen. (In our experience, markets seem to accelerate to the downside even more quickly than they rise—witness the stock market in 1987, which lost in two days what it had taken a year to gain.)

Since the oil market is subject to extreme overnight moves based on political conditions, we felt that stop loss orders provided inadequate protection against a drop in the market. A stop placed too close to the position could cause us to miss out if the market continued on in our favor, while placing the stop order far from the market could subject us to much larger losses. Luckily, there was a much easier way to protect profits while still allowing us to make additional profit if the market continued in our favor. And, for no additional out-of-pocket cost! Imagine being offered a free insurance policy to cover all of your assets from any disaster; this is what the proper use of options can do.

How? In the case of the crude oil market, where we are long a futures contract (expecting the price to go higher), we first purchase a put option, which becomes more valuable as the price goes lower. Let's assume we purchased a futures contract at $20, and after crude oil rose to $40 we purchased the 35 put option for $1,000. If oil were to drop, this would provide absolute protection of any profits below our put's strike price of $35. Since we had purchased our futures contracts at under $20, we are in effect "locking in" most of our profits.

Overnight, large, previously unknown oil fields are found, and the price of crude drops by more than one-half, to $15. This would cause the original contract we purchased at $20 to have a loss of 500 points times $10 a point, or $5,000. However, our $35 put would now be worth $20,000 ($35 strike price minus $15 actual price, or $2,000 times $10 a point or $20,000). Even this type of catastrophe leaves us with a profit of $15,000, and, best of all, we will still be able to profit if oil continues higher.

The second part of this strategy is to sell a call to pay for the put we purchased. We do this because if we continue to pay for protection by way of the puts alone, it can become pretty expensive if the market stays in a trading range. Since the options expire in a definite amount of time, we would have to continue purchasing new puts and paying substantial amounts in premium. Therefore, to pay for the put we purchased, we recommend selling an out-of-the-money crude oil call option. In our example, we could sell a $45 call, which would not only entirely pay for the purchase of the $35 put, but would still allow us $5,000 additional profit if the market continues moving in our favor. Profits are limited to $45 if the market moves past that level. However, since the market had already moved over 100 percent from its lows at the beginning of the year, and we were still allowing for another rise in prices of 10 percent or more, this small risk of having future profits limited is well worth the financial and emotional protection provided. A win-win situation no matter what happens!

With the no-loss, cost-free hedging,

- If the market goes down, all of our capital and a good percentage of our profits are protected from loss.
- If the market moves sideways, we have neither gained nor lost from the strategy, since we received a credit when we initiated this position.
- If the market moves in our favor, the insurance turned out to be unnecessary but at least we didn't pay for it, we were not stopped out of our position as we could be with a stop order, and we are still able to make additional profits on our trades.

In all cases, we can sleep well at night knowing our capital and much of our profits were protected.

## TRADING OPTIONS BASED ON GOVERNMENT REPORTS, INDEXES AND MEETINGS

Large, unexpected moves in the markets are often caused by the immediate news of major reports, figures, and government meetings. The more you know about these reports, the better you can assess their impact on the markets. I think the market's reaction to a report that is significantly different than expected is the most important indicator of the market's strength or weakness. For example, when an unexpectedly favorable report fails to cause any significant move in the market, I can tell that the market is "tired" and I'd be cautious about initiating new positions.

In 1984 and 1985, the markets eagerly awaited the money supply figures, which would significantly affect the metals markets and, to a lesser degree, the stock and financial markets. In 1987–88, the trade deficit figure resulted in major moves in the currencies, causing 300-point to 400-point ranges in the Swiss franc and Japanese yen in a matter of minutes, then causing movement in all the other markets. Anticipated raising and lowering of the discount rate has caused similar reactions in the financial and S&P 500 markets. Finally, the agricultural and livestock markets are always greatly influenced by the release of government reports and figures.

Markets are also affected by the lack of action after a report. In the last week of 1987, the currency markets rose substantially when foreign

**Figure 4.10**    Relative Volatility Levels of Swiss Franc Options and Futures Before and After February 1988 Trade Deficit Report. (0 = Lowest Volatility Level; 100 = Highest)

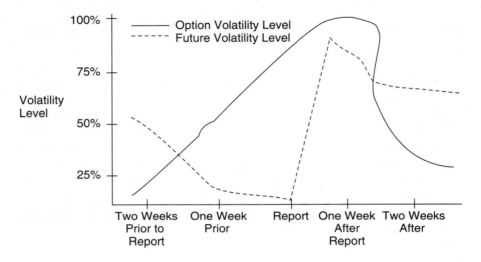

Volatility Level Centered around Report Date

governments failed to support the dollar after a G-5 meeting. The traders took this to mean that they had decided not to support the dollar, so this nonaction was interpreted bearishly for the U.S. dollar. However, the governments had actually agreed to support the dollar but decided to wait until after the first of the year to make their announcement.

There is, however, a major difference between the actions of the futures and options markets, both before and after these events. The futures markets become stagnant prior to the release of government reports, then quite volatile right after the release, stabilizing shortly thereafter. The options markets, however, do not stabilize in price before a report to correspond with the lack of action in the futures market. Instead, options volatility and premium rise rapidly before a report, peaking during the last hour of trading before its release. Afterwards, options pricing becomes random until the true market direction is shown, usually in the first hour after the report. However, due to the thinness of the markets and the tendency of options sellers to wait to determine the velocity of the move, it is difficult to buy options at a reasonable price until the market has stabilized. (See Figure 4.10.)

Another difference between options and futures is that the out-of-the-money options increase greatly in value prior to the report. Then, after the report is issued and it is determined that these options are still out of the money, they lose their value even more quickly.

An example of this is an April 1988 Swiss franc neutral options position I initiated one day before the February trade deficit report. At that time, I collected a premium of $1,000 for selling a far-out-of-the-money put and call. After the report, although the Swiss franc had moved 100 points lower, the put had gained only 5 points in value while the call had lost 27 points, for a net gain of 22 points or $275.

I initiated this position not only because I felt these strike prices would be out of the range of the Swiss franc during the next month, but also because they were the most overpriced options. My computer analysis showed that the fair value of this combination was 65 points (I received 80 points). However, further computer analysis showed that a move of 250 points in either direction on the day of the report would not have caused a loss in this position. (See Figure 4.11.)

While I had this 400-point window of profit, futures traders were having a much harder time. Shortly before the report was issued, the Swiss franc moved up 100 points, potentially stopping out many short futures traders. Then the market immediately plummeted 300 points.

This type of action also occurred before and after January's trade report. Out-of-the-money calls that became substantially overvalued the day before the report were almost totally worthless the next day. Even the out-of-the-money puts gained very little in value, despite the fact that the market moved more than 200 points lower that day.

As we have seen, purchasing out-of-the-money options close to the release of reports can provide us with a trade that moves in the direction we predicted but is still only slightly profitable, if at all. However, purchasing an option approximately one week prior to a report allows us to obtain a more fairly valued option. I recommend purchasing options at the money or no more than one strike price out of the money, because these are usually the most fairly valued and responsive to a move in your favor.

The month purchased is also significant. If you're interested in a longer-term trade, I recommend an option of between three and six months' duration. If you're purchasing an option just to take advantage of a report, get one closest to expiration because it will have the largest percentage move if the report is favorable to your position. However, if you've guessed wrong, it will also lose the most premium. Traders undecided between these two positions might purchase an option between two and three months' duration to combine the effects of both.

Other reports that traders watch include: gross national product, unemployment report, consumer and producer price index, index of leading economic indicators, consumer spending, factory orders, industrial production and factory capacity utilization.

**Figure 4.11**  Theoretical Option Valuation at Various Underlying Prices

SFJ—Swiss Franc - Apr
Volatility = 14.82%    Days Out = 53
Interest Rate = 6.50%    2-16-88

SFJ—Swiss Franc - Apr
Volatility = 14.82%    Days Out = 53
Interest Rate = 6.50%    2-16-88

CALLS

| | 76 | 77 | 78 |
|---|---|---|---|
| 70.00 | .14 | .08 | .05 |
| 70.25 | .16 | .09 | .06 |
| 70.50 | .18 | .11 | .06 |
| 70.75 | .20 | .13 | .08 |
| 71.00 | .23 | .14 | .09 |
| 71.25 | .26 | .16 | .10 |
| 71.50 | .30 | .19 | .12 |
| 71.75 | .34 | .21 | .13 |
| 72.00 | .38 | .24 | .15 |
| 72.25 | .42 | .27 | .17 |
| | 76 | 77 | 78 |
| 72.50 | .47 | .31 | .20 |
| 72.75 | .53 | .35 | .22 |
| 73.00 | .58 | .39 | .25 |
| 73.25 | .65 | .44 | .29 |
| 73.50 | .72 | .49 | .32 |
| 73.75 | .79 | .54 | .36 |
| 74.00 | .87 | .60 | .41 |

PUTS

| | 68 | 69 | 70 |
|---|---|---|---|
| 70.00 | .75 | 1.10 | 1.56 |
| 70.25 | .68 | 1.01 | 1.44 |
| 70.50 | .61 | .92 | 1.33 |
| 70.75 | .55 | .84 | 1.22 |
| 71.00 | .50 | .77 | 1.12 |
| 71.25 | .45 | .69 | 1.03 |
| 71.50 | .40 | .63 | .94 |
| 71.75 | .36 | .57 | .86 |
| 72.00 | .32 | .51 | .78 |
| 72.25 | .28 | .46 | .71 |
| | 68 | 69 | 70 |
| 72.50 | .25 | .41 | .65 |
| 72.75 | .22 | .37 | .59 |
| 73.00 | .20 | .33 | .53 |
| 73.25 | .17 | .30 | .48 |
| 73.50 | .15 | .26 | .43 |
| 73.75 | .14 | .23 | .39 |
| 74.00 | .12 | .21 | .35 |

We use computer evaluations of options prices to determine which options have the greatest overvaluation. These trade sheets were compiled several days before the United States trade deficit report that caused severe overvaluation of the Swiss franc options. Based on this, with the contract at 7,300, we were able to initiate neutral options positions in the Apr Swiss franc 69 put and 78 call at a total premium of 80 points ($1,000). Its fair value was computed at 58 ($625). Our computer evaluation showed us that we would not lose money if the futures moved 250 points in either direction. One week later, as volatility subsided and premiums dropped for both puts and calls, this combination was trading at 36 points ($400) for a profit of $600.

Source: Data from Com-Tech Software.

# CHAPTER 5

# Nine Steps To Designing a Winning Game Plan

*BY VAN K. THARP, PhD*

**Editor's Note:**

Dr. Van K. Tharp is a trained psychologist. Who else knows better about the flaws of personality when it comes to trading the markets successfully?

The logical and consistent way in which our author attacked the problem of successful trading is based on the creation of a constant environment for our successful trader. The author lists the following nine steps to design such an environment:

1. Know yourself.
2. Know and understand your beliefs about the markets.
3. Design a system to fit you.
4. Check for biases.
5. Develop a money management plan.
6. Test your system.
7. Develop a set of rules.
8. Develop a daily business procedure.
9. Check your plan periodically.

As the reader can surmise from the listing, the author tries to instill the fact that, to succeed in trading relatively erratic markets, a trader must be pretty solidly ensconced with proper trading techniques and money management plans. It's basically the trader against the world, and a trader who doesn't have his or her own act together is going to be hard-pressed to master market action.

Once a trader becomes successful enough to make money consistently, the solid plan will serve as a guide to continued trading success. A trader who does not have such a plan in place will be tempted to tamper with his or her market approach, to fine-tune parameters that cannot be optimized, all to the detriment of his or her trading success. A guide developed ahead of time will forestall this eventuality.

After being exposed to many, many successful trading strategies in my years of consulting, I believe the one element they all share is that they generate low-risk ideas. Since many methods can generate low-risk ideas, there really is no holy grail trading system. Instead, the grail amounts to finding a trading system that fits a trader's personality and then clearing away the mental blocks that may exist to following that system.

Many traders claim that their decision making is largely intuitive. My research suggests that these traders fall into two categories. For many of them, their intuition is really "into wishing." The remainder are simply not consciously aware of how they make decisions, so they call their unconscious decision-making process "intuition." I have devised a way to assess the validity of intuition, and it is incorporated in the check-list method given in this chapter. All types of traders—options, futures, stocks, institutional and money managers—can use this procedure.

A game plan for traders is equivalent to a business plan. Most businesses fail because they do not plan adequately. Trading is no different from any other business. Your game plan is a way of putting everything you know about the psychology of successful trading plus your method of trading into a comprehensive plan to make money in the markets. A game plan is also the best protection you can give yourself. You preplan every contingency while you are away from the stress of trading. You program new choices into your brain. When stress starts to build, you will have useful responses at your disposal immediately. You will behave more intelligently and avoid common mistakes. As a result, I recommend that you develop a *written* game plan.

Your game plan will, of course, include your trading system. My bias is that it is much easier to trade or invest using a system to help you make decisions. First, a sound trading system is a shortcut for human decision making, which is often flawed with biases. Second, you can follow a trading system with a very simple mental strategy: *See the signal; recognize that it is familiar; feel good about it; and then act.* The more complex one's mental strategy is, the more difficult it is to make consistent, profitable decisions.

There are four precautions to using a trading system. First, your decision process has to be thorough enough so that you select something that both works and stands the test of time. You cannot be that thorough every time you make a decision, so you must verify your methodology before you use it to make decisions. Second, once you select a system, you must use it in the manner intended. Third, you must periodically review your system to make sure that it is working for you. Finally, your system must be part of a comprehensive game plan. A system without an overall game plan will not work. This chapter gives you specific suggestions for developing such a plan.

## STEP 1: KNOW YOURSELF

The first part of your game plan should include a thorough self-evaluation of your strengths and weaknesses. Since part of your plan involves developing a successful system, pay attention to those aspects of self-knowledge that are important to designing a system that fits you. These include: knowing how easily you make decisions; knowing how active you want to be in the market and knowing your overall philosophy toward the markets.

### Ease in Making Decisions

Traders generally fall into two categories: Either it's easy for them to make trading decisions, or it's difficult to make trading decisions. Into which of these two categories do you fall? Do you make decisions to enter the market easily? Are you a borderline gambler? Are you perhaps too active in the markets? Or, in contrast, do you have a difficult time making decisions? Does everything have to be perfect for you to trade effectively? Do you tend to let numerous opportunities pass you by while you make up your mind?

You can improve your decision making by adopting a trading system that fits your personal strategy. If making decisions is difficult for you, then you need a very mechanical trading system. Use your natural tendency to be thorough in the testing phase of your system. If you are not a programmer, use one of the available software packages that make this task easy even for nonprogrammers. Once you are satisfied that your decision-making system works, let your decisions be mechanical. The more mechanical your decisions are at this point, the better. If decision making is normally difficult for you, then develop a computer-based system that sends out trading signals by modem or have your broker execute your system for you.

On the other hand, if making decisions is easy for you, you need a complex hierarchy of decision criteria to enter the market. These criteria could be programmed into a computer, or they could simply be a series of checklists. A decision tree of this type makes your normal tendency of jumping into the market with little thought much more difficult for you.

Although this approach may cause you to lose a few good winning trades, it will help you in the long run.

In this chapter, I describe how to develop a decision tree method of trading. The decision tree can be a simple checklist, or it can easily be programmed on a computer to produce a mechanical trading system.

## Activity Level

What is your time frame for making profits? Do you want to jump in and out of the market several times each day? Are you a day trader? Do you want to get in and out of the market a couple of times each week? Each month? Or are you looking for those few really good trades that come along in every market once or twice a year?

If you trade occasionally, you still need to monitor the market daily without any expectation of trading. You could forget to look at the market on the one day of the year when the big trade comes along and subsequently miss that trade. When you do put on a position, you will probably hold it for a much longer period of time than the average trader. This means holding on to large paper profits waiting for them to get bigger. It also means going through minor market fluctuations without changing your position. When you trade in this manner, you will keep your position until the market sends you signals to get out. You may have to wait a long time for your big profits, but at the same time, your transaction costs will be low.

If you trade more frequently, you will have numerous occasions when you sell out of a position at a loss or at scratch only to watch the market take off without you. Your losses will generally be quite small, but so will your profits. In addition, your transaction costs will be higher because you will be in and out of the market often. As a result, you will have to make a much higher percentage of profits. If you can be right 70 percent of the time or more, for example, then you probably can be a successful day trader.

Short-term trading requires that you be constantly alert. If you periodically take time off to refresh yourself as I recommend, then you may temporarily lose your feel for the markets. The need to constantly be on top of the markets will tend to produce stress and lead to careless mistakes. One major mistake, from carelessness or oversight, can cost you a tremendous amount of profits. And when you are continually in the market, you have more opportunity to make that kind of mistake. Some of the best traders in the world remain on top because they understand that somewhere a career-ending trade exists with their number on it. Their job is to avoid taking that trade, but it is very difficult to do when you are a short-term trader.

Short-term trading also has several advantages. You will be more likely to be in tune with the market, since you will be trading actively. In addition, you will catch small moves that the longer-term trader will miss.

Although short-term trading is right for some people, I favor the longer time frame for most traders. Most good traders make their money in the long time frame. Although many floor traders make a decent income from arbitrage or scalping, the big money is made on those occasional longer-time frame trades that happen once or twice a year. Most off-the-floor traders with a short time horizon do not make big profits unless it is on huge volume.

In addition, short-time frame trading gives one a greater exposure to the disastrous effects of mistakes. Since you are always active, the possibility always exists for you to make a careless or stress-related mistake. When you become less active, you only take the trades that have a good chance to make significant profits. You have fewer, smaller losses and your overall profits are up.

I recently had a call from a trader who claimed that, by applying the principles detailed in my course, he had increased his account size by 287 percent during the past year! That was the good news. At the same time, he had just made a horrendous, careless mistake that had cost him a lot of money. He claimed that he made several like that each year, and he wondered why they occurred. *It is because short-time frame trading allows greater exposure to mistakes.*

Finally, the long time frame allows one more freedom, while the short time frame is more likely to produce or magnify conflict. Many clients express an interest in day trading yet have other jobs such as being a broker or a doctor. Most of these people have a number of conflicts between day trading and their other responsibilities. First, they might not be certain that they could carry out their other responsibilities if trading is full time. Second, they might not feel sure that they could have the kinds of relationships they want if they are preoccupied with full-time trading. All of these conflicts can be solved, with the same or even greater profit potential, by shifting to a longer time frame.

## Overall Market Philosophy

Most people have difficulty selling when prices are low (or going down) and buying when prices are high (or going up), yet this strategy is essential for most successful trading strategies. Behaving in this manner goes against people's natural tendencies. Instead, they would rather buy when prices are at bargain levels and sell when prices seem high. If you are one of these people, then there are several possibilities for you.

First, this strategy can be used to trade options with some success. You can buy puts when the price is high and buy calls when the price is low. Such a strategy is generally successful, and your risk is limited (to the price of the options) as long as you follow sound money management principles.

Second, you can trade successfully in consolidating markets. As long as you can recognize when you are in a consolidating market, this procedure works well.

Systems based on this approach are called trend-fading systems. Here one assumes that prices move within a normal band. The rules are that you buy at the low end of the band and sell at the high end of the band. Certain technical trading indicators such as oscillators, the relative strength index (an oscillator that moves between 0 and 100), stochastics, contrary opinion indexes, etc., are designed to help people use trend-fading systems. This type of system has some advantages for most people.

First, you will be right more often than you are wrong. You will get good fills on limit orders. However, these systems appear to be easier to follow than they actually are. When you look at a chart in hindsight, you can easily draw a band around the prices. Band trading has not worked that well over the past decade. Furthermore, I do not know many traders who are doing it successfully.

In contrast, if you can buy when prices are going up and sell when prices are going down, you will make a good trend follower. You simply go with the trend until it changes. In this type of system, you will *never* buy the bottom or sell the top. You will be wrong more often than you are right, but most of your losses will be small (if you follow the rules). And occasionally, you will get a substantial piece of a long move. Trend following is based on the premise that once a trend begins, it tends to persist. This type of strategy requires patience and the ability to go with the flow. Trend following has been a very profitable strategy over the past two decades, but there are not many people using trend-following systems in the market.

Trend-following and trend-fading systems are not mutually exclusive. If you are skilled enough to determine what type of market you are in, you can use whichever system is appropriate for that type of market. In other words, you fade the trend in responsive markets, buying and selling at the upper and lower ends of the band, respectively. But when the market breaks out of the band, you switch to a trend-following system. Doing both can be very profitable, but it also introduces another variable: being able to recognize the type of market that currently exists. And if you trade for the wrong kind of market, your results will be disastrous.

## STEP 2: KNOW AND UNDERSTAND YOUR BELIEFS ABOUT THE MARKETS

The super traders whom I know have a deep understanding of the markets. They have spent years observing relationships between market phenomena, developing expectation models about the markets and testing and refining those models. If you would like to be a super trader, or even a successful trader, you need to be willing to devote the same kind of time and effort to market study. Develop your own understanding of the markets. The caveat here is that the time must be well spent. The information that most people study, from highly promoted seminars to magical trading systems, is useless. Furthermore, successful trading has nothing to do with market analysis. You can generate statistics about the market every day for a year and not come up with a low-risk idea. *Successful trading requires that you generate low-risk ideas and act upon them.*

In evaluating the market for low-risk ideas, pay attention to three performance variables. First, look for something that consistently makes profits. Remember that being right and making profits may not be the same, since systems or indicators that are right 30 to 40 percent of the time can be tremendously profitable if you are a long-term trader. If you are a short-term trader, your rate of profitable trades needs to be much higher. Second, look for the maximum equity drawdown, the largest overall downtrend in your capital, over the period of time tested. A system or set of indicators that sustains very large losses is simply not tradable for most people, even if the total profits are high in the end. Third, look for the overall risk/reward ratio of the system. This would be the total profitability of the system divided by the maximum equity drawdown. Since the risk/reward variable takes into account the profitability and the maximum equity drawdown, this might be the only variable you need. Nevertheless, knowing the overall profitability and the overall risk is important to most traders.

The key to fitting a trading system to your personality is to gain market understanding so that you can generate low-risk ideas using the criteria given above. First, write down your beliefs about the market. Once you know your beliefs, look for indicators that fit those beliefs.If you try to trade without matching indicators to your beliefs, you will not have a system that matches your personality and your trading probably will not be successful.

### Key Elements of Low-Risk Ideas

I have found that traders' beliefs about the markets generally fall into the following key elements of low-risk ideas:

1. *Price.* Price refers to such factors as the direction of movement within a time frame (trend); the rate of change of the movement (momentum); differences in various markets, contracts or indexes (divergences) or sharp movements (breakouts).
2. *Activity.* Activity refers to such factors as the number of contracts or shares sold (volume), the number of contracts outstanding (open interest) or the variation in price over a particular time period (volatility).
3. *Time.* Time refers to such factors as the duration of a particular market move, regularities in the rise and fall of price (cycle) or patterns that typically occur at certain time periods (seasonality).
4. *Sentiment.* Sentiment refers to the strength of opinion about a particular market. At extremes, the crowd is usually wrong.
5. *Value.* Value is a measure of supply and demand used by fundamentalists.
6. *Technical patterns.* Technical patterns include various technical indicators that might measure the type of market that exists, support and resistance, the character of the market or trader psychology.
7. *Floor trader signals.* Floor trader signals consist of unique information available only to floor traders, such as the body posture and facial expressions of other traders as they buy or sell, the tone of voice of other traders or the amount of noise in the pit.
8. *Intuition.* Some people trade because they just know what to do. Intuition may either mean that the trader is very good at picking up signals that most people are unaware of (i.e., but he or she is not aware of how it's done), or that the trader is "into wishing." In either case, if it is an important element for you, then include it as a factor in your decision tree.

Figure 5.1, shown on page 114, presents a more detailed discussion of the various subelements and beliefs that traders might hold. Take a sheet of paper and rank the importance of each element in generating low-risk ideas on a scale of zero to five, with zero meaning no importance and five being very important. If you give an element a ranking of three or higher, then list what you believe about that element and what indicators you follow that fall under that element.

For example, you might believe that price is a key element and rate it a five. Under price, you might list as beliefs:

• The trend is your friend; always go with it. I typically measure it with a moving average crossover.
• There are one or two good moves in each market each year in which I can catch a long-term trend and ride it. I will probably have to take six trades in each market to be sure of catching those two moves.

You might believe that sentiment is also important and give it a rating of four. Under sentiment, you might list the following beliefs:

- An extreme value in sentiment occurs just before the market turns.
- Investment advisors are generally wrong as a group.
- The media, in reporting the market news, will reflect sentiment extremes; in fact, they help produce them.

Complete this step for each key element that you think is important for you.

## STEP 3: DESIGN A SYSTEM TO FIT YOU

Begin to design your specific trading system by using what you know about yourself: 1) your decision-making capabilities (whether you make decisions easily or with difficulty), 2) your overall trading philosophy, 3) your desired activity level and 4) your beliefs about the market and what is important. Once you understand these important elements about your personality, you can find indicators that fit *you*—rather than using indicators just because someone says they might work. Thus, first search for indicators that fit you and your beliefs about the market.

You will encounter so many indicators that you'll be able to make infinite combinations of them. These combinations, however, will not necessarily perform any better than just one or two individual indicators. While the temptation is always present to add one more indicator to produce a holy grail system, I believe that you will lose money if you constantly change your system by adding or deleting indicators. *When you find a workable system that fits you, stick to it consistently and you will make money over the long run.*

Following is a general outline of how to design a system specific to your needs; an example of this process appears at the end of this chapter.

First, find a set of indicators that fits your beliefs about the market, your philosophy of trading and your desired activity level.

Next, assign a value to each indicator based on its strength (how that indicator is predicting a bullish or bearish move). For example, if it is definitely bullish, then give it a value of $+4$; probably bullish, $+2$; neutral, 0; probably bearish, $-2$; or definitely bearish, $-4$.

Assign a weight to each indicator according to how important that indicator is for you. For example, do you consider it essential that a particular indicator have a strong bearish or bullish signal for you to take a short or long position? If so, give the indicator a high weighting of around five points. On the other hand, if the indicator is important, but not critical, give it a moderate rating of two or three points.

Multiply the value of each indicator by its weighting. Add the resulting products to get a specific number. This number, depending upon

**Figure 5.1**    Key Elements of Low-Risk Ideas and Useful Beliefs You Might Hold about Them

---

**PRICE**

Price is meaningless; only your equity before and after a trade and the stop levels you set during a trade are important.

- *Trend* is the direction of movement within a time frame. Trends may last anywhere from a few hours to years, depending upon the time frame under consideration. Trends are typically measured with moving averages. Your trade should be in the direction of the predominant trend.

- *Momentum* refers to the rate of change in price and is typically measured by various types of oscillators. Momentum changes before price. Oscillators are particularly good tools if your philosophy of trading is to catch tops and bottoms (i.e., band trading).

- *Divergences* refer to differences in related indexes, markets or contracts. For example, gold may be compared with silver; the most active bond contract may act a little differently than the cash market, or the Dow Jones Industrial Average (30 stocks) may act differently than the Investor's Daily Index of 6,000 stocks (i.e., the broader market). When one market, contract or index starts to move differently, it may signal a change in trend. People holding a strong cash position may be selling futures contracts. The broad market will fall prior to a movement in the Dow.

- *Breakout* is a sudden, sharp move out of a trading range or area of resistance. It indicates a strong force in the market. The market usually returns to fill in gaps.

**ACTIVITY**

- *Volume* refers to the number of options, contracts or shares sold during a specific interval of time. Volume precedes price. Peak activity tends to occur in the middle of a move. When prices move up on slight volume (after heavy volume), it is a sign that few buyers may exist.

- *Open interest* refers to the number of options or contracts outstanding. Patterns of volume and open interest give you important information about whether or not a lot of interest exists for a price trend to continue in a particular market.

**Figure 5.1**    Key Elements of Low-Risk Ideas and Useful Beliefs You Might Hold about Them (continued)

- *Volatility* refers to the variation in price over a particular period of time. Most people are attracted to high volatility, but highly volatile markets are dangerous because you can be right and still lose money.

**TIME**

- *Duration* refers to the length of a particular move or lack of move. When you have a position that does nothing for a long time, get out or raise your stop.
- *Seasonality* refers to patterns that typically occur at certain time periods.
- *Cycle* is a regular rise and fall of price. There are common rhythmic patterns to market moves.

**SENTIMENT**

- *News media sentiment* refers to consensus of information from radio, television or newspapers. If the media reports that a particular market is strong, it usually indicates that everyone knows about it. As a result, those who plan to play the move are already doing so and the lack of new buyers or sellers will result in change in trend.
- *Advisory sentiment* refers to consensus of information given by investment advisers to the public. If public investment advisers, especially the most widely followed, are predicting a particular market to move in a given direction, it is another indication that everyone knows about the move.
- *Fellow trader sentiment* refers to the consensus of emotion by other traders about the market. If most people around you are excited about a market, they are probably wrong.

**VALUE**

- *Value* is a measure of supply and demand used for trading by fundamentalists. If you buy below value, then you will make money if you are patient. If you sell above value, then you will generally make money if you are patient.

**Figure 5.1** Key Elements of Low-Risk Ideas and Useful Beliefs You Might Hold about Them (continued)

---

**TECHNICAL PATTERNS**

Technical patterns include various technical indicators that might measure the type of market that exists, support and resistance, the character of the market or trader psychology.

- In a consolidating market, trend fading works best.
- The third wave of an Elliott Wave pattern is generally the most profitable wave to trade.
- Support and resistance levels indicate where most traders have their stops.

**FLOOR TRADER SIGNALS**

Floor trader signals consist of unique information available only to floor traders, such as the body posture and facial expressions of other traders as they buy or sell, the tone of voice of other traders or the amount of noise in the pit. If other traders are buying or selling out of panic, I have the advantage. When the pit is noisy, it indicates a lot of activity and a continuation of the trend. When the pit is quiet, the trend is likely to change.

**INTUITION**

Some people trade because they just "know" what to do. Intuition may either mean that the trader is very good at picking up signals that most people are unaware of (i.e., but he or she is not aware of how it's done), or that the trader is "into wishing." When I have a particular feeling about the market, I'm almost always right.

---

whether it is high or low enough to suggest that a low-risk trade is imminent, can be used to tell you whether to buy, sell or do nothing. As a result, you will have developed a method of generating low-risk trades based on your personal beliefs about the market.

## STEP 4: CHECK FOR BIASES

People make decisions in a vague, unconscious manner. Often, they are unaware of either the content or the structure of their thinking. As a result, human decision making is frequently biased by selective perception, sequential information processing and judgmental shortcuts. Although a thorough discussion of these biases is beyond the scope of this chapter, I can offer you the following steps to help reduce biases in your trading.

- Know the probabilities of a trade being successful under the various conditions in which you will trade. Also know what to expect from your system each month, each quarter and each year. Express these probabilities as a number, such as .40 or .65. Being able to know your system's results in terms of probabilities is one of the purposes of testing it (Step 6).
- Are you avoiding any sources of uncertainty because you think they do not apply to you? For example, you might have heard that 90 percent of all speculators go broke, but you are certain that it does not apply to you at all.
- Trading indicators are simply your way of representing trading opportunities. The reading on any particular indicator is not the opportunity per se. Most traders tend to act as if their indicators are the trading opportunity instead of a representation of the opportunity or a symbol of reality. As a result, they find it difficult to get out when the market proves them wrong.
- How big are your testing samples? Do you use sample sizes of 30 or larger in your system tests? For example, if you have a system that trades only five times a year, you will need a minimum of six years of data when you test it. However, I recommend that you use more than ten years of data, if possible.
- To what extent do your initial estimations (i.e., the first numbers you thought of) determine your assessment of the probability? Are you considering all the information that comes to mind or just the information that seems most obvious? Do you vary the order in which you consider indicators, or do you always consider them in the same order?
- Is there any evidence that your estimate of the situation is wrong? If so, are you avoiding that evidence?
- What are the sources of information in your system? Are you missing any important ones? Write down each source, and then determine how reliable it is. Can you trust that source to give you accurate information? Are you listening to friends or brokers who spread rumors? Could the information in your business paper be a misprint?

## STEP 5: DEVELOP A MONEY MANAGEMENT PLAN

Trading success has little to do with market analysis. Instead, it has to do with generating and carrying out low-risk ideas. Low-risk ideas will make you money if you practice sound money management, but will lose money if you don't. For example, even if you have a system that is correct 90 percent of the time, you will go broke on your first losing trade if you risk all your capital on each trade.

Decide on the maximum amount of capital you will risk per trade. Your risk on any given trade is the maximum loss divided by your capital. I strongly recommend that you limit your risk to 10 percent of your current equity for any given trade (or for a group of related trades). Despite your best efforts, you cannot avoid the possibility of your maximum loss exceeding 10 percent if you have to suffer through one or more limit down days. Avoid adding paper gains or losses to your equity. In other words, change your equity only when you lock in profits with a stop or you get out of the trade.

I also recommend that you limit your coverage, the capital to margin ratio, to no less than 3.5. Once again, this gives you a reasonable margin of safety. You must determine your own comfort level, however.

Once you decide how much money you are willing to risk on a single trade, you might consider some sort of pyramiding plan. One example of such a plan might be to adjust your equity every time you lock in a profit, while continuing to maintain a 10 percent equity position in the trade. In other words, if you lock in a profit, increase the position—especially if it still is a buy—so it is still 10 percent of your equity.

Part of your money management plan should also include a worst-case contingency plan. Conduct a brainstorming session in which you evaluate everything that can possibly affect your trading: a string of severe losses, disability, the disability or death of a loved one, an unplanned financial emergency unrelated to trading or health, etc. Have your spouse help you with this, if possible. Even though it is tempting, do not hold back. When you have thought of every possible scenario, write down your three best behavioral solutions for dealing with each one. Keep these solutions as part of your overall game plan. The point of this exercise is that if you know what to do in each worst-case scenario, you don't have to worry about them. You already have planned for them. And since these are the worst things that can happen, you are prepared for anything.

## STEP 6: TEST YOUR SYSTEM

Take a period of about ten years and use that data to refine the parameters of your system. Once you have parameters you like, test your system over another ten-year period of data. When you test your system, determine its profitability per trade and the maximum drawdown during a period of losing streaks. Also notice how often it trades; does it fit your desired level of activity? Once you have done this, you will have a good idea of the conditions you must live with if you trade this system. Is this a system you can trade comfortably? Can you follow it? Remember that you developed it around conditions ideal for you.If you have trouble following it, then you are definitely the problem.

Paper trade your system. Remember that paper trading will give you the maximum performance level you can expect to achieve. Thus, if you can't make good profits paper trading, you need to start again.

Your system might get you into a single market three times each year with only one of those trades expected to be profitable. That single profitable trade, however, might make you 50 percent on your capital. If your system has these kinds of characteristics, you might go several years trading a single market without making a profit. At that point, you might become discouraged and abandon your system. On the other hand, if you trade five or six different markets with the same expectation, you could expect to trade about 15 times per year with about five profitable trades. Suddenly, your chances of going a whole year without making money are greatly reduced. Based on the characteristics of your system, determine the degree of diversification necessary to successfully trade your system over a year and be profitable. Include in your game plan the different markets that you will follow. Since your capacity is seven, plus or minus two chunks of information, I suggest that you limit yourself to no more than five markets.

## STEP 7: DEVELOP A SET OF RULES

Write out the trading rules that you developed earlier. Review them at the beginning of each day. The more you review them, the more automatic they will become and the easier you will find them to follow.

The most important part of your written rules should be your psychological rules. Some possible rules that you might want to include on your own checklist of psychological trading rules are given below.

- I will keep a psychological trading diary.
- I won't trade unless I am ready. There's always another opportunity.
- My job is to avoid the big losing trade with my number on it.
- I will continue to read my *Investment Psychology Guides* and work on self-improvement.
- Trading problems arise when I neglect other important aspects of my life.
- I will suspend trading if I have two consecutive months (fill in appropriate time frame for you) of losses. At this point, I will do a complete inventory of myself and my game plan. Every six months I will do such an inventory regardless of my market performance.
- Each year I will take at least one fun vacation.
- I will exercise regularly.

- I will reward myself periodically for good performance.
- I will preplan my actions each day in order to anticipate what might go wrong. Planning ahead will give me choices in case those events do happen.
- I will review procedures for overcoming my weaknesses.
- I will continue to be open to beliefs that are more useful to me than those I hold now.
- I will develop and follow a daily plan for trading after I analyze the market for each day.

## STEP 8: DEVELOP A DAILY BUSINESS PROCEDURE

The last rule above is so important that I have included it as a separate step in your business plan. A typical daily procedure that I recommend for my clients is as follows:

*AM Procedures*

- Review psychological and trading rules.
- Review daily plan for trading.
- Preprogram yourself to carry out the plan.
- Self-analysis: Are you ready to trade?
- Carry out the plan.

*PM Procedures*

- Review the day.
- Did you follow the rules?
  If yes (even if you lost money), pat yourself on the back.
  If no, program yourself so that you will not repeat that mistake again.
- Analyze the market and develop a plan for the next day.
- Visualize your goals.

Once you have developed a simple daily procedure like the one described, the only thing left for you is to do it. Follow your game plan, follow your daily plan, and follow your daily procedure. Once you have something that works, success requires consistency. After going through this chapter and designing a plan that works, using it should be easy. If you have trouble doing it, then either admit that you do not belong in the market and stay away, or get help removing your psychological blocks to trading.

## STEP 9: CHECK YOUR PLAN PERIODICALLY

As your achieve your goals, revise and update your business plan. Similarly, as you evolve, reappraise your strengths and weaknesses and revise that part of your plan.

Periodically update your list of things that could go wrong and the plan of action for each possibility. Doing so yearly will help you avoid excess worry.

You will also want to check your trading rules periodically. Throughout history we have had different types of markets. During the late 1920s, those who profited most were fearless, high-leverage plungers. Conservative, slow bears profited the most during the crash period from 1929 to 1932, which may be the kinds of markets we are having today in the 1990s. During the depression, when prices were low, fortunes were made by those who could buy, accumulate and hold bargains. From the end of the depression until the early 1960s, people who bought stocks and held on did well. From the late 1960s until the early 1980s, the people who made fortunes were the commodity and currency trend followers. Currently, large profits are being made by the stock and bond leveraged buyout crowd. Each of these strategies works very well for a certain period of time, but then it stops working well or doesn't work at all. That is where many system followers get into trouble.

In your search for a system that fits you, you might even develop a great system. But systems may work for only limited periods of time. When market conditions change, you need something else, so review your trading method periodically. If you are a day trader, review your system once each month. If you trade once each month, then review your system yearly. Is it working for you? Do you need to adjust your system? Do you need to adjust yourself? Revise your written trading rules and psychological rules periodically to make sure they are effective for you.

## AN EXAMPLE OF DESIGNING A LOW-RISK IDEA GENERATOR

Let's look at an example of how to put these steps into practice and develop a low-risk idea generator that meets your personality and beliefs. In this case, we will be designing such a generator for Jim, a hypothetical OEX options trader.

Jim was very thorough in his decision making. Often, he agonized over such decisions as where to go on vacation or what kind of suit to buy. Because of his thoroughness, trading decisions were also difficult. When Jim tried to trade, he had trouble acting before a move was over.

Jim basically was a trend follower who wanted to be in one or two good moves in OEX options each year. However, he knew that if he kept an option position for more than three weeks, the erosion of premium over time would destroy him even if he were right about the market.

The first step in designing your low-risk idea generator is to determine what your time frame is for trading. Do you trade long-term trends lasting a year or two? Are you an options trader who must be out of a position within a month or so because of expiration dates and a declining premium? Do you like to make several trades a week that only last a few days? Or do you make several trades a day that only last a few hours? In determining what time frame you wish to trade, remember that the shorter your time frame, the more often you need to be right.

Jim liked moves that last two to six weeks in the OEX options. And, because he had trouble making decisions, he needed a fairly mechanical trading system.

Second, look at a chart of the contract, stock or option that you are trading. Look at a full page of daily bar graphs (or weekly bar graphs if your time frame is really long) to determine if there is an obvious long-term trend or if there could be one. If so, you are probably in an overall bear market. Determine what this direction is and (even if you are trading bands and only picking tops and bottoms) resolve not to go against the long-term trend.

Since Jim traded OEX options, he first looked at long-term trends in the overall stock market. When the price of the Investor's Daily Index of 6,000 stocks was above its 200-day moving average and the slope of the average was also positive, Jim looked for bullish positions. When the price was below the average and the slope of the average was negative, he looked for bearish positions.

Next, Jim listed the critical elements and his beliefs for each one. He then determined which indicators accurately reflect each of those beliefs within the time frames he wished to trade.

Armed with his list of indicators, Jim determined the following information about each indicator:

*What is the range of values for each indicator?*
Let's look at a few examples. Since Jim was trading the stock market, he elected to follow several stock indicators. One such indicator was the Investor's Intelligence Index of the percentage of New York stocks whose prices were above their ten-week moving average. Theoretically, these numbers could range from zero percent in an extreme bear market to 100 percent in an extreme bull market. More realistic extremes, however, might be 25 percent in a bear market climax and 75 percent in a bull market climax.

**Figure 5.2**   1: Giving Meaning to an Indicator

| Indicator Value | Meaning | +4 Rating |
|---|---|---|
| Over 70 | Definitely Bearish | -4 |
| 61 – 69 | Probably Bearish | -2 |
| 40 – 60 | Neutral | 0 |
| 30 – 39 | Probably Bullish | +2 |
| Under 30 | Definitely Bullish | +4 |

Let's look at another indicator Jim might have followed, the McClelland Oscillator. This oscillator ranges from about –150 in a selling climax to +100 in a buying climax. Plus or minus 90 might be more realistic extremes.

Jim also had a sentiment indicator in which he took the total volume of CBOE calls sold each day and divided that by the total volume of CBOE puts sold that day. He then repeated the process using OEX calls and puts. Finally, he added the two ratios together and calculated a three-day moving average. Over the previous four years, the values of this index had ranged from about 3.8 to about 1.7. Jim considered 3.3 and 2.1 to be high and low extremes, respectively.

### What are the significant levels within each range?

At what level does an indicator become meaningful for you? At what level would you call your indicator definitely bullish? Assign any value at or above that level a +4. What range of the indicator would you consider probably bullish? When the indicator is in that range give it a value of +2. What is the neutral range of the indicator? Assign values within that range a score of zero. What range of the indicator would you call probably bearish? Give that range a score of –2. Finally, determine the value of the indicator at or below which you would be definitely bearish. Give the indicator a –4 when it falls to that extreme range.

Jim was using the Investor's Intelligence Index of the percentage of New York stocks over their ten-week moving average as a predictor. Based on experience, he considered the ranges given in Figure 5.2 to have significance for him.

Let's look at one other example of Jim's three-day call/put moving average, which ranged from about 1.7 to about 3.8. The weights he assigned to that indicator are given in Figure 5.3.

Notice that the ratings in Figure 5.3 are somewhat different from the ones we suggested earlier. Since Jim was designing a personalized trading system, he wanted some flexibility.

**Figure 5.3**    2: Giving Meaning to an Indicator

| Indicator Value | Meaning | Rating |
|---|---|---|
| Over 3.3 | Definitely Bearish | −3 |
| 3.1 – 3.3 | Probably Bearish | −2 |
| 2.9 – 3.1 | Slightly Bearish | −1 |
| 2.5 – 2.9 | Neutral | 0 |
| 2.3 – 2.5 | Slightly Bullish | +1 |
| 2.1 – 2.3 | Probably Bullish | +2 |
| Under 2.1 | Definitely Bullish | +3 |

*How important is each indicator?*

Are you willing to trade if an indicator is not giving you a signal to trade? That is, rate the relative importance of each indicator to your trading. Look at your first one. Are you willing to trade if this indicator is not giving you a very strong signal? If it is essential, give it a high weighting. If it is important, give it a moderate weighting. If it is interesting but not that important, give it a low weighting.

Jim had eight beliefs about the market that he translated into market indicators, as shown in Figure 5.4. Three of those indicators were crucial, and Jim would not trade unless all three were at significant levels. As a result, Jim gave each of those indicators a weighting of 5. Jim also had three indicators that he considered to be important, but not critical. As a result, he gave two of those indicators a weighting of 3 and the third one a rating of 4. Jim considered the remaining two indicators to be interesting, but not that important. Those two indicators received a weighting of 1.

I have not discussed Jim's specific indicators in Figure 5.4 because I do not wish to mislead any of you into thinking that certain indicators are critical or important. Instead, I have given the indicators a number so that you understand how to weight them according to how important *you* think they are without being biased by any specific ones that I might mention.

*Evaluate the overall significance of your checklist.*

At what level are you willing to make a trade? At what level are you willing to initiate a long position? At what level are you willing to initiate a short position?

First, determine the range of values of your checklist. You can do this by multiplying the top rating of each indicator by the "importance" weighting given to it. When you have all those values, add them up to de-

**Figure 5.4**   Rating the Significance of Jim's Indicators

| Indicator | Significance | Assigned Rating |
|---|---|---|
| 1 | Critical | 5 |
| 2 | Critical | 5 |
| 3 | Critical | 5 |
| 4 | Very Important | 4 |
| 5 | Important | 3 |
| 6 | Important | 3 |
| 7 | Interesting | 1 |
| 8 | Interesting | 1 |

termine the maximum value of your checklist. Next, multiply the lowest rating of each indicator by its importance. Once again add the values to determine the minimum value of your checklist. In most cases, the minimum and maximum values will simply have different signs (e.g., the scale might range from + 68 to –68).

Let's look at Figure 5.5, which illustrates how Jim might do this. Jim arrived at the highest level of this set of indicators, 104, by multiplying the total assigned rating (i.e., 26) by the maximum score of 4, since the maximum score is constant. As a result, since we know that the minimum score is –4, we know that the lowest level of this set of indicators will be –104 (i.e., 26 times –4).

**Figure 5.5**   Determining the Range of Your Checklist

| Indicator | Assigned Rating | Max. Score | Product |
|---|---|---|---|
| 1 | 5 | + 4 | + 20 |
| 2 | 5 | + 4 | + 20 |
| 3 | 4 | + 4 | + 16 |
| 4 | 4 | + 4 | + 16 |
| 5 | 3 | + 4 | + 12 |
| 6 | 3 | + 4 | + 12 |
| 7 | 1 | + 4 | + 4 |
| 8 | 1 | + 4 | + 4 |
| Totals | 26 | | + 104 |

*Determine significant trading levels within that range.*

Suppose Jim tested his set of indicators over a period of time and discovered that whenever he had a score over + 70, he had a low-risk bullish trade and that whenever he had a score of –85 or less, he had a low-risk bearish trade.

Jim also developed another checklist, within a day trading time frame, for lowering his risk even further. That is, he determined the long-term trend and then used his first checklist to generate a trading idea within the time frame in which he felt most comfortable. He elected to lower his risk even more by adding a shorter-time frame checklist (i.e., day trading) and waiting until both sets of indicators generate compatible trading ideas. Since Jim could generate low-risk ideas on a short time frame at better-than-chance levels, he lowered his overall risk substantially. He now had the structure of a low-risk idea generator designed around his specific personality and beliefs about the market. At this point, he had completed the first three steps in developing his low-risk game plan.

As the next step, Jim tested his checklist for biases. He noticed that some of his indicators were very subjective (e.g., Elliott Wave count), while others were much more objective (e.g., advance-decline line). Jim decided to evaluate his objective indicators first so that his subjective evaluation of the market would have less chance of biasing his reading of the more objective indicators. In addition, he decided to evaluate each indicator in a random fashion to counteract any tendency to form an opinion about the market from the first few indicators he looked at.

Jim developed some strict rules about money management. He decided that he would make the biggest profits and suffer the least risk if his position size were based on his account equity rather than his starting capital. He also decided that his equity changed only when he closed out a position, was stopped out or had locked in a profit by raising his stop.

The OEX option positions that Jim would open would have potential losses of no more than 10 percent of his equity. Jim determined that with five straight losses his account would be down only about 40 percent, whereas he would double his account with four straight wins.

Keeping these money management principles in mind, Jim tested his plan. He reviewed his system for each year in which OEX options were available and determined that his average loss would be 10 percent of equity and that his average gain would be 22 percent of equity. His data also suggested that he would average eight trades each year and that three or four of them would be profitable. In addition, he estimated that his yearly profit would be between 20 percent and 60 percent.

Jim also discovered that he could computerize his checklist method of trading by using a common spreadsheet program. He set up the program so that it asked him 12 questions and then told him the size of his position and a course of action: Buy, sell or do nothing. Jim had a fax board in his computer, so orders from the spreadsheet program went directly to his broker via fax.

Finally, Jim developed a set of trading rules and a daily business procedure modeled after the suggestions given in this chapter. In addition, he agreed to review his plan every six months or after five consecutive losses. As a result, Jim has an ideal trading plan for his personality.

# CHAPTER 6

# A Dynamic Approach to Options

*BY JOHN GFELLER*

**Editor's Note:**

John Gfeller writes this chapter from Switzerland. After communicating with him on the subject of this chapter over the past year, I have gained insight into how Gfeller thinks when he trades.

As a professional trader using options strategies, the author reveals what options he uses and what levels of extended forecasting he goes into when he plots his strategy. This chapter is a brief synopsis of a series of options plays and the reasoning behind them.

The core of Gfeller's decision making rests on conventional bar chart analysis. Surprising as it may be, the conventional bar charts do work! The reader might ask how one can trade successfully merely using bar charts when so many advanced analytical techniques are available for the modern trader. Let's pause and consider this question: Were there traders who made money in the 1910s? 1920s? 1930s? 1940s? 1950s? 1960s? 1970s? 1980s?

The answer is an obvious yes. A second question: Were there not analytical techniques used in the 1910s that are now used in the 1990s, and vice versa? The answer is also yes.

The answer to the last question is the key to market success. What is it about past trading techniques that is similar to current trading techniques that allows traders using these techniques to make profits?

Read this simple chapter to find what makes a trader successful in all markets, under all conditions. Additional clues can be found in some of my past works. I could give you the answer, but for heuristic purposes you will benefit more by coming to the answer on your own terms.

## INTRODUCTION

This chapter is intended to provide the reader with practical ideas and applications in the area of speculative trading using exchange-listed options. Although theoretical constructs are important, it is through hands-on examples that one can best obtain a feel for trading, especially where two or more options are involved. We will emphasize what some call a *dynamic* approach to options—that is, adding or reducing options positions, modifying option strikes, expiration dates, buying back short options and so on. Dynamization of options strategies yields vastly superior results than a simple "hold until expiration" approach, provided one stays on top of the markets.

On the other hand, dynamization has several drawbacks. First, commissions paid to brokers can be prohibitive, and will in any case affect the bottom-line performance of your strategy. Discounted commissions, wherever they may be had, go a long way toward solving this problem. Second, the positions can become somewhat difficult to follow, especially if one follows a number of markets. Fortunately, you can use a personal computer to do your position management; inexpensive options pricing programs and option-related software can help with margin calculations and keep track of the basic elements of options and how they react under different conditions. Third, overtrading and impulse trading, although tempting when using options strategies, can be costly and fatiguing. A disciplined game plan is absolutely essential.

Perhaps the most insidious aspect of dynamization is the tendency to think that trading options is less dangerous than trading futures and thus requires less commitment, as you can always "come back" in a nonzero sum game environment like options. Nothing could be further from the truth. If anything, walking away from the markets a net winner is more difficult with options than with futures. Realistic stop loss levels and thorough scenario planning from the outset and for the entire holding period of the strategy are important in this regard.

Other considerations of all options traders are: the development and unbiased testing of a serious trading plan with clearly defined rules; the frequency of signals, with provisions as necessary for intraday market-following technology; and the time commitment needed to effectively implement the trading program. Until these last factors are analyzed, options traders are best advised to engage only in paper trading and to hone their skills in preparation for live trading.

For those who are impatient with this philosophy, it should be noted that the expected survival rate and life expectancy would be rather low. As discipline is one of the key factors for long-term success in the futures and options markets, the first test of potential success is whether or not one has the necessary discipline to develop and test a sound methodology. If it seems too difficult to go this route, ask yourself why you are or want to be in the markets. The answer—independence, wealth, power, self-validation, revenge—may surprise you, and it will either raise your level of commitment or prompt you to head for the hills, thereby saving you a great deal of money.

Whatever the challenges of options trading, however, the rewards for the successful trader can be enormous. Just remember that the money is secondary and will spring only from your effort and love of the profession; for trading *is* a profession. Some may take it lightly, as merely a way to earn fast money, instead of as a highly challenging profession, pitting intellect, preparation, nerve and mastery of self against the aggregate wisdom of the market. This attitude is something like that of a certain pop star who was quoted as follows after his umpteenth divorce: "Yeah, sure, we ran around a little, had a couple of laughs, did the whole romantic bit and all, but it was never, like, serious stuff or anything, you know?"

## PART I: THE BASICS

### Buying Options

Options, if properly used, can provide more profit potential and more flexibility than the straight use of futures. In fact, perhaps the most alluring feature of options is their tremendous leverage, depending on strike price, time to expiration and volatility. The trick in using options is that the timing has to be very good, as options are a "wasting asset" and subject to time value decay. That is, a buyer of options would have to see a move large enough to pass the break-even point at expiration in order to realize a profit. And then the commissions must be factored in.

### Selling Options

Sellers of options, on the other hand, would benefit from time value decay, as the premium they collect at the outset will, all other factors being equal, only decline in value and ultimately be cheap to buy back, or expire worthless. So why not sell options instead of buying them? Simply stated, the case against selling options is that, although one has a larger statistical chance of coming out ahead, one has a predetermined and limited maximum profit (the difference between the premium collected and zero), and one has an unlimited risk. Of course, there are numerous instances where selling options is very interesting. As a general rule, however, unless one has the underlying asset, or is willing to purchase the underlying asset, selling options for private accounts is a risky proposition.

The rule of thumb in comparing options buying and selling has best been expressed as, "To make money buying options you have to be very right; to make money selling options all you have to be is not very wrong." But are you willing to bet that you won't be very wrong? So we come back to options buying, with its necessary emphasis on precise market timing. Now if you're an options trader and are very good at market timing, chances are that you'd already be managing a commodity fund and be a regular guest at Barron's Roundtable. At the very least, you'd have a well-funded private speculative account and the luxury of taking time off from the markets. In any case, you might not be reading this book. Although quite a few people have good timing, they use inappropriate options strategies, lax money management techniques or poor trading psychology. It is options strategies that concern us here.

### Combining Buying and Selling

In deciding upon an options strategy, consider many factors in addition to directional analysis and market timing. Thinking a market is getting ready to go up is insufficient. It is equally important to look at the expected magnitude and duration of the move and, if possible, the strength of the expected initial move. Then factor in current options volatility levels and leverage, with the desired delta.

Why not combine the advantages of buying and selling options? This is a nice idea, provided you've done the above preparatory work. Only at this point should you look at the possibility of putting on a strategy using more than one option. In other words, do your homework before you get fancy, spinning glittering webs of high-return, low-risk strategies. *Caveat emptor*: All that glitters is not gold. A complicated strategy involving numerous options may make you a hit at cocktail parties, as you regale a bunch of poor fools leading Walter Mitty–like lives with your plans to conquer the financial markets using your raw intellect and strategic brilliance. But come morning, your seemingly no-fail six-way strategy can come crashing down on your head, magnifying your champagne hangover by the insistent ring of the phone demanding margin money, making you wonder who the real fool is. The clear winner after you grudgingly liquidate your positions, minutes before the market starts the monster rally you'd been waiting for all along—is your broker, who pockets the hefty commissions on all six options.

### Factors Contributing to Your Approach

The antidote to the above sad tale is simply to realize that, attractive as options strategies may sound, they are no panacea for careful planning and understanding of all the elements involved. "Most men lead lives of quiet desperation," the saying goes. Options can provide formidable speculative leverage. Just keep in mind that, for every perceived advantage in initiating an option strategy, there is a trade-off that may or may not be perceived. Getting into a strategy with your eyes open from the beginning may save you some quiet desperation at the end. With this duly noted, let's embark on a brief tour of the options approach that this chapter will employ.

First decide what kind of trading personality you have. There are two clearly defined styles of trading that characterize most market participants. The first style is what I call the "Che Guevara approach" (political implications aside)—jungle hit-and-run tactics, guerrilla warfare, small-arms tactics. The idea is to survive long enough against vastly superior odds by harassing the enemy through low-risk actions so as to eventually win your cause by attrition. The second style of trading is what I call the "General Westmoreland approach"—saturation bombing using high technology, designed to stun the enemy into submission with overwhelming firepower and pave the way for ground troop assault.

The advantage of the first approach is that almost anybody can engage in this type of activity because the means required are minimal. A good supply of household ingredients—including rope, bottles and gasoline—will do. The problem arises if you don't fully understand the terrain, or if you needlessly expose your position, in which case you'll get ferreted out and liquidated in short order. Also, your tactics as well as your strategy must be very good. That is, you must have an excellent game plan and then carry it out in the most efficient manner possible, making the best use of the tools at your disposal. Because of this double requirement, not everyone is cut out to be a jungle fighter, although most individual speculators are just that, given their limited firepower, whether they realize it or not.

The advantage of the second approach is that you have more flexibility and can engage in different types of action as the situation arises. You're not limited to crouching in the jungle, waiting for a passing column to snipe at, but you can blow the entire jungle away if it suits your needs. The problem is that much concentrated and coordinated effort is required, with a good deal of sophisticated equipment, and the expense involved—assuming it can be shouldered at all—makes quick success an important objective. Also, there is the distinct possibility of not being able to mow down resistance even with strong firepower. The markets seem to have a mind of their own, and even if one piggybacks the heavyweights, there is no guarantee of success. Another drawback of the second, blanket approach is losing sight of the enemy. This lack of perception can be very costly, as it encourages munitions to be expended in a scattershot approach.

## My Approach

Since I operate from an individual trader's standpoint, and since this chapter is written mainly for individual traders, I naturally gravitate toward the Che Guevara approach. The essence of this approach is keeping your ear to the ground, lying very still for as long as necessary (which can be a long time), concentrating intensely on the objective, seeing the opportunity come into view, then acting with utter speed before the window of opportunity closes. "In skating over thin ice, our safety is in our speed," notes American philosopher and poet Ralph Waldo Emerson. In other words, you have to be patient and aggressive at the same time. This is not a combination in high supply with the average trader, or anyone else for that matter. But it is the only hope for the aspiring jungle fighter, in addition to Goethe's adage that "He is dangerous who has nothing to lose."

How does this jungle fighter approach work in practice? It means seeing an emerging opportunity first. That in turn implies buying options—most of the time going long options—when volatility levels are low and the market hasn't yet stumbled upon what will soon become obvious. This is, of course, the crux of the matter. This is what most of the holy grail–type trading systems try to fathom—the as yet undiscovered opportunity. But when is any opportunity undiscovered?

This is merely a reflection of the fact that most market participants feel differently about the market than you do. By definition, then, this type of trading is contrarian and requires going against the crowd. Note, however, that this in turn implies picking tops and bottoms, which is a notoriously quick way to the exit as a would-be trader. So what is the solution? Is there any way out of the labyrinth? Fortunately, yes, provided one monitors technical indicators, does some elementary charting and waits for relatively low volatility levels before buying options. This is what we will look at now.

Let's assume that it's August 1989 and you're looking for a place to buy gold, for whatever reason. The first thing you can do is look at a weekly chart, which will give you several years' worth of information. (See Figure 6.1.) You should be able to draw a clear trendline on the downside, connecting all the high points made from December 1987 to June 1989. When this weekly down trendline is broken on the upside, you tell yourself, that will be your first indication to go long gold. Moreover, since this particular down trendline connects four points in this time period, it can be considered a valid line. (The more points the better, since everyone will then be looking at the same line and will jump on board as soon as the line is broken. This then becomes a form of self-fulfilling prophecy.)

**Figure 6.1**   Daily Bar Chart of August 1990 Comex Gold Prices from August 1989 to April 1990

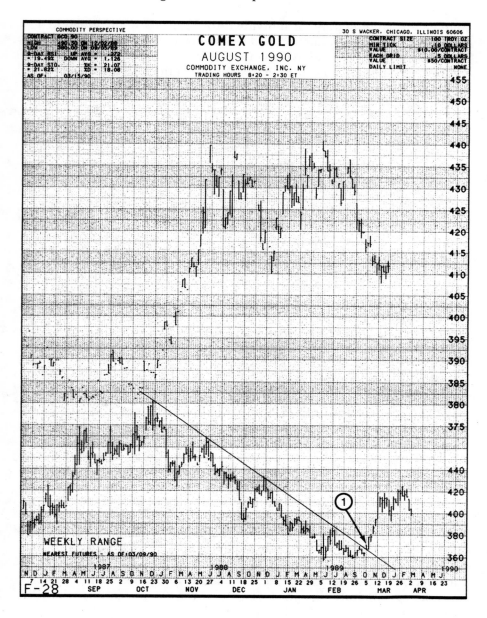

Source: Reprinted with permission, ©1992 Knight-Ridder Financial Publishing, 30 South Wacker Drive, Suite 1820, Chicago, Illinois 60606.

How do you know to stay out until the weekly chart gives you a signal by trendline violation? That is, aren't there cases when something would prompt you to take a position before an official signal is given? Of course there are, and that's precisely the point. Once you start making exceptions to the rules, it's all over. The idea is to develop a game plan that you can live with and that works, provided you follow it. If you don't like following weekly chart trendlines, so be it; find something else to look at. But look at it consistently. Better still, write down your complete game plan and look at it daily. Whether or not you trade any given day, week or month is not important. The important thing is to develop and test your game plan, then put it into action. If your game plan gives you only five trades a year, but each trade makes you a 20 percent profit, that's 100 percent a year, not including the effect of compounding.

Since I look at weekly trendlines, this is the approach I'm outlining here. Don't take my approach if you prefer another one, but make sure that your approach is simple and makes sense. The nice thing about trendlines is that they are incredibly easy to use, yet very effective, if only because everybody looks at them. Still, try to look at tools in a slightly different way than the majority. For example, if the majority prefers to look at daily chart trendlines but practically ignores weekly chart trendlines, you might elect to use trendline analysis on both charts as one of your signals.

Use your weekly chart trendline as the main orientation, and zero in on the actual trade opportunity using trendlines on the daily chart, in the same direction as the anticipated movement on the weekly chart. Surprisingly, few investors really look at both daily and weekly charts together. If more did, they might be surprised at the positive results. But it seems to be human nature to complicate things. In this technological age, when computerized trading systems abound that make NASA headquarters look like preschool, it may seem presumptuous to claim that something as simple as trendline analysis can be the foundation of an effective trading system. And of course it's not quite as simple as that. But the truth of the matter is that people have made fortunes trading with tools as simple as these. What's the catch? There's little glory in telling your crowd that you caught a $50 move in gold using trendlines. On the other hand, you caught a $50 move, period. And that just might be a good deal more than the people at the forecasting institutes and think tanks got out of that particular move.

Let's go back to our example and see how it would have unfolded, using trendlines and a couple of other handy tools that we'll explain as we go along. Around the third week of October 1989, the weekly trendline was broken on the upside. (See #1 on Figure 6.1.) The only problem might be that it gapped up. The question then becomes whether to go long anyway and risk getting whipsawed by a down move.

This is where the daily chart comes in handy. The daily chart shows, in effect, a two-week downtrend that was broken on the upside on October 16, at the same time the weekly long-term down trendline was broken on the upside. (See #3 on Figure 6.2.) The advantage of looking at the weekly chart first and the daily chart second, instead of the other way around or (worse still) looking only at the daily chart, is that once a signal occurs on the weekly and is confirmed by the daily chart, the ensuing move has a good chance of being very powerful.

On average, you will have fewer trades to choose from but more powerful signals, and this trade-off should work well in your favor. You won't be constantly chopped up by the market while taking small stabs at what might or might not be a potentially good move. You'll also pay less in broker commissions. Last but not least, you'll sleep better at night because you should generally be on the right side of the market, having waited for the long-term signal from the weekly chart. "Boring but safe" is the best way to describe this approach. It's amazing how many people will try to fade the trend by isolating a trend, then going against it—a sure recipe for disaster.

I hear the question, "So where's the exciting bottom and top picking, and the heroic contrarian investing this guy preached a couple of pages ago?" Hold on, because for those of you who want guts and glory, you'll have more than your share before this is over. Before going long gold, you should also look at technical indicators. My favorites are the 9-day and 14-day relative strength index (RSI) and stochastics. On October 10, 1989, both of these indicators reached low levels, which from a contrarian point of view suggested that the gold market was oversold and likely to stage a rally.

In retrospect, of course, it all looks rather obvious. But if you had asked people in October 1989 whether gold was a good buy, the answer would have been about fifty-fifty. In fact, the bullish consensus on October 10 was only 56 percent, as recorded by Commodity Perspective Chart Service. You'll find that in many cases the bullish consensus will reach a peak just before a large drop. In this case the bullish consensus was neutral, but the fact that gold was sitting on its lows for the previous several years might well have given one room for pause. In any case, it would have taken some intestinal fortitude to go long gold at precisely that juncture.

When gold did break its weekly and daily trendlines on the upside on October 16, 1989, with the nine-day RSI and nine-day stochastics oversold, the signal to go long was already valid. One or two more conditions for entry would, however, increase the chances of success, at the risk of restricting the number of valid entry signals. The first condition is Williams's %R indicator (for explanation and formula, see *How I Made One Million Dollars... Last Year... Trading Commodities* by Larry R. Williams,

**Figure 6.2**   Daily Bar Chart of June 1990 Comex Gold Prices from August 1989 to April 1990 with Stochastic Chart and Bullish Consensus Chart at Bottom

Source: Reprinted with permission, ©1992 Knight-Ridder Financial Publishing, 30 South Wacker Drive, Suite 1820, Chicago, Illinois 60606.

©1973 by Conceptual Management), which would have given the green light for a long position on or around October 10. The second condition I like to use is Welles Wilder's reaction trend system. (See *New Concepts in Technical Trading Systems* by J. Welles Wilder, Jr., ©1978 by J. Welles Wilder.) As it happens, this indicator gave a signal on October 16 at approximately $385.

For purposes of illustration, let's assume that we would have gone long gold with futures instead of with options.

## Stops: My Thoughts

Getting into a trade, even if done at an ideal level, is often easier than getting out with a profit. For one thing, there is the problem of where to place the stop loss. And if you work without stop losses, you are courting a swift demise, calling to mind Thomas Hobbes's dictum: "Life is nasty, brutish and short."

Herewith a brief aside about stop losses. No proper stop loss guidelines are applicable in all cases. Some people use a given percentage of their account worth as a stop, which seems to me rather arbitrary. A better stop loss level is a given percentage move against your position, although this is still somewhat arbitrary. The only kind of stop loss that makes real sense to me is the violation of a meaningful support or resistance level. This way, in case you do get stopped out, at least you have the consolation of knowing that the initial position was probably wrong anyway, but that you played the move the right way.

It's more than just a question of salvaging some dignity: It's a matter of discipline. And discipline is what will get you through the rough times and keep you intact to enjoy the good times. There is nothing more frustrating than patiently watching an impending move develop for weeks or even months, carefully getting into a perfectly executed trade, basking in warmth as the move starts to unfold, only to get stopped out on some minor reaction at a poorly chosen stop loss and then have the market begin its real move without you. In other words, to have been right and lost money; to have won the battle and lost the war. This frustration is compounded by the logical suspicion that if one cannot make money given the ideal scenario, one will only do worse in less ideal circumstances. This is analogous to not being able to win the serve in tennis, or, to a lesser degree, not winning in chess when playing white.

So where do you place this well-chosen stop loss? Is it a mythical flight of fancy, inscrutable to all mere mortals and accessible to only the most seasoned market wizards? Fortunately, stop loss levels are quite easy to choose, provided one waits for a period of low volatility to put on the position. That is, with volatility low, you can usually find a meaningful stop, close enough to keep your shirt on your back, yet far enough to require a decisive move to trigger it. Looking at our gold example, the stop loss chosen on October 16 would have been slightly below the previous low made on October 11, at around $376.50 on the June 1990 contract.

It's no coincidence that waiting for low volatility gives you not only good stop loss placement, but also the advantage of paying less for the options you buy, since low volatility by definition implies that most market participants haven't yet seized upon the upcoming move, and probably think the market will stay in a trading range. Thus, when you come across brokerage firm research with nebulous statements like, "Based on a mix of fundamental and technical factors, we expect the gold market to remain flat to sideways, in a narrow trading range, although with possibly slightly lower prices for several months to come," it's probably wise to look into buying some options, provided you have a strong directional view.

**Riding the Move**

Having judiciously selected our stop loss, we are now well positioned to ride the move. Let's see how this situation would have unfolded.

With the buy signal on October 16 being generated on a "gap" day (see Figure 6.2, with price at $380 to $385), the natural human tendency to wait for a retracement to obtain a better entry price comes into play. There are several problems with this tendency. First, if a signal isn't immediately acted upon, the chance to get on board may evaporate, and with it potentially large profits. You are in fact risking a potentially great trade for the hope of a slightly better entry price. Assuming you have confidence in your signals, the trade-off simply isn't worth it.

This brings us to the second drawback: If you have a workable system, any signal should be viewed as an opportunity to be seized immediately. If you don't feel your system is workable enough to take signals even on a gap day, then you shouldn't be using that system. So we're back to basics again: Don't trade unless you've found or developed and thoroughly tested a trading system.

The third drawback is that by deciding not to act on a signal, you're doing more than deciding not to decide. You are, in fact, deciding not to trade the signal, which is actually going against your system. "No decision is a decision," as they say in politics. Since you've spent so much time, money and energy developing a trading approach, why sabotage it at the last minute, just when it stands a chance of paying off? That's like designing a spacecraft and then deliberately blowing it up by remote control just as it starts to lift off, heaving a sigh of relief while contentedly telling yourself: "Well, at least this way we know the darn thing could have worked. . . . In fact, it probably would have worked. That was a great spacecraft, all right. Let's break out the champagne, boys." Not a few traders have a subconscious death wish of this kind.

The final drawback to waiting for a pullback for a better entry price upon receiving a signal has to do with discipline. Once you start to interpret your own signals, everything goes out the window. You quickly become prey to the twin emotions of fear and greed. And if you don't take your signal at the outset, at what point do you take it? Trading is difficult enough without complicating things. Your trading system is there to help you—don't short-circuit it. If your system says to buy on a gap day, then buy on the gap day.

So, we have now bought gold via a long futures contract position on October 16, and have our stop loss in place. If we don't get stopped out and our position starts to become profitable, at some point we should move up the stop loss order to protect our profits. The big question, of course, is when and how. If you do it too soon, the stop will be too tight and you'll risk getting stopped out. If you do it too late, you'll risk giving away a large chunk of profits. Since for purposes of convenience we are using futures in this example, we can keep the initial stop losses in place without worrying about losing time value, unlike with options (we'll go through the same example later using options).

Perhaps the easiest way to deal with moving the stop loss is not to move it until the 14-day RSI reaches overbought territory—in the case of a long position. At this stage, there should be enough of an uptrend to clearly discern and draw an up trendline. You may then move up your original stop loss, which was below your entry price, to a little below the up trendline. This then becomes a profit stop. It's called a trailing profit stop, since you ratchet it up every day to reflect the upward movement in the trendline.

By following this approach, our trailing profit stop would have been triggered on December 27, at around $415. The profit from the trade would therefore be:

(L) $385 (Oct. 16, 1989)

(S) $415 (Dec. 27, 1989) (See #1 on Figure 6.2.)

The profit is $30 per ounce per 100-ounce contract, or $3,000 per contract. On speculative margin of, say, $2,500 per contract, this represents a profit of about 120 percent (less commissions) in ten weeks.

Notice how the price of gold starts moving up slowly, then steadily picks up steam in November, with several gap days to the upside, culminating in a closing high around $435 on November 24. This situation is well described by an analogy quoted in *The Wall Street Journal*: "The market is like a cat. . . . It spends a lot of time lolling around, but when it starts to move it can move very fast."

Is there any way to play this increasing upward momentum? Yes, and one of the easiest and most effective ways to do so is with the steeper trendline approach. This simply means using each trendline until a steeper trendline favorable to the direction of the move can be drawn. Initially, a trendline should comprise at least two or three points to be considered valid. When the trendlines become steeper and the price starts to move more quickly, then fewer points are necessary. The thing to remember is that when the market goes wild, we want to assure some profits while still trying to hang on for further profits. Bear in mind the danger inherent in the market/cat analogy. This way you avoid running into, for example, a buzz saw of stop loss orders coming the other way at you.

Using our steeper trendline approach, we would have exited the market with our trailing profit stop a little below the trendline, on the open at around $424 on November 28. The profit from the trade would be:

(L) $385 (Oct. 16, 1989)

(S) $424 (Nov. 28, 1989) (See #2 on Figure 6.2.)

This gives $39 per ounce per 100-ounce contract, or $3,900 per contract. On the same speculative margin of $2,500, this equates to a profit of about 156 percent (less commissions), this time in only six weeks. This means more profits in less time, which has the advantage of freeing your funds for other trades in the meantime.

Although this gold example is admittedly very clear in retrospect, with the weekly chart, daily chart, technical indicators and trendlines all coming together very nicely, such situations are not at all that unusual, provided one looks at 20 or more commodities, scanning for opportunities on a daily basis. With this approach, several excellent occasions should present themselves every year.

### Monitoring a Portfolio and Using Indicators

The obvious question is, "Sure, John, that's the ticket—simply watch four or five different indicators plus the daily and weekly charts on more than 20 different commodities, all on a daily basis, to get into a trade; then select and implement a winning strategy, then follow up on the whole thing with judicious stop losses and well-timed exit techniques. No problem. Oh, just one small question: Who's going to pay the private, full-time technical research staff to watch over my meager $25,000 account? And by the way, aren't these technical indicators you outlined just a little archaic in this day and age, when you have fund managers going crazy trying to keep up with the latest technical systems and trading software?"

Luckily, a private, full-time technical research staff is now available. It's called System Writer Plus™, and has been described as the "trading software equivalent of landing a man on the moon." So if your broker—understandably—won't bend over backwards to give you continuous and up-to-date technical support, and if you'd rather keep your independence than hand over your money to a fund manager even with a great track record, look into this package to help you develop and test your systems and give you trading signals. The tremendous advantage of this system is that the small traders now have a chance to compete with the big fund managers and maintain their traditional autonomy, but this time with effective firepower. It's like giving Stinger missiles to Afghan rebels to help them ward off helicopter gunships. In short, it's cost-effective and it works.

What about the second question: Why should we use "normal" indicators in this crazily competitive financial arena? Just "act normal, that's crazy enough" (Dutch proverb). Some of the best trading approaches are among the simplest. In fact, keeping it simple should be a key goal in developing your system. Using well-worn formulas need not be tantamount to flogging a dead horse. Nor should looking for new ways to use these same tools be considered mere blind thrashing about.

It's not so much a question of raw gray matter and sophistication as it is of methodology and rigor. To paraphrase one street-smart savant, "Success isn't a matter of intelligence, it's a matter of determination. The bright guys are in cafés discussing how the world should be. The dumb guys are in the office, changing the world." Besides, in this era of the demise of the Golden Boys, with fast cars and fancy women—or was that fancy cars and fast women?—and lavish good times and desperate frenzy reminiscent of the last days of Pompeii, relying on sound basics is perhaps not such a bad idea. Besides, trading is arguably the world's oldest profession, despite popular legend; traders were swapping camels for spices in the shadow of the pyramids at the dawn of recorded times. Although these nomads are relegated to the dustbin of history, their spirit survives today in an open-air market in Bombay, a swap meet in Topeka, Kansas, or the T-bond pit at the CBOT. There's nothing dishonorable about using old methods—just make sure you know how to use them.

One effective and "normal" method for gauging market movement, which can be applied to the run-up in gold from October to December 1989, is a momentum indicator. One such indicator could give the following perspective: When the indicator crosses the zero line and moves up, there is increasing upward momentum; when the indicator starts to come down again in toward the zero line, there is decreasing upward momentum (although momentum is still upward). When the indicator crosses the zero line and drops below it, there is increasing downward momentum; and when it starts to come up again toward the zero line, there is decreasing downward momentum. This approach gives you a good perspective on the real strength or weakness of the market.

A word about retracements is in order. If for some reason your system fails to give you an entry signal for what initially turns out to be a nice trade, and you're convinced for sound technical reasons that the ensuing movement will be a nice profit maker, then retracements are very helpful. The best levels to watch are the 38.2 percent, 50 percent and 61.8 percent retracements of the preceding move, whether up or down, although the 23.6 percent and 75 percent levels are also sometimes looked at. Used together with trendlines, retracements can be very powerful tools. A precision ratio compass can be helpful in this regard, although quote systems and trading software increasingly incorporate this feature.

Before going through our gold trade with options, let's talk about the value of fundamental analysis to the trader. While a great many traders swear by fundamental analysis when it comes to trading, say, agricultural commodities, the financials seem to be a different story (although here again, such theories as purchasing power parity can sometimes effectively be used as a sort of "fundamental overlay.") Personally, I prefer to leave the entire thing aside, as fundamental analysis in any case doesn't purport to provide timing for trades, and timing is everything in trading. When one sees eagerly awaited economic figures and releases disseminated with contradictory effects, coupled with revisions of previous months' data, one can only shake one's head and wonder how to make sense of it all. To paraphrase Harold MacMillan, former British prime minister, "The most pressing problem in making economic policy is forecasting the recent past."

However, an excellent tool exists in this regard: Watch the market's reaction to fundamental news or data to help determine its real directional desire. If a strong bull market cannot get help from a fresh bullish report, use this fact together with your technical indicators to determine if the bull market has peaked. Another example: A flat rising market is now technically overbought, and a very bullish report comes out. But the market cannot gather steam from the report. It is probably a sign of an impending market tumble. Using economic data with this approach is often extremely effective and easy to implement.

A last note: Follow net trader position reports, which are updated regularly, to know where the large speculators, small speculators and commercials have positioned themselves. This information can be found in various chart services, such as Commodity Trend Service, Palm Beach, Florida.

## PART II: APPLYING STRATEGIES

There is a danger inherent in using option strategies as a panacea. Either a real or an opportunity cost is involved in even zero cost strategies, and this cost must be paid either at the outset or somewhere down the line. The point is, you *will* pay the cost.

### Buying Options Outright

With this in mind, let's look at our trade with options. On October 16, we might have bought a gold call option with a strike of, say, 405, or roughly $20 out-of-the-money. Volatility at the time for out-of-the-money call options was running at about 15 percent. For purposes of graphical clarity, we'll refer to the June 1990 gold futures chart, even though in October 1989 we would have considered options two or three months to expiration. We'll simply make adjustments as necessary to reflect the different basis. On October 16, then, our call option, with a fictitious January expiration, would have cost roughly $4 (using an option calculator, with the appropriate volatility levels). Its worth on December 27, at our futures exit price of 415, would have been $12. The profit would be $8, or 200 percent before commissions. This is vastly superior to the profit we made using futures contracts. Also, the risk is limited.

By using our *steeper trendline-plus* approach and exiting earlier and at a better price, the value of the same option on November 28 would have been roughly $21, for a profit of $17, or 425 percent in six weeks, before commissions. This is quite a return, you will agree. Also notice the way that time value decay affects the option's value between November 28 and December 27. This is an excellent illustration of the "jungle fighter" strategy—not overstaying a position. Speed is essential when dealing with purchased, or long, options.

### Looking at Volatility in Outright Buys

Now let's see if we can achieve even better results using options combinations with the straightforward, long call, "no frills" idea just described. First, let's keep in mind that volatility levels rose between October 16 and December 27. Implied volatility on out-of-the-money gold call options, with three months to expiration, around 14 to 15 percent as mentioned on October 16, rose to 18.3 to 19.9 percent on November 28, and stood at 18.2 to 18.8 percent on December 27. A quick look at the June 1990 gold chart shows that price moved from $372 to a little over $435, a 17 percent move equivalent to $63 per ounce. Therefore, merely on a volatility basis, buying options in August (to minimize cost) and selling options in November or December (to maximize return) would have been the thing to do. Of course, you're not limited to selling the same option you bought. This is where the rule of thumb of "buy low volatility, sell high volatility" becomes interesting when combined with options strategies.

One possibility is to keep the original 405 strike call option until it becomes deep in the money, then "roll up" by selling it and buying a call with a higher strike. The original call will have mainly intrinsic value and will therefore act more like a futures contract than an option at that point. *Since the idea of options is to achieve high leverage, we should always look to protect profits, especially when they are substantial.* So, with gold at $424 on November 28, we could sell the 405 call (which by now has lost one month of time value and still has two months to go) at $21 and buy, say, an $11 out-of-the-money call with a strike price of 435, with only two months to expiration, at then-higher volatility levels of 18.3 to 19.9 percent, for a price of $7. The advantage in rolling up (or down, as the case may be) is that now that you don't have as much at stake. Gold can keep going up, down or sideways, but you'll have taken good profits, with a chance to make much more money. This gives you peace of mind.

In case this rolling approach sounds like the best of both worlds when one has large profits, "it ain't necessarily so." One disadvantage of rolling is that you've sold your original option at a price that doesn't really reflect the increase in volatility from October 16 to November 28 (since it's deep in the money), and you've now bought an option that does reflect this higher volatility. *In other words, you have in effect sold low and bought high.* Another disadvantage of rolling is that you are tacitly admitting that the market may be winding up its move. If that's your view, you might consider getting out altogether on an appropriate exit signal and keeping all your profits. So the jury's out for me where rolling is concerned.

The counterargument from rolling proponents might be: "Yes, but by rolling you have the latitude to widen your exit signals and thereby give yourself a better chance of weathering a momentary adverse reaction. You can then go on to make huge profits." The logical answer to this is that widening your exit signals is fiddling with the system, which takes us back to the drawing board and my introductory tirade concerning discipline.

### Rolling Over by Buying a Spread

One noteworthy alternative to the above is to roll by buying a spread. For example, you might first sell to liquidate the 405 call, then buy (go long) the 435 call as in the prior example, for a debit of $7, and at the same time sell (go short) the 445 call, for a credit of $4. This way you are selling as well as buying volatility, somewhat neutralizing the drawback presented by the higher volatility levels previously mentioned. Because you are getting a credit on the sell side, you reduce the premium paid for putting on the spread.

In buying a spread, you also have the advantage of eventually being able to buy back the short 445 call at some point. You get added strategic flexibility by simply staying long the 435 call in case you think the underlying contract—gold—will surge to new highs, allowing you to either cash in your chips on an unfettered long call, or keep it and go short the 445 call a second time. (As strategies go, legging in or out of a spread is simple but potentially very effective, although here again there is a trade-off in that if you buy back the short call and gold fails to move up, you'll incur an opportunity cost.)

All in all, spreads sound quite nice. So what's the catch? Although by buying a spread we are partially neutralizing the volatility cost implied in our roll-up example, as well as taking in a credit by selling an option and even gaining added flexibility, as long as the spread is in place, the profits from an upward move in gold will be limited by the short option. This is a disadvantage if you expect much higher futures prices. If, on the other hand, your studies indicate that we are approaching key resistance levels, it might be wise to sell a call with a strike at or close to your projected resistance point(s). Following our much-vaunted discipline and rigorous trading logic, you might question the wisdom of paying a net debit for a call spread when you expect an imminent down move in any case. The valid reason for doing so has more to do with the dynamics of options than with market direction because at key resistance or support levels there is often a tendency for the market to pause while deciding where to go next. This pause works in your favor because time value decay and possibly lower volatility should reduce the short 445 call's value, thus allowing you to buy it back for a profit. You would then elect to stay long the 435 call or sell it as your signals dictate. This "dynamization" can add significantly to the bottom line of your options trading, but only if you do it in accordance with your system.

### Other Spreads To Consider

Let's examine some other option strategies, starting with our original signal. On October 16, since we were anticipating a potentially strong move, the appropriate move was to buy a simple call, not a call spread. But purchasing a call outright or a call spread costs money, even when volatility is low. If a subsequent move fails to develop, you will eventually lose your entire premium, through the time decay factor that makes options a wasting asset. One way around this obstacle is to put on a *call ratio backspread*, for example, shorting one 395 call and going long two 405 calls, with a January expiration. The strategy could have been implemented on October 16 for a debit of only $1. The idea is that gold will go higher than the second strike, or 405. If that happens, everything beyond the break-even point of $415 plus the original debit is a clean profit (after deducting the triple commission). Of course, if at expiration gold is between 395 and the break-even, you will have a net loss. You therefore need to be confident that gold will stage a decent rally beyond 405, at which point you can unwind your position as you see fit before or at expiration.

Another play that I like is to buy the usual 405 call for a debit of $4, then sell a 375 January put for a credit of $7 to reduce the cost of the call, even making a credit of $3 overall. If gold is below 375 at expiration, you will find yourself long one futures contract at $375, which will be *marked to the market* on a daily basis, meaning that you'll have to put up the cash represented by the unrealized losses on the contract. Since we thought that everything looked great for an upside move, a break below 375 (see Figure 6.2) would obviously mean that all bets are off, and the real strength, if it develops, should be to the downside. At that point, you would be seriously inconvenienced by a long futures position at 375.

Is there a solution? Well, you could try cushioning yourself by putting the strategy on for a larger initial credit. This can be achieved by shorting an additional 415 call for a credit of $2.50, to the original position generated by being long the 405 call and short a 375 put. You can replace the 375 put with a 365 put, in which case you will limit your upside (the 415 call sold) but also decrease the downside risk (the 365 put sold). Granted, for a moderate up move you'll come out a winner, but no matter how good the charts look, this strategy is like picking up dimes in front of a moving steamroller. (If you like risky business, and are of the opinion even after seeing the evidence of an impending gold rally that gold should go up but not too much, a nice strategy to get embroiled in is the *call ratio spread*, which involves, say, buying the 395 call and selling two 405 calls. If gold goes beyond 405 at expiration, you'll find yourself short one contract of gold at 405. There are more wicked plays around, but there's still a tangible "Sword of Damocles" aspect to this one. Actually, the call ratio spread has its uses, but given the chart pattern and the major buy signals generated by our system, you would be ill-advised to put on this strategy on October 16.)

This brings up the point of choosing the right strategy at the right time. There seems to be a common myth that as long as you can get the timing of the market right (an extraordinarily difficult thing to do consistently), the rest will take care of itself. Nothing could be further from the truth, although it is my conviction that good market timing combined with mediocre strategies is better than mediocre market timing combined with good strategies. The fact remains that you must integrate timing and strategies (not to mention money management and psychology) in a synergistic manner, instead of via a schizophrenic patchwork quilt method that will only get you into trouble. It's tough to make consistent winnings in the market—if you want a friend on Wall Street, you're better off getting a dog—but the more well honed the strategy tools at your disposal, the better your chances will be.

Getting back to gold on October 16, an excellent play is to go long the 405 call for a debit of $4 and sell a put spread (not a put): You sell the 385 put and buy the 375 put, for a credit of $3.50. The complete strategy will cost $0.50 ($3.50 – $4.00, without commission costs). Your risk on the put spread is $6.50 ($10 between the two strikes of the 385/375 put spread minus the $3.50 credit). Your profit potential on the upside is open-ended due to the long call position. On the other hand, if the price of gold should fall, you will lose the value of the call, $4, and the risk on the put spread, $6.50, for a total of $10.50 on the whole play.

Because you think the chances are high that gold should rise, it shouldn't bother you to sell an at-the-money put spread and collect a higher premium for apparently higher risk; if gold doesn't rise as expected, it could instead tumble severely to well below 375, at which point it would turn out to have been not much less risky to sell an out-of-the-money spread.

The big advantage of this long call/short put spread idea, aside from the predetermined, limited downside risk, is that your initial cash outlay is greatly reduced. The delta (increase in value of the strategy for a percentage move in your direction in the underlying) of your position is thus increased versus that of the simple long 405 call example. Another way to look at it is that you have greater leverage because your cash outlay is reduced.

The profit picture using the long call/short put spread is as follows: From October 16, at which time the cost of the strategy was $0.50, or almost zero, the strategy rose in value to around $20 on November 28, when we would have closed out the strategy using the steeper trendline method for a profit of 3,900 percent before commission. The profit is higher than with the straight long call, but keep in mind that there is a margin call at the outset that is at risk, which means that your 3,900 percent profit is really only $2,000/$1,000, or 200 percent of your capital risked. The point is that in trading options you must distinguish between capital outlay and total risk.

Another advantage of selling a put spread instead of a put is that, while more costly, its lower risk entails correspondingly lower margin requirements. This will save you a lot of headaches, as your total risk is paid up at the outset. Although some people seem to enjoy wrestling with daily margin calculations and having to question margin calls, this is usually counterproductive and can lead to frustration and high cash outflow. (Many of these may be the same traders who insist on inappropriate strategies and jump the gun on their own systems, then blame the markets when things go sour.) Besides, what starts off in theory as a straightforward set of formulas for margin calculations often degenerates in practice into a Gordian knot. Try to avoid protracted turf battles with bureaucratic warlords on this issue, as you will invariably lose. Better to pay predetermined and limited margin at the outset and have done with it.

If you insist on implementing this strategy for a credit, it can be done, but generally only by buying a farther-out-of-the-money call, which reduces your delta, or by buying a call closer to expiration, which decreases your chances for profit. This last idea is useful only if you're confident that the move will take place very soon, as time value decay starts slowly and accelerates as expiration nears, approaching a logarithmic curve several weeks to expiration. You'd then conceivably be hampered by an expired worthless call option and a still very much alive short put spread.

## Straddles and Strangles

Rather than explore a number of other strategies, I'll just conclude here by mentioning straddles and strangles. The purchase of these implies thinking volatility will rise, with a breakout in price but with direction unknown. These are relatively expensive to implement, as you're not forced to take a directional view. Buying a straddle is the more aggressive—and expensive—volatility play of the two, and involves buying an at-the-money call and an at-the-money put. Buying a strangle, on the other hand, involves buying a call and a put at slightly out-of-the-money strikes. In our gold illustration, however, these would not be appropriate strategies to use, as we have a strong directional view. The other way to play straddles and strangles is to sell them for an initial credit, thinking that volatility should fall or remain flat, and letting time value decay work in your favor. This approach, though, is even less appropriate for our example, as we think volatility will rise, not fall.

These strategies, like all others, have their utility. My point here is that you will invariably find that the trading approach you develop will often be suited more to one kind of strategy than another. In my case, since I look for situations with a strong directional view and where volatility should rise, one of the strategies I prefer is the long call/short put spread outlined above when going long (or long put/short call spread when going short). Your risk is predetermined and limited, your profit potential is unlimited, and you pay a very low premium to get into the strategy. The other strategy I like very much is the call ratio backspread, in which you anticipate a strong move in your direction but pay little or nothing and lose little or nothing if the market goes in the other direction. Experiment on paper until you get a good feel for the strategies that best suit your trading style.

## PART III: THE HARDEST PART

The hardest part of trading is not developing and testing a viable approach, or finding your way through the numerous strategies available, or racking up an impressive string of paper trade gains. Nor is it haggling for discount commissions after you break your back finding a good broker who'll hear your story and work to make your money—instead of merely his earnings—grow, or checking on fills and getting confirmations straight, or even elaborating a good money management program to make sure you survive. The hardest part of trading is sticking to your trading program. In short, total commitment to your predetermined approach.

This commitment will help you avoid getting stuck in a quagmire of disconnected options positions that will result in unwitting diversification and a dilution of your options leverage—in effect, an expensive and useless insurance policy. This commitment will also help you avoid getting wiped out in your first months of trading, keeping in mind Mao's guerrilla formula of never directly confronting the enemy, but surviving long enough to come out ahead. Finally, this commitment will keep your ego in check, which will go a long way toward keeping you in the black. Note that you cannot bully the market—instead, you have to finesse it. Much ink has been spilled on this subject of late, much of it very helpful. Sitting permanently glued to a screen and furiously hurling insults at it each time the market moves a tick against you may make you feel better, but it probably won't add much to your financial bottom line, although it may add to the other bottom line.

Quite a few traders have large egos for reasons of financial power and independence. This is the other bottom line. Large egos are often masks for deep-rooted fears or insecurities. Investment psychology is indeed crucial.

Once you have your timing tools (i.e., analysis) under control and have worked on your investment psychology, cap your efforts by mastering money management via mathematical formulas that provide the link between gaming theory (odds forecasting, probability and so on) and concrete market success in futures/options trading.

Not to confound the number-crunching crowd, but I must admit the imponderable or $x$ factor in investing. A little luck at the right time can make a large difference. According to traditional German financial wisdom, there are four requirements for success: (1) Geld (money); (2) Gedanken (ideas); (3) Geduld (patience); and (4) Gluck (luck). Money management gives the capital (or money) to work with per trade. The game plan, market analysis, scenario planning and option strategies provide the ideas. Investment psychology techniques lead to the emotional staying power (or patience) before, during and after the trade— the setup, execution and debriefing components. So all that is needed is luck!

# CHAPTER 7

# An Introduction to Swaptions

*BY KEITH SCHAP*

**Editor's Note:**

Keith Schap has professional writing credentials that serve him well in the world of financial writing. For this reason, he was asked to contribute this chapter on a leading edge strategy using sophisticated products such as interest rate futures and options. It is not a methodology chapter, but an overview of swaptions.

Jon Najarian's chapter on program trading with options points out that those strategies cannot be implemented without two crucial components: access to a relatively large amount of capital and executions of orders. In a similar vein, this chapter outlines several impediments to implementing swaptions strategies—namely, access to cash dealers in the banking network and access to the buy side. Despite these drawbacks, this arcane set of strategies is important. Sometime in the near future, you are likely to have access to this trading strategy, either through the services of a professional money manager or through insiders wishing to find backers to implement the strategy.

## GROWTH OF THE SWAP MARKET

The decade of the 1980s was an especially fruitful period for financial engineers. Yet of all the new derivative products introduced during that time, none caught the fancy of risk managers like swaps, especially swaps on interest rates. And perhaps none holds out more potential for managed futures fund traders and other portfolio managers than swaptions.

By the end of the 1980s, swap market growth had outstripped even such fast-growing futures contracts as the Chicago Board of Trade T-bond and the Chicago Mercantile Exchange Eurodollar. (See Figures 7.1 and 7.2.) Since then, the gulf has widened with the total, including swaptions, reaching $923.4 billion notional value in the first half of 1991, a 41 percent increase in activity over the first half of 1990.

From the first, swaps attracted corporate financial managers for reasons that should be obvious. Here they could, in relative secrecy from their competitors, design transactions that met their needs with regard to size and longer-dated maturities. In many cases, that couldn't be done as well in the futures markets. Except for Eurodollar futures, which are largely a creature of the swap market, hedging more than a few months or a year using futures seems almost impossible. Swaps also offered freedom from margin calls, mark-to-market accounting and other noisome aspects of futures trading.

## CONSIDERATIONS IN USING SWAPS OR FUTURES

The total derivatives market is complex, with no single class of instrument offering an across-the-board advantage over another. A survey of some of the major concerns of commercial traders shows that on some grounds swaps seem better suited to the needs of commercial traders, while on others the advantage is with futures.

Let's look at some of the main points traders use to evaluate swaps and futures: term, liquidity, basis location, secrecy, pricing, spread effects, transaction cost, financial protection, accounting, regulation and delivery mechanism.

- *Term.* From the outset, the possibility of extending coverage over a term of several years attracted risk managers to swaps. Due to their longer terms, swaps involve less rollover cost than hedging with futures. They also allow commercials to lock in spreads; futures do not.
- *Liquidity.* Futures are especially liquid for relatively smaller deals. But futures traders tend to be "nonfundamental," short-term thinkers, so futures lose liquidity in deferred markets. And, in the cases of very large size, swaps are probably more liquid.
- *Basis location.* Swaps, like other over-the-counter (OTC) deals, create an opportunity to move the basis of the contract. In certain cases, Chicago grain basis may not reflect Iowa or central Illinois markets adequately. New York harbor oil may not reflect Gulf, or Cushing, Oklahoma, or Rotterdam realities. Neither the German bund market nor the T-bond may capture the complexities of an international

**Figure 7.1**    Growth Markets in Interest Rates

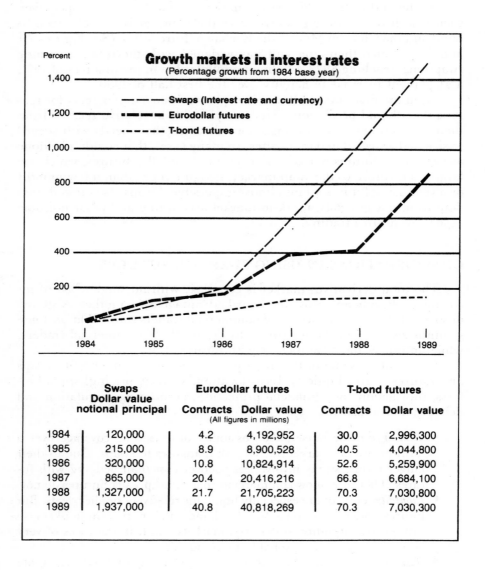

Source: Reprinted with permission from *Futures* magazine, August 1990. Sources for figures: Exchanges for futures; *Euromoney* and *United States Banker* for swaps before 1987 and International Swap Dealers Association for Swaps after 1987.

**Figure 7.2** International Swap Dealers Association Market Survey (Activity January 1 through June 30, 1991)

| Currency | Interest Rate Swaps | | | Currency Swaps | | |
|---|---|---|---|---|---|---|
| | $ Equivalent (mills) | Currency as % of Total ($762.1 bill) | % Change First Half of 1990 | $ Equivalent (mills) | Currency as % of Total ($322.6 bill) | % Change First Half of 1990 |
| U.S. Dollar (USD) | 447,994 | 58.78% | 52.04% | 115,501 | 35.80% | 85.21% |
| Yen (JPY) | 73,456 | 9.64% | 8.85% | 50,389 | 15.62% | 19.14% |
| Sterling (GBP) | 62,601 | 8.21% | 5.10% | 13,235 | 4.10% | 63.50% |
| Deutschemark (DEM) | 48,439 | 6.36% | 0.12% | 15,104 | 4.68% | 23.83% |
| Swiss Franc (CHF) | 29,994 | 3.94% | 40.73% | 37,773 | 11.71% | 145.90% |
| French Franc (FRF) | 17,356 | 2.28% | 40.90% | 4,853 | 1.50% | 50.25% |
| Australian Dollar (AUD) | 17,092 | 2.24% | (3.71%) | 15,156 | 4.70% | (7.40%) |
| Canadian Dollar (CAD) | 15,946 | 2.09% | (7.69%) | 11,961 | 3.71% | 65.53% |
| European Currency Unit (XEU) | 13,059 | 1.71% | 4.41% | 12,659 | 3.92% | 51.03% |
| Italian Lira (ITL) | 10,721 | 1.41% | 451.78% | 11,727 | 3.63% | 128.77% |
| Swedish Krona (SEK) | 10,464 | 1.37% | 11,398.90% | 8,787 | 2.72% | 1,924.65% |
| Dutch Guilder (NLG) | 5,564 | 0.73% | 42.92% | 3,362 | 1.04% | 119.74% |
| Belgian Franc (BEL) | 2,187 | 0.29% | 127.34% | 1,668 | 0.52% | 28.11% |
| New Zealand Dollar (NZD) | 1,404 | 0.18% | 35.00% | 1,725 | 0.53% | 15.00% |
| Danish Krone (DKK) | 779 | 0.10% | 32.71% | 841 | 0.26% | 53.19% |
| Hong Kong Dollar (HKD) | 434 | 0.06% | 28.78% | 251 | 0.08% | 65.13% |
| Other Currencies | 4,631 | 0.61% | 240.26% | 17,655 | 5.47% | 455.01% |
| | $762,121 million | | | $322,647 million | | |
| | | | | *$161,324 million* | | |

* Total adjusted for double counting of both sides of a currency swap.

Source: International Swap Dealers Association.

financial transaction. Increasingly, commercial traders see such factors as an extra risk management problem. Swaps offer commercials an opportunity to locate the basis that suits their needs.

- *Secrecy.* Commercials can execute OTC deals—swaps among them— quietly, away from the public eye. This can cut down on slippage and avoid giving away a competitive position.
- *Pricing.* Futures markets provide a remarkable pricing mechanism, a crucial factor in any major trading activity. Without this kind of readily available benchmark, managing risk becomes a touch-and-go enterprise (as junk bond traders have sorrowfully discovered).
- *Spread effects.* Futures spreads can be uncertain, especially when deferred contracts experience thin trading. Swaps can lock in those spreads. More to the point, swaps may afford a different percent of carry than futures due to the term (it's far easier to decide that a market will reward storage for the next six months than for the next five years).
- *Transaction cost.* Short, simple contracts are cheap to execute. Like futures, cash grain deals including trains (which are subject to National Grain and Feed Association rules) are simple to construct and therefore inexpensive to execute. Barges are a little trickier. Because OTC transactions such as swaps lack the precedents of tradition (though the International Swap Dealers Association is striving to remedy that), they tend to require more contractual structure and can be more expensive in terms of transaction cost.
- *Financial protection.* Default risk becomes a major concern with OTC deals, and remedies and sanctions occupy significant contractual space in swap deals. While futures exchanges do not guarantee the futures commission merchant or the account, they do guarantee the counterparty (something a holder of Drexel paper might especially value). Bank letters of credit could substitute for swappers.
- *Accounting.* Because OTC markets may not trade regularly, there may not be a regular quote. In addition to practical trading considerations, this may create accounting problems by providing ready closets for the hiding of skeletons.
- *Regulation.* Swaps are essentially an unregulated market. Proponents support this state of affairs by pointing to the fact that deal size alone rules out participation by any but those with the resources and sophistication to look after themselves. Even though the arbitration and other regulatory mechanisms of the futures trade sometimes appear subject to domination by some of the participants, the combination of government and self-regulatory oversight exerts a stabilizing and protective influence on those markets. As swaps reach into more markets, that kind of protection may increasingly seem a good thing.

- *Delivery mechanism.* The Commodity Futures Trading Commission allows cash trading off exchanges because those trades involve a "reasonable anticipation of delivery." As a paper market, that anticipation disappears and, under regulations currently in force, could render swaps illegal.

Commodity Trader Advisers (CTAs) and other institutional futures users have recently begun to sound more like their corporate counterparts. The positions some managers want and need to trade are so large that even relatively liquid futures markets struggle to absorb them. Already, numbers of the larger CTAs have begun to use the interbank currency market because it offers a single price for size on a 24-hour basis. Traders increasingly mention the analogous possibilities available in the swap market.

For traders steeped in traditional futures and options markets, swaps and swaptions should seem only a next logical step, not an entirely new venture. After all, the options traded in the pits at the CBOT, CME, New York Mercantile Exchange and other world exchanges are technically options on futures. While futures contracts convey an obligation to buy or sell a given quantity of goods at an agreed-upon price and time, option purchasers have the right, but not the obligation. In theory, a holder of corn futures ultimately takes possession of corn, while the holder of an option on corn futures may take possession of a corn futures contract—should he or she choose to exercise the right. This is true for all options on futures. To emphasize, the futures contract itself may settle through physical delivery or cash settlement. But option exercise entails delivery of a futures contract.

Traders new to the swap market but familiar with futures or their ancestors, forward contracts, should be able to orient themselves quickly. A forward contract, after all, simply involves two people agreeing to make and take delivery of specific goods at a negotiated time, place and price. Like any other OTC trade, the terms of the forward can be whatever the two agree on. The major drawbacks are that forward contracts are illiquid and, like all OTC instruments, entail significant counterparty credit risk.

Over a century ago, traders realized that a kind of generic forward contract could make life easier by allowing for a vibrant secondary market. With standardized terms and a centralized trading arena, traders could still take a position to make or take delivery at a future time, as with a forward. The difference was that the liquidity and standardization of the new futures contracts allowed traders to change their minds. As needs changed, they could easily trade out of a position or into a new.

Futures were the final link. Suppose a pension fund manager, anticipating a major influx of funds in 30 days, knows he or she will be investing a portion of it in U.S. Treasury bonds. Given a favorable current price and expecting lower interest rates within a month, he or she might buy T-bond futures because the futures price appreciation in the interim will compensate for the price increase in the cash market. The futures trade locks in the price of the bond.

Options allow pension traders to defer the decision. Buying a T-bond call with a strike price at or close to the current price gives the traders a choice. When the anticipated funds arrive, they can look at the bond market again. If the price has risen as expected, they can exercise the option (or trade it) and acquire the bond below market price. However, should interest rates have risen in the meantime (perhaps because of a surge in inflation) and T-bond prices have dipped, they can let the option expire and pay the lower market price. That is, traders can benefit from the asymmetrical payoff pattern of the option markets. (See Figures 7.3 and 7.4.) More and more, portfolio managers seek that advantage.

Implicit in all forward contracts and many futures contracts is the intention to make or take delivery. While almost no futures contracts see delivery, that possibility remains at the heart of every trade. Not so with swaps.

## SWAPS, FORWARDS AND FUTURES

Much has been made of the fact that swaps, forwards and futures are special cases of the same idea. Standard swap pricing (for currency, interest rate and commodity swaps) regards swaps as strips, or sequences, of forward contracts. Still, swaps differ from those other financial transactions in one important respect. No principal amount changes hands as with bond issues or other loans. No physical goods change hands as with forward contracts. Swaps are strictly paper trades.

To underline that point, contrast a simple bond issue with an equally simple interest rate swap.

If a corporation wants to raise $50 million, it can issue a five-year bond with a 10 percent coupon, to pull a number out of the air. As with any other lending agreement, the bond involves both an interest payment and an exchange of principal. At the start, the lender transfers the money to the borrower. During the term of the loan, the borrower makes periodic payments for the privilege of using the money. Then the borrower pays back the principal amount at the end.

For simplicity, let's assume annual coupons. So lenders who buy that bond will receive five interest payments and one final payment of the principal. Thus, a pension fund that buys $10 million of the issue will receive $1 million a year and, on the maturity date, its $10 million principal.

**Figure 7.3**   Payout Diagram: Short Futures

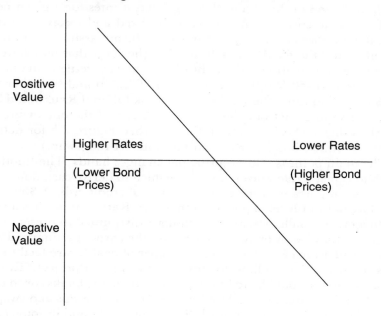

**Figure 7.4**   Payout Diagram: Long Call

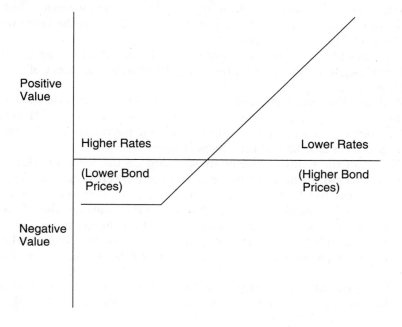

In contrast, an interest rate swap involves an agreement to exchange cash flows based on fixed and floating interest rates for a given period.

If the same corporation agrees to pay fixed and receive floating on $50 million notional principal for five years (again assuming annual settlements), and the fixed rate is 10 percent (however that may have been derived) and the floating is the LIBOR rate, at each settlement one party pays $5 million (50,000,000 × 0.10 = 5,000,000) and the other whatever $50 million times the London Interbank Offered Rate would be. In practice, swappers net out the two payments, and the one owing more pays the other a check for the difference. (See Figure 7.5 for details of forward contract, bond transaction and interest rate swap.)

The main point is that no principal changes hands. The "notional" principal is just a reference point from which to derive cash flows. (That fact is also important in the determination of credit risk. A $50 million swap does not imply an exposure of that size. Rather, it implies an exposure to a much smaller stream of cash flows discounted to present value.)

To see what swaps or swaptions add to the corporate financial repertoire, consider the case of a major developer of health care facilities who wants to borrow $50 million for five years to fund a project. Two common approaches would be to borrow from a bank (or banks) or to issue a bond. In either case, the availability of interest rate swaps and swaptions affords the developer greater flexibility of approach, and in some cases it allows him or her to reduce the cost of funding.

If the developer were to take the bank loan route, he or she would prefer to borrow fixed for planning and budgeting purposes, but the banks much prefer to pass their interest rate risk on to the borrower in the form of floating-rate loans.

In cases like that, the developer can take out the floating rate loan and then negotiate an interest rate swap to achieve the effect of a fixed-rate loan.

Still pulling numbers out of the air, if the interest rates on the loan at the annual reset periods are 8 percent, 9 percent, 12 percent, 11 percent and 10 percent, then the five annual interest payments will be for $4, $4.5, $6, $5.5 and $5 million, respectively.

To offset the floating rate he or she paid on the loan, the developer enters into a swap where he or she pays a fixed interest rate and receives floating. If the fixed interest rate is 10 percent, the developer will pay $5 million at each annual settlement. Assuming the floating-rate side of the swap is the same as the bank payments and that the swap payments are netted, the developer will be a net payer in the first two years and a net receiver in the second two. The fifth year will be a wash. (See Figure 7.6.)

Taking the loan payments together with the swap, the end result is that the developer pays $5 million a year in interest for each of the five

**Figure 7.5**  Essential Structures of Forward Contracts, Bonds and Swaps

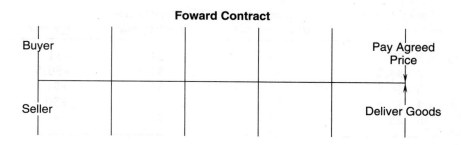

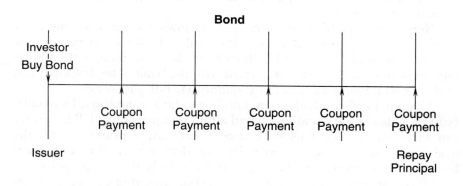

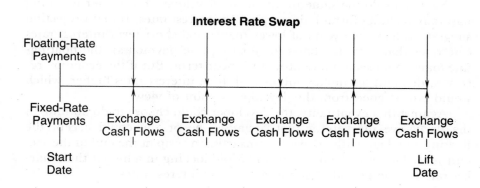

**Figure 7.6** Comparison of Loan and Swap Cash Flows

| Loan developer pays bank floating rate | Swap developer pays 10% fixed rate | Developer receives floating rate | Net difference |
|---|---|---|---|
| 1. $4 | $5 | $4 | -$1 |
| 2. $4.5 | $5 | $4.5 | -$0.5 |
| 3. $6 | $5 | $6 | +$1 |
| 4. $5.5 | $5 | $5.5 | +$0.5 |
| 5. $5 | $5 | $5 | — |

years. To be sure, in the first year he or she pays only $4 million to the bank, but he or she also pays $1 to the swap counterparty. In the third year of the loan, he or she pays the bank $6 million, but gets $1 million from the swap. And so on.

Note also that the swap in no way removes the need for the bank loan. The developer still deals with the bank, which may or may not be aware of the swap. But the cash flows from the swap remove the uncertainties of the floating-rate instrument with the bank. The developer can base financial planning on known quantities, not guesswork.

That application should seem familiar to futures hedgers. In parallel fashion, a dealer long heating oil and afraid that prices will fall by winter can short futures and lock in a price. That way, if prices do fall, the dealer gets his or her target price, less transaction costs. The one drawback is that if prices rise, the dealer still gets only that target price.

Of course, options allow a remedy for the unwanted part of the heating oil hedge result. If long heating oil, the dealer can buy a put. Then, if prices rise, the dealer is out the price of the put but still participates in the rally. Yet if prices do fall, the put protects against the downside.

Swaptions do the same thing for the developer. His or her planning naturally includes formulating a view on interest rates. If that projection suggests at least two years of lower than usual short-term interest rates (the rates that form the basis for floating-rate payments), the floating-rate loan would seem more attractive, near term. But if the economy recovers, demand for money might well drive interest rates higher, which would not be good from the developer's point of view.

Against that eventuality, the developer could choose to do nothing in the derivative markets at first. That is, he or she could accept the floating-rate loan with an eye to transacting a swap at the end of the second year. That way, he or she would avoid locking in a higher than market rate for the period of supposedly lower interest rates.

The developer also could engage in a "two, three swaption"—a two-year option on a three-year swap. Basing the eventual swap on current spreads and rates would allow the developer to take delivery of the swap when and if he or she needed it in two years. On the other hand, if interest rates in the market at exercise time are lower than what the swap specifies, the developer forfeits the premium on the swaption and pays the market rate, or contracts for a swap at the new market rates.

Thus, for traders who deal primarily with options on futures, thinking about OTC options takes some mental agility; OTC financial derivatives typically deal directly with interest rates, whereas financial futures deal with price. For example, long a call on interest rates is equivalent to long a put on price. Short a put on interest rates is equivalent to short a call on price.

Carrying that to swaptions adds yet another layer of complexity, for a swaption buyer must decide also whether to pay or receive the fixed interest rate. All of this has created a terminological morass. But usage seems to be settling on the convention that the buyer of a call swaption will receive fixed and pay floating, while the buyer of a put swaption will pay fixed and receive floating.

By embracing the derivatives markets from the outset, though, the developer can create extra financial benefits. Rather than borrow from a bank, suppose the developer issues a five-year bond callable at two years and sells a two-year call swaption to a bank for 20 basis points a year. The bank gains the right to a three-year swap in which it receives the fixed rate and pays floating. (See Figure 7.7.)

Investors will buy that kind of bond because it pays higher coupon interest than a similar noncallable issue. Banks will take their side of the swaption because, if interest rates go down, they can exercise the swaption and so receive a higher than market return.

If the bond coupon derives from five-year Treasuries that are trading at 8.75 percent (still strictly hypothetical numbers), noncallable debt might trade at a spread of 50 basis points over the Treasury rate, while callable debt might trade at 60 basis points over. That means investors who buy the bonds are short a call option for which the debt issuer pays 10 basis points a year for five years. (See Figures 7.8, 7.9 and 7.10.)

If interest rates decline during the first two years, the bank can exercise its swaption and so receive a higher than market return for the last three years. The developer, in turn, can call in the bond to offset the fixed-rate payments to the bank. The combination of the swap and a floating-rate debt reissue results in maintaining almost the same cash flow sequence as before. The developer still has a fixed-rate borrowing at about 9.35 percent. However, if interest rates rise, the bank will not exercise the swaption nor will the developer call in the bond. The developer continues to pay the same coupon rate as before.

**Figure 7.7**    Corporate Bond with Swaption

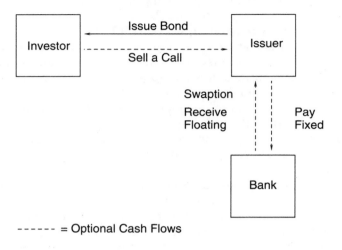

**Figure 7.8**    Payout Diagram: Callable Bond

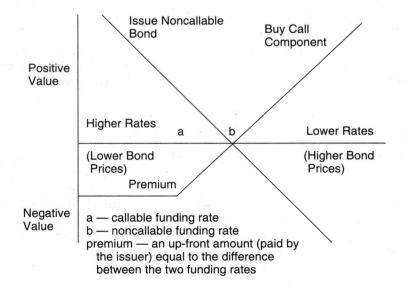

**Figure 7.9**  Payout Diagram: Short Call Swaption

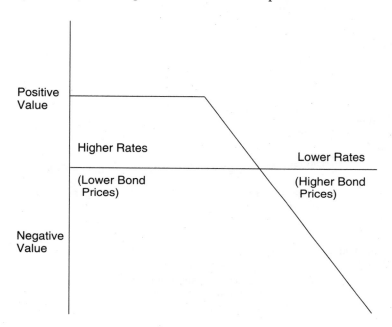

Not to be overlooked is the fact that the swaption premium collected from the bank results in a total cost of funds that is ten basis points lower than the original interest rate for noncallable debt. That reduction in the cost of the debt issue, thanks to the sale of the swaption, highlights the fact that the goals of swaption users closely resemble those of commercial participants in the more familiar futures and equity options markets. Portfolio managers, corporate treasurers and bankers might buy or sell puts or calls to reduce the cost of funding, enhance yields, adjust portfolio duration and convexity, cover embedded options in mortgages or other securities or hedge anticipated fundings.

Similarly, market users can buy swaptions in anticipation of a debt issue to lock in a favorable interest rate or to offset the embedded option of a mortgage issue or a callable bond. They can sell swaptions to reduce the cost of borrowing or to enhance portfolio yields. And they can use combinations to control portfolio duration or to facilitate asset-liability management. Indeed, the uses for swaptions among corporate and institutional market users seem potentially without limit.

Swaps and swaptions differ from forwards in yet another important way—liquidity. Forward contracts remain, for the most part, highly individual buyer-seller transactions. If the needs of either party change

**Figure 7.10**    Payout Diagram: Callable Bond Issue with Short Call Swaption

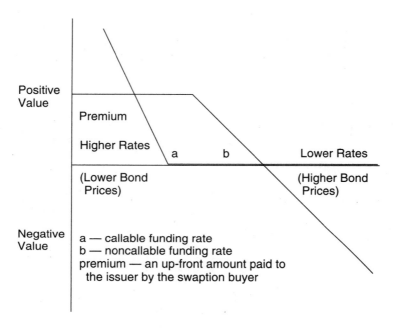

before the contract comes due, it is almost always necessary to renegotiate with the original counterparty.

### SWAP MARKET STRUCTURE

The first swaps were similar in that the swap dealer helped a customer find a counterparty in need of a mirror-image position. But the dealer only got the two sides together in those transactions and didn't take a position. (See Figure 7.11.)

As the market grew, exactly matched dealer books became hard to maintain. The exigencies of time and market balance required that dealers increasingly be willing to take positions. Furthermore, as dealers came to play greater roles, swap customers grew less likely to know who took the opposing position—beyond the dealer. Yet increased market activity has made it possible to trade out of positions by assigning them to a third party, much as futures traders can do. In liquidity, swaps no doubt resemble futures more than they do forwards.

The fact that from time to time most swap participants naturally gravitate to one side of the market creates myriad speculative opportuni-

**Figure 7.11**    Evolution of Swap Market Structure

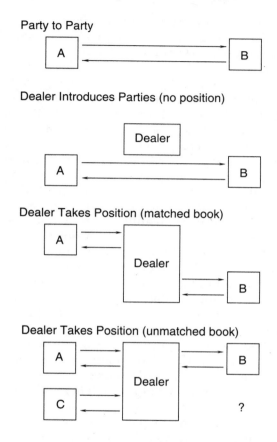

ties for traders willing to handle size and the relatively longer time periods of these markets.

For example, in late 1990 and early 1991, the German government sold large issues of putable bonds to help finance the reunification of Germany. It was fairly common practice among the buyers of those bonds to strip out the embedded put option and sell it as a swaption. Huge supply, uncertainty about volatility and a lack of "natural buyers" of long-dated swaptions, though, resulted in relatively cheap swaption premiums.

Also not surprising is the fact that swaption traders identify cheap and expensive options in much the same way as traders do in other markets. With varying degrees of sophistication, they relate the volatility of the underlying instrument to that implied by the pricing of the option professionals.

The complexity of swap option pricing lies beyond the scope of this discussion. Suffice to point out that pretty much the same factors that interact to shape the prices of options on futures operate in the swaption markets: the underlying market price, the strike price, time to expiration, volatility, and the maturity of the underlying swap.

As with any other option, the longer the time to expiration and the higher the volatility, the more the option is worth. But again, the focus on interest rates, rather than price, requires attention. The higher the strike rate, the higher the call premium; for a higher strike gives the call holder the right to receive higher fixed payments. Conversely, the higher the strike rate, the lower the put premium. Also, assuming two swaptions with the same time to expiration (and all else equal), the longer the maturity of the underlying swap, the higher the premium.

Again, of all the factors, volatility is most critical—as with other kinds of options. In fact, "street talk" concerning the German debt issue mentioned earlier ran to the effect that the original swaption sellers were offering cheap volatility. As veteran option traders are well aware, the sellers' prices implied volatility levels lower than the market's estimates of historical volatility, with a resulting lowering of swaption prices.

A commonplace of the futures trade is that while a futures trader must take a view on price, an options trader must take views on price and volatility. And the trading principle is the same for both—buy low, sell high. Volatility is so critical that options traders can be wrong about the underlying market and still make money if they're right about volatility. That is no less true with swaptions. Therefore, situations like the German debt issue often create speculative opportunities.

The drift of "natural" participants from one side of the market to the other is no rare phenomenon. In the natural rhythm of a seasonal market like heating oil, the balance between longs and shorts often shifts to one side, as a study of documents like the CFTC's report of commitments of traders reveals. In the T-bond market, similar patterns occur around Treasury refundings.

An important difference, though, is that relatively informal OTC markets lack some of the reporting and monitoring facilities of futures. Traders who wish to locate those opportunities have to be alert to less formal signals. They especially must develop relationships in the swap dealer community that will wire them into current talk about who is doing what in risk management circles so opportunities become quickly apparent.

Swap dealers strive to locate mirror-image transactions. The ideal book would contain a series of matches between pairs of risk managers or investors, one wishing to pay fixed, the other to receive it.

Ideally, futures hedging would operate the same way. Producer and end-user would come to market simultaneously with offsetting positions. One, a natural (physical market) long, would sell futures. The other, a natural short, would buy futures. Clearly, that happens but seldom. Hence the need for speculators to take the other side as hedgers enter the market.

Swaptions are no different. If world economies do begin to recover from recession in late 1992 and in 1993, as many economists project, ostensibly a multitude of corporate market users would surge to fund expansion and development. Then there would be swaptions for sale in plenty. Yet it is difficult to see who in the corporate sector would be natural buyers of those instruments, especially if most of the corporates have similar, not mirror-image, needs. Ordinarily, banks might be, but what with new capital requirements and the big banks' generally weakened financial state, there seems to be a gap in the market. Gaps like that are the bread and butter of speculation.

Arising out of situations like the one outlined is a useful bit of technical market data. The swap spreads, published through several screen services, show when imbalance occurs between the bids and offers, like any other measure of overbought-oversold conditions.

Just as those patterns create opportunities for fund managers in more familiar futures markets, so the swaption market may often provide analogous opportunities of special interest. For like the interbank currency trade, swaptions can absorb vast sums of investment capital, given a willingness to engage in longer-term trades.

## MAKING RISK MORE PALATABLE

Risk is a little like energy in classical physics: It never goes away.

In the popular view, friction robs a machine of mechanical energy. Actually, it transforms some of the mechanical energy into heat. (It's amusing to recall that the original Black-Scholes options pricing paper points out that the pricing formula is equivalent to an equation physicists use to figure the transfer of heat.) In like manner, hedging doesn't make price risk disappear but converts it into risk of another kind. There is still risk, which hedgers accept in the belief that the new risk is more manageable or otherwise less threatening.

A company that has to finance a $25 million project with a floating-rate loan faces interest rate risk, which can make budgeting a nightmare. Since the mid-1980s, companies have used the swap market to sidestep interest rate risk. Swapping variable for fixed rates transfers that risk to the counterparty, allowing planning and budgeting. However, in getting out from under rate risk the company accepts credit risk. Unlike futures transactions, where the exchange clearing corporation guarantees a counterparty, the OTC swap market provides no assurance that a swapper will "be made whole" if the counterparty goes bankrupt or otherwise defaults on his or her end of the deal. For corporate swap customers, the swap dealer serves the clearing function, in a way. Yet, the swap dealer can fail to make good, too.

One solution to the credit risk problem, for both swap customers and dealers, is to create a synthetic swap with U.S. Treasury instruments. The zero default risk of Treasuries solves the credit risk problem. But it does introduce swap spread risk, which derives from the two financing approaches the swap and Treasury markets use.

The standard swap rate is based on the LIBOR. Bond and note traders, however, use the repo rate for financing. To the extent that the two rates don't move in parallel fashion, the Treasury seller faces risk. If the spread narrows, a dealer will gain who is short Treasuries to hedge his or her swap position. If the spread widens, the dealer loses. A better solution, in the minds of many commercial tacticians, is the synthetic swap using Eurodollar futures. Because Eurodollar pricing derives from LIBOR, that kind of synthetic eliminates both the credit risk of the standard swap and the spread risk of the Treasury synthetic. Very large swap traders may deal directly with the "synthetic system." Then, to the extent that cash and futures do not converge, they face basis risk.

Going through a swap dealer eliminates this basis risk, but synthetic swaps also expose the swap party to date mismatch risk. Much depends on the timing of the swap reset dates (when the swap parties determine the new floating rate). If they coincide with the Eurodollar futures delivery dates at the International Monetary Market division of the CME (IMM dates), no problem. For, as with any cash-futures expiration, cash and futures rates converge on IMM dates.

If the reset falls within a day or two of the IMM dates (say, September 15 when the IMM date is the 18th), the difference will be negligible. But a reset on August 30 introduces enough of a date mismatch that there can be a rate convergence problem. And it's impossible to guess where the rate will be between IMM dates.

# CHAPTER 8

# Stock Market Hi-Lo Poker

*BY JIM YATES*

**Editor's Note:**

The author of this chapter, Jim Yates, is a "numbers" man. His approach reflects the application of sound statistical probabilities. This is the basis of comparison to the game of hi-lo poker: Both are statistically connected.

He discovered the concept of applying a normal bell-shaped distribution to market action before it was applied in the form of Market Profile developed by Peter Steidlmayer. Yates's approach centers on distributing the volatilities of options premiums over the normal bell shape (See Figure 8.1). Given a large enough population of different optionable stocks, the whole spectrum of volatilities will be confined by the normal bell shape. As time progresses, there will be continuing shifts of positions of these optionable stocks inside the bell, moving, for instance, from extremely oversold to extremely overbought. All the analysis would be based not on typically used tools of technical analysis, but rather on the changing volatilities of the options.

The author then suggests options strategies for particular stocks, based on where the volatilities of their options are found in the spectrum. For instance, overbought stocks, as based on volatilities, will be suited for put purchases, vertical put spreads, call sales, etc.

The editor cautions about the use of the distribution data. The approach works best when one is able to incorporate more data from this type of analysis on more stocks, as the author intended. The ideal situation is to develop a portfolio that contains the whole population of stocks and stock options.

**Figure 8.1**    The Option Strategy Spectrum

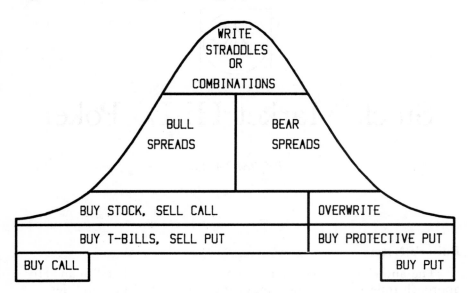

Does this mean one should not be selective of the stocks and act on generated signals for a handful of stocks? The problem in doing this lies in picking what stocks will behave as forecasted. The key to success with the author's approach rests with the fact that the *total* population of optionable stocks is used in managing assets. This approach is best suited to someone like a mutual funds manager, who would be able to create a complete portfolio of optionable stocks.

Listed options are a relatively recent development. The first exchange-traded options changed hands in 1973. I had some experience trading options in the over-the-counter market, so I was immediately drawn to the market when it opened at the Chicago Board Options Exchange.

Options are stock market derivatives, and they have been traded for years. They come in two forms: call options, which represent the right to buy the underlying stocks or futures at a set price and for a period of time, and put options, which represent the right to sell the stocks or futures at a set price and for a period of time.

In days prior to exchange listing, they were strictly tools for speculation. Once you owned a contract you either exercised it or let it expire worthless. With the introduction of exchange-listed options, the options could be bought and sold in a liquid secondary market. Options trading was born.

Trading listed stock options is, in many ways, like playing hi-lo poker.

- Both are "games" based on random events.
- Both are also zero sum games; each is probability based.
- And finally, both offer two ways to win.

Options trading is just another form of gambling in the minds of many investors, and my comparison to poker simply confirms their opinion. But, these investors are quick to question the characterization of the market as a random game. They point out that the stock market is not a zero sum game, but one in which all may benefit. A zero sum game is one in which winners win what losers lose—in other words, a perfectly fair market.

What lends credence to a poker game comparison is the theoretical foundation on which the listed options market is based. *Options are a product of the efficient market hypothesis.* Options prices are based on models that assume that stock price changes are random, just like the cards dealt from a well-shuffled deck in a poker game.

The goal of these pricing models is to find a fair price, one that favors neither the buyer nor the seller, sometimes referred to as a zero sum game.

Probability theory plays an important role in option pricing models and the game of poker. Another assumption of option pricing models is that the percentage stock market changes are "normally" distributed. The distribution provides the basis for a probability analysis in options trading similar to that used by poker players.

With so many similarities, a closer comparison of the two "games" might provide some insight that would be valuable for successfully playing each.

## HI-LO POKER AND OPTIONS TRADING

I recently had a chance to play hi-lo poker in the probability capital of the world, Las Vegas. I shared a card table with a retired bus driver from Cleveland and a young college student from San Francisco.

Hi-lo poker has been one of my favorite pastimes since I was in high school. This version of one of the world's most popular card games produces two winners in each game: the best poker hand (the high hand) and the worst poker hand (the low hand).

There is a variation of hi-lo poker I like: five card stud. The game starts with each player receiving two cards, one face down and the other face up. Based on an analysis of their developing poker hands, players then elect to stay in the game or quit (fold). The game continues until each remaining player has received five cards. The player with the best poker hand wins one-half of the pot, the total amount contributed to the game by the players. The player with the worst hand wins the other half.

As I played and watched the game in Las Vegas, I became fascinated with the similarity of the card game to options trading. The way in which both are played also drew my interest. The college student played every hand to the end, betting the maximum all the way. The bus driver sat back and threw in almost every hand. He waited for the right opportunity and bet conservatively when it arrived.

I had seen options traders approach the market in both manners: one, insensitive to risk, and the other, very risk sensitive. Some attempted to trade every day. Others took a more conservative approach and picked their spots. Need I say who walked away from the poker table with all the money? This is repeated in the options market. Recklessness does not pay in either game.

## GAMBLING

The more I watched the card game, the more fascinated I became with the options market comparison. I began to ask myself if I was coming to the conclusion that options trading was just another form of gambling.

This musing caused me to turn to the dictionary to find the real definition of the word *gambling*: "to play any game of chance for stakes; to stake or risk money or anything of value on something involving chance or unknown contingencies; to take a risk."

Both the card game and any form of stock market trading fit that definition. I could see a vast difference between the way my newfound friends from Cleveland and San Francisco played poker. Both might be considered gamblers, but one was certainly a lot more conservative than the other. I concluded that what one considers to be gambling or not is related to the degree of risk undertaken relative to what would be considered to be the norm.

## POKER AND THE STOCK MARKET: DEGREE OF RANDOMNESS

Most would agree that the stock market is more than just a game of chance. The value of a stock must be directly related to the fundamental condition of the company the shares represent. There is obviously a relationship between the earnings of a company and the value of its shares. So how can the game of five card stud, which is not based at all on fundamentals, be compared to the stock market?

Over the long term, stock prices reflect the underlying fundamentals of the company. International Business Machines (IBM) did not become one of the world's largest companies by chance alone. Its success is based solely on sound fundamentals.

The short term is an entirely different matter. Stock price movement over short time frames has been determined to be random. The daily price fluctuations of IBM doesn't make it worth $2 less today than it was worth yesterday. *This fact is the basis for all option pricing models*.

In a poker game, the cards are shuffled to produce a random distribution. Based on the random distribution of the cards, the probability of being dealt any particular combination of cards can be determined. We can, therefore, estimate the probability of being dealt a pair of aces, or three of a kind or, for that matter, a royal straight flush. The more specific the card combination, the less likely the hand.

Randomness takes on a different look in the stock market. It is the *percentage price changes* that are expected to be randomly distributed. Three of the charts that accompany this chapter illustrate what I mean. Figure 8.2 shows the S&P 500 Stock Index for a one-year period of time.

Figure 8.3 is a bar chart of the percentage price changes for the index on a daily basis. As you can see from the bar chart, the daily price changes appear random, with no observable pattern to their occurrence.

The third chart in our series (Figure 8.4) shows a bar graph of the distribution of the percentage price changes. The bell-shaped distribution shows the probability link that the market and the game of poker have in common.

## LESSONS LEARNED AT THE POKER TABLE

So what can we learn at the poker table about trading stocks and listed options? The answer is, a lot.

First, let me get back to the five card stud example. Recall that the best five card high hand and five card low hand split the pot. At the start of the game, the dealer deals each player two cards, one face down and one face up. The players examine their cards to estimate the probability of winning. If the first two cards are two of a kind, such as a pair of aces, the player knows that the probability of winning the high half of the pot is very good. Having a strong opening hand does not, however, guarantee a win. If the first two cards dealt are an ace and a six of a different suit, the player is in an excellent position to win the low half.

As the game continues, two skills become increasingly important.

The first is a knowledge of probability as it relates to poker. The ability to estimate the probability that the hand you are holding is better, or worse, than your opponent is key to long-term success.

Figure 8.2   S&P 500 Stock Index over One Year

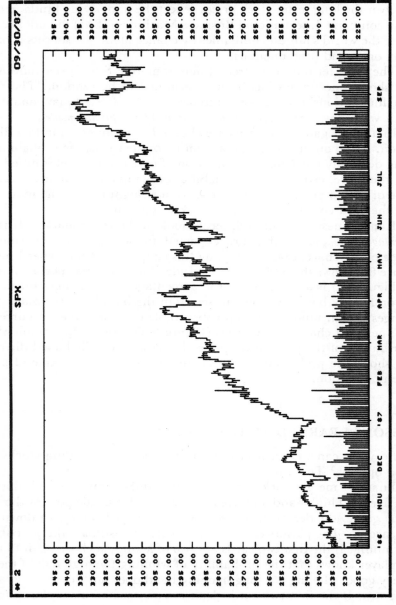

Source: MetaStock-Pro by EQUIS International Data provided by Historical Data Services, Inc.

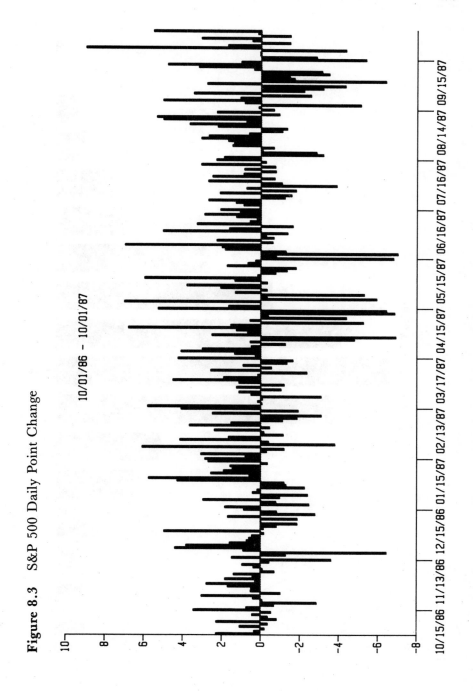

**Figure 8.3**    S&P 500 Daily Point Change

10/01/86 – 10/01/87

**Figure 8.4**  Distribution of S&P 500 Daily Point Changes

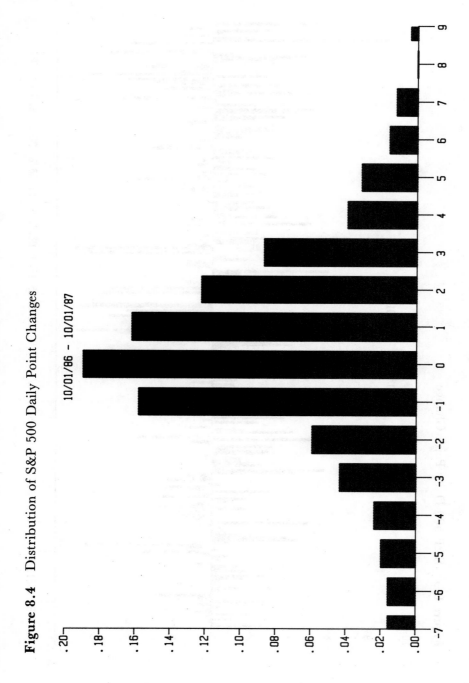

The stock market is viewed by random walkers much like a poker game. Every day the market "deals a hand." Opening "hands" vary in attractiveness, and there is no assurance that a good opening hand will be a final winner. Traders must decide each day to play or fold based on their analysis of their hands. In the case of options traders, there are two ways to win: Call buyers win if the market advances, and put buyers are winners if it declines.

A second skill that good poker players seem to have is the ability to read the emotions of their opponent. Some poker players are unable to hide their joy when they have a good hand or their despair when they fear the hand is a loser. A good poker face is important for the successful player.

Many stock market players also study the reaction of their opponents, who are actually other investors. They call it "reading the sentiment" of the market. Sentiment indicators are popular because most investors think most investors are wrong most of the time. This may be just an expression of their own confidence. Perhaps the most widely known options market sentiment indicator is the put/call ratio. This indicator compares the volume of put trades to that of call trades. The concept is that a rise in the volume of puts traded versus calls is actually bullish because option buyers are wrong most of the time.

Many stock market indicators that are thought to be purely technical in nature are actually sentiment indicators in disguise. An example is the popular Elliott Wave theory championed by Bob Prechter. In presentations, Prechter explains that the five wave concept can actually be seen in any time frame because it is really a picture of the emotional reactions of investors.

## ADD MATHEMATICS TO HONE TRADING SKILLS

As valuable as sentiment indicators are in both the game of poker and the stock market, I feel they are not nearly as important as an understanding of the mathematics of the game. Poker players know this and combine sentiment analysis with their knowledge of probability. Options traders seem to place most of their emphasis on market sentiment. While valuable, it would seem that combining the information with a mathematical analysis would lead to better results.

## AN OPTIONS TRADER'S ODDS TABLE

With the above in mind, I set out to see if a way might be found to calculate an odds table for the market. Savvy poker players approach their card game a lot more conservatively than most options traders do their trading. Poker players know the probability of any one hand developing during the course of the games. The reason for their conservative play is that they understand the mathematics of the game. If I, however, could establish a set of odds tables for options trading, I might be able to improve my performance in the game of "stock market hi-lo."

The first step in creating an odds table for options traders is to understand the assumptions that form the basis for options prices. Options are valued using one of several mathematical models. All models employ:

- stock price
- exercise price of the option
- time until expiration of the option
- current interest rate
- dividends to be paid by the stock
- volatility assumption for the stock

The most famous option pricing model, the Black-Scholes model, is seen in Figure 8.5.

Of the variables in the model, the volatility factor is the most critical in valuation of the options. The volatility factor is also the potential source of data from which an odds table might be created.

The volatility factor is defined as the daily standard deviation of the price of the stock, annualized. The listed options market assumes that stocks are efficiently priced. This means that all available information about the company is almost instantaneously incorporated in the price. Stated another way, the efficient market theory assumes that the price of the stock reflects all available information. The theory also assumes that any further price movement will be random and the *price changes are lognormally distributed*. The volatility estimate attempts to determine how much the stock may deviate from its current price over any time period.

Option pricing models assume that the stocks' percentage price movements, in addition to be being random, will be "normally" distributed. This means that two-thirds of the price change observations will be within one standard deviation of the stock price for a finite time period of observation. The options market assumptions concerning efficiency and randomness are of major concern in developing an options trading odds table. If I could convert the normal distribution assumption into an odds table, it would allow me to determine the probability of any particular percentage price movement.

In the game of poker, the odds change as the game is played because once the cards are dealt they cannot be dealt again. A savvy poker player keeps a mental record of the cards that have been dealt and incorporates this information in the probability decision. As more and more cards are dealt, the resulting hands are more and more predictable.

**Figure 8.5**    The Black-Scholes Valuation Formula

$$\text{Fair value of options} = P_s\, N(d_1) - Se^{r(t-t^*)}\, N(d_2)$$

$$\text{Where } d_1 = \frac{\text{lognormal } (P_s/S) + (r + \tfrac{1}{2}\, v^2)\,(t^*-t)}{v\sqrt{(t^*-t)}}$$

$$\text{and } d_2 = \frac{\text{lognormal } (P_s/S) + (r - \tfrac{1}{2}\, v^2)\,(t^*-t)}{v\sqrt{(t^*-t)}}$$

$P_s$ = stock price
S = strike price of option
N(d) = cumulative normal density function
r = risk-free interest rate
t = current date
$t^*$ = expiration date of option
$v^2$ = variance rate of stock return
e = natural logarithm base of 2.71828

Following are ten key assumptions of the Black-Scholes model (Fischer Black and Myron Scholes, "The Pricing of Options and Corporate Liabilities," *Journal of Political Economy*, May–June 1973; 637–54. ©1973 by the University of Chicago. Reprinted with permission of the University of Chicago Press):

1. Short-term interest rate is constant.
2. Stock prices are random.
3. Stock price distribution is lognormal.
4. Stock pays no dividends.
5. Stock has a constant rate of returns.
6. Options are exercised at maturity.
7. No commissions are paid on transactions.
8. Partial acquisition of the underlying stock is possible.
9. Prices at settlement are the same for both buyers and sellers.
10. Tax rates do not enter into calculation of returns.

The options market assumption that stock price changes are random would eliminate any possibility of incorporating past stock price change data into the option trading decision process. Under that assumption, there is no need to "keep track of what has been played," which is what a historical chart does. If I accepted the option pricing assumptions, I would probably conclude that I have to rely on a sentiment indicator to make trading decisions.

On the other hand, if I could somehow estimate the probability and direction of stock price movements, I might be able to enhance my stock trading success. The potential for the use of options would be greatly enhanced because the derivatives would allow me to change the distribution outcome.

The question becomes what new assumptions must I make to allow me to design such a table and what happens if my new assumptions are wrong.

## REGRESSION TO THE MEANS

Suppose I assume that the stock price changes are randomly distributed, but around a *trend* of the price rather than the price itself. What I am saying is, suppose I assumed that past price movement *was* meaningful. That simple additional assumption would permit me to determine how much a stock had deviated from the trend, rather than from a point. It also would allow a determination of the probability of the stock regressing to the mean.

If I could determine that a stock was two standard deviations above its mean (the mean being the trend), I could assume that there was a strong probability that the stock would regress to the trend. I might further be able to determine the probability of any price change amount.

Two questions are of immediate concern. What makes me think I can make such an assumption? What if I am wrong?

A possible clue that stock price changes are trend-related may be seen in a chart of stock volatility. Many stocks, especially the large capitalization issues, have volatility charts that are remarkably consistent.

Another clue may be found by looking at a long-term price chart of the stock. While short-term movement may be random, longer-term charts certainly seem to indicate trends. If I am wrong? The key here may be the medical doctor's motto: "Do no harm." As long as the risk of being wrong about the nature of price movement is no more than if I assume it was random to begin with, I will "do no harm."

The feature of the options market that makes it most comparable to hi-lo poker is its two-sided nature. Option buyers can buy calls if they think the market is going to advance or puts if they think it will fall. In hi-lo poker, a player can continue to participate if the hand held is thought to be the best or the worst. The poker player usually determines which way he or she is going, a good hand or a bad hand, after the first two cards are dealt. In the same manner, an option trader usually first determines which way he or she is going, bullish or bearish. On occasion a poker player may hold a hand that is a potential winner both ways. An option player may also assume such a position by buying both a call and a put. Unlike the poker game, determining which way to go in the market is a much tougher task.

After a period of trial and error, I have determined that a 10-day price trend is best for my short-term options trader's odds table, and a 90-day trend seems to work best for hedging strategies. The 10-day trend provides sufficient price movement to justify the cost of trading. Ninety days is necessary to overcome costs when strategies employ stock transactions. Using the above assumptions, Figures 8.6 and 8.7 can be used to estimate the probability of advance or decline of the underlying stock. The tables require three inputs: the price of the stock, the 10-day or 90-day average of price and the options volatility assumption. To use the tables you must first determine the percentage deviation of the price of the stock from its 10-day or 90-day average. Then determine where this places the stock on the +100 to -100 scale at the right of the table. Do this by locating the percentage price change in the appropriate volatility column.

Figure 8.8 compares the options odds table to beginning five card stud poker hands. The table says that a score of +100 or -100 is similar to being dealt a pair of aces at the beginning of the game. The odds of winning are extremely high if our assumptions are right. The table also serves to remind us that while the odds are high and we have the best possible chance of winning, future events may change the picture. This is a warning not to approach any trade too aggressively.

## USING THE OPTIONS ODDS TABLES

In the game of five card stud a player must continuously reassess the winning probabilities as more cards are dealt. The same is true in option trading. Most option traders forget that trading is a two-step process. Step one is a buy decision. Step two is a sell decision. If the probability of being right is 50 percent for both the buy and sell decision and both must be present to constitute a win, the overall probability of winning is only 25 percent. To have a 50 percent chance of winning such a game, each decision must have a 70 percent chance of being right.

The problem of being 70 percent right on buys and 70 percent right on sells is greater than one would initially think. The Options Trader's Phase Chart gives you some idea just how difficult it is. It is a chart of the table readings for the S&P 100 Index (OEX) during calendar year 1990. While the market does move to the +70 percent or -70 percent area on a rather consistent basis, the swings between the two extremes appear to be random.

I have found that the best way to solve this problem is to wait for a market score of +90 percent or -90 percent and then look to exit when

**Figure 8.6**    Percentage Deviation from 10-Day Trend Necessary To Reach High or Low Extremes of Expected Trading Range

*Implied Volatility*

| 5 | 10 | 15 | 20 | 25 | 30 | 35 | 40 | 45 | 50 | 55 | 60 | 65 | 70 | 75 | 80 | | |
|---|----|----|----|----|----|----|----|----|----|----|----|----|----|----|----|---|---|
| 1 | 2 | 3 | 4 | 5 | 6 | 7 | 8 | 9 | 10 | 11 | 12 | 13 | 14 | 15 | 16 | H | 100 |
| | | | | | | | | | | | | | | | | I | |
| | | | | | | | | | | | | | | | | G | |
| .6 | 1.3 | 2 | 2.6 | 3.3 | 4 | 4.6 | 5.3 | 6 | 6.6 | 7.3 | 8 | 8.6 | 9.3 | 10 | 10.6 | H | 67 |
| .3 | .6 | 1 | 1.3 | 1.6 | 2 | 2.3 | 2.6 | 3 | 3.3 | 3.6 | 4 | 4.3 | 4.6 | 5 | 5.3 | P | 33 |
| | | | | | | | | | | | | | | | | E | |
| | | | | | | | | | | | | | | | | R | |
| 0 | 0 | 0 | 0 | 0 | 0 | 0 | 0 | 0 | 0 | 0 | 0 | 0 | 0 | 0 | 0 | C | 0 |
| | | | | | | | | | | | | | | | | E | |
| | | | | | | | | | | | | | | | | N | |
| -.3 | -.6 | -1 | -1.3 | -1.6 | -2 | -2.3 | -2.6 | -3 | -3.3 | -3.6 | -4 | -4.3 | -4.6 | -5 | -5.3 | T | -33 |
| -.6 | -1.3 | -2 | -2.6 | -3.3 | -4 | -4.6 | -5.3 | -6 | -6.6 | -7.3 | -8 | -8.6 | -9.3 | -10 | -10.6 | | -67 |
| | | | | | | | | | | | | | | | | L | |
| | | | | | | | | | | | | | | | | O | |
| -1 | -2 | -3 | -4 | -5 | -6 | -7 | -8 | -9 | -10 | -11 | -12 | -13 | -14 | -15 | -16 | W | -100 |

the score reverts to a reading of 50. If you think about it, all I am doing is establishing a discipline that forces me to wait for a significant deviation from the trend (90 percent of the deviation expected according to market volatility assumptions) and then trading out when the market reverts to the trend.

## FACTORS AFFECTING WHAT TO TRADE

The question of when to trade the markets leads directly to a second question—what to trade. Most traders report disappointing results when they attempt to trade the market using options. Some say that prices are not predictable. Others say liquidity is lacking. They complain that while they make money trading stocks or futures, they always seem to end up on the losing end in the options market. As a result, most professional traders would rather trade the underlying stock or, in the case of the indexes, index futures. They simply don't trust the listed options market.

What they are really saying is that they don't understand the listed options market. If they did, they would see that, properly used, options will make a good stock or futures trader better. There are two features of listed options that work against traders. The first disadvantage—limited liability—is usually seen as an advantage. The second is the clock, the countdown to the option expiration date.

### False Security: Overstaying

Traders know that the buyer of an option can lose only the purchase price. This limited liability is widely reported as one of the advantages of the contracts. The advantage may work as a disadvantage to the trader.

**Figure 8.7**  Percentage Deviation from 90-Day Trend Necessary To Reach High or Low Extremes of Expected Trading Range

|  |  |  |  |  |  |  | *Implied Volatility* |  |  |  |  |  |  |  |  |  |  |
|---|---|---|---|---|---|---|---|---|---|---|---|---|---|---|---|---|---|
| 5 | 10 | 15 | 20 | 25 | 30 | 35 | 40 | 45 | 50 | 55 | 60 | 65 | 70 | 75 | 80 |  |  |
| 3 | 6 | 9 | 12 | 15 | 18 | 21 | 24 | 27 | 30 | 33 | 36 | 39 | 42 | 45 | 48 | H | 100 |
|  |  |  |  |  |  |  |  |  |  |  |  |  |  |  |  | I |  |
|  |  |  |  |  |  |  |  |  |  |  |  |  |  |  |  | G |  |
| 2 | 4 | 6 | 8 | 10 | 12 | 14 | 16 | 18 | 20 | 22 | 24 | 26 | 28 | 30 | 32 | h | 67 |
| 1 | 2 | 3 | 4 | 5 | 6 | 7 | 8 | 9 | 10 | 11 | 12 | 13 | 14 | 15 | 16 | P | 33 |
|  |  |  |  |  |  |  |  |  |  |  |  |  |  |  |  | E |  |
|  |  |  |  |  |  |  |  |  |  |  |  |  |  |  |  | R |  |
| 0 | 0 | 0 | 0 | 0 | 0 | 0 | 0 | 0 | 0 | 0 | 0 | 0 | 0 | 0 | 0 | C | 0 |
|  |  |  |  |  |  |  |  |  |  |  |  |  |  |  |  | E |  |
|  |  |  |  |  |  |  |  |  |  |  |  |  |  |  |  | N |  |
| -1 | -2 | -3 | -4 | -5 | -6 | -7 | -8 | -9 | -10 | -11 | -12 | -13 | -14 | -15 | -16 | T | -33 |
| -2 | -4 | -6 | -8 | -10 | -12 | -14 | -16 | -18 | -20 | -22 | -24 | -26 | -28 | -30 | -32 |  | -67 |
|  |  |  |  |  |  |  |  |  |  |  |  |  |  |  |  | L |  |
|  |  |  |  |  |  |  |  |  |  |  |  |  |  |  |  | O |  |
| -3 | -6 | -9 | -12 | -15 | -18 | -21 | -24 | -27 | -30 | -33 | -36 | -39 | -42 | -45 | -48 | W | -100 |

**Figure 8.8**    Comparison of Options Odds to Beginning Five Card
Stud Poker Hands

| Call Buyer's Poker Hand Equivalent | Hi-Lo Table | Put Buyer's Poker Hand Equivalent |
|---|---|---|
| Deuce and an eight | 100 | Pair of aces |
| Deuce and six | 67 | Pair of jacks |
| Nine and ten (same suit) | 33 | Pair of sevens |
| Ace and a deuce | 0 | Ace and a deuce |
| Pair of sevens | −33 | Nine and ten (same suit) |
| Pair of jacks | −67 | Deuce and six |
| Pair of aces | −100 | Deuce and an eight |

It may lead to a tendency to overstay the position—in other words, to cease being a trader. The limited liability may also cause the trader to seek "cheap" options because they offer greater percentage gains and smaller losses. Again, this in effect turns the advantage into a disadvantage and may convert a trader into a speculator.

**Expiration Date**

The expiration date is sometimes a problem because option buyers feel they are forfeiting some of their purchase price when they sell an option before it expires. The result is that they tend to hold the options until expiration date and again are turned into speculators. Traders must learn to use options in a trading mode, rather than as speculators.

**Delta**

The first step a potential options trader must take is to learn exactly how options work. Trading options is comparable to flying an airplane, with the option pricing model providing "instrument readings." As I discussed earlier, options are priced by mathematical formula. The first output of the formula is the value of the option. The second derivative is the rate of change of the price of the option. The mathematical definition of the rate of change in the option price is *delta*. A deep-in-the-money option has a delta approaching 1.00, which means that the option changes almost point for point with the price of the underlying stock. A far-out-of-the-money option has a delta approaching zero. At-the-money options have deltas close to 0.50. The delta reading may be viewed as an instrument reading reflecting market exposure and is the equivalent of an airplane gauge showing rate of climb. Stock and futures traders are not accustomed to ever-changing rates of increase or decrease in the underlying. In the stock and futures business, the rate of change is a constant, similar to driving a car versus flying a plane.

### Theta

Another instrument reading provided by an option pricing model is called *theta*. Theta is the rate of change of the time premium. Time premiums decay at an ever-increasing rate. The most rapid rate of decay occurs near expiration date. A savvy options trader needs to keep an eye on the theta instrument to avoid being long an option when premium is rapidly eroding. Figure 8.9 illustrates the price decline of an option over time. It shows an option that has a value of $3.50 with 90 days until expiration. If all other factors remain the same, the option will be worth $2.75 when it has 60 days to go. Then with 30 days left the premium will shrink to $2. Thirty days later the option has zero value. The important point to see is that for the first two months the rate of decay of the option was $0.75 per month. For the last month it was $2.

### Correctly Buying Time

The first lesson options traders must learn is to buy time correctly. They should make it a rule not to own an option that has less than one month until expiration. This is hard to do because longer-term options cost more than short-term options and generally have less trading volume. Since lower trading volume means less liquidity, traders are going

**Figure 8.9**   Premium Decay Curve

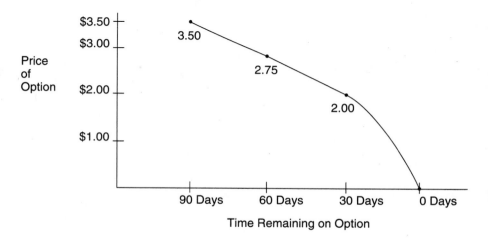

to have to find the optimum strike price to trade, which leads us to the second lesson options traders must learn.

Option writers tend to concentrate on the at-the-money option. This is the option that provides the best combination of return and protection under most circumstances. The fact that most writers concentrate on these options means that liquidity will be relatively high for buyers. The negative is that the same high premium that attracts the writer works against the buyer. The problem of high premium can be substantially reduced by selling the position before the rapid premium decay of the final three weeks of the contract.

## CONCLUSION

Most investors see options as tools of speculators. The derivative instruments may be used to speculate. Those who speculate can expect speculative results—a few large winners but many losers. The options market offers conservative traders an entirely different opportunity. Using a disciplined approach that incorporates an understanding of option pricing theory and control of market exposure, a good stock trader may be able to improve performance. The keys to success in nonspeculative options trading are the same found with good poker players: discipline and patience combined with an understanding of the game and a good game plan.

# CHAPTER 9

# Using Overlapping Straddles

*BY GARY DUFIELD*

**Editor's Note:**

Gary Dufield devised a systematic strategy to take advantage of underlying market action. This action is extended into option's movement. Of all the trading strategies in this book, this method considers the impact of timing on market action most extensively.

The author's approach is based on the simple application of moving average crossovers. The author fine-tunes the length of the averages to fit "average" market action. He also applies other momentum-based timing approaches.

At the *core of his decision making* is timing. From this start, the author applies the buying of call or put options to take advantage of such underlying market action. One feature of the systematic approach is that the trader is always in the market: either long or short.

At the *core of his strategy* is the creation of strangles by legging into them, one side at a time. The first side is executed based on signals generated from moving average crossovers. The second side of the strangle is entered into to protect profits. A simple straddle involves buying a call and buying a put with the same strike price. The author's approach involves the buying of a call in a bullish move, followed by the buying of a put after the bullish move has been made. This strategy locks in a strangle with two different strike prices.

Several benefits result. One is that the trader does not have to enter stop buy or stop sell orders to protect from losses. Another is that he or she does not have to worry about errant market action. Both benefits are based on the fact that the trader is buying call or put premiums.

The primary difficulty with this chapter rests with the charts the author has created to illustrate his strategy. Since this approach requires constant monitoring of positions and assessing which positions to close out, the author's charts are crammed with information.

The editor reviewed the charts and determined that there was no practical way to redraw them to illustrate all the information without drawing 15 new charts for each one of the author's original charts. If you find the charts and text to be difficult to comprehend at the same time, as the editor did initially, then put the charts aside and reread the chapter later, with the charts.

Many strategies can be used to trade the futures markets and their options. All have their flaws and weak points that can expose you to either occasional large losses, runs of small losses, needless commission costs or any combination of these. In the course of trading over the years, I have experienced all of these difficulties and, in working to overcome them, have developed a trading method that is designed not just to make money, but also to preserve it. In spite of the defensive nature of this system, net profits usually amount to between 15 percent to 30 percent per quarter, and in volatile markets often exceed that geometrically.

If you are new at commodity trading, or experimenting with trading systems, it won't take long to figure out that you need to find a trading approach that works both in trending and in choppy, whipsaw markets. This is a difficult task because the two efforts are mutually exclusive, and it will inevitably lead you to more sensitive short-term trading and eventually to day trading. I have yet to meet a broker or individual who can consistently day-trade at a profit, covering both losses and full commissions, and do it from off the exchange floor. You will inevitably have to face the fact that overnight position trading is the only answer to covering commissions with big gains.

Nevertheless, the problem with standard trend trading techniques— even in a trend—is that of always being "stopped out" due to minor market fluctuations. Having stop loss orders hit "unnecessarily" will, of course, force you back into short-term trading because you then have to decide whether or not to reenter the market, and in which direction. To avoid this, and to achieve the desirable goal of always being in the market (in order not to miss sudden good moves), you must give up the use of stop loss orders and replace them with a good technical market direction signaling system.

This is easier said than done because such a system is the goal of all system designers. Thus, you must also look for something more than simply a signaling system; it must be accompanied by a trading vehicle to go with it—a vehicle that will not only control and snare the market, but also control your emotions.

You will find that the two emotions of fear and greed will cause dissatisfaction with any system and cause you to deviate from the trading rules, tamper with the system or abandon it. To protect the discipline of the system, I have developed a vehicle, a spread system, through which the signaling system can be applied. The result is an overall trading system with the following attributes:

- It is never stopped out.
- It never misses sudden big moves.
- It can make profits on big moves in the wrong direction, such as crashes or spikes.
- It never gets in or out of the market too late or too soon.
- It works in both trending or whipsaw markets.
- It enables you to enter any market—anywhere, anytime.
- It allows you to sleep at night!

To understand this (or any other) trading system, you must first understand the principles of some simple directional signaling systems. This is because markets must be traded; it is very rare for a person to simply buy and hold a position without incurring losses.


## MOVING AVERAGES BASED SYSTEM

To take an unbiased and disciplined approach to trading, a simple moving average system is very useful. However, you will find most of them are too slow: They lag the market too much. Also, most attempts to use shorter-duration moving averages will result in the generation of too many false signals. But by experimenting with different types of moving averages and their uses, it is possible to develop a good middle-ground approach that also works well in whipsaws. The trading approach we will look at here uses such a system for long-term signals. In addition, we use an early warning system for short-term signaling to leg in and out of hedges.

The short-term system, as you will see, is merely a higher-speed (shorter-duration) duplicate of the long-term signaling system, and it is both timely and reliable. But more on this later. As mentioned before, even good market-following systems can take occasional big hits. And fear of these big hits, even if they are merely loss of profits, can lead to the bad habit of "jumping the signals," making it impossible for the trader to follow the system no matter how simple and mechanical. You will then find yourself prejudging the signals, predicting the market and wandering from system discipline into "seat of the pants" trading. The end result is usually that the system proves right, leaving you wrong—with losses.

## MODIFICATION TO LONG-TERM OR SHORT-TERM-ONLY POSITION: USE OPTIONS

Since our trading system is always in the market, reversing from long to short and short to long, and making more money than it loses, we must find a way to ensure that we follow it. The feature that does this controls emotions by controlling risk, adding a profitability potential even to wrong way moves. It also hedges by locking in profits. This is, then, a self-hedging system.

In experimenting with both long-term and short-term signaling systems, you will find that, in a trend, the short-term system can be used to put on and take off hedges during times of uncertainty, when a major reversal signal is threatened but not yet in effect. The hedge will give you the confidence to stick with your main trade. However, you will find that using a futures contract to hedge a futures contract, especially in nonagricultural markets, has the effect of not being in the market, and is the same as getting in and out. The result is that, again, you would be short-term trading—with all the bad timing errors and Murphy's Law tricks that implies (such as when you decide where and whether to lift the hedge or not).

Hedging with a purchased put option against a long future, or a purchased call option against a short future, works much better. The option hedges the position and gives you the lead time and lead space you need until a confirmed reversal signal is proven. At the same time, it doesn't stop the futures contract from making money if the trend continues. This means you don't have to be so quick to lift the hedge (exposing the position to premature risk), and that lifting it too late is meaningless. Therefore, you avoid quick-guess short-term trading.

This is a good approach, but we can do better. For one thing, although we can't lose much money if the market goes the wrong way, we can't make much either using this approach. But if we replace the future with an option, we can make money either way, right or wrong, up or down, because an option straddle (a put versus a call) can make money either way the market goes.

Of course, options are more sluggish than futures, and they decay with time. But if you want to offset that and make fast money, you can create synthetic futures by combining long and short options of opposite types. You can even long-term trend trade by short-term trading, legging in and out of your hedges in a series of overlapping straddles.

Thus far we've examined the concepts that have led to the development of this direction-neutral, self-hedging, market-following system. Now let's see exactly how it works, starting with some simple diagrams of these concepts and evolving into the fully developed, more flexible system and its rules.

## DEVELOPING A MARKET-FOLLOWING SIGNALING SYSTEM FOR TRADING DISCIPLINE

### First Filter: Moving Average Crossover of Bands

In seeking a moving average that would track the trend without giving too many false signals, yet not lag the market so much as to be late in signaling sizeable corrections, I have found the 20-day moving average of closes too slow, and the 9-day or 10-day moving average good, but subject to frequent false signals. Therefore, I settled for 15 days, which seems to be the best compromise. I see no advantage to using exponential or weighted moving averages, since they simply generate more false signals. In whipsaws, moving averages tend to move horizontally, and as a result buy and sell signals occur at the same (or worse) price, resulting in a series of losses. For this reason, I use a band system: parallel lines made up of a 15-day moving average of the highs and a 15-day moving average of the lows.

Most books will tell you to sell only if the market breaks below the *lower* moving average, and to buy only when the market breaks out above the *upper* moving average. I think this is wrong. Do it earlier, sell when the market moves down to the *upper* moving average and buy when it comes up to cross the *lower* moving average. In addition, I use a 2-day close moving average to represent the market, not intraday prices. I found 3-day moving averages smoother, but too slow. So, when your 2-day close average comes down and touches the 15-day high average, get short. When the 2-day close average comes up and touches the 15-day low average, get long. The width of the band can be of help in a whipsaw—especially since it tends to get wider in a whipsaw. Note, as shown in the following diagram, that if you get a signal and the two-day average then recrosses the same moving average, you must reverse.

In conjunction with the above, I also use a 10-day moving average of the closes as an interpretative aid. Note the following rules: If the 2-day moving average is crossing into the band, but the 10-day is a long way from doing the same, *the market will probably whip back*. Likewise, if the 2-day moving average is giving one signal and the 10-day is crossing the band in the opposite direction—giving the opposite signal, you are also in a whipsaw. However, if the 2-day and 10-day moving averages enter

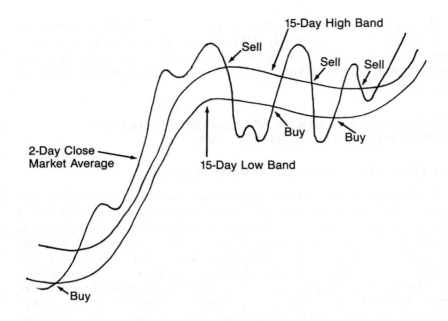

the band at approximately the *same time* and the *same direction,* as shown in the following diagram, you have a good strong signal that indicates a major move.

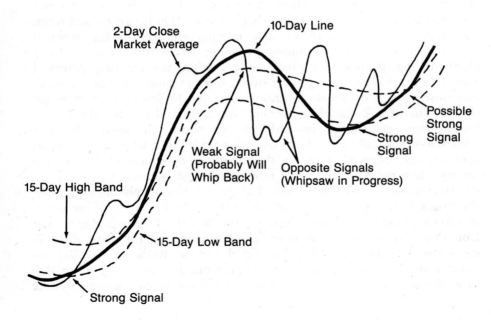

The following diagram illustrates that the 10-day moving average and 15-day band outline the entire whipsaw as a possible large bull flag.

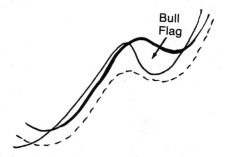

Bull Flag

Also note that when the 15-day band is narrow and sloping, you are in a run; when it is fat and turning horizontal, you are in a congestion range.

These moving averages are used only for the main trend, in order to determine whether our main orientation should be long or short. A 10-day moving average is basically a 2-week moving average, and the 15-day high/low band is a 3-week band. For our short-term signals we will replace "week" with day and use a 2-day close moving average oscillating back and forth inside a 3-day high/low band.

In an uptrend, the 2-day moving average will overlap or be slightly above the 3-day high moving average, and in a downtrend it will overlap or be slightly below the 3-day low moving average. As shown in the following chart, whenever the 2-day moving average pulls off of one of the 3-day moving averages and moves toward the center or the opposite side of the 3-day band, a short-term signal is generated.

These signals are usually just minor corrections and outline minor flags, and the 2-day close may not always go completely to the other side of the band. Therefore, they are merely warning signals, and good points to initiate a hedge, but *not* points to reverse your main position. On the other hand, a steep reversing flag and sudden movement of the 2-day line to the opposite wall of the band often warn that a major move in the opposite direction is immediately under way. As shown in the following chart, if the 10-day moving average is well outside the 15-day band when this happens, it is most likely a sudden, deep whipsaw move, but if this occurs with the 10-day line crossing the 15-day band, a crash could be underway.

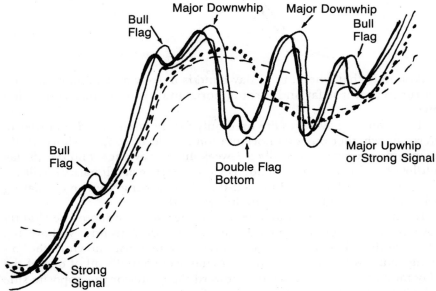

During bull or bear flags all you have to do is hedge your main position with an option, but during whipsaws you may want to go into a neutral spread such as a straddle until a trend resumes.

The bull and bear flag patterns in the 3-day system do not always occur one above (or below) the other, as they do in a trend. Sometimes they occur side by side, and it is important to recognize these patterns. A bull flag followed by a bear flag can indicate a double top (as in first figure next page):

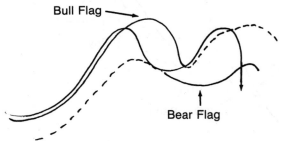

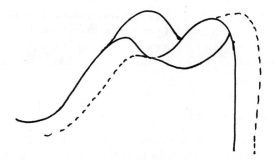

It can also turn into two bull flags, which is very bullish:

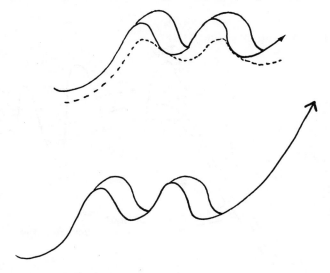

In some cases, it can be the beginning of a whipsaw:

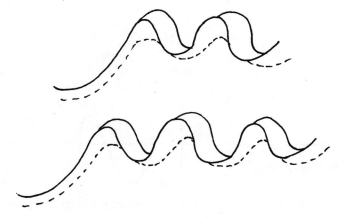

Of course, the opposite of these patterns should be recognized also: A bear flag followed by a bull flag can be a double bottom, or it can turn into a double bear flag and be very bearish, or it can turn into a narrow whipsaw. To determine which of these is most likely, we need to look at our oscillators.

**Second Filter: An Oscillator**

An oscillator of the main system as a whole is best, one that measures the plus or minus distance between the two-day close moving average and the center of the 15-day band (15-day close). (See Figures 9.1 and 9.2.)

**Figure 9.1**    Moving Averages

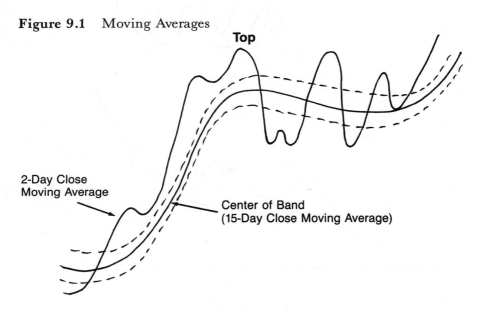

**Figure 9.2**    Oscillator

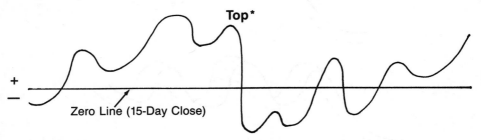

*This point on the oscillator chart corresponds with Figure 9.1 price top.

In an oscillator, the 15-day line is "straightened out" to be the mid or zero line, and the 2-day line is shown oscillating above or below it according to how far away the 2-day moving average gets from the 15-day moving average. Note that the final high (marked "Top" on both charts) is higher than the previous high on the moving average charts but lower than the previous high on the oscillator chart. This is known as *divergence* and usually indicates the start of a major reversal, a whipsaw or slowing of the trend.

Note also that when the whipsaw is actually underway, the oscillator comes back to the zero line and stays near it. When the oscillator is near the zero line and oscillating in smaller and smaller waves, signals given by the moving average system are usually best considered to be minor whipsaws rather than buy or sell signals.

Another way to interpret an oscillator is to draw a support line connecting the wave bottoms of an upslope, or resistance lines connecting the wave tops of a downslope, as shown in the following chart.

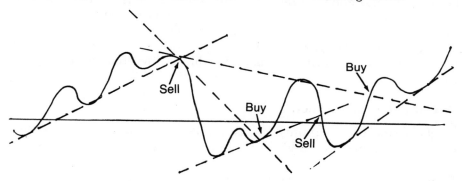

If the oscillator breaks one of those support or resistance lines (the most recent line in use), you can consider it to be a buy or sell signal, rather than waiting for the oscillator to cross the zero line, which is the conventional interpretation.

Another way to do this is to track the oscillator with a 10-day moving average of itself and use that to generate signals:

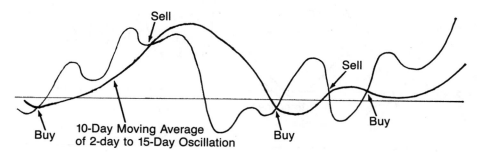

Most of the signals generated above were valid except the one sell signal that occurred with both the oscillator and 10-day moving average at the zero line. That was a whipsaw.

### Third Filter: Relative Strength Indicator

Besides oscillators of the system, you can also use momentum oscillators, such as a 9-day or 10-day relative strength index (RSI). Again, use the RSI like the oscillator and draw in support and resistance lines, watching for divergence as well. (See Figure 9.3.)

If you cannot tell which bottoms (or tops) in the zigzagging line to connect because of minor fluctuations in the RSI, use your 2-day to 15-day oscillator's 10-day moving average as a guide. Note that when the RSI is near the 50 percent line, reversals are often whipsaws. Also, while it is customary to consider a market with an RSI above 75 percent to be overbought and about to sell off, or one with an RSI below 25 percent to be oversold and about to rally, the opposite can be true. The RSI can max out at 100 percent or 0 percent and the trend can pick up speed. Or, the RSI can retreat toward the 50 percent line, with the market trend slowing but relentlessly marching on. The RSI can also retreat toward the 50 percent line with the market whipsawing, then resuming its trend.

### Fourth Filter: Stochastics

This kind of uncertainty can be ironed out by use of a stochastic. Even slow stochastics are like RSIs but much more sensitive and whip

**Figure 9.3**   Relative Strength Chart

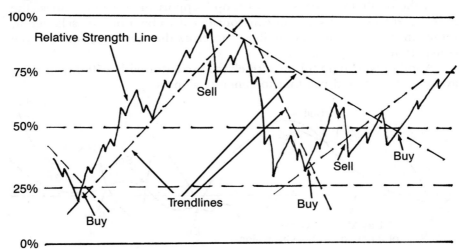

**Figure 9.4**  LEFT: Relative Strength Index; RIGHT: Stochastic

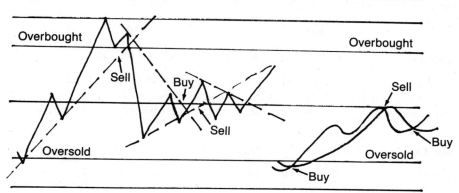

back and forth from 100 percent to 0 percent even on minor moves. For that reason, we don't want to use a 9-day or 10-day stochastic, but a smoother, more sluggish 9-week or 10-week (45-day to 50-day) slow stochastic. It will give you far truer overbought and oversold signals. It also gives fewer and truer buy and sell signals for your major trend. A regular 9-day slow stochastic can be used for short-term swing signals. (See Figure 9.4.)

## Putting Everything on Paper

All these moving averages and oscillators should be kept for two sets of charts. One chart (your main one) will be your daily bar chart based on daily closes, highs and lows. The second chart (for the big picture) uses 1-week bars, based on the high and low of the week and Friday's close. All the oscillators, etc., for the weekly bar chart will be formed in the same way as for the daily bar chart. The weekly chart gives you the big picture. A whipsaw on the daily charts shows up simply as a bull or bear flag on the weekly. An overbought or oversold condition on the daily chart may show the opposite on the weekly, and so on.

Therefore, if you are getting a sell signal while overbought on the daily chart and a buy signal while oversold on the weekly, you may consider that the sell-off will not last long, and the bull trend will eventually return, while support on the weeklies may tell you how deep the correction will be. Chart patterns, of course, must be interpreted on all charts.

While all of these things can help you in trading, keep this thought foremost to maintain your trading discipline: *When the 2-day moving average crosses the edge of the 15-day band*, especially as the 10-day line is about to cross it too, *a trend reversal signal is in effect and must be followed* or at least hedged to neutral.

We will now set aside signaling systems and look at what will give us the courage to follow our signals, as well as protection from false signals or interpretations: the trading vehicle.

## TRADING A HEDGED SYSTEM FOR RISK CONTROLS

Along with trend identification, risk control is the other, equally important factor in successful trading, and the most difficult. The object of risk control is to reduce both the size and number of losing trades.

### Use Options To Replace Stop Loss Orders

Most systems assign the control of the number of losing trades entirely to their trend identification (or signaling) system. However, it is important that your risk control (or money management) approach also attempt to control frequency of loss.

The most common risk control technique is the use of stop loss orders, which control size of losses but not their number. The normal way of using a stop loss (if you are not stopped out right away and you do get a successful trade underway) is to move the stop loss up or down periodically (depending on trend) with the market, locking in your accumulating profits in the trade. Theoretically, when the market finally reverses, your stop loss order is hit and you are out of the market with your profit.

Besides the fact that a sudden crash or limit move may result in your order not being filled, or at least not being filled where you wanted it to be, stop losses can result in there being no successful trade in the first place.

The problem is that markets do not move in straight lines, either day to day or minute to minute. In fact, they zigzag, often hitting your stop loss unnecessarily—causing either a smaller profit than you intended or deserved, or an inability to get the trade off the ground at all, and a series of small losses instead. In the end, after each stop loss hit, you are left uncertain as to how, when, whether or where to get back into the market and in which direction. And in the meantime, you miss much or most of the move you'd hoped to catch.

To avoid this, simply do not use stops. Instead, if you are long, buy an at-the-money put option and periodically move it up (replace it) as the market moves upward. If short, do the same with a call option.

### The Impact of Deltas on Options Used in Risk Control

In a big or sudden move against you, an option can make about as much money as your futures position can lose. The option offsets, or hedges, your real or potential losses in a bad trade effectively enough to give you the confidence to follow your trading system. Yet an option does not prevent you from making money if the futures trade goes right (as hedging with a futures position can). This is not only because the hedging option can lose only a fixed amount of money, while the futures contract is unlimited in profitability potential, but also because a losing at-the-money option loses money at a rate approximately 50 percent or less than the futures contract makes money. The option also continues to lose money at a slower and slower rate each day as it moves out of the money. Conversely, a winning option makes money at a faster and faster rate per unit move each day it moves further into the money.

This effect is known as *delta*. The delta of a futures contract is a constant 100 percent per unit move all the time, win or lose. As the options move into the money, the delta values will decline until they reach 0 percent. Profitable options, however, have ever-increasing deltas as they move into the money, until their deltas reach 100 percent, and then they match the futures contract's movement one for one. A profitable option can offset losses in a losing futures contract. However, the decaying value of a losing option will only minimally affect a winning futures position.

At maximum, on a small move in an active market, the cost of insuring with an option might offset around 50 percent of your profits, but this is a spread trading system and therefore is expected to be more conservative and less aggressive than the gamble of a straight long or short trade. The point is, you can hold the trade and make 50 percent or better of the gain the trend will give you, rather than being stopped out or reversed and suffering losses and no gains.

## Starting Position: Underlying Cash and Option Position

To utilize this approach, if your main system gives you a buy signal, go long a future and buy an at-the-money put. If, further up the trend, you get a minor sell signal on the short-term moving averages, buy a new put at the new, higher market level and sell the old put. This brings your put up to near the current high and locks in the profits in your futures contract. Any minor move further down can be ignored until the market resumes its uptrend. Should the market continue down and cross the main, long-term moving average band, you can simply add a second put and you will actually make additional profits if the market crashes.

You can do this even more simply and effectively by not even using the short-term moving averages as a signal for moving up your hedging put, but by automatically moving it up as the market reaches each new and higher option strike price line. Then, you only have to watch the main long-term moving average, and if it is crossed to the downside, you can then add your second put.

However, there are two problems with this: (1) If the main trend becomes bearish, we have two puts being used to make money while they are hedged by a futures contract, which is backward from our original philosophy; and (2) if the market begins to whipsaw, how do we determine on which side of the market the futures position should be, and on which side the options?

One solution is this: When the market falls through the long-term moving average, instead of buying a second put, buy a one-strike-lower, in-the-money *call* and take profits in (sell) your long futures contract. This leaves you with one put (near the swing high) and a call at least a strike price below it. Thus, you have a straddle that has a value locked in between the put and the call. You also have a straddle that can make additional profits whether the market moves up to new highs or drops to new lows. As a result, the straddle cannot decay to nothing, even if the market were to go flat. The straddle also has a fairly high delta because the profitable option is in the money.

### Second Position: Shift to All-Options Position

Now we're in an all-option trading vehicle. In fact, that is the basis of this trading approach. It is a system of trading a series of overlapping locked-in-value straddles. Before getting into the mechanics of the system, let's examine the characteristics of this kind of straddle.

## SHIFT TO THE OVERLAPPING STRADDLE

### How Straddles Work

A simple straddle is best described as an at-the-money or near-the-money long put and call at the same strike price. Because each option has a considerable potential to make money in its favorable direction and only limited loss potential in the opposite direction, the winning side of the straddle spread (the winning option) can make more money than the losing side (losing option) can lose. Therefore, a straddle can make money either way a market moves—up or down. (See Figure 9.5.)

The maximum risk in a straddle is the cost of both options and occurs if the market either doesn't move or returns to the place of purchase without your taking profits. Another factor that affects a straddle's potential profitability is delta. Because the winning side of a straddle will experience an ever-increasing delta (or rising rate of earnings), while the losing side will experience an ever-decreasing delta (that is, it will lose less and less at an ever-decreasing rate of change), the straddle can make some money on the first day, or effective increment, of market movement. If the trend and strength of market volatility continue, the strad-

**Figure 9.5**   Put + Call = Straddle

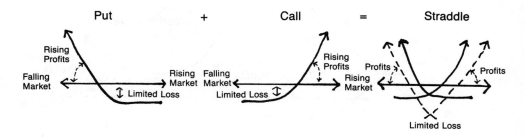

dle will make money at an ever-increasing rate, until eventually it can make money as fast as a futures contract.

To illustrate this, let's say the delta increases 10 percent every 100 points the market moves. In this example the market moves up in a trend 100 points per day. The delta of the call over five days would rise from 50 percent to 60, 70, 80, 90 and finally, on day five, reach an earning rate equal to 100 percent of a futures contract. Conversely, the put's losses would drop from 50 percent of a futures contract, to –40, –30, –20, –10, and on day five reach 0 percent, or no further losses. If you net out the difference of the two deltas each day you get: 60–40, 70–30, 80–20, 90–10, 100–0; or 20 percent, 40 percent, 60 percent, 80 percent, and 100 percent for each of the first five days of a major move. If each point equals $10 in the futures market, then on day one the straddle made $200 on a 100-point move, day two made $400, day three $600, day four $800 and day five $1,000. The straddle would then continue to make $1,000 a day for each day the market continued to move up 100 points.

Of course, if the market began to fall back at 100 points a day it would give up the profits at the same rate in reverse order, plus some time decay. For that reason it is important to take profits or lock profits into your straddle at certain points.

Let's say you didn't take profits, and the market fell 1,000 points rapidly; although you would give up your profits in the first five days, the put would then become profitable over the next 500 points and the straddle would make money again at a similar ever-increasing rate until delta reached 100 percent, or $1,000 a day (in this example).

But if the market runs up 500 points, then drops 1,000 points, it would be nicer to take profits in a straddle on the extreme end of each swing and make two successful trades.

Markets, of course, don't usually run in straight lines, but zigzag back and forth, moving slowly in a given direction. For this reason (and because out-of or at-the-money options values—which are mainly based on time value—tend to decay as the time until option expiration draws

**Figure 9.6** Combining Call and Put Movements Yields Combined Curve of Straddle's Price Action

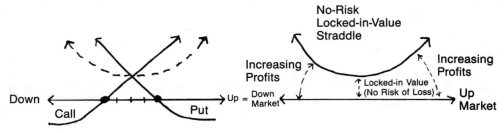

nearer), we don't want to hold options forever but trade them over short-term bursts in the back-and-forth market and quickly take or lock in profits.

Naturally, even the total straddle can lose money through time decay if the market doesn't move at all, as both options approach their expiration date. In this case, you can lose at expiration what you paid for both options.

There is a way to avoid this, however. In fact, there is a better way to form a straddle—one that *cannot* decay away to nothing (because it has a locked-in value), but which nevertheless has a built-in high minimum delta.

This is how we do it. After buying an at-the-money call the market runs up 100 points. Now you buy an at-the-money put. You have legged into a straddle with the put 100 points above the call and $1,000 value locked in between the two options. This means that the straddle can only decay, at worst, down to $1,000 and not to zero. It also means that you have a straddle with a locked-in winning side minimum delta (either way, up or down) that starts at 60–40 instead of 50–50, so that on the first 100-point move into the money it jumps to 70–30. If instead you initiated an outright straddle after the 100-point move, you would need a 200-point move to cause the straddle to jump to 70–30 from 50–50.

In fact, if you have a straddle with, say, 400 points locked-in value between the put and call, you can have a straddle with a locked-in value of $4,000, which is as much or more than both options cost. This straddle would not only have a winning delta of near 100 percent, but also no risk. That is to say, it can't lose money. (See Figure 9.6.)

Now, it's not always possible to build locked-in-value straddles with locked-in profits that are great enough to cover all or most of the cost of both options, but it is almost always possible to build locked-in-value straddles of at least 1/4 to 1/2 the total cost. You can therefore greatly reduce your risk while increasing minimum winning delta (and decreasing maximum losing delta).

What we want to do in this system, or trading vehicle, is *trade a series of overlapping, locked-in-value straddles* over a series of short-term market moves, rolling them over on each significant zig or zag the market makes, while keeping maximum winning delta in the direction of the main trend. It is possible to sell off calls at higher points, and puts at lower points, thus legging in and out of each straddle and maximizing profits even further.

If you are wondering what "overlapping" straddles means, it is this: You begin to "leg into" (buy half of, or one option of) your next straddle before you get out of any or all of the options of the previous straddle. Then, when the second straddle is completely formed, only half (one option) of the previous straddle is dropped and the other half is retained.

This, then, is a *three-option system*, made up of a call and a put plus one additional option oriented in the direction of the next expected move. Plus, at least two of the options form a locked-in-value straddle.

## How the Three-Option System Works

Let's say you're using two moving averages to determine trend reversal signals: a fast moving average of two or three days and a slow moving average of, say, 15 days. Whenever the fast moving average crosses the longer-term average, you buy an option in that direction: a call if it is a buy signal, a put if it is a sell signal. You continue to buy an option on each subsequent signal until you have built up to three options. From then on, whenever you buy a new option, you drop the oldest (and always opposite) option, thereby maintaining no more than three options. (See Figure 9.7.)

This system keeps two out of three of your options favorably oriented in the direction of the current trend. It also allows the winning option to carry over through two up (or down) thrusts, thus making more money. In addition, the winning trades will overlap on the charts, while the losing trades will not. This, too, gives you more profit-making coverage on the chart's movement.

But there are some problems with this approach. One is that in a steep, fast market it may be difficult to sell profitable options that are four or more strike prices in the money. The market for expensive options is thin, and bids may not be equivalent to what you deserve to get. You may have to exercise the option, then offset the resulting futures contract. This makes for added complications.

Second, and more likely, the market may move slowly, or have a shallow angle, or whipsaw back and forth, so that the time decay of your options results in a greater loss than the intrinsic profit ever builds up. Worse, the option may even expire before you get a fourth-wave reversal

**Figure 9.7**   Diagram and Legend Showing How Put and Call
Positions Are Initiated and Offset

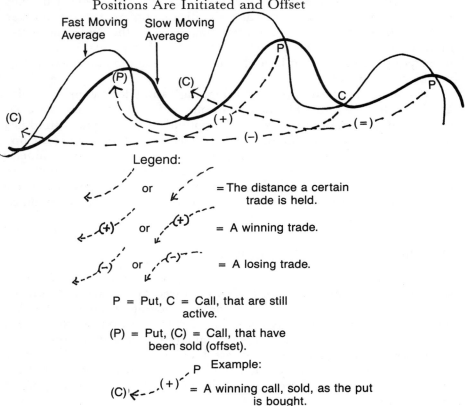

on the moving averages and the signal to take profits in your oldest option.

Therefore, you will want to use a system that gets you in and out of the options faster and over shorter distances on our charts. To accomplish this, simply use the short-term moving average system (the 2-day close inside the 3-day high/low band) instead of the 10-day or 15-day band or any other long-term moving average. (See Figure 9.8.)

As you can see, this works just as well and with the same results, but we get a lot more trades in during the same time period that the longer system would have taken just to build up to two options. The options don't have time to decay, plus the profitable options we sell off are not so deep in the money that they are difficult to sell.

The only real defect here is slippage. The market itself is, of course, even faster than these fastest of moving averages. Therefore, we can never buy our put at the exact high of a wave, or our call at the exact low.

**Figure 9.8**    The Effects of Using Shorter Moving Averages: More Signals To Get in and out of Positions Are Generated

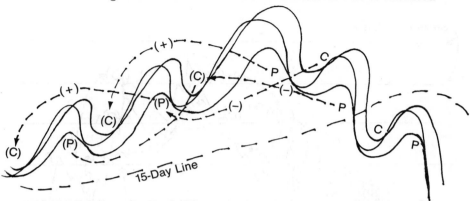

In fact, if you look at the illustration you can see that the calls are bought slightly higher than their neighboring put. This results in a strangle (one or both of the options out of the money, or a call higher than a put), which is like a straddle, but with a locked-in cost instead of value, and a low delta. This is not ideal. Now, you could "fix" this by buying *calls* on *sell* signals and *puts* on *buy* signals; this might work for a while until a true reversal happened, and then you would be in the market backward. And, in the case of a wide whipsaw, as opposed to a shallow one, all your trades would begin to lose. So going opposite the signal is not the answer.

The answer is this: On each signal buy both a put and call (a straddle) at once, and drop two options—the oldest, plus the losing one of the closest pair. Doing this prevents you from building strangles. However, it still does not let you lock in a put at or near the high of each wave, or a call near the low. To fix that, *simply don't wait for a signal*. At each new high (or low) strike price, automatically add a new straddle and drop two options.

**Editor's Note:**

As you can see, figures starting at 9.9 onward contain some very difficult graphics. The author and I discussed how we could make them easier to understand. We considered completely redrawing the graphs using conventional ideas, but after evaluating the length of the chapter, we decided against it.

Beginning with Figure 9.9, the charts attempt both to show a static picture of buying and selling calls and puts and to explain a sequentially dynamic strategy. First, find the letters C and P. The Cs represent call transactions and the Ps represent put transactions. Then

**Figure 9.9**    Chart Showing the Opening and Closing of Call and Put Positions over the Course of a Market Move

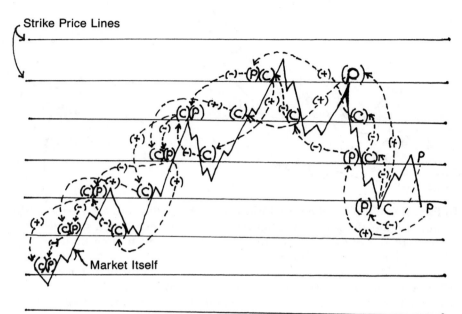

find the Cs and Ps distinguished from the *bracketed* Cs and Ps. Looking at Figure 9.9, you will find that most of the Cs and Ps are bracketed but that the few closest to the right are not. The author is merely showing that as of the creation of the graphic, the bracketed Cs and Ps are call and put transactions that have been closed out; that is, there are no open trades. Toward the right of the graphic, the nonbracketed Cs and Ps represent trades that are still open.

This is all the author is trying to show. The alternative was to show separate graphs for each time a call or a put option was first opened, and then another graph for the closing out of the trade. But imagine how many more graphs would have been required. Figure 9.9 alone would have been represented by more than 22 separate graphs!

You do not even need to chart the market itself, just its strike line-to-strike line moves. (See Figure 9.10.)

You might wonder what the moving average-oscillator signaling system is for, now that we seem to have totally abandoned it in favor of a

**Figure 9.10**   Conceptualized Market Move from Perspective of
Strike Prices of Options and How Open/Closed
Options Positions Enter into Overlapping Straddle
Approach

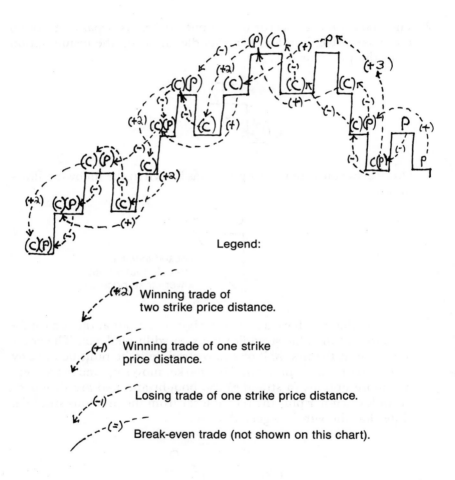

Legend:

_(+2)_ Winning trade of
two strike price distance.

_(+1)_ Winning trade of one strike
price distance.

_(-1)_ Losing trade of one strike price distance.

_(=)_ Break-even trade (not shown on this chart).

simple step chart. The answer is that there are many complex moves a
market can make, even between strike lines, and we will need to consult
the technical charts for general direction to make sure we keep the majority of our options arranged favorably toward the next most likely major move in the market.

But for now, let's concentrate on the basics of the trading approach,
and look at a simplified example.

1. To start out, you buy an at-the-money or near-the-money straddle (put and call).

2. The market moves up (or down) one strike. As it passes through the strike price, buy another straddle and drop the losing option from the previous one.

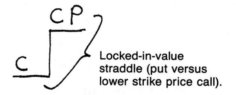

3. This leaves you with three options, as shown in the following illustration.

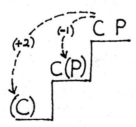

Locked-in-value straddle (put versus lower strike price call).

Note that you have a call at the bottom, a put at the top (making a locked-in-value straddle), plus an additional call. The additional call is the first half of a new straddle to be built before any of the old one is dismantled. The market moves up one more step, two more options (a straddle) are bought and two are dropped: the oldest winner plus the recent loser from the previous straddle. Note that the win is bigger than the loss.

4. From now on, you repeat the same process as the market trends.

Net profit = + 10 − 6 = +4.

If +1 = $500, then 4 × 500

= $2,000 profit.

Note in the above example that the winning trades overlap and are of a value of two strikes each, while the losing trades do not overlap and are of a value of one strike price. In other words, there are approximately equal numbers of winning and losing trades, but the winners are twice as big. And all the while you are hedged (protected from a crash) by a put placed at the most recent high, locking in the value of the oldest call.

The following guidelines will help in trading the many patterns and reversals a market can make other than a straight trend, but with a put at the last high and a call at the last low you will always have a winning position off which to play.

## RECOGNIZING PATTERNS IN THE STEP CHART AND BEST WAYS TO TRADE THEM

### Simple Trend Reversal

Buy a put and drop an extra call. As shown in the following diagram, this keeps a locked-in-value straddle intact, plus an extra leading option in the direction of the trend. If you think the reversal is temporary and shallow (a one-backstep correction), buy a call instead of a put on the setback.

Buy a put and drop extra call.

This leaves a locked-in-value straddle plus an extra at-the-money call.

Then, if the market rallies you have a winning trade.

This is a way to handle a short-term bull flag. If the market falls, you also have one more winning trade. But the market must go up from here for the next trade to add equity.

## Trading Whipsaws

A narrow, one-strike-wide whipsaw is handled the same way as a flag: A call is bought on the backstep, except that on the following rally, a put is bought.

(Locked-in-Value
Straddle)

(New Locked-in-Value
Straddle)

After the first trade, all trades win.

If the whipsaw widens, another profit can be taken. Execute the strategy outlined in the following diagram while buying a call and put on the breakout.

If a genuine breakout occurs, drop both losing options and keep the deep-in-the-money winner.

Then take a large profit on the next move.

The idea is to keep two options oriented toward the next move and only one option as a hedge.

If you know in advance that the whipsaw is ending, buy an option favorable to the breakout *before* the whipsaw breaks out.

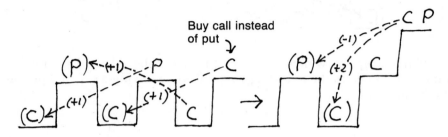

## Another Way of Handling Whipsaws

If you enter a whipsaw and take a *profit* on the backstep, and buy a put at the low instead of a call, as shown in the following diagram, you have not left behind a locked-in-value straddle.

If the market falls further, you will have to take a loss to straighten out the position.

If the market whipsaws, you can then start buying puts on highs and calls on lows, and take all profits.

But you will have to take a loss on the breakout.

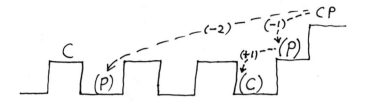

## Wider Whipsaws

Two-strike-wide whipsaw can be handled like this:

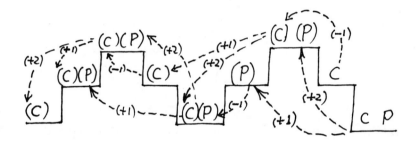

Twelve units (strikes) of profits, minus three of loss = +9, or, at $500 per strike, as in our examples = +$4,500 in two waves.

A three-strike-wide whipsaw can be handled like this:

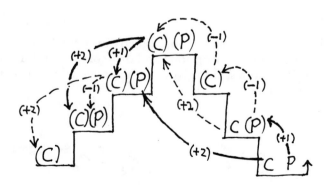

10 – 3 = +7, or $3,500 profit in one wave. The object here is, on the last move before the reversal, to drop both profitable options, reorienting the remaining triad of options for a reversal.

By studying past market moves, one can determine what the most common market patterns are and statistically what best tactic to use in any given pattern. However, for safety, it is usually best to try to keep a locked-in-value straddle in place, as shown in the following illustration,

(C) P
C ⌐(-1)⌐ P     or:     (C) P     C ⌐(-1)⌐ C

rather than not:

C (P) (+1)
C          P

Taking a profit and eliminating a locked-in-value straddle reduces the winning power (winning delta) of your remaining position and increases the chance of option time decay. However, as we have seen, sometimes it is best to take all profits. Your signaling system can determine when.

### "Cheating"

Since signals are unlikely to come exactly on strike price lines (where you ordinarily buy your new options and drop old ones), but more often occur between strike lines, this gives you a chance to readjust a position in time to avoid a loss.

(+2) (-1) C P
C (P)
(C)

→

(+1) C P     Sell Signal
(+2) (C) P
(C)

Take profit in call instead, and...
buy back out-of-money put just dropped.

Resulting in:

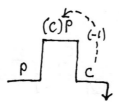

Or, you can do it this way, to keep in the locked-in-value straddle:

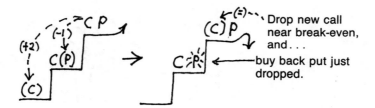

Drop new call near break-even, and . . .

buy back put just dropped.

Resulting in:

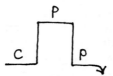

Or, if you can tell the reversal is only a shallow flag, try this strategy:

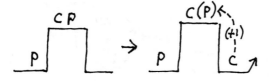

Take profit in higher put and buy a call at the lower level.

Or, from the other example:

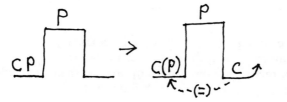

Drop lower put at break-even and buy another call.

This results in:

Or:

However, all this is "jumping the system" based on prejudging the market, and it can be dangerous.

If the market moves faster than the signals, then resort to the standard pattern recognition rules and execute the best possible moves at the next strike price. Some moves can even be ignored if you think they're phony, as shown in the following diagram.

But with the help of signaling systems and correct judgment, it is possible to get the same results in the same number of market moves, regardless of market pattern, by leaving both options of the last straddle in place until a signal is given, as shown in Figure 9.11.

**Figure 9.11**

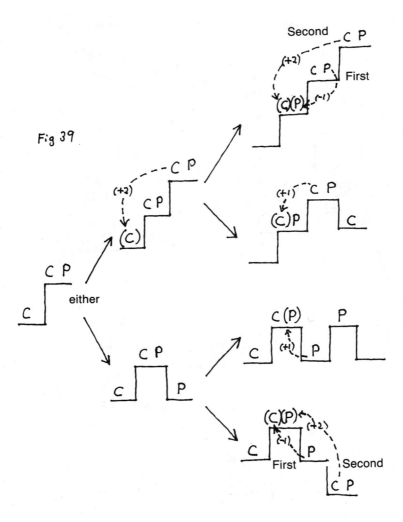

The secret above is to leave four options intact (just drop one of the five at a new strike), or none of the four after buying new option(s) until a signal is given; then drop the second *correct* option, reducing holdings to three. This can give you the following results, which generate the same profits in any pattern:

**Figure 9.12**

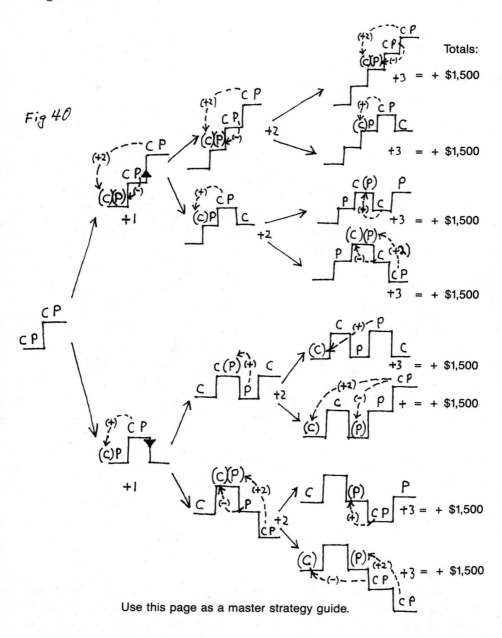

Use this page as a master strategy guide.

## SUMMARY

Basically there are two ways to trade this three-option system: When you add two options you must drop two, so either drop both winners or drop the big winner and the small loser. Do the former if you suspect a reversal, the latter if the trend continues:

Dropping one of each:

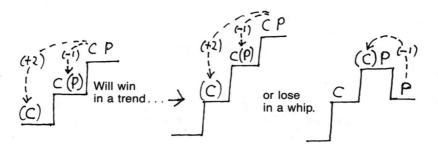

Taking both profits:

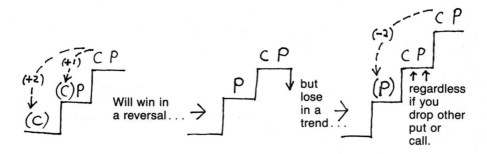

Taking all profits works in erratic markets:

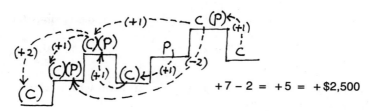

$$+7 - 2 = +5 = +\$2,500$$

But in trending markets, you must let profits ride one extra strike:

$$+4 - 2 = +2 = +\$1,000$$

or you get losers twice as big as winners:

$$+2 - 4 = -2 = -\$1,000 \text{ (loss)}$$

And, of course, in one-step backsteps and other one-step whipsaws you buy only one option and drop one option:

(with locked-in straddle)

(with locked-in straddle)

(*no* locked-in straddle)

The decision of which option to drop depends on which way the market is supposed to move next.

## VARIATIONS

### Trading Superfast Bull Markets

If a market is skyrocketing the limit up each day, you can move one put up each day, just as you would raise a stop, and let a call ride:

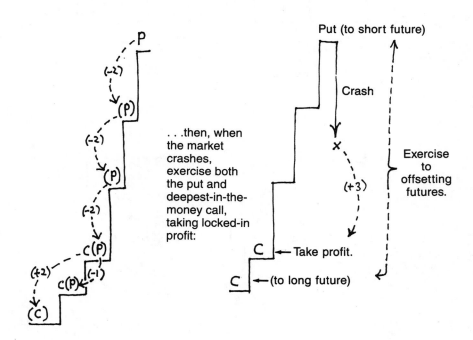

The problem with this is that you need extra money in your account to finance rolling over the hedging put because the profits in the call do not accrue to the account until the call is sold or exercised. Therefore, if possible, it is better to use the regular system, periodically taking profits.

### Writing Options in Slow Markets

While you do not want to write options in a fast market (because they would limit your hedging option), in slow markets a put, call or both can be written covered against the system, a few strikes out of the money, while continuing to trade the long system:

SC = short call, SP = short put

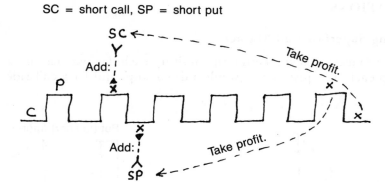

Or:

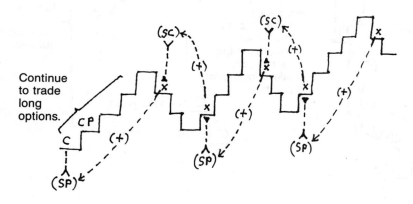

Stochastics, RSI, oscillators or moving averages can be used to signal entry and exit points for shorts.

Many spread configurations can be built around our triad of long options. Here are a few based around the upward-biased straddle, the locked-in straddle, plus a call:

which =                A straddle plus a call.

## Covered Writes

*Out-of-the-Money Debit Spreads:*

A straddle (a short synthetic future plus two calls).

Two bull spreads plus a put. Similar to a put ratio backspread. Maximum profit potential blocked to upside.

A straddle versus a long synthetic future. Acts like a call ratio backspread or a call. Full hedging potential blocked off.

Behaves like a short butterfly. Maximum profits of straddle blocked in both directions, but some offset protection from decay during flat whipsaw. Mild upward bias.

SC

CP

C

SP

=

Similar to a call ratio backspread. Full hedging potential blocked.

*In-the-Money (all, or partial) Credit Spreads:*

CP

C

SC

=

A straddle plus a bear spread. Acts like a strangle.

CP

C

SC   SC

=

Two credit bear spreads, plus a put. Acts like a put. Upside potential blocked.

SP

CP

C

SC

=

A bear and bull spread, plus a call. Acts like a call or a call ratio backspread.

Two credit bear spreads plus one credit bull spread. Similar to a short butterfly with a downward bias.

*Mixed Spreads (in and out of the money):*

Like a put ratio backspread, or a put.

Like a call ratio backspread, or a call.

Like a short butterfly with an upward bias.

The same spreads, upside down, can be made if the long option triad is in the more bearish mode:

P
⌐
 └⌐ c P
  └

All of these spreads can be even more subtle by writing time spreads (buying and writing options of different expiration dates).

Note that writing in-the-money options has an effect similar to buying or shorting a futures contract against the main option straddle triad. It tends to slow or block off one side of the straddle and augment the other side.

Writing out-of-the-money options can help offset some time decay, but it may also block off maximum potential of the hedging side of the position or slow the optimal side.

The short options, especially the in-the-money shorts, may have to be adjusted with each trade adjustment in the long option triad during regular trading.

This can become as complicated as the quantum mechanic dance of subatomic particles, and may necessitate a computer. In general, it is best to keep things simple and write out-of-the-money options one or two at a time to offset decay in flat, whipsaw markets that are near their lows or not volatile. Such spreads do not have to be adjusted daily.

## CONCLUSION

This system works best in volatile, high-priced markets that you would like to trade but are afraid to, such as the S&P in 1987, soybeans in the 1988 drought, gold in 1979–80 or petroleum in 1990. Also, you can determine a good market by looking at a 10-year chart of a commodity. By seeing the average price line where bull markets in that commodity top, and the price at which the bear markets usually bottom, you can draw a line halfway in between to get an average, or midprice. When a market is *above* the midline, whether in a bull or bear trend, the market will probably be volatile enough to trade this system successfully.

This system is designed to protect you. In a choppy, erratic market, you can lose if half your decisions are wrong, but you will lose slowly—because for every losing decision you make, a hedging option is partially making up for the loss. But in volatile markets it is hard to lose if you follow the rules and the signals.

A crash, even if you are in backwards, can be profitable. In the 1987 stock crash, two calls that lost all their money would have lost $10,000 each, while one put (the hedge) would have made over $30,000. The purpose of this system is to give you the confidence to follow the signals and rules with discipline.

And remember, round-turn options commissions should be less than futures commissions. Insist on it.

# CHAPTER 10

# Using Options Instead of Futures

*BY RONALD J. FROST*

**Editor's Note:**

When I first approached the original contributing author, David Dupont, he was fresh from a long stint at the Chicago Mercantile Exchange. I requested a chapter that followed our guideline that the information had to be practical and hands-on. As time passed, Dupont got sidetracked developing a brokerage business at Merrill Lynch, so he asked Ronald Frost to flesh out his outline and write this chapter. Frost did all the writing and chose all of the examples to illustrate his analytical process.

Frost is a spread trader who has fine-tuned his approach with options. The author compares the options strangle or straddle positions with the results of the futures spread position in all the examples. The three examples that he works with are progressively more complex. The first example starts with a simple cattle and hog spread. The last ends with the use of option time spreads. Along the way, the author explains his approach carefully so that readers can discover: Why does the expert do this?

In an industry where there are enough perception problems, terminology adds to the confusion. We have strangles, straddles, flying condors (sometimes with wheels), caps, collars, fences and butterflies. Why not add another—opspreads!

Opspreads are simply futures spreads that use options instead of futures.

Traders will usually put on a futures spread when they believe the price difference between two futures contracts in the same commodity (intramarket) or between related commodities (intermarket) are out of line. Therefore, they are more concerned with the *absolute difference* in prices than with the direction of prices. Spreads are often traded instead of outright positions because they are perceived as less risky. However, the risk is not limited because the contract bought can decline and the contract sold can go up, causing a loss on both positions.

One of the reasons options trading has become popular is the limited risk concept in buying options. Option spreads using bullish call or put spreads, bearish call or put spreads, calendar spreads and butterflies are popular because of limited risk. One might also use options for trading purposes to buy options when implied volatility is perceived as very low or to sell them when implied volatility is perceived as very high. Time decay works against the buyer of an option but in favor of the seller.

If the trader is interested in limiting risk and increasing probabilities of making money, why not combine the elements of futures spreads with options trading? This chapter examines some of those possibilities.

## SIX REASONS WHY OPTIONS MAY BE USED IN PLACE OF FUTURES

Here are six reasons why options may be used to take advantage of spread relationships.

1. Buying calls and puts limits the risk to the premiums paid for the options plus the commissions. If a live cattle call is purchased for $1.50 per 100 pounds or cwt. and a live hog put is purchased for $1.00 cwt., the debit is $2.50 or $1,000 (since cattle and hog contracts are quoted in dollar amounts per hundredweight, we have 40,000 pounds × $0.025 cents per pound = $1,000).

2. There are no margin requirements when buying options. The premium must be paid at the time of purchase.

3. The different strike levels allow the trader to create strategies that are either neutral or slightly biased in one of the commodities.

4. Unlike a futures spread, the trader can actually be wrong on the spread forecast and still make a profit on the options if the prices move sharply in either direction.

5. By monitoring implied volatility levels in the options contracts, the option spreads may outperform a spread in the underlying future's delta equivalent if prices move sharply and quickly. As a

result of sharp and quick moves, the implied volatility of the options will increase.

6. If advantageous, the options can be exercised into a futures position. This can happen if the options are trading below intrinsic value and the trader believes the spread will continue to act favorably after options expire and wants to hold the position longer.

## COMPARATIVE EXAMPLE OF FUTURES VERSUS OPTIONS

Before proceeding with actual examples of trades, an overview will set the stage. Live cattle (as opposed to feeder cattle) versus live hog futures will be used in this set of seven theoretical outcomes.

- Current market assumptions:
  Live cattle futures = $76 cwt. (hundredweight)
  Live hog futures   = $52 cwt.
             Spread = $24 premium the cattle futures contract

- Outlook:
  The spread can do only one of three things: widen, stay the same or narrow. Cattle prices are too high relative to hog prices. The spread is expected to narrow.
- Call and put valuations on cattle and hogs:
  Live cattle 76 put option = $1.25
  Live hog 52 call option  = $1.50
  Both options are at-the-money options. The live hog options are higher priced because they almost always trade at higher implied volatilities than live cattle options.

With these facts, a trader who wants to make money based on future expectations can do either of the following:

1. Intermarket spread of futures: Sell live cattle futures and buy live hog futures.

2. Strangle with options: Buy live cattle 76 puts and buy live hog 52 calls.

## SEVEN MARKET OUTCOMES

Let's look at the seven possible outcomes. To simplify the example, round numbers will be used and the outcomes of the spread or strangle plays will be evaluated at options expirations only. (Livestock options expire a few weeks prior to the futures' last day of trading.) I will also make the options spreads equal to the futures spreads by using two options to make the options position closer to the delta equivalent of a futures contract. At-the-money options trade with a delta of about 0.50 so that two such options would have an approximate delta of 1.00, equivalent to one underlying futures contract.

As background, live cattle and live hog contracts are quoted in one hundredth cents per pound or dollars per hundredweight (cwt.). Both the cattle contract and hog contract are 40,000 pounds. (The live hog contract contained 30,000 pounds prior to the first quarter of 1991 but was increased to 40,000 pounds thereafter.) A price quote of $76.35 per hundredweight means 0.7635 cents per pound. Options on live cattle and live hogs are therefore quoted as follows: $1.75 means 1.75 cwt. or $0.0175 cents per pound. Strike prices are quoted in even numbers.

## 1. Prices Rise and Intermarket Spread Stays the Same

| *Futures at Options' Expiration* | *Options Pricing at Expiration* |
|---|---|
| Live cattle = $84 or + $8 | Live cattle 76 put = 0 or − $1.25 |
| Live hog = $60 or + $8 | Live hog 52 call = $8 or + $6.50 |

Spread = $24, or unchanged

| *Futures Net Results* | *Options Net Results* |
|---|---|
| Short live cattle = − $8 | Long live cattle 76 put = − $1.25 |
| Long live hog = + $8 | Long live hog 52 call = + $6.50 |
| Net = 0 | + $5.25 |

+ $5.25 × 2 =    $10.50

(Note: Two of each option were purchased so that they are nearly equivalent to one futures contract.)

Advantage: Opspreads: $10.50

## 2. Prices Stay the Same and Intermarket Spread Stays the Same

| *Futures at Options' Expiration* | *Options Pricing at Expiration* |
|---|---|
| Live cattle = $76 or unchanged | Live cattle 76 put = 0 or −$1.25 |
| Live hog = $52 or unchanged | Live hog 52 call = 0 or −$1.50 |

Spread = $24, or unchanged

| *Futures Net Results* | *Options Net Results* |
|---|---|
| Short live cattle = 0 | Long live cattle 76 put = −$1.25 |
| Long live hog = 0 | Long live hog 52 call = −$1.50 |
| Net = 0 | −$2.75 |

−$2.75 × 2 = −$5.50

Advantage: Futures: no loss

### 3. Prices Fall and Intermarket Spread Stays the Same

*Futures at Options' Expiration*
Live cattle = $66 or -$10
Live hog = $42 or -$10

Spread = $24, or unchanged

*Options Pricing at Expiration*
Live cattle 76 put = $10 or + $8.75
Live hog 52 call =   0 or - $1.50

*Futures Net Results*
Short live cattle = + $10
Long live hog = - $10
Net =   0

*Options Net Results*
Long live cattle 76 put = + $8.75
Long live hog 52 call = - $1.50
+ $7.25

+ $7.25 × 2 =   $14.50

Advantage: Opspreads: $14.50

### 4. Intermarket Spread Narrows

*Futures at Options' Expiration*
Live cattle = $70 or - $6
Live hog = $60 or + $8

Spread = $10, or it narrows
by $14

*Options Pricing at Expiration*
Live cattle 76 put = $6 or + $4.75
Live hog 52 call = $8 or + $6.50

*Futures Net Results*
Short live cattle = + $6
Long live hog = + $8
Net = + $14

*Options Net Results*
Long live cattle 76 put = + $4.75
Long live hog 52 call = + $6.50
+ $11.25

+ $11.25 × 2 =   $22.50

Advantage: Opspreads: $22.50, or $8.50 better than futures spreading

### 5. Spread Narrows, Both Prices Fall

*Futures at Options' Expiration*
Live cattle = $60 or -$16
Live hog = $48 or -$4

Spread = $12, or it narrows by $12

*Options Pricing at Expiration*
Live cattle 76 put = $16 or + $14.75
Live hog 52 call =   0 or - $1.50

| *Futures Net Results* | *Options Net Results* |
|---|---|
| Short live cattle = + $16 | Long live cattle 76 put = + $14.75 |
| Long live hog = – $4 | Long live hog 52 call = – $1.50 |
| Net = + $12 | + $13.25 |

+ $13.25 × 2 =    $26.50

Advantage: Opspreads: $26.50, or $14.50 better than futures spreading

## 6. Prices Rise, Spread Widens

| *Futures at Options' Expiration* | *Options Pricing at Expiration* |
|---|---|
| Live cattle = $83 or + $7 | Live cattle 76 put = 0 or – $1.25 |
| Live hog = $54 or + $2 | Live hog 52 call = $2 or + $0.50 |

Spread = $29, or it widens by $5

| *Futures Net Results* | *Options Net Results* |
|---|---|
| Short live cattle = – $7 | Long live cattle 76 put = – $1.25 |
| Long live hog = + $2 | Long live hog 52 call = + $0.50 |
| Net = – $5 | – $0.75 |

–$0.75 × 2 = – $1.50

Advantage: Opspreads: –$1.50 loss, or $3.50 better than futures spreading

## 7. Prices Fall, Spread Widens

| *Futures at Options' Expiration* | *Options Pricing at Expiration* |
|---|---|
| Live cattle = $73 or –$3 | Live cattle 76 put = $3 or + $1.75 |
| Live hog = $42 or –$10 | Live hog 52 call = 0 or – $1.50 |

Spread = $31, or it widens by $7

| *Futures Net Results* | *Options Net Results* |
|---|---|
| Short live cattle = + $3 | Long live cattle 76 put = + $1.75 |
| Long live hog = – $10 | Long live hog 52 call = – $1.50 |
| Net = – $7 | + $0.25 |

+ $0.25 × 2 = + $0.50

Advantage: Opspreads: $0.50, or $7.50 better than futures spreading

Even though the above examples showed that opspreads plays had the advantage over futures six out of seven times, I have three cautions to offer to readers.

1. Although the risk is limited when buying options, stable markets or dropping implied volatilities can put the options trader at a disadvantage.

2. If selling options is part of the strategy, margins are incurred because there is unlimited risk in the options sold. Furthermore, if an option is sold initially and the market moves against the trader, the option that was sold might be exercised.

3. The spreads used here are significantly out of line. Intracommodity spreads are not used because the cost of buying the options for small moves often will not overcome the cost of the premiums, making the trade less attractive.

There are two instances in which the futures position will outperform the opspreads, even if the spread narrows: when the prices paid for the options are too high or when the spread does not narrow enough to offset the time decay. An example will be shown later.

## THREE CASE STUDIES WITH OPSPREADS

This section will examine the following popular spreads used by futures traders:

- live cattle versus live hogs
- wheat versus corn
- Swiss franc versus Deutsche mark

These spreads will be viewed by three different traders, each with a different approach. The first will be the outright futures spread trader whose analysis is rather cut and dried. The results of the outright spreads will be the benchmark against which to compare our opspreads strategies.

The other two are opspreads traders who will use options to implement the analysis the futures spreader applies. The valuation of the options within the opspreads strategies will define the risk levels. Two strategies will be illustrated: Trader B (for buyer) will always be a buyer of options, regardless of their volatility. Trader V (for volatility) will always implement opspreads strategies with volatility considerations.

### First Case Study: Cattle Gains or Loses to Hog Spreads

Let's look at the live cattle versus live hog spread. (See Figure 10.1.) Seldom have cattle futures prices been more than $25 per cwt. higher than hog prices. Using futures only, the spread trader can sell cattle and

**Figure 10.1** Live Cattle/Live Hogs Monthly Spread

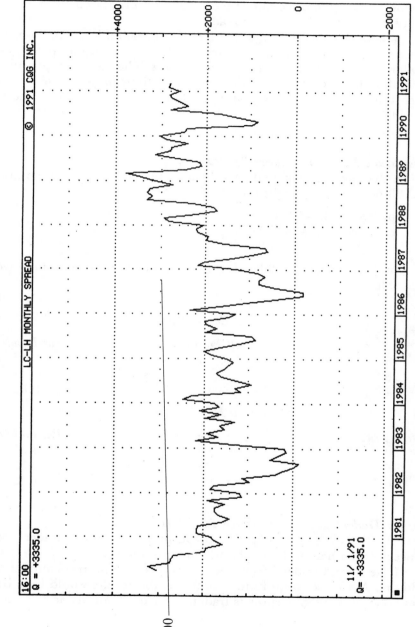

buy hogs when the price difference is $25 or more. It will work most of the time, but it will fail occasionally.

In fact, early in 1991, after the New Year celebrations were over and heads were clearing, two traders were discussing that same spread. One thought hog prices would gain on cattle prices. The other thought fundamentals indicated that cattle prices would continue to gain on hog prices. Each trader made the other cautious about the spread strategy he was considering.

### Case Study Data for January 3, 1991

In the beginning of 1991, April cattle were selling at a premium of $29.88 per hundredweight over April live hogs.

Apr live cattle = $76.35
Apr live hog = $46.47
Spread = $29.88

On January 3, the following futures and option premiums were available:

#### April Cattle Options

| Strike Price | Call Premium | Put Premium |
|---|---|---|
| 78 | 0.95 | 2.55 |
| 76 | 1.75 | 1.47 |
| 74 | 3.10 | 0.82 |

#### April Hog Options

| Strike Price | Call Premium | Put Premium |
|---|---|---|
| 50 | 0.60 | 4.35 |
| 48 | 1.05 | 2.85 |
| 46 | 1.95 | 1.45 |

### Spread Trader's Results on March 26, 1991

First, let's take a look at the spread play. The spread trader's only concern is the narrowing or the widening of the spread.

If the spread trader bought one April live hog futures contract and sold one April live cattle futures contract, the results would have been these on the day the opspreads trader also closed out his or her trades:

Apr live cattle futures = $80.82
Apr live hog futures = $52.45
Spread = $28.37, narrowed slightly from $29.88

*Original Positions*

Sell Apr live cattle futures at          Buy Apr live hog futures at
$76.35 cwt.                              $46.47 cwt.

*Close-Out Positions*

Buy Apr cattle futures at               Sell Apr live hog futures at
$80.82 cwt.                             $52.45 cwt.
Net = $4.47 cwt., or -$1,788            + $5.98 cwt., or $2,392
Profit = $604

The spread did narrow slightly because hog prices moved up more quickly than cattle prices. The futures strategy worked because prices moved significantly. In futures spreading, the cattle losses almost offset the hog gain.

### Opspreads Scenario A: Hogs To Gain on Cattle

Unlike spread traders, opspreads traders have several choices to make in executing a trading decision, but first they must evaluate the following factors.

#### Volatility

The implied volatilities on the live cattle options ranged from 10.4 to 11.5 percent. This meant that the live cattle options were relatively low priced.

The implied volatilities on live hog options were as follows: 50 calls were at 19.3 percent, 48 calls were at 18.3 percent and 46 calls were at 18.7 percent. The puts were at the following levels: 50 puts were at 22.9 percent, 48 puts were at 21.5 percent and 46 puts were at 19.3 percent. In relative terms, the hog options had higher volatilities than the cattle options.

Since live hog options volatilities can range from 13 percent to 35 percent, the option premiums for hogs were moderately priced within the context of past pricing. Both cattle and hog prices were expected to become more volatile. Buying options for both cattle and hogs was therefore calculated to be favorable because the volatile underlying futures price moves were expected to overcome time decay.

#### Which Options To Buy?

The next problem was to find which strike price to buy. Buying the wrong ones would lose money even though the analysis and forecast would be right.

In this case, buying the out-of-the-money live hog 48 call was selected by opspreads Trader V. The reader might wonder why out-of-the-money calls were purchased when at-the-money calls, the 46 strike, were available. The forecast was that the futures spread would narrow from $29.88 because hog prices would gain on cattle prices, not because hog prices would stay unchanged while cattle prices fell. In this case, buying the out-of-the-money live hog call executed that forecast better.

In fact, the trader bought two calls and two puts to bring the total delta closer to a futures position. Two live cattle 76 puts were bought. The 76 put was almost at the money. As an extra measure of comfort, the acquired options did not show extreme implied volatilities; this meant that opspreads Trader V did not buy overpriced options.

The cost for the hog call options was:

$$2 \times \$1.05 = \$2.10 \text{ or } \$840$$

($1.05 cwt. × 40,000 pounds × 2 options contracts = $840)

Cattle puts were:

$$2 \times \$1.47 = \$2.94 \text{ or } \$1,175$$

($1.47 cents per pound × 40,000 pounds × 2 options contracts = $1,175)

In effect, this is an options strangle, buying a call and a put, both out of the money.

### Profit Potential
The profit potential is unlimited because one or both of the options could move deep in the money: Hog prices could move up, or cattle prices could move down.

### Risk
The maximum loss would occur if both options expired worthless. That would be $2,015 plus commissions (cost of two live hog call options at $840 plus cost of two live cattle put options at $1,175).

Unlike futures spreads, there is also the risk of the options spread remaining constant and the prices of cattle and hogs also remaining constant while time decay takes its toll on the options positions.

### Results on March 26, 1991
Both cattle and hog prices dropped immediately, favoring the cattle puts at the expense of the hog calls. (See Figures 10.2 to 10.4.) Then both markets turned around and soared.

On March 26, it was time to liquidate the position. Here were the futures and options prices on that day.

**Figure 10.2** Live Cattle and Live Hog Monthly Bars

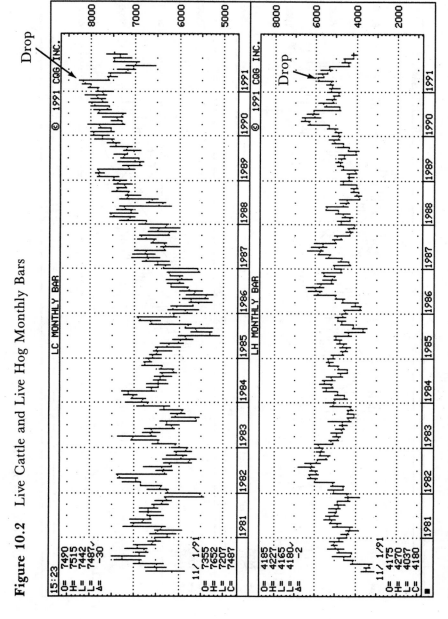

© 1991 CQG Inc. Reprinted with permission.

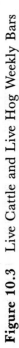

**Figure 10.3**   Live Cattle and Live Hog Weekly Bars

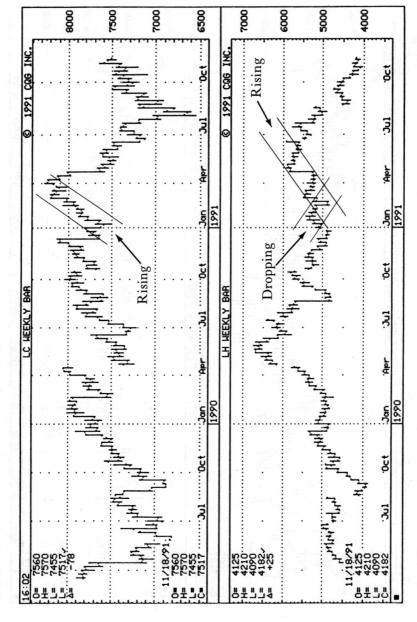

© 1991 CQG Inc. Reprinted with permission.

**Figure 10.4**  Live Cattle/Live Hog Weekly Spread

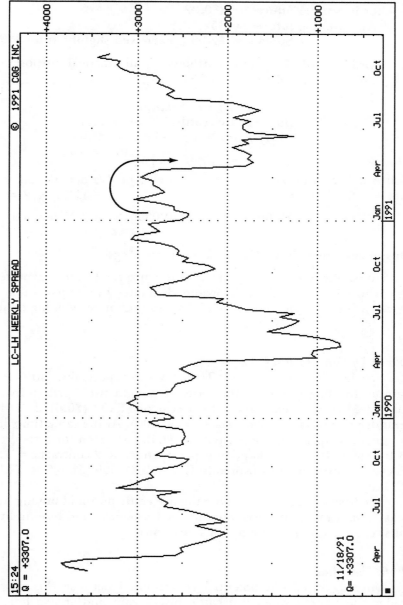

© 1991 CQG Inc. Reprinted with permission.

Apr live cattle futures = $80.82
Apr live hog futures = $52.45
            Spread = $28.37, narrowed slightly, from $29.88

Apr live cattle 76 put = worthless for all practical purposes
Apr live hog 48 call = $4.50

*Original Positions*
Buy Apr live cattle 76 put = $1.47
Buy Apr live hog 48 call = $1.05

*Close-Out Positions*

Sell Apr live cattle 76 put = 0         Sell Apr live hog 48 call = $4.50
Net = -$1.47 × = -$2.94                          +$3.45 × 2 = $6.90

Profit = +$3.96, or $1,584 ($0.0396 × 40,000 pounds)

## Opspreads Scenario B: Cattle To Gain on Hogs

Unlike the first scenario, in which the opspreads trader expected hog prices to gain on cattle, this opspreads strategy anticipates that cattle prices will go to unending new highs and hog prices will lag behind or drop.

### Which Options To Buy?

Now let's look at opspreads Trader B who expects live cattle prices to gain on live hog prices. In this case, he bought two April 76 live cattle calls at $1.75 cwt. each for a total cost of $1,400 ($0.0175 × 40,000 pounds per contract × 2 contracts = $1,400). At the same time, he also bought two April live hog 46 puts at $1.45 cwt. each for a total cost of $1,160 ($0.0145 × 40,000 pounds per contract × 2 contracts = $1,160). The total position cost opspreads Trader B $2,560 ($1,400 + $1,160 = $2,560).

The first strategy involved buying live cattle puts and buying live hog calls. This strategy involves buying live cattle calls and buying live hog puts, exactly the opposite options positions.

### Profit Potential

Once again, profit potential is unlimited because this opspreads trader can benefit when live cattle prices gain and/or live hog prices drop.

### Risk

Risk is limited to the cost of the options, in this case, $2,560.

*Results on March 26, 1991*

The live cattle prices rallied as live hog prices fell, and the trader felt great. (See Figures 10.2 and 10.3.) Then hogs rallied, eroding the profits on that side of the spread. Nonetheless, the move in cattle was making money. These were the prices of the calls and puts on March 26, 1991:

Apr live cattle 76 calls = $4.82 cwt.

Apr live hog 46 puts = worthless for all practical purposes

Time to liquidate: Sell live cattle calls and sell out live hog puts.

*Original Positions*

Buy live cattle 76 call = $1.75          Buy live hog 45 put = $1.45

*Close-Out Positions*

Sell live cattle 76 call = $4.82      Sell live hog 46 put =   0

Net: =  + $3.07 × 2 = $6.14                    -$1.45 × 2 = -$2.90

Profit =  + $3.24, or $1,296 ($0.0324 × 40,000 pounds)

Even though the spread narrowed instead of widening, the trader made money because of the major up move in cattle. The loss on the hog options was limited to the cost of the premiums.

## Comparative Analysis

In the first case, by taking the outright short live cattle futures and long live hog futures, the spread trader made a profit of $604.

In the opspreads cases, the profits were larger. In the first such case, opspreads Trader V was bullish on hogs by buying calls and bearish on cattle by buying puts. The profit on this strategy was $1,584. In the second case, opspreads Trader B was bearish on hogs by buying the puts and bullish on cattle by buying the calls. The profit was $1,296.

The options profits occurred in both cases because of big moves in the underlying futures. Even though opspreads Trader B was wrong about the direction of the spread, he made money.

## Second Case Study: Wheat To Gain on Corn

Looking at a chart of the wheat/corn spread (see Figure 10.5), the traders noticed that wheat seldom traded at less than 40 cents over corn. Exceptions occurred in 1983–84, 1986 and again in 1990–91.

In fact, the pattern in early 1991 closely resembled that of 1984. By August 1991, traders figured the spread was about to widen to a more normal spread. Why? Perhaps because wheat would become more desirable as a livestock feed. Perhaps the wheat would be more attractive as

**Figure 10.5**   Wheat/Corn Monthly Spread

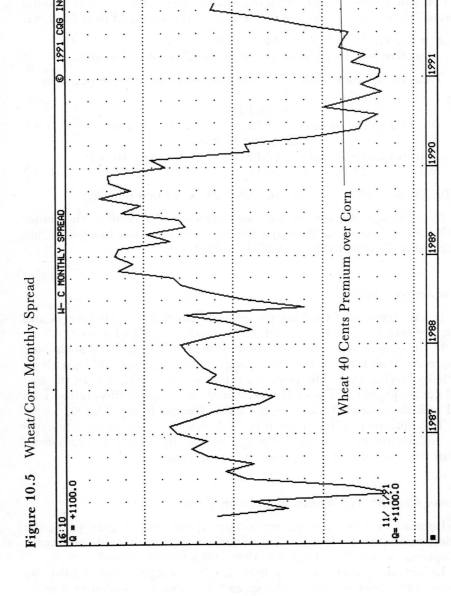

© 1991 CQG Inc. Reprinted with permission.

an export commodity. Perhaps someone who knows all the fundamental factors as well as the insides of politicians' and traders' minds would have a better handle. In any case, the traders thought the spread would widen considerably. The only caveat was that both markets were in bull moves and the spread could in fact narrow again.

As background, wheat futures and corn futures are both traded in 5,000 bushel contracts. Prices are quoted in dollars, whole cents and eighths of cents per bushel: $4.52$^{1/8}$. Wheat and corn options are traded in strike price intervals of 10 cents per bushel and are also quoted in whole cents and eighths of cents per bushel. "250 calls at 24$^{1/2}$" means 24$^{1/2}$ cents per bushel or $1,225 (5,000 bushels × 24.5 cents = $1,225).

### Case Study Data for August 1, 1991

The prices of wheat and corn futures contracts on August 1, 1991, were as follows:

Dec wheat futures = $3.08 bushel
Dec corn futures = $2.68$^{1/4}$ bushel
Spread = $0.39$^{3/4}$

On the same day, August 1, 1991, the following wheat and corn futures options premiums were available:

#### December Wheat Options

| Strike Price | Call Premiums | Put Premiums |
|---|---|---|
| 320 | 11$^{3/4}$ | 23$^{1/2}$ |
| 310 | 16 | 17$^{1/2}$ |
| 300 | 20$^{1/2}$ | 11 |
| 290 | 26 | 7$^{1/2}$ |

#### December Corn Options

| Strike Price | Call Premiums | Put Premiums |
|---|---|---|
| 280 | 12$^{1/2}$ | no trades |
| 270 | 16$^{1/8}$ | 17 |
| 260 | 19$^{1/2}$ | 10$^{1/2}$ |
| 250 | 24$^{1/2}$ | 6$^{1/4}$ |

### Spread Trader's Results on November 1, 1991

The futures spread trader bought December wheat and sold December corn futures. Wheat futures moved from $3.08 to $3.64$^{3/4}$ a bushel, or a gain of $0.56$^{3/4}$ profit. Corn futures moved from $2.68$^{1/4}$ to $2.54 a bushel, or a gain of $0.14$^{1/4}$ cents on the short sale.

#### Original Positions

Buy wheat futures at $3.08        Sell corn futures at $2.68$^{1/4}$

*Close-Out Positions*

Sell wheat futures at $3.64³/₄         Buy corn futures at $2.54
  Net = + $0.56³/₄ per bushel            + $0.14¹/₄ per bushel
        or $2,837.50                           or $712.50

Profit = + $0.71, or $3,550 ($0.56³/₄ + $0.14¹/₄ = $0.71 profit;
                $0.71 × 5,000 bushels = $3,550)

## Opspreads Scenario A: Wheat To Gain on Corn

Rather than buy wheat futures and sell corn futures because of the unlimited risk, opspreads Trader B said the play was to buy the wheat calls and buy the corn puts.

Opspreads Trader V pointed out that wheat and corn futures showed implied call volatilities in the 24 percent to 28 percent range. The hot weather and bullish trending wheat and corn were causing the grain options to have high volatilities, not unusual for that time of year. It could be expected that grain volatilities would probably fall as December approached. Because of this, opspreads Trader V did not want to buy the high premiums. Instead, he chose to offset part of the high premium by creating a synthetic wheat/corn option position. More will be written about this later.

### Which Options To Buy?

Undaunted, the first opspreads Trader B bought two December wheat 310 calls at $0.16 each and two December corn 260 puts at $0.10¹/₂ each for a total cost of $2,650 (2 call options × $0.16 per bushel × 5,000 bushels plus 2 corn put options × $0.10¹/₂ × 5,000 bushels). The lower the strikes for both commodities, including calls and puts, the lower the implied volatilities. Both choices were slightly out of the money. Net debit is $0.53 per bushel, or $2,650. Two options of each were purchased to reach a delta closer to one futures contract.

### Profit Potential

Profit potential is unlimited if one or both markets go deep in the money.

### Risk

Risk is limited to the cost of the options, $2,650, plus commissions.

*Results on November 1, 1991*
    Wheat prices rose as expected, while corn futures shot up immediately
and then dropped. The Mikhail Gorbachev kidnapping in Russia failed
and caused the grain markets to drop temporarily, but then wheat continued trending up, while corn prices became choppy. On November 1 (see
Figures 10.6 and 10.7), the spread had widened and it was time to take
profits. Here were the prices:

$$\text{Dec wheat} = \$3.64 \; ^3/_4 \text{ per bushel}$$
$$\text{Dec corn} = \$2.54 \text{ per bushel}$$
$$\text{Spread} = \$1.10^3/_4, \text{ widened considerably from } \$0.39^3/_4$$

$$\text{Dec wheat 310 calls} = \$0.54^3/_4$$
$$\text{Dec corn 260 puts} = \$0.08$$

The option position, on the other hand, had moved as follows:

*Original Positions*
Buy wheat 310 call = $0.16        Buy corn 260 put = $0.10$^1/_2$

*Close-Out Positions*
Sell wheat 310 call = $0.54$^3/_4$        Sell corn 260 put = $0.08
Net = $0.38$^3/_4$ × 2 = $0.77$^1/_2$        −$0.02$^1/_2$ × 2 = −$0.05
Profit = + $0.72$^1/_2$, or $3,625 ($0.72$^1/_2$ × 5,000 bushels)

## Opspreads Scenario B: Wheat Gains over Corn, But...

Because of the currently high implied volatilities on August 1, 1991
for both the wheat and call options, acquiring the options would mean
opspreads Trader B would be buying high-priced options. In the above
opspreads strategy, the violent move to the upside in wheat overcame the
initial acquisition of high-priced premium.

*Which Options To Buy or Sell?*
    There is a way to diminish the amount of premium paid, but it
comes with a greater risk. If the futures spread were to narrow, opspreads Trader V's strategy would be to buy two December wheat 310
calls at $0.16 each for a $0.32 debit and sell two December corn 260 puts
at $0.10$^1/_2$ each for a $0.21 credit. Adding the $0.32 debit to the $0.21
credit, this strategy incurred a debit of $0.11 ($0.21 − $0.32 = −$0.11),
or $550 ($0.11 × 5,000 bushels). Note that the premium bought is offset
partially by the premium sold. In effect, this is a synthetic long wheat
versus corn spread.

**Figure 10.6**   Dec Wheat and Dec Corn Daily Bars

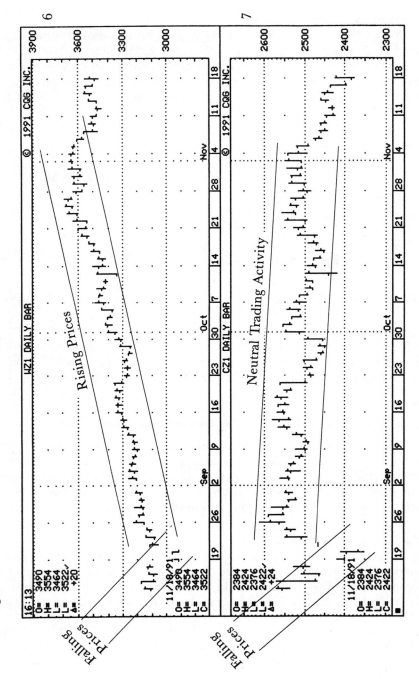

© 1991 CQG Inc. Reprinted with permission.

**Figure 10.7**  Dec Wheat/Dec Corn Daily Spread

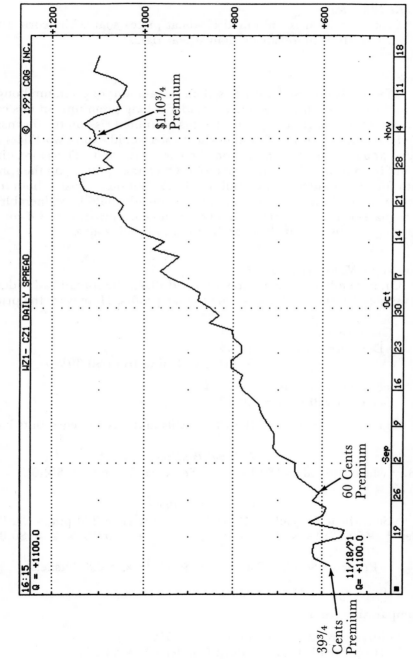

© 1991 CQG Inc. Reprinted with permission.

## Profit Potential

Profit potential is unlimited if wheat prices soar while corn prices stabilize or drop more slowly than wheat rises.

## Risk

The risk is now no longer based on the amount of premium bought, as in the other examples where the trader is long premium. In this case, because of the short put option, there is unlimited risk on the downside. If wheat and corn prices fall, the wheat calls would expire worthless and there would be unlimited risk on the corn puts sold. Therefore, there would be margin calls on the puts sold. Of course, putting on the spread with futures would also have unlimited risk, but on August 1, both markets were in a bull move and the futures spread would be vulnerable on both markets if wheat prices would dive and corn prices soar. Of course, stops can be used, but they can be used in options also.

## Results on November 1, 1991

On November 1 (see Figures 10.6 and 10.7), the spread had widened as we noted earlier and it was time to take profits. Here were the prices.

$$\text{Dec wheat futures} = \$3.64^3/_4$$
$$\text{Dec corn futures} = \$2.54$$
$$\text{Spread} = \$1.10^3/_4, \text{ widening from } \$0.39^3/_4$$

$$\text{Dec wheat 310 calls} = \$0.54^3/_4$$
$$\text{Dec corn 260 puts} = \$0.08$$

Time to liquidate: Sell the wheat calls and buy the corn puts back.

*Original Positions*

Buy wheat 310 call = $0.16          Sell corn 260 put = $0.10$^1/_2$

*Close-Out Positions*

Sell wheat 310 call = $0.54$^3/_4$          Buy corn 260 put = $0.08$

Net = +$0.038$^3/_4$ × 2 = $0.77$^1/_2$          +$0.02$^1/_2$ × 2 = $0.05$

Profit = $0.82$^1/_2$, or $4,125 ($0.82$^1/_2$ × 5,000 bushels)

## Comparative Analysis

Futures spread trader's profit = $3,550
First opspreads trader's profit (Trader B) = $3,625
Second opspreads trader's profit (Trader V) = $4,125

Recall that the second opspreads trader position (Trader V for volatility) was long the wheat calls and short the corn puts. Much of the cost of the wheat calls was offset by the sale of corn puts. The trader used the spread difference and implied volatility as the determining factors in selecting a trade. That offset unlimited exposure on the downside of the corn puts and the possible loss of the option premium on wheat. There was a terrible time in mid-August as both prices fell, the worst-case scenario was unfolding and margin calls were occurring. (See Figure 10.6.) Tension was high and the position close to being liquidated.

Opspreads Trader B had an advantage over the other two strategies because of limited risk. Recall that Trader B was long both wheat calls and corn puts. Going close to delta neutral, this strategy outperformed the futures spread despite the loss on the corn puts. The sharp move up in wheat and the increasing volatility overcame the high-priced options at the initiation of the trade. During the mid-August drop in the prices of both, there was peace of mind because corn put profits were offsetting losses on the wheat calls.

The futures spread trader would have been able to survive the mid-August crisis, as the spread did widen slightly.

The financial trophy, however, belongs to opspreads Trader V, with peace of mind advantage to opspreads Trader B and the futures spread trader.

### Third Case Study: Deutsche Mark To Gain on Swiss Franc

The final example, a Swiss franc and deutsche mark (D-mark) trade, showed an entirely different result than the previous two examples. The probability seemed strong in 1991 that the D-mark would gain on the Swiss franc, as it did in late 1987 and early 1988.

As background, Swiss franc contracts are traded in units of 125,000 francs. Each franc is quoted as $0.0001 fraction of a cent: 77.14 means each franc is worth $0.7714. Deutsche mark contracts are also traded in units of 125,000. Each mark is quoted as $0.0001 fraction of a cent, worth $12.50: 64.90 means each mark is worth $0.6490.

On January 7, 1991, March Swiss franc futures were at $77.14 and March D-mark futures were at $64.90, a spread of $12.24. The Swiss franc contract (see Figure 10.8) seldom traded at a premium of more than $12 in the past decade.

#### Case Study Data for January 7, 1991

The implied volatilities were high for both the Swiss franc and the D-mark, the Swiss franc at 14.2 percent and the D-mark around 13.5 per-

Figure 10.8    Swiss Franc/Deutsche Mark Weekly Spread

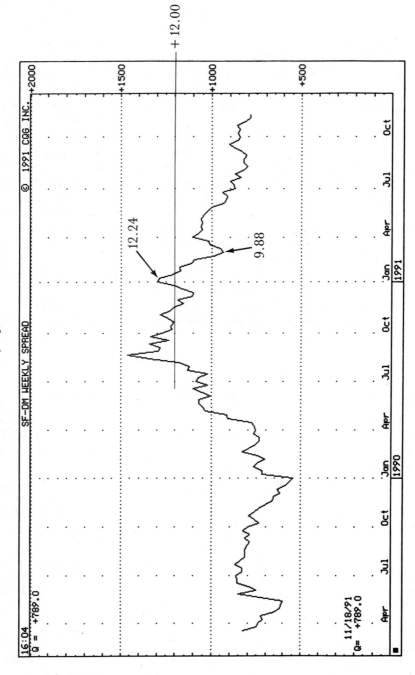

cent. Here were the prices of Swiss francs and D-marks on January 7, 1991:

$$\text{March Swiss franc futures} = 77.14$$
$$\text{March D-mark futures} = 64.90$$
$$\text{Spread} = 12.24$$

### March Swiss Options

| Strike Price | Call Premium | Put Premium |
|---|---|---|
| 77.50 | 1.59 | 1.94 |
| 77.00 | 1.82 | 1.68 |
| 76.50 | 2.00 | 1.45 |
| 76.00 | 2.37 | 1.25 |

### March D-Mark Options

| Strike Price | Call Premium | Put Premium |
|---|---|---|
| 65.50 | 1.13 | 1.73 |
| 65.00 | 1.35 | 1.45 |
| 64.50 | no trades | 1.21 |

### Spread Trader's Results on March 3, 1991

The trader who disdained the options, shorted the Swiss franc and bought the D-mark profited handsomely.

January 7, 1991
Sold Swiss franc at 77.14        Bought D-mark at 64.90
March 1, 1991
Bought Swiss franc at 74.79      Sold D-mark at 64.91
                                                        + .01

Net = +2.35
Combined Profit = +2.36, or $2,950

The spread did narrow from 12.24 to 9.88. (see Figures 10.8 and 10.9.)

### Deutsche Mark To Gain on Swiss Franc

The forecast was for the D-mark to gain on the Swiss franc. The spreads between the two currencies were at historically high levels, and it appeared they would narrow.

### Which Options To Buy?

Opspreads Trader B was excited about the wide spread and recommended the following strangle: Buy the D-mark 65.50 call at 1.13 and the Swiss franc 76 put at 1.25 for a debit of 2.38 or $2,975 ($0.0238 ×

**Figure 10.9** Swiss Franc and Deutsche Mark Weekly Bars

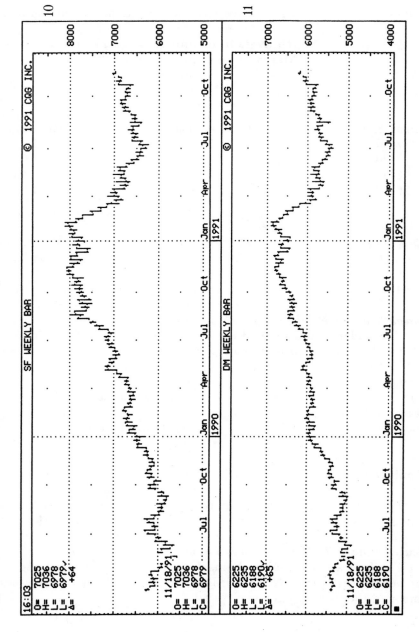

125,000 units per contract = $2,975). Both options were out of the money. To reduce costs, only one of each was purchased because of the high premiums. Previous examples dealing with options required two options each.

### Profit Potential
Profit potential of this strategy is unlimited.

### Risk
Risk is limited to the initial premium, $2,975, plus commissions.

### Results on March 3, 1991
The spread did narrow by March 1. The Swiss franc did fall, and the D-mark was near the price at which the trade was initiated. (See Figures 10.8 and 10.9).
Here are the prices on March 1:

$$\text{Swiss futures} = 74.79$$
$$\text{D-mark futures} = 64.91$$
$$\text{Spread} = 9.88, \text{ narrowed from } 12.24$$

$$\text{Swiss franc 76 put} = 1.79$$
$$\text{D-mark 65.50 call} = 0.18$$

This was not a good options trade.

*Original Positions*
Buy Swiss franc 76 put = 1.25        Buy D-mark 65.50 call = 1.13

*Close-Out Positions*
Sell Swiss franc 76 put =    1.79        Sell D-mark 65.50 call =    0.18
Net = +.54                                                            −.95
Loss = −.41, or 512.50 (0.0041 × 125,000)

Both markets were choppy, and although the spread worked, too much was paid for the options (the option sellers wouldn't agree). If the implied volatilities on January 7 were 10 percent, the Swiss franc 76 put would have been priced at 0.735 instead of 1.25, and the D-mark 65.50 call would have been priced at 0.77 instead of 1.13, a combined difference of .87!

## Premiums Too High

The high volatilities concerned the second opspreads trader, Trader V. However, he is intrigued with calendar spreads. Agricultural commodities are quite different from financial commodities when it comes to calendar spreads. June cattle are not the same animals as October cattle, July wheat is not the same as December wheat. Financials are more closely correlated between months. This trader looked at the June Swiss franc and June D-mark futures as well as the March expiration choices. In fact, the June options on both the Swiss franc and the D-mark were at *lower* volatilities than the March options.

Prices on January 7, 1991:

*Futures*

| | March | June |
|---|---|---|
| Swiss Franc | 77.14 | 76.92 |
| D-mark | 64.90 | 64.55 |

*Swiss Franc Options*

| Strike Price | March Put | June Put |
|---|---|---|
| 77.00 | 1.82 | 2.48 |
| 76.00 | 1.25 | 2.07 |

*D-mark Options*

| Strike Price | March Call | June Call |
|---|---|---|
| 65.00 | 1.35 | 1.82 |
| 64.00 | 1.88 | 2.32 |

The main purpose of a calendar spread is to take advantage of the time decay on the nearby option. Therefore, the trader sells the nearby option and buys the longer-term option. If the options are at the money, the spread is considered neutral. If the calls sold and purchased are out of the money, the spread is bullish, and if the puts utilized are out of the money, the spread has a bearish bent to it.

The currencies were in choppy markets, and opspreads Trader V opted for the calendar spreads. Out-of-the-money puts were selected for the Swiss franc: Sell the March 76 put and buy the June 76 put. For the D-mark, the choice was sell the March 64 call (at the money) and buy the June 64 call (in the money).

*Swiss Franc Put Positions*
Sell One Mar 76 put = +1.25
Buy One Jun 76 put = −2.07
$\qquad\qquad$ Net = −0.82 for a $1,025 debit

*D-mark Call Positions*
Sell One Mar 64 call  =  + 1.88
Buy One Jun 64 call  =  -2.32
                Net  =  -0.44 for a $550 debit
        Total debit  =  -1.26 or a total $1,575 debit

Opspreads Trader V was expecting the spread to narrow but didn't know when or how quickly. He did not want major moves up or down initially as the spreads between months would narrow and cause losses, albeit limited ones.

### Profit Potential

Profit potential is technically unlimited because the nearbys could expire worthless and then the more distant months could move in the "right" direction (i.e., Swiss francs down and D-marks up). Recall that if the March options expire worthless, this will leave Opspreads Trader V long a June Swiss franc 76 put and long a June D-mark 64 call.

### Risk

No set formula is used because different months are involved, but for practical purposes, the net debit is $1,575 (plus commissions).

### Results on March 1, 1991

Again, by March 1 the Swiss franc had fallen, but the D-mark had leveled into a trading range.

Prices on March 1, 1991:

|  | *Futures* | |
|---|---|---|
|  | *March* | *June* |
| Swiss franc | 74.79 | 74.54 |
| D-mark | 64.91 | 64.56 |

*Swiss Franc Options*

| *Strike Price* | *March Put* | *June Put* |
|---|---|---|
| 76.00 | 1.79 | 2.49 |

*D-mark Options*

| *Strike Price* | *March Call* | *June Call* |
|---|---|---|
| 64.00 | 1.05 | 1.72 |

Here are the results of the calendar spreads trying to take advantage of the spread between the Swiss franc and the D-mark.

*March Swiss Franc*
    Sell 76 put 1.25
    Buy 76 put 1.79
      Net = -.54

Profit = +.11

*June Swiss Franc*
    Buy 76 put 2.07
    Sell 76 put 2.70
      +.63

*March D-mark*
    Sell 64 call 1.88
    Buy 64 call 1.05
Net = +0.83
Profit = +0.33

*June D-mark*
    Buy 64 call 2.32
    Sell 64 call 1.82

−0.50

Profit on D-mark calendar spread = 0.33
Profit on Swiss franc calendar spread = 0.11
Total Profit = +$0.44, or $550

These are the results as of March 1. Look what would have happened by holding on to the June options. By June 3, the June Swiss franc had fallen to 67.01, and the D-mark had faded to $57.16. The profits of the Swiss franc put would have been fantastic, offsetting the loss of the D-mark calls and even outperforming the March futures spread. Such is the value of hindsight.

After March 1, the Swiss franc could have risen, losing all the value of the put, and the D-mark could have fallen (they did), eroding all the value of the call, but the Swiss franc didn't go higher.

## Comparative Analysis

Advantage all the way to the futures trader in this situation. Why? First and foremost, the premiums paid for both the Swiss franc and D-mark options were overpriced in January. Even the narrowing of the spread could not overcome the time decay and high volatility in the premium prices.

The calendar spread did not work as well as expected because of the price movement of the D-mark. However, had the June currency options been held to June, that would have been better than the March spread.

## SUMMARY

Using options instead of futures offers many alternatives to the spread trader. This chapter has shown the pros and cons of various strategies. Therefore, examine the following questions before doing the spreads.

1. Is the spread historically at levels seldom reached, either highest or lowest? You can feel more comfortable doing the options spread knowing that you can expect the wide spread to narrow, or the narrow spread to widen.

2. Is there a fundamental reason why the spread may continue out of line? Did events in the Soviet Union create an undue relationship in the Swiss franc versus the D-mark? If there are no sound, fundamental reasons to be out of line, then any aberrations can be expected to be only temporary. These situations offer prospective windfall profits.

3. Are the premiums overpriced? Are implied volatilities unusually high? If the premiums are overpriced, buying would mean that you are overpaying. The chances of making money on both figuring out the right direction of the markets and buying the right options would be that much more against you.

4. Are some strikes more reasonably priced than others? Even within series of options, there are biases causing the farther-out-of-the-money options to be more overpriced. The maximum optimized situation is to buy the option that has the cheapest inflated value.

5. Do you want to go delta neutral with the options? If you want to trade the equivalent of a futures contract, you can easily shift from the outright options positions to a futures hedged position.

6. How liquid are the options you're considering using? Liquidity is important because you can unload your options positions more easily if the options are more tradable.

7. Which months offer the better opportunity? Frequently, more distant options have lower volatility and therefore are better values to buy. Nearer options are more sensitive to the underlying's movements and therefore have greater implied volatility and are more overpriced.

8. Which strategy offers you more peace of mind? Only you can answer that. Some people don't feel comfortable having naked positions on and subject to margin calls. These traders would rather pay a premium to get no surprise margin calls. Others can take the risk.

# C H A P T E R   1 1

# Program Trading
# with Options

## BY JON NAJARIAN

**Editor's Note:**

Program trading is not new, for it came into being when the first stock index was tradeable as a futures contract. The concept is another class of arbitrage activity, this time played only between stocks indexes and either stocks or their derivatives, such as options or warrants.

Jon Najarian presents the concept of program trading in a simple manner. It's well thought out and emphasizes index futures features that make program trading workable. The implementation of program trading is presented pedagogically in this chapter.

The use of options in program trading is not a necessity. Options can be used as building blocks to create synthetic stock positions. Options, when applied in such a fashion, can be used as a proxy for the underlying stocks. Because of this unique feature, options are now an integral part of program trading.

Program trading strategies between commodities-type futures or options and commodities-type indexes are not as popular as those created between stocks or stock options and the stock indexes. This is due to the different expirations among the underlying commodities-type futures contracts. The program trader would have a difficult time aligning expirations of the commodities-type futures, options and index.

This is one particular strategy employed only by traders who have access to a huge capital base and excellent order executions.

$P$rogram trading is one of the most talked about, least understood forms of trading on Wall Street today. Just listen to the evening news and you're sure to hear something like, "Computer-driven sell programs eclipsed the morning's gains and sent the Dow down 35 points on heavy volume."

Can program trading be as bad as its headlines lead us to believe? Are there really rooms full of computers and greedy traders manipulating the stock market to suit their fancy?

This chapter explores some of these questions, poses additional questions and seeks to familiarize the reader with the concepts behind program trading and how they could be turned to the investing public's advantage.

## HISTORY AND DEVELOPMENT OF STOCK INDEX FUTURES

### Cash Settlement Boosts Popularity

Listed futures on cash commodities have been trading for over 100 years. In the original futures contracts there was no exchange of cash, but the ownership of actual slabs of pork bellies stored somewhere in a refrigerated warehouse, or thousands of bushels of soybeans stored somewhere in a granary. The relatively new stock index futures contract is similar to its agricultural-based brothers because it represents the future value of a product. The key difference is that the stock index futures contract settles into cash instead of actual cash products such as pork bellies or soybeans. At settlement, the difference in cash value between the inception and expiration of the trade is transferred from seller to buyer and vice versa.

The cash settlement feature elevated the stock index futures contract from the seat-of-the-pants, naked long or short strategies of typical commodity futures into an art form.

The stock index future is a cash-settled contract that represents an equivalent position in the actual stock index, and it is not settled until the contract's expiration date. This type of contract has several unique features. One feature is that it doesn't pay dividends. Another is that it doesn't require the full margin that would be required for the actual stock purchase. Hence, at expiration, when cost of carry and dividends payable or receivable are zero, the futures price will trade at parity with the actual cash value of the underlying stocks. Otherwise, an extra set of calculations and assumptions about dividends yet to be paid, or cost of money borrowed, must be factored into expiration value. Therefore, the futures value becomes exactly equal to the value of the actual stock index at the moment of expiration.

## Limitations on Early Program Trading

When index futures contracts were first developed, two problems arose that impeded the expansion of program trading. First, it took too long to execute orders, and second, the *downtick* rule restricted short sellers of stock.

### Immediate Executions

Until the Kansas City Board of Trade listed the *Value Line* Index contract, a trader wishing to place a bet on the direction of the stock market could only execute imprecisely through stocks or stock options. The technology to execute a significant percentage of stocks in a given index simultaneously did not exist in the marketplace. The individual stocks or stock options orders had to be placed through an order room, and the time spent waiting for their execution impaired the ability to trade profitably.

### Avoiding Downticks in Executions

Another barrier was the so-called downtick rule for listed stocks. After the stock market crash of 1929, the Securities and Exchange Commission ruled that a short seller of stocks could not establish a price lower than that of the immediately preceding sale. All listed stocks trade on either an uptick or downtick from the last trade of the security. A person who doesn't own the security he or she is selling can sell only on an uptick or unchanged price, never a downtick. This limitation on short sellers was designed to deter them from bullying a security to a lower price.

The new futures contract, however, would enable traders to sell the *Value Line* Index contract and "get short" the market very quickly at times when they might not be able to sell the stocks individually due to the downtick rule. Thus, the key to the initial success of the contract was not only its ability to serve as a surrogate for the market, but its ability to eliminate the risk of not being able to hit the bid on a group of stocks.

## First Index Is Not the Best: *Value Line*

Program trading has been driving the stock market since the *Value Line* Futures Index, the first stock futures contract, was introduced at the Kansas City Board of Trade in 1982. It allowed an investor to buy or sell the future price of an index of 1,800 stocks with a single transaction. The attraction for the investor and speculator was that, for the first time, they had the ability to go long or short the market in a single transaction. This feature was to become the key to the early success of the contract. The *Value Line* futures contract became one of the most actively traded futures contracts in the world.

The *Value Line* was traded physically in the traditional commodity-style trading pit. Brokers sought bids and offers from locals who tried to use their intuition and sense of market timing to buy or sell at the appropriate moment. A majority of the pit traders who supply the broker with two-sided markets are known as scalpers. The scalper seeks to purchase futures on the current bid and sell at the current offer, thus capturing the difference in price between the bid and offer. A steady, static market clearly favors the scalper, while an actively moving, volatile market favors the position trader. The contract would swing wildly as large buyers or sellers entered orders.

### The Successful Second Index: The S&P 500

It turned out that the Kansas City Board of Trade had brought out their *Value Line* futures contract mere weeks ahead of the Chicago Mercantile Exchange's introduction of its stock index future—the Standard & Poor's 500 Index.

The popularity of the S&P 500 quickly surpassed that of the *Value Line* contract. There were several reasons for this, but the most generally accepted was that the Chicago trading arena was already the center of the world's options markets, with the personnel and expertise to accommodate volume growth already in place. The Chicago Board Options Exchange provided a quick, efficient way for futures traders to hedge large futures sales or purchases. The Chicago Mercantile Exchange's product also had an additional edge: its contract size. The Kansas City *Value Line* Index future is based on the cash value of 1,800 stocks, while the Chicago Mercantile Exchange's S&P Index future is based on the cash value of only 500 stocks. The S&P product allowed traders greater participation due to the smaller margins on its 500 stock index.

The S&P 500 quickly became the benchmark futures contract. Open interest grew at an astonishing rate. During the boom or bust days of the 1920s, an investor had to put up 10 percent margin for stock purchases. But with the advent of stock index futures, traders, investors or hedgers could control $120,000 of stock market index value for as little as $6,000. This effective benefit was even more advantageous: it was only 5 percent "margin." (In the futures trading arena, the partial money used to control the futures contract is not considered margin, but "good faith deposit.")

## PRICING THE FUTURES CONTRACT

Before any stock index future was listed, scholars had argued that such an instrument would always trade at a premium to the underlying cash value of the index. Their theories were quickly disproven. Futures traded with oscillations in premiums. This was attributable to simple supply and demand. A large seller or buyer of the futures could cause the S&P 500 to rocket to either a substantial premium or discount from the cash index. As the average daily volume grew in the S&P 500, the need to effectively hedge and price the future became more important.

The first problem to address was the pricing of the futures contract.

### Program Buying and Selling

Since index futures contracts trade around the price of the cash index, the difference triggers buy and sell decisions for program traders. We can project the approximate additional premium or discount needed in the price of the future to trigger a trader's reaction to the disparity.

Upstairs traders were the first to start calculating the *fair value* of a given futures product. Once they were able to formulate a fair value, they created arbitrage plays against it. The term "fair value" of a future referred to its projected premium level.

Fair value is highly dependent on the players' perceptions. For instance, if you were trying to project the premium level a future should trade above its cash index value, you would calculate the value of the underlying cash value of the stocks, multiply that by the number of days until the future expires (and turns into the underlying cash value of the future), divide that by 365 (the number of days in a year), multiply that by the interest rate or cost of funds and, finally, add or subtract the dividends you would receive if you were long the stocks, or pay if you were short the stocks. (See Figure 11.1.)

## COSTS AND BENEFITS TO PROGRAM BUYERS AND SELLERS

First, let's take a look at the costs from the perspective of the two basket trading players:

1. The buyer of a basket of stocks versus short the futures
2. The seller of a basket of stocks versus long the futures

The cost to the buyer is not equal to the benefit of the seller and vice versa.

**Figure 11.1**   Long and Short Stock Formulas and Explanations

$$\text{Long stock value} = \left( \frac{\text{Stock value} \times \text{Days until futures expiration}}{365 \text{ days in a year}} \right) \left( \text{Interest rate} \right) + \text{Dividends}$$

$$\text{Short stock value} = \left( \frac{\text{Stock value} \times \text{Days until futures expiration}}{365 \text{ days in a year}} \right) \left( \text{Interest rate} \right) - \text{Dividends}$$

| **Short Basket** | **Long Basket** |
|---|---|
| • Program trader buys the futures contract and sells the underlying stocks. | • Program trader sells the futures contract and buys the underlying stocks. |
| • Trader receives interest on the value of the short stock. | • Trader pays interest to carry long stock position. |
| • Trader owes the dividends to the lender of the stock. | • Trader receives the dividends on the stock. |

**Cost to Buyer of Basket**

One of the key components in the pricing of the futures contract is the interest rate we use. When program trading became possible, the interest rate (broker loan rate) charged to a buyer of stock was approximately 10 percent. We use the following formula to calculate the fair value of the futures contract:

$$(R \times D \times I) \div (365 \text{ days in a year})$$

R = Risk-free interest rate
D = Number of days to hold positions
I = Cash value of index

We arrive at:

$$10\% \times 90 \times 200 \div 365 = \$4.93$$

$$\$4.93 - \$2.50 = \$2.43,$$

$2.50 being assumed dividend in this example

We find that the buyer of stocks versus a short futures position would expect to pay $4.93 to carry a long position. The program buyer would also receive the dividends paid on the stocks in his or her basket. For the sake of this example, we will say that the basket of stocks will pay $2.50

in dividends over the three-month period of the play. These dividends help defray the buyer's costs and reduce the total carry cost to $2.43.

### Income to Seller of Basket

The money received by the seller of stocks versus a futures purchase is different from the $2.43 buyer's costs. There are several obvious reasons for this. First, the seller doesn't pay to carry long stock, but rather is paid interest on the short value of the stock he or she has sold. Interest is paid to the seller on a percentage of the broker loan rate on the dollar value of the short stock. A standard arrangement would be 85 to 90 percent of the broker loan rate (large customers and firm traders can get even higher loan rates). Again using the fair value formula:

$$(R1 \times D \times I) \div (365 \text{ days in a year})$$

R1 = Risk-free interest rate credited
D  = Number of days to hold positions
I  = Cash value of index

We find the following:

$$(10\% \times .85) \times 90 \times 200 \div 365 = \$4.19$$
$$\$4.19 - \$2.50 = \$1.69$$

We find that the seller of stocks versus a long futures position would expect to receive $4.19, or $0.73 less than the buyer of stocks would have paid. Since the seller is short the stocks, he or she owes the dividends ($2.50), so the total credit would be $1.69 ($4.19 - $2.50 = $1.69).

A wirehouse often has a significant long stock position because of its clients' positions in stocks. One such wirehouse frequently found it necessary to trade the short basket position in order to offset the tremendous cost of financing its customers' long stock positions. Firms that could match long and short positions in-house could capture the full difference between the rate they charged their customers for stock purchases and their own cost of money. (In a firm the size of the now-defunct E.F. Hutton, generating a 2 percent spread on several billion dollars of long stock positions could be one of its largest profit centers.)

### Public Perceptions of Program Sellers

Another factor that sets program sellers apart from program buyers is the idea that program sellers are hurting individual investors by unscrupulously selling securities against their long futures. Rather than being viewed as a benefit to the marketplace by tightening the bid/ask spread and keeping the futures contract in line with fair value, program sellers are viewed as immoral thugs who care only about their own profit and nothing about the companies behind the stocks they are selling. Basically, program sellers are hated for the same reasons as short sellers. Although program sellers are not going naked short against their sale of the stocks, they are preying on the times of fear that send the S&P to a discount from fair value.

## TRADE EXECUTIONS: COST AND TIMING

There are significant costs to be considered by the program trader. The largest program traders will trade approximately 15 million shares of stock per month. Figure 11.2 illustrates the volume of program trading for a one-week period.

The stock transactions, then, are the single greatest cost associated with program trading. The costs of stock execution can be staggering, even though traders can negotiate very favorable rates. The cost of executing a basket of stock versus only 100 S&P 500 futures could be as much as $21,000. This commission cost is based on the assumption that there are transactions involving 1,000,000 shares of various stocks bought or sold at a cost of $0.02 per share. With entry and exit costs so high, there must be extreme profit potential in the trade to set the program trading machines into motion.

At other times, program traders buy all the futures they can get and sell a corresponding number of shares of stock in the companies that make up the basket.

The reader should now be aware that there are actually three different "fair values" for any given futures contract: the long stock value, the short stock value and the risk-free value of the futures contract. If a firm was carrying a long portfolio of stocks, their fair value would be vastly different from a firm with no long stock position.

### Costs of Executions Factored into Premium Value

The costs of trade executions are equal for both buyers and sellers of programs, so they do not affect the decisions to execute. However, commission costs must still be factored in once the decisions are made.

As a rule of thumb, the costs of establishing a "perfect basket" (that is, the exact replication of the underlying stocks in the index by buying or selling all the stocks) should be about $0.50 per futures contract.

If we assume a given future's fair value is $2.43 premium to the cash index, we would add the stock execution costs to arrive at a triggering value. Therefore, the computer-driven buy programs would kick in at a premium of greater than $2.93 ($2.43 + $0.50 = $2.93). At any pre-

**Figure 11.2**   Program Trading Volume by 15 Most Active Member Firms (Millions of Shares) from November 18–22, 1991

|  | Index Arbitrage | Other Strategies |
|---|---|---|
| Nomura Securities | 20.3 | 0.3 |
| Morgan Stanley | 0.7 | 18.3 |
| Kidder Peabody | 16.7 | 1.0 |
| First Boston | 7.9 | 7.1 |
| Susquehanna | 9.3 | 0.2 |
| UBS Securities | 6.9 | 0.6 |
| Bear Stearns | 3.4 | 3.1 |
| PaineWebber | 1.8 | 4.4 |
| Merrill Lynch | . . . | 5.8 |
| LIT America | 5.0 | . . . |
| W & D Securities | 0.1 | 4.4 |
| Goldman Sachs | 0.9 | 3.6 |
| Walsh Greenwood | 2.6 | . . . |
| Salomon Brothers | . . . | 1.7 |
| Swiss Bank | . . . | 1.5 |
| Total for 15 Member Firms | 75.6 | 51.7 |
| Total for All Firms Reporting | 77.9 | 55.1 |

Source: Reprinted by permission of *The Wall Street Journal*, © 1991 Dow Jones & Company, Inc. All Rights Reserved Worldwide.

mium level greater than $2.93, the program buyers could buy stock and sell futures and lock in a profit.

Conversely, sell programs would be triggered by a drop in premium to $1.93 ($2.43 − $0.50 = $1.93). Once the premium of the futures over the cash dropped to less than $1.93, program sellers would step in and sell stock and buy the futures and lock in a profit.

The program trader is merely seeking to capture an edge of as little as $0.20 per contract. The spreads between the futures and cash are margin-thin, but when executed in the large volume provided by this type of market, the rewards can be tremendous.

**Figure 11.3**   Path of a DOT System Order

DOT system allows trader to buy or sell
thousands of shares in a single keystroke.

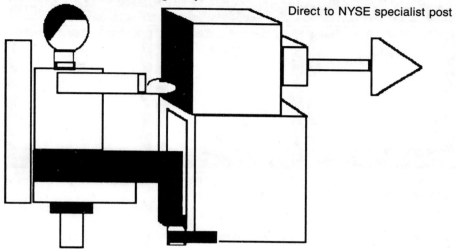

Direct to NYSE specialist post

## Speeding Up Trade Executions

The next hurdle to overcome was speed of stock trade execution. The question was how quickly a program trader could hedge his or her market risk from the futures markets by executing the other side in the stock market.

The New York Stock Exchange's Direct Order Transmission (DOT) system was the answer. Even in its crude, preliminary form it allowed a program trader to simultaneously send hundreds of stock buy or sell orders to the NYSE in a single keystroke. (See Figure 11.3.) Suddenly, NYSE specialists were no longer in total control of orders executed in their pits. DOT buy or sell orders needed no runner to carry the order from a stock booth on the periphery of the exchange to the specialist. The DOT system brought the order electronically to the specialist's post. (See Figure 11.4.)

Response time to initiating trades was reduced from minutes to seconds. Now a more risk-averse trader could consider program trading as a viable option: Position risk could be almost immediately offset. This tightened the spread between the futures bid and ask even further.

## STOCK WEIGHTING—ALTERNATIVES TO THE PERFECT BASKET RETURNS FROM PAST PROGRAM TRADING

In the early 1980s, pioneer program traders were earning triple-digit investment returns. As competition narrowed the markets, yields

**Figure 11.4**    DOT Screen

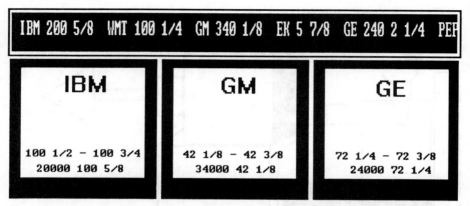

Program traders execute stock trades on the NYSE in seconds. Timing is critical to the profitable execution of the basket.

dropped correspondingly. The program traders had to take greater and greater risks to get smaller and smaller rates of return.

By the late 1980s, program traders all but abandoned the perfect basket. By trading selected, high-correlation stocks from the basket and eliminating low capitalization (and thus low-weighted) stocks from the basket, traders were able to cut their costs on stock execution and thereby increase returns.

The capitalization of a company is determined by multiplying the number of shares outstanding by the market price of the stock. For example, the capitalization of IBM would be determined by multiplying 571,391,000 outstanding shares by the stock price of $104 per share to get the capitalization of $59,424,664,000.

In a *weighted index* (not the futures contracts) such as the S&P 100 (OEX) or the S&P 500, the price of the index is determined by the price at which the various stocks are trading, weighted by their valuation. Put more simply, the more expensive and widely held the company, the greater its percentage of the index. Therefore, in a capitalization-weighted index such as OEX, 1,000 shares of IBM will have a greater effect on the price of the index than 1,000 shares of CCB (a company with 16,783,000 shares outstanding, trading at $419 with a capitalization of $7,032,077,000).

## Modified Baskets

As program traders began moving away from the perfect basket, the buzzwords became "tech-weighted" or "oil-weighted" baskets. Traders would remove the stocks that underperformed relative to the index and replace them with high-tech or oil stocks. This "weighting" process would accelerate the movement of their baskets. Their goal was at least partially achieved. They would go through quarters when their projections were accurate and the returns wonderful. Other quarters were not so profitable; program traders would lose if they incorrectly estimated the right balance of stocks in the modified basket.

## FUTURES VERSUS OPTIONS (SYNTHETIC FUTURES)

The most aggressive traders began trading the Chicago Board Options Exchange's S&P 100 Stock Index option (CBOE OEX) versus the Chicago Mercantile Exchange's S&P 500 future. Compare this with the instruments that were originally used in program trading: index futures against the identical cash index.

The program traders created synthetic long or short futures contracts in the CBOE's OEX option pit against which they could trade in other markets.

They established a synthetic long futures contract by buying an at-the-money call option and then selling the corresponding at-the-money put option in the S&P 100 Stock Index (the inverse would create a synthetic short futures contract). Once this synthetic long or short was established, the trader would take the opposite side in either the actual futures contract or the underlying stocks themselves.

If the aggressive trader elected to trade the synthetic long futures in OEX versus the short S&P 500 future, the arbitrage was far from a perfect basket. The S&P 100 Stock Index is made up of the top 100 capitalized stocks from the S&P 500, in effect a subset of the S&P 500. A primary difference is that the S&P 500 Stock Index future is much more heavily oil-weighted.

A typical trade might be made assuming that a given move in the OEX Stock Index implied an equal move in the S&P 500 future. Although the two indexes do track each other rather nicely, the relationship is not static, but constantly changing. A decline in the price of crude oil may cause all stocks to rise, but the spread between the OEX and S&P 500 would contract due to the more heavily oil-weighted S&P lagging the OEX.

### Rolling the Basket

Whether the program trader was trading the S&P future or OEX index versus the basket of stocks, at expiration either surrogate will turn into the cash value of the underlying stocks. Obviously, this will destroy the hedge against the long or short basket of stocks. Faced with this eventuality, the program trader must either roll the hedge to the next available month or close the position by buying or selling his or her basket of stocks on the close at expiration.

Since both the S&P 500 future and OEX options settle in cash, the purchase or sale of stocks on the close at expiration will establish the closing value of the trader's long or short S&P 500 future or OEX index. If, on the other hand, the trader elects to keep the position on, he or she must price the fair value of the next available OEX or S&P 500 and then close the near-term position and open a position in the next available term.

If the trader has a long synthetic in OEX versus the short basket of stocks, the position would look something like this:

Long 10,000 OEX Nov 365 calls
Short 10,000 OEX Nov 365 puts

Short $365,000,000 in the underlying stocks

To roll the position from November expiration to December expiration, the trader would execute the following trades:

Sell long Nov 365 calls    Buy short Nov 365 puts

Buy Dec 365 calls    Sell Dec 365 puts

short $365,000,000 in underlying stocks, untampered with.

This will effectively close the long synthetic in November and roll it to a long synthetic in December.

## Front-Running

A program trader who is unable to profitably roll a long or short position from the near term to the next available term is faced with the certainty that the expiring future or index options will turn into the cash value of the underlying. As discussed earlier in this chapter, the trader knows he or she must enter orders to buy or sell the stock hedge on the closing points to effectively close the position.

How could a trader use this information to disadvantage others in the marketplace? Let's take a program trader who has the long synthetic future against the basket of short stocks as an example. This trader has been unable or unwilling to roll the position from November to another cycle. The trader knows he or she is going to have to purchase $365 million worth of stock on the close of expiration Friday or else be forced to come up with $365 million cash.

Armed with this "inside information," the unscrupulous trader could wait until the last 20 or 30 minutes of trading on expiration Friday and start aggressively buying either futures, call options or actual stock (or a combination of all three). As the program trader's buy programs are executed on the close, the stock specialist makes adjustments that reflect the imbalance of buyers. The underlying stocks gap up and the expiring cash-settled options and futures are driven higher. There are rules in effect to limit the extent of this front-running, but there are so many entry points that it is extremely difficult to monitor and control this sort of activity.

## THE FUTURE OF PROGRAM TRADING

There is an old Chinese proverb, "You can never do but one thing." Anything that affects the stocks will impact both the futures and index options as well. Whether a seller elects to enter the short side of the market by selling stocks, selling S&P 500 futures, selling OEX 100 calls or buying OEX 100 puts, the seller's entry into one of those instruments will directly impact all.

The program trader's actions tighten the markets in the futures and the options. The short-term effects can move the market for brief periods of time, but even the largest program traders are not bigger than the market.

The CBOE's recent introduction of OEX caps (an option that has a fixed or capped total potential value) will provide yet another vehicle for the program trader. As both futures and options execution becomes available through electronic delivery systems (similar to the stock DOT systems), the spreads between futures and options prices will narrow.

These effects of program trading allow the marketplace to become more efficient and a more equal environment for all participants.

# CHAPTER 12

# Exploiting Volatility for Maximum Gain

*BY LEONARD S. YATES*

**Editor's Note:**

This chapter discusses one of the more difficult concepts for readers to understand—volatility.

The more difficult a strategy is to uncover and understand, the fewer the players. How does this philosophy play in the face of the age-old axiom that the simpler the concept is, the better it is? In this manner: There is knowledge that is knowable by a majority of the people, and there is knowledge that only a few can know. Simple concepts are created for most people to know, and as a result they all benefit; complex concepts benefit only a few.

The concept of playing the markets based on an expected valuation movement of options is not new. From the time standardized options were created by the Chicago Board Options Exchange, options valuations have played a valuable part for professional traders.

Stocks and stock options are related by several common denominators. One tie-in is based on the fact that options can be converted to the underlying stocks. Another relationship deals with the *expectations* of either market, stocks or their options, to move in a certain direction by investors and speculators. This is lumped under the all-inclusive term, *market sentiment*. This expectation can be seen in the change from inflated to deflated valuations of options or vice versa. From the perspective of the underlying stocks, overvaluation or undervaluation can be seen in other evaluation tools: momentum studies or breakout studies.

Len Yates uses valuation change as an indicator to execute decisions to buy or sell options. If premiums are inflated, he "fades" them by selling, expecting values to return to normalcy. If options premiums are deflated, he "fades" them by buying premium, expecting values to return to normalcy by picking up in premium value.

The author's strategy is to plot the change in premium valuation over time. When such charts show especially high or low volatility valuation relative to historical data, he acts on it. In this chapter, the reader discovers how the application of an advanced evaluation technique can be employed for above-average rates of returns. Where possible, price bar charts have been inserted to help readers correlate volatility changes with price changes.

When the *Voyager* spacecraft gave scientists a closer view of the planets and moons than they ever enjoyed before, it was supposed to answer questions and confirm theories. Instead, it opened up additional possibilities and showed us that our universe is more wonderful than we imagined. In the same way, close examination of the historical volatility graphs of a number of popularly traded assets reveals a variety of new possibilities in the area of volatility-based trading. There are many more ways of taking advantage of volatility than we've ever known.

## VOLATILITY-BASED TRADING

Almost everyone tends to think of options trading in terms of price-based trading: You buy or sell calls or puts based on what you think the price of the underlying instrument is going to do. If you're good at calling the turns and trends in the market, you can do very well at price-based trading.

But this is not the only way to make money. Volatility-based trading can also be very profitable, more reliable and less risky than price-based trading. Moreover, it does not require good price forecasting skills. It is more sophisticated than price-based trading, requiring more sophisticated tools such as computer software. Current volatilities are not printed in the newspaper, nor are they displayed on the screen of any quote monitors we know of.

The mechanism for profiting from volatility fluctuations is the option premium. Option premium levels rise and fall with expectations of how volatile the underlying asset is going to be. Essentially, you buy options when their premium levels imply "too low" a volatility relative to their underlying. You sell options when their premium levels imply "too high" a volatility for their underlying.

The most obvious kind of volatility-based trading uses the observation that volatilities, unlike prices, often tend to move within observable bounds. After moving to one extreme, volatility often returns, sometimes within a short time, to "normal."

Historical volatility charts can make it easy to see what "normal" volatility is for a given asset. They can also uncover assets whose options are chronically overvalued or undervalued, reveal special lead-time/lag-time situations and identify many exciting short-term opportunities.

In this chapter we will examine a number of historical volatility charts produced using OptionVue IV™ software. OptionVue IV™ provides implied and statistical volatility charts for every optionable asset in the U.S. While the charts used in this study cover a six-month period, the methods of interpretation are the same no matter how much data you have. More data will simply broaden your basis of observation and make for sounder decisions.

### Types of Volatility

Since option premium levels rise and fall with expectations of how volatile the underlying asset is going to be, a useful gauge for measuring premium levels is implied volatility (IV for short). Option premiums imply a level of volatility for their underlying asset. The more inflated the option premiums, the greater the expected volatility level in the underlying asset.

Statistical volatility, on the other hand, is a measure of how volatile the price behavior of the asset itself has been in recent days, weeks or months. This is often referred to as historical volatility, but we make this distinction between statistical and historical volatility: While both types can have a history, we reserve the term *historical* to mean how either of these volatilities has behaved over a period of time.

Options do not always behave according to statistical volatility. For one thing, statistical volatility has to do with the past (up to the present). Options premiums inherently reflect perceptions about the near-term future volatility of the asset. Hence the need for these two separate terms: implied volatility and statistical volatility.

## TAKING ADVANTAGE OF VOLATILITY

In looking at the charts for all of the most popularly traded assets, it is clear that there are more opportunities to do volatility-based trading than one might expect. Not only do the equity indexes and many individual stocks exhibit very "playable" volatility swings with observable floor levels, but there are also several instances of chronic overvaluation or undervaluation, obvious advantages of certain indexes for selling strategies and other indexes for buying strategies. There are also stocks where implied volatility lags actual volatility by a week or two, other stocks where the lag time is several weeks, and several unusual situations where implied volatility took a dip and came right back in less than a week.

Commodity option volatilities have a tendency to trend. In many cases the volatility can go to a low level and stay low for a long time. Volatilities for bond and currency options do not change much over time and might not be very useful for volatility-based trading.

In my opinion, volatility-based trading can be most lucrative in the equities and equity indexes. In the following pages we will look at charts, observe patterns and discuss which option strategies we can use to take advantage of them. We will also give some rules of thumb on when to close out a profitable position and when to cut losses.

We will discuss five different ways to take advantage of volatility:

1. chronic over/undervaluation
2. differences among the indexes
3. playing volatility fluctuations
4. miscellaneous special situations
5. volatility skewing

## Chronic Over/Undervaluation

In the category of chronic over/undervaluation of option premiums, the index options stand out. All index options seem to be chronically overvalued. Their implied volatilities ride higher than their statistical volatilities throughout the period under study. (See Figures 12.1 to 12.4.)

For example, the chart for the OEX (the S&P 100 Index option traded on the Chicago Board Options Exchange) shows that options typically trade at an implied volatility level four percentage points above the actual volatility level. This can make a substantial difference in the price of a typical option.

To illustrate, an at-the-money OEX call option with 50 days to go is worth $5^3/_4$ at a 12 percent volatility level and $7^5/_8$ at a 16 percent volatility level. This is a difference of $1^7/_8$ points, or about 30 percent. Out-of-the-money comparisons are even more dramatic. A 15-points out-of-the-money OEX call option with 50 days to go is worth $1^1/_4$ at a 12 percent volatility level and $2^1/_2$ at a 16 percent volatility level. This means that you can sell an option at $2^1/_2$ that is really worth $1^1/_4$ according to the way the underlying index really behaves.

What this says is that you should sell premiums and take advantage of these overpriced options. Some good strategies for selling premiums are:

**Figure 12.1**    S&P 100 Index Volatilities

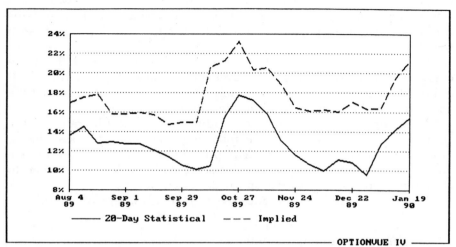

Source: OptionVue IV™.

**Figure 12.2**    S&P 100 Price Bar Chart

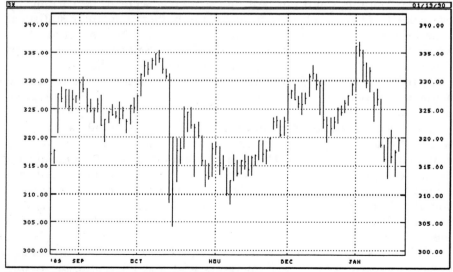

Source: MetaStock-Pro by EQUIS International.

**Figure 12.3**    NYSE (cash) Volatilities

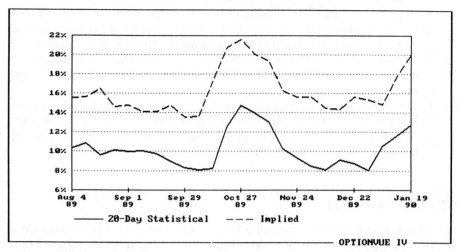

Source: OptionVue IV™.

**Figure 12.4**    Major Market Index Volatilities

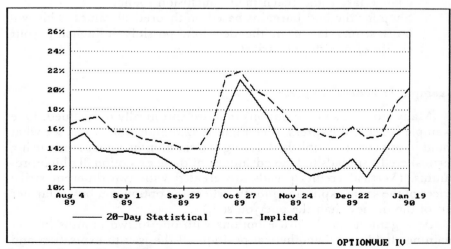

Source: OptionVue IV™.

- Out-of-the-money credit spreads. The credit spread strategy is perhaps the purest and most conservative way of selling premium.
- Butterflies. Butterfly spreads can be just as good but often provide less flexibility than credit spreads in picking the separate strike levels of your two sides (calls and puts) to take advantage of temporary bargains.
- Naked writing (preferably both sides, i.e., strangles). The sale of naked strangles is riskier and not as feasible as it used to be due to high margin requirements.
- Covered writing, in the case of assets where you could buy the underlying; covered writing is a completely different kind of strategy with unique characteristics, more appropriate for the investor who already holds optionable stocks.

## CREDIT SPREADS

Many of the specific examples in the remainder of this chapter deal with credit spreads. In selecting which strikes and months to use for a credit spread, you will want to do three things:

1. Go as far out of the money as it takes to make you feel comfortable. The farther out of the money you go, the more room you give the underlying to fluctuate without the need to adjust your position (i.e., cut losses). Going too far out of the money, however, can lower your prospective returns because the option premiums will be less than those closer to the money.
2. Choose a month you're comfortable with. The nearby months change faster and reach their conclusion sooner.
3. Shop for the best bargains based on theoretical values. This will be a strong factor in the decision, possibly influencing your choice of month and strike(s).

### Example 1: Federal Express

Many stocks also have options that are chronically overvalued. One example is Federal Express. (See Figures 12.5 and 12.6.) Let's see what could have been accomplished during the six months under study using vertical credit spreads to take advantage of these exceptionally high premiums. (Vertical credit spreads are created with two different strike prices of the same expiration month, where the option you buy is farther out of the money than the one you sell.)

As a game plan, we'll use options with one to two months life remaining, hold each hypothetical position all the way to expiration and then immediately put on another. [Editor's Note: Prices from newspa-

**Figure 12.5**    Federal Express Volatilities

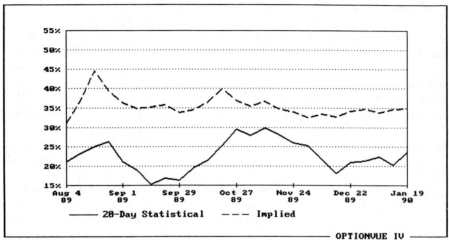

Source: OptionVue IV™.

**Figure 12.6**    Federal Express Price Bar Chart

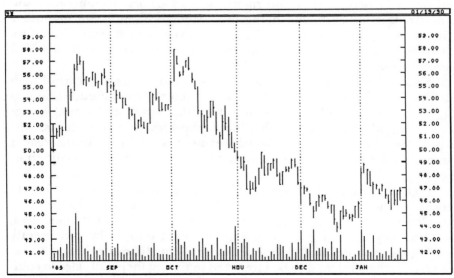

Source: MetaStock-Pro by EQUIS International.

pers may not adequately reflect actual market prices because they are merely the last sale prices of the options.]

On August 4, 1989, our first date of record in the charts, Federal Express stock was at 50¹/₈. We concentrate our spreading activity around the 50 strike price because the price of the underlying was closest to it. The Sep 50 calls were 2⁵/₈, the Sep 55 calls were ³/₄, the Sep 50 puts were 2, and the Sep 45 puts were ³/₄. Putting on credit spreads in both the calls and the puts would have netted a $312.50 credit per spread. (You sell the Sep 50 call at 2⁵/₈ and buy the Sep 55 call at ³/₄ for a credit of 1⁷/₈. You also sell the Sep 50 put at 2 and buy the Sep 45 put at ³/₄ for a credit of 1¹/₄; the total credit is 1⁷/₈ + 1¹/₄, or 3¹/₈.) Collateral requirement for the combined position would have been $1,000 ($500 for each spread).

At expiration the stock was 52. The Sep call has to be bought back in at 2, at a cost of $200. Since it was sold at 2⁵/₈, there was a profit of ⁵/₈. The Sep 55 call, which was purchased at ³/₄, went out worthless for a loss of that amount. The Sep 50 put was sold at 2, and it also went out worthless for a profit of 2 points. The Sep 45 put was purchased at ³/₄, and this went out worthless for a loss of that amount. Netting all four profits and losses (⁵/₈ − ³/₄ + 2 − ³/₄ = 1¹/₈), we are left with a profit of 1¹/₈ points, or $112.50 per spread. On a margin requirement of $1,000, this gave us an 11.25 percent (not annualized) return on collateral (commissions not included).

This and three other subsequent positions in Federal Express are summarized with their results in Figure 12.7.

Totaling the results, we would have a $606.25 gain on the $1,000 collateral, or 61 percent over four quarters. This ignores commissions and other transaction costs, but doing these spreads in sufficient quantities (five or more) will minimize the relative impact of such costs. Even if we factor in all these costs and reduce the annual return by half, the 30.5 percent return is very good.

Figures 12.8 to 12.10 list various assets and stocks in terms of high and low volatility as of October 11, 1991. [Editor's Note: Figure 12.8 lists high-volatility stocks that illustrate the author's text and strategy. Figures 12.9 and 12.10, on the other hand, show low-volatility stocks, currencies and indexes. These two figures are inserted to help the reader compare volatility differences only, not to be used with this specific strategy.]

Figures 12.11 to 12.16 are graphic plots of chronically high volatility stocks for the period from August 7, 1989 to January 19, 1990.

Covered writers should be very interested in finding stocks like these, because they can achieve much higher overall returns by consistently writing call options at slightly higher premiums than they ought to be. Covered writers might also be interested in timing their call sales to coincide with implied volatility peaks.

**Figure 12.7**  Closing Prices from *Investor's Business Daily*

Date:

| Aug. 4 | Sept. 18 | Oct. 24 | Nov. 20 |
|--------|----------|---------|---------|

Stock price:

| | | | |
|--------|----------|---------|---------|
| 50¹/₈ | 51⁷/₈ | 51 | 48 |

Option price:

| | | | |
|--------|----------|---------|---------|
| Sep 50c 2⁵/₈ | Oct 55c 1¹/₈ | Nov 50c 2¹/₂ | Jan 50c 2 |
| Sep 55c ³/₄ | Oct 60c ⁷/₁₆ | Nov 55c ⁹/₁₆ | Jan 55c ⁹/₁₆ |
| Sep 50p 2 | Oct 50p 1³/₈ | Nov 50p 1⁷/₁₆ | Jan 50p 3³/₄ |
| Sep 45p ³/₄ | Oct 45p ¹/₈ | Nov 45p ⁵/₁₆ | Jan 45p 1¹/₄ |

Net credit:

| | | | |
|--------|----------|---------|---------|
| 3¹/₈ | 1¹⁵/₁₆ | 3¹/₁₆ | 3¹⁵/₁₆ |

Stock price at expiration:

| | | | |
|--------|----------|---------|---------|
| 52 | 53¹/₄ | 49¹/₈ | 46⁷/₈ |

Position closed for net debit of:

| | | | |
|--------|----------|---------|---------|
| 2 | 0 | ⁷/₈ | 3¹/₈ |

Net profit:

| | | | |
|--------|----------|---------|---------|
| 1¹/₈ | 1¹⁵/₁₆ | 2³/₁₆ | 1³/₁₆ |

Source: Reprinted by permission of INVESTOR'S BUSINESS DAILY, *America's Business Newspaper*, (1989), ©INVESTOR'S BUSINESS DAILY. 1989.

## EQUITY VERSUS INDEX

If you prefer "higher octane" option plays than covered writing, then despite the large selection of stocks with chronically overvalued premiums it is probably best to use index options instead of stock options for three reasons:

1. Based on the historical volatility charts, the indexes have a more consistent, attractive differential, as discussed earlier.
2. Indexes are not subject to surprises such as mergers or bankruptcies, which can ruin a good premium writing strategy in stock options.
3. The large selection of available strikes and nearby months that you have with index options provides a great deal more flexibility to fine-tune a position and make adjustments when necessary.

### Differences Among the Indexes

The charts reveal another interesting observation about the indexes. Among the several most popular broad-based indexes, implied volatility

**Figure 12.8**    20 Best Assets in Terms of High Implied Volatility*

| | | | Current | | Historical | |
|---|---|---|---|---|---|---|
| Symbol | Type | RDVO | S.V. | I.V. | S.V. | I.V. |
| SCIS | Stock | 0 | 41.0% | 126.0% | 47.1% | 50.2% |
| RCSB | Stock | 2 | 94.7% | 111.0% | 44.9% | 50.5% |
| BLR | Stock | 2 | 60.4% | 93.8% | 72.9% | 77.9% |
| U | Stock | 35 | 65.1% | 89.3% | 44.6% | 52.5% |
| DIGI | Stock | 3 | 65.4% | 85.6% | 73.7% | 68.4% |
| CHPS | Stock | 11 | 75.7% | 83.6% | 66.4% | 64.0% |
| ZE | Stock | 2 | 49.1% | 83.6% | 46.1% | 59.6% |
| SQNT | Stock | 18 | 77.6% | 82.3% | 70.7% | 73.1% |
| GLN | Stock | 170 | 54.3% | 81.0% | 52.7% | 62.1% |
| MNTR | Stock | 35 | 86.1% | 79.4% | 61.8% | 60.7% |
| TATE | Stock | 231 | 35.1% | 79.4% | 59.4% | 64.3% |
| NSM | Stock | 3 | 65.7% | 78.0% | 59.6% | 62.9% |
| BLY | Stock | 1 | 62.1% | 77.5% | 77.7% | 86.3% |
| SNPX | Stock | 36 | 105.0% | 77.4% | 67.5% | 66.4% |
| SSI | Stock | 2 | 30.2% | 75.0% | 46.0% | 60.5% |
| CNF | Stock | 211 | 60.7% | 72.3% | 41.3% | 53.7% |
| TBY | Stock | 7 | 47.7% | 72.0% | 55.1% | 67.9% |
| WEN | Stock | 11 | 37.2% | 71.1% | 48.5% | 50.5% |
| CLIX | Stock | 60 | 60.8% | 70.8% | 72.3% | 67.7% |
| OCTL | Stock | 30 | 80.0% | 70.0% | 54.0% | 56.0% |

*Report based on data as of Oct. 11, 1991.

Source: OptionVue IV™ Database Survey

Note: RDVO (relative dollar value of options traded) is OptionVue's normalized ranking of specific option liquidity. A ranking of 2400 would be twice as "liquid" as a ranking of 1200.

levels are fairly equal, yet actual volatilities differ considerably, creating discrepancies to be exploited. (See Figures 12.1, 12.3 and 12.4.)

The Major Market Index (XMI) is the most volatile index, with actual volatility readings ranging between 12 percent and 21 percent. The New York Stock Exchange Index (NYSE) is the least volatile with readings between 8 and 15 percent. The S&P 100 Index (OEX) is in the middle, with readings between 10 and 18 percent. This means that if you want to sell premium, you should do it with NYSE options. If you want to buy premium you should use XMI options. The difference this can make is remarkable.

**Figure 12.9**  20 Best Stocks in Terms of Low Implied Volatility*

| Symbol | Type | RDVO | Current S.V. | Current I.V. | Historical S.V. | Historical I.V. |
|--------|------|------|------|------|------|------|
| HOU | Stock | 7 | 11.9% | 12.0% | 14.3% | 18.9% |
| D | Stock | 26 | 13.1% | 14.7% | 11.1% | 16.6% |
| SCE | Stock | 5 | 9.4% | 15.2% | 14.1% | 17.4% |
| TXU | Stock | 1863 | 11.3% | 15.2% | 15.9% | 18.8% |
| ED | Stock | 17 | 13.7% | 15.3% | 15.9% | 20.3% |
| CWE | Stock | 85 | 9.9% | 16.1% | 17.3% | 19.5% |
| XON | Stock | 248 | 16.4% | 16.3% | 19.6% | 19.2% |
| AEP | Stock | 14 | 12.9% | 16.6% | 14.7% | 18.4% |
| UN | Stock | 8 | 9.7% | 16.7% | 12.5% | 21.8% |
| NMK | Stock | 1 | 16.9% | 18.0% | 23.8% | 26.4% |
| MOB | Stock | 27 | 12.2% | 18.2% | 18.1% | 21.0% |
| PCG | Stock | 0 | 16.7% | 18.2% | 17.2% | 18.4% |
| TX | Stock | 42 | 13.6% | 18.5% | 18.4% | 20.2% |
| ETR | Stock | 3 | 13.0% | 18.6% | 16.7% | 19.7% |
| MMM | Stock | 63 | 14.4% | 19.2% | 17.2% | 21.5% |
| CQ | Stock | 5 | 11.6% | 19.8% | 18.7% | 30.0% |
| NYN | Stock | 41 | 12.4% | 19.8% | 15.2% | 19.9% |
| PEG | Stock | 5 | 14.5% | 19.8% | 18.2% | 20.8% |
| SO | Stock | 5 | 18.2% | 19.8% | 17.9% | 23.8% |
| TY | Stock | 0 | 11.7% | 19.9% | 16.9% | 21.0% |

*Report based on data as of Oct. 11, 1991.
Source: OptionVue IV™ Database Survey

For example, with NYSE options trading at a typical implied volatility level six percentage points above the actual volatility level, selling 5 percent out-of-the-money calls with 50 days remaining life allows you to collect a 1 1/2 point premium on an option that is really worth only 5/16, a 4.8:1 advantage.

With XMI options trading at a typical implied volatility level just two percentage points above the actual volatility level, selling 5 percent out-of-the-money calls with 50 days remaining life allows you to collect a 4 3/8 point premium on an option that is really worth 3 1/4, a 1.3:1 advantage.

In the middle ground, OEX options, trading at a typical implied volatility level four percentage points above the actual volatility level, selling 5 percent out-of-the-money calls with 50 days remaining life allows you to

**Figure 12.10**    20 Best Stocks in Terms of Low Implied Volatility*

| Symbol | Type | RDVO | Current S.V. | Current I.V. | Historical S.V. | Historical I.V. |
|---|---|---|---|---|---|---|
| CD | Currency | 306 | 1.5% | 2.7% | 3.0% | 4.4% |
| XCD | Currency | 28 | 1.6% | 4.7% | 2.2% | 5.3% |
| TY | Bond | 2978 | 5.0% | 5.5% | 5.0% | 6.5% |
| FC | Commodity | 80 | 6.6% | 8.1% | 6.7% | 8.9% |
| US | Bond | 44422 | 6.8% | 8.3% | 8.1% | 9.6% |
| AD | Currency | 21 | 4.2% | 8.9% | 4.5% | 9.8% |
| LC | Commodity | 625 | 9.4% | 10.3% | 9.6% | 10.9% |
| XAD | Currency | 58 | 3.4% | 10.4% | 3.9% | 10.4% |
| DX | Currency | 1163 | 8.0% | 10.5% | 9.4% | 12.2% |
| JY | Currency | 3236 | 6.2% | 10.8% | 7.7% | 10.7% |
| GC | Commodity | 1059 | 8.1% | 11.3% | 12.2% | 16.4% |
| UTY | Index | 132 | 7.7% | 11.6% | 9.7% | 11.4% |
| XJY | Currency | 583 | 5.2% | 11.6% | 5.7% | 11.3% |
| BP | Currency | 1070 | 9.3% | 11.9% | 9.0% | 12.0% |
| HOU | Stock | 7 | 11.9% | 12.0% | 14.3% | 18.9% |
| DM | Currency | 8049 | 9.6% | 12.2% | 9.7% | 12.1% |
| SF | Currency | 1287 | 9.4% | 12.3% | 11.1% | 12.5% |
| XBP | Currency | 430 | 6.4% | 12.4% | 6.6% | 12.2% |
| XSF | Currency | 449 | 6.6% | 13.3% | 8.0% | 13.4% |
| XDM | Currency | 2060 | 7.0% | 13.4% | 7.3% | 12.5% |

*Report based on data as of Oct. 11, 1991.
Source: OptionVue IV™ Database Survey

collect a 2¹/₂ point premium on an option that is really worth 1¹/₄, a 2.0:1 advantage.

Traders with sufficient collateral might like to work both sides of this for a really pure volatility play—a kind of "volatility arbitrage," if you will. You would buy straddles in the XMI and simultaneously sell straddles in the NYSE. By making each straddle delta neutral with the appropriate ratio between puts and calls, plus doing an appropriate ratio between the two indexes (inversely proportional to their relative prices and betas), you can establish a position that is immune to market price changes and overall volatility changes. As you approach expiration, this position is bound to pay off: If there is little movement in the market, your NYSE straddle will gain more than the XMI straddle loses; if there is much movement in the market, your XMI straddle will gain more than

**Figure 12.11**    Litton Industries Volatilities

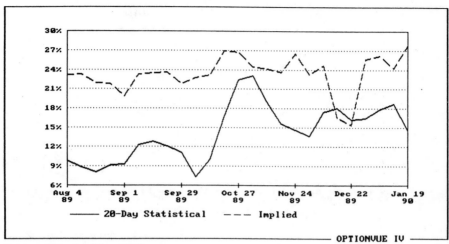

Source: OptionVue IV™.

**Figure 12.12**    St. Jude Medical Volatilities

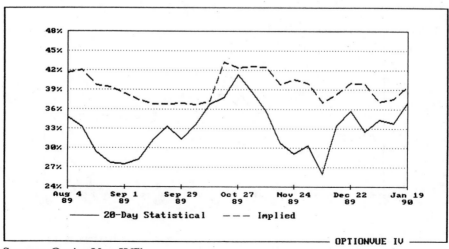

Source: OptionVue IV™.

**Figure 12.13**    Aluminum Co. of Am. Volatilities

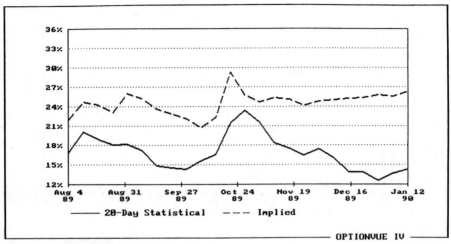

Source: OptionVue IV™.

**Figure 12.14**    American Cyanamid Volatilities

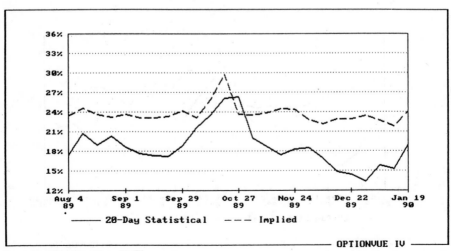

Source: OptionVue IV™.

**Figure 12.15**    Aristech Chemical Volatilities

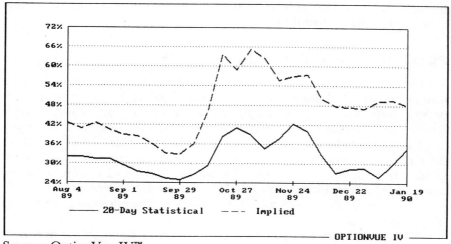

Source: OptionVue IV™.

**Figure 12.16**    Coca-Cola Co. Volatilities

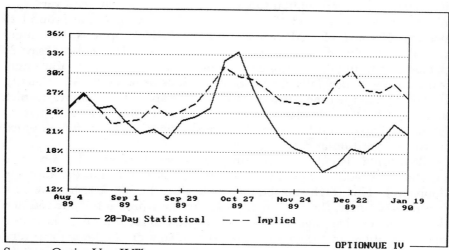

Source: OptionVue IV™.

the NYSE straddle loses. Sufficient collateral is required to cover for the naked writing of NYSE options. (Brokerages will not be able to recognize the long XMI options as a cover for the NYSE options, even though that is practically what they do.)

## PLAYING VOLATILITY FLUCTUATIONS

From the charts, you can see that almost every asset has its own unique volatility characteristics—how subdued it gets during a quiet period, how active it gets during a volatile period and whether there seem to be observable volatility cycles. You can also observe how its implied volatility behaves relative to its statistical volatility. Implied volatility levels often depend on the kind of control exerted by the market makers in each asset's options. The market makers in Exxon stock options, for example, hold implied volatility at a relatively constant 16 to 19 percent, even while the stock itself exhibits volatilities ranging from 14 to 27 percent.

Unlike ordinary price fluctuations, volatility fluctuations are more likely to exhibit observable floor levels, transition times and even ceiling levels. It stands to reason that volatility patterns would be this reliable. Fischer Black, coauthor of the Black-Scholes model, observes: "Changes in volatilities are often temporary; after a significant change up or down, volatilities seem to revert back toward their previous levels." (See *Options Markets* by Cox and Rubinstein, Prentice-Hall, p. 280, "Fischer Black's Approach to Estimating Volatility.")

Quite a number of stocks and indexes exhibit volatility patterns that can be used for handsome gains. For example, from the historical volatility chart for the ever-popular OEX (Figure 12.1), you can see a very definite floor level at around 16 percent as well as two peaks at around 23 percent. If you preferred to sell premium in OEX options, you might time the opening of such positions to coincide with levels above, say, 20 percent. (I wouldn't recommend trying to catch the peaks. You might miss out if volatility falls just short of previous peak levels. Additionally, it appears that the time between peaks can be about three months, which could be a bit long. Notice that implied volatility stays above 20 percent for more than a month in one of the peaks, which is long enough to exhaust one position and open another.)

You could also play the volatility upswings. For example, you could purchase a straddle when implied volatility settles down to the apparent floor level. This might not be advisable with the indexes, however, for two reasons: first, the perpetually high options premiums put you at a theoretical disadvantage, and second, as you can see from the charts, implied volatilities in the indexes can tend to stay on the floor for several weeks. Without knowing when the next upswing might occur, one or two straddle positions could rot on your shelf before the movement you need finally arrives. It might be possible to hold back and try to catch an upswing in its early stages, but this would require close monitoring because volatility can increase suddenly.

Among stocks, some especially promising fluctuation patterns are those of Bolar Pharmaceutical, Philip Morris, Disney, Wal-Mart Stores and Dow Chemical.

### Example: Bolar Pharmaceutical

Bolar Pharmaceutical is an especially good example. (See Figure 12.17 and 12.18.) From the volatility chart you can see that its implied volatility swung several times between 49 and 70 percent. If you had bought a straddle every time implied volatility was at 49 percent and sold it as soon as implied volatility reached 70 percent, the results would have been impressive. Refer to the Bolar Pharmaceutical chart for the indicated buy and sell points. Using old option prices from the newspapers, here is what reasonably could have been done:

Aug 4, 1989, with stock at $27^3/_4$ and volatility at 49 percent:
Buy Oct 30 call at $1^3/_4$
Buy Oct 25 put at $1^1/_8$
Debit = $-2^7/_8$

Aug 7, with stock at 21 and volatility at 70 percent:
Sell Oct 30 call at $^3/_4$
Sell Oct 25 put at $5^3/_8$
Credit = $6^3/_8$

Profit = $3^1/_2$ ($6^3/_8 - 2^7/_8$), or a 122 percent gain in 3 days

Aug 28, with stock at $26^1/_4$ and volatility at 51 percent:
Buy Oct 25 call at $2^5/_8$
Buy Oct 25 put at $1^5/_8$
Debit = $-4^1/_4$

Sep 11, with stock at 19 and volatility at 69 percent:
Sell Oct 25 call at $^1/_4$
Sell Oct 25 put at $6^1/_4$
Credit = $6^1/_2$

Profit = $2^1/_4$ ($6^1/_2 - 4^1/_4$), or a 53 percent gain in 17 days

**Figure 12.17**    Bolar Pharmaceutical Volatilities

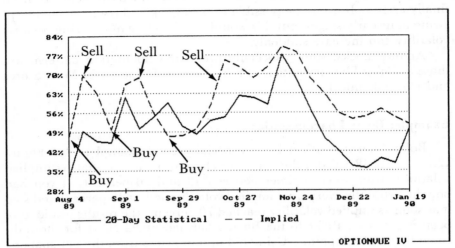

Source: OptionVue IV™.

**Figure 12.18**    Bolar Pharmaceutical Price Bar Chart

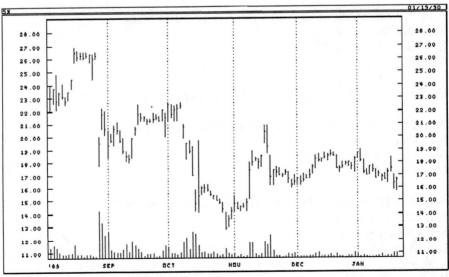

Source: MetaStock by EQUIS International.

Sep 25, with stock at 21³/₈ and volatility at 48 percent:
Buy Nov 22¹/₂ call at ⁷/₈
Buy Nov 20 put at ⁷/₈
Debit = -1³/₄

Oct 20, with stock at 15¹/₂ and volatility at 69 percent:
Sell Nov 22¹/₂ call at ¹/₄
Sell Nov 20 put at 5
Credit = 5¹/₄

Profit = 3¹/₂ (5¹/₄ - 1³/₄), or a 200 percent gain in 26 days

**Example: Philip Morris**

Another good example is Philip Morris (Figures 12.19 and 12.20),
which seems to swing back and forth between levels of 21 percent and 35
percent. Refer to the chart for the indicated buy and sell periods. Based
on actual option prices at the time, you could have made the following
trade:

Sep 25, with stock at 155¹/₂ and volatility at 21 percent:
Buy Nov 155 call at 6¹/₈
Buy Nov 155 put at 4¹/₈
Debit = -10¹/₄

The stock is now split and the number of options positions is four
times the original.

Oct 19, with stock at 44¹/₂ and volatility at 34 to 35 percent:
Sell 4 Nov 38³/₄ call at 6¹/₂
Sell 4 Nov 38³/₄ put at ¹/₈
Credit = 26¹/₂

Minus 10¹/₄ + 26¹/₂ Profit = 16¹/₄ (26¹/₂ - 10¹/₄), or a 159 percent gain
in 25 days

Having four times the number of option contracts than you started
with, the net profit would be (6.625 x 4) - 10.25, or a 159 percent gain.

However, the next apparent buying time in Philip Morris—mid-
December—would not have led to a profitable trade. Your straddle
would have languished as the stock price went nowhere for weeks. Fortunately, with straddles you seldom experience a total loss because that

**Figure 12.19**    Philip Morris Volatilities

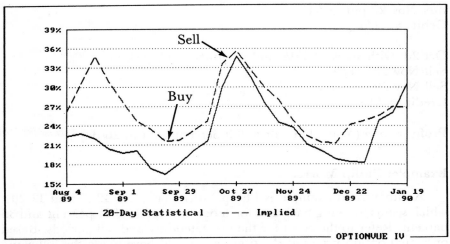

Source: OptionVue IV™.

**Figure 12.20**    Philip Morris Price Bar Chart

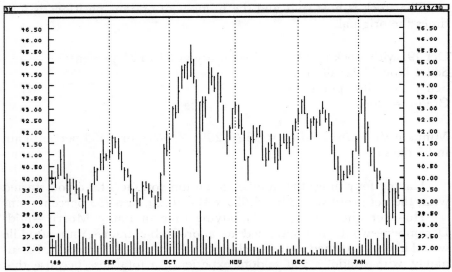

Source: MetaStock-Pro by EQUIS International.

would require the stock to land precisely on the strike price at expiration.

We've been using straddles in these examples, but you can use other strategies, including out-of-the-money vertical debit spreads and horizontal debit spreads, to take advantage of a volatility upswing. In the author's opinion, however, the most powerful strategy, for its return on investment and limited risk, is the simple straddle purchase.

When buying a straddle, you will want to purchase options with six to eight weeks or more remaining life, provided that they are liquid. This is to ensure the needed time frame (the charts show that it sometimes takes as long as five weeks for implied volatility to rise again after it has come down). Don't be discouraged by the higher price of longer-term options. While they cost more, longer-term options always exhibit a higher *vega*—volatility sensitivity, as well as a lower *theta*—time decay rate. This is exactly what you want. You want high vega so that when volatility goes up you have the options that will respond the most. You also want low theta so that your position loses little to time while you wait.

Your choice of strike depends on risk preferences and possible available bargains. At-the-moneys are more conservative than out-of-the-moneys and have higher vegas. Because of their higher leverage, out-of-the-moneys are potentially more rewarding if the underlying itself makes a volatile move.

A good rule of thumb for timing a straddle sale is when implied volatility has swung to the upper extremes or at least returned to normal, depending on the pattern and how you want to play it, or when the straddle has achieved your profit objective. You don't want to continue holding a straddle after one side has become deep in the money and the other side is almost worthless. Then, for all practical purposes, it is no longer a straddle but a single-option position with its attendant risk. Since deep-in-the-money options and far-out-of-the-money options exhibit almost no vega, your options will not respond when your stock finally does have a volatility increase. So, if the stock is still a good straddle-purchase candidate, sell your old straddle and buy a new one.

As for a losing position, while this is a subjective matter, I would not use a stop loss. I would continue to hold on to the straddle until implied volatility returned to normal. If implied volatility did not return to normal before the options had less than 20 days to go, I would close out (or adjust) the straddle early because its vega will have deteriorated.

### Example: Disney Productions

As a final example, we will look at Disney (Figures 12.21 and 12.22). It has an apparent implied volatility floor level of 24 percent. If you were to have purchased a Disney straddle both times Disney's implied volatil-

**Figure 12.21**   Disney Productions Volatilities

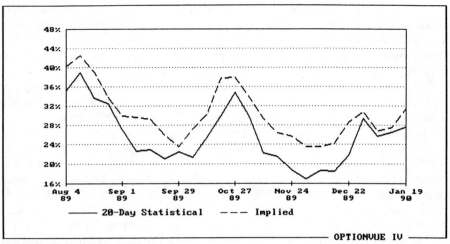

Source: OptionVue IV™.

**Figure 12.22**   Disney Price Bar Chart

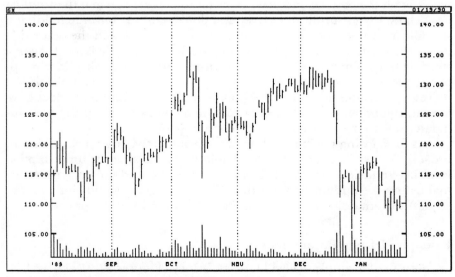

Source: MetaStock-Pro by EQUIS International.

ity fell to 24 percent, and then sold when the implied volatility rose to about 30 percent, your results would have been as follows:

Sep 29, with stock at 120⅞:
Buy Nov 120 call at 5⅛
Buy Nov 120 put at 3¼

Oct 9, with stock at 134⅛:
Sell Nov 120 call at 15⅛
Sell Nov 120 put at ¾
90 percent gain.

Nov 29, with stock at 128¾:
Buy Jan 130 call at 4¾
Buy Jan 130 put at 4¾

Dec 27, with stock at 109⅞:
Sell Jan 130 call at ⅛
Sell Jan 130 put at 21¾
130 percent gain.

Thirty percent was selected as the upside target because, while volatility went as high as 38 percent one time, it reached only 30 percent another time. This illustrates the point that sometimes it might be safer to set your volatility target at about average and not wait for volatility to swing all the way to its previous extreme.


## SPECIAL SITUATIONS

When looking through charts, you sometimes come across unique situations. We picked out two to demonstrate here:

### Example: BellSouth Corporation

This stock shows an interesting "lag" tendency. Its implied volatility seems to lag behind statistical volatility by approximately one month. (See Figure 12.23.) With statistical volatility very high at the end of this period and still rising, we would consider buying a straddle to benefit from the increased option premiums when implied volatility eventually catches up, presuming it will. (Even if implied volatility never rises, the increased volatility now evident in the stock should help our straddle.)

On January 19, 1990, with BellSouth stock at 52⅝, we may have

**Figure 12.23**    BellSouth Corp. Volatilities

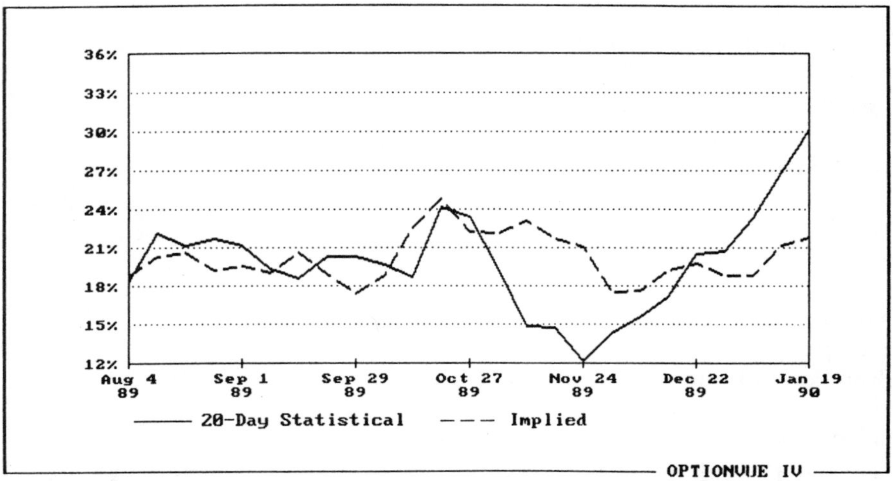

Source: OptionVue IV™.

bought the Feb 50 calls at $3^{1}/_{4}$ and the Feb 55 puts at $2^{5}/_{8}$. As of January 30, 1990, this position was still open and looks even more profitable.

**Example: Ford**

If you look at Figure 12.24, you will see that even though the volatility of the market in general has risen dramatically by the end of this period, Ford volatilities haven't risen at all. They should. One of Fischer Black's easily confirmed observations about volatility is that "volatilities of different stocks tend to change together in the same direction." The implication is to buy a Ford straddle immediately, expecting that Ford options will eventually rise in sympathy with the rest of the market.

So, on January 19, with the stock at $44^{3}/_{4}$, we may have bought the Feb 45 calls at $^{5}/_{8}$ and the Feb 45 puts at $1^{1}/_{2}$, for a net cost of $2^{1}/_{8}$. Implied volatility soared the following week as Ford stock dropped to $41^{1}/_{2}$. At this point, we may have sold the straddle for a net $3^{1}/_{2}$, a gain of 65 percent.

**VOLATILITY SKEWING—THE "OUT-OF-THE-MONEY PHENOMENON"**

Ever since the panic of 1987, index options have exhibited what is generally called *volatility skewing*. Out-of-the-money puts trade at pro-

**Figure 12.24**   Ford Motor Volatilities

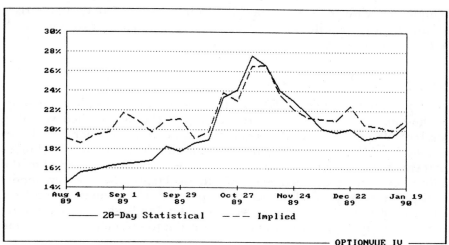

Source: OptionVue IV™.

gressively higher implied volatility levels the farther out of the money you go. At the same time, out-of-the-money calls trade at progressively lower implied volatility levels the farther out of the money you go. At times this skewing is worse than at others, but at the time of this writing, a difference of six percentage points from at the money to far out of the money is typical.

One explanation for this is that institutional portfolio managers buy protection for their long stock positions through purchased puts and/or sold calls, continually driving the market makers near their position limits in these options. Being near their position limits and not wanting to take on additional short puts and/or long calls, the market makers shift their prices accordingly.

Another plausible explanation is that the market seldom makes an upward move as dramatic as many of its downward moves. Maybe so, but does Wall Street have that good a memory? The first explanation seems more solid. Why did October 1987 mark the starting point for this phenomenon? Probably because the panic sell-off did such terminal damage to "portfolio insurance" as a method of risk control, increasing the need for index puts and calls.

Whatever the cause, however, this volatility skewing is unnatural and represents a profit opportunity. The first strategies that come to mind are put debit spreads and call credit spreads, since both of these would involve selling an option that is priced too high relative to the option you are buying. Unfortunately, both strategies are inherently bearish, and unless you are bearish on the market you may have to do some ratioing to take out the bearish bias. Ratioing will introduce naked options into the picture, with their high margin requirements and undesirable risk. Consequently, we will look at the following example in two ways: with and without ratioing.

### Example: OEX Spread

On January 2, 1990, OEX was trading at around 336. The just-out-of-the-money Jan 330 puts were trading at $2\frac{3}{8}$, an implied volatility level of 19 percent. At the same time, the much-farther-out-of-the-money Jan 315 puts were trading at $\frac{3}{4}$, an implied volatility level of 24 percent. If the 315s had been trading at the same volatility level as the 330s, they would have been nearly worthless. Hence, there was an opportunity to buy a spread between these puts for $1\frac{5}{8}$, which should have cost $1\frac{1}{2}$ or more. (This trade was not found in hindsight. The author actually noted the opportunity and mentioned it to several people the same day.)

In subsequent days, with the market moving briskly lower, the value of this spread grew to its eventual maximum of 15 points (the difference between the strike prices: $330-315 = 15$). The fact that the market moved the right way, however, was just luck as far as we're concerned. If the market had moved higher, we may have lost money. The point is that with options on the same asset trading at levels so disparate from each other, probabilities in the long run favor the investor who takes such positions (perhaps with a success rate of 60 to 70 percent). It's like spinning quarters on a table: They come up tails some of the time, but because of a slight weight displacement they come up heads much more often.

You can play the spread this way (1:1) and count on losing 30 to 40 percent of the time, or you can ratio away the market risk. This involves selling a greater number of the far-out-of-the-money options than the near-the-money options bought. The optimum ratio can be computed easily with computer software to tell you the delta of each option. On the day we opened this position, the delta of the near-the-moneys was 42 and the delta of the out-of-the-moneys was 11. This indicates a nearly perfect 4:1 ratio. You sell four out-of-the-moneys for each near-the-money you buy.

This gives you temporary immunity to price changes in the underlying—temporary because the passing of time and new price levels in the underlying bring new option deltas. Hence, you will have to keep an eye on this kind of investment and make occasional adjustments to bring it back to delta neutral.

With the market falling so rapidly after January 2, a ratio spread between the two options cited above would have probably fared worse than a simple 1:1 spread because the falling market would have forced you to adjust your position one or two times—buying in the 315s at a loss or buying more of the 330s at increasingly higher prices. This occurrence is probably more the exception than the rule, however. Ratioing can be worth the trouble for those who have sufficient collateral to do naked writing because it amplifies the advantage of the mispricing while reducing your exposure to price changes in the underlying. Those who do naked writing should be fully aware of the risks.

## CONCLUSION

Options trading has been compared to playing a 3-D chess game. Indeed, there are three primary dimensions to options trading: price, time and volatility. Everyone is familiar with thinking of options in terms of price—using one strategy or another to take advantage of an expected price change in the underlying. This is referred to as price-based trading. Success with price-based trading requires good skills at predicting price swings.

There is very little that can be done with the second dimension—time—because it has no fluctuations, only a steady forward progress. Certainly we have to deal with time, and we can pick a strategy that we believe places time on our side, but we cannot trade time.

The only other thing we can trade is volatility. Very few traders are used to thinking of profiting from options in this way. However, volatility itself ebbs and flows as price does, and you can take advantage of these fluctuations using options.

# APPENDIX A

# Options Trading Fact Sheet

| Option | Exchange | Tick Value | Trading Months | Trading Hours (CST) | Last Trading Day (subject to change) |
|--------|----------|-----------|----------------|---------------------|--------------------------------------|
| | | | **Financial** | | |
| Treasury Bonds | CBT | 01 = $15.63 | All | 7:20–2:00 5:00–8:30 | Friday (12:00 CST) that precedes contract month by at least 6 business days |
| Treasury Notes | CBT | 01 = $15.63 | All | 7:20–2:00 5:00–8:30 | Friday (12:00 CST) that precedes contract month by at least 6 business days |
| Eurodollar | IMM | 01 = $25.00 | H, M, U, Z | 7:20–2:00 | First Monday preceding third Wednesday of contract month |
| S&P 500 | CME | 05 = $25.00 | All | 8:30–3:15 | Third Thursday of contract month (quarterly) Third Friday of contract month (serial) |
| NYFE | NYFE | 05 = $25.00 | All | 8:30–3:15 | Third Thursday of contract month (quarterly) Third Friday of contract month (serial) |
| NIKKEI | CME | 05 = $25.00 | All | 8:00–3:15 | Second Friday of contract month (quarterly) Friday preceding third Saturday of contract month (serial) |
| TOPIX | CBT | 1/100 = ¥2,000 | H, M, U, Z | 7:00–2:00 5:40–8:15 | Second Thursday of month |
| Japanese Govt Bonds | CBT | 1/2 pt = ¥2,500 | H, M, U, Z | 7:00–2:00 5:40–8:15 | Friday (12:00 CST) of month preceding contract month by at least 6 business days |

**Metals, Currencies and Oils**

| | | | | | |
|---|---|---|---|---|---|
| Copper | CMX | 05 = $12.50 | H, K, N, U, Z | 8:25–1:00 | Second Friday of month preceding contract month |
| Gold | CMX | 01 = $10.00 | All | 7:20–1:30 | Second Friday of month preceding contract month |
| Silver | CMX | 01 = $5.00 | H, K, N, U, Z | 7:25–1:25 | Second Friday of month preceding contract month |
| Platinum | NYMEX | 01 = $5.00 | F, J, N, V | 7:00–1:30 | Friday preceding first Saturday of contract month |
| Swiss Franc Deutsche Mark British Pound Japanese Yen | IMM | 01 = $12.50 | All | 7:20–2:00 | Second Friday preceding third Thursday of contract month |
| Canadian Dollar | IMM | 01 = $10.00 | All | 7:20–2:00 | Second Friday preceding third Thursday of contract month |
| U.S. Dollar Index | NYCE | 01 = $25.00 | H, M, U, Z | 7:20–2:00 | Second Friday preceding third Wednesday of contract month |
| Crude Oil Heating Oil Unleaded Gas | NYMEX | 01 = $10.00 | All | 8:45–2:10 | Second Friday of month preceding contract month |

**Agriculture and Livestock**

| | | | | | |
|---|---|---|---|---|---|
| Sugar | CSC | 01 = $1.20 | H, K, N, V | 9:00–12:43 | Second Friday of month preceding contract month |
| Orange Juice | NYCE | 01 = $1.50 | F, H, K, N, U, X | 9:15–1:45 | First Friday of month preceding contract month |
| Cotton | NYCE | 01 = $5.00 | H, K, N, V, Z | 9:30–2:00 | First Friday of month preceding contract month |
| Cocoa | CSC | 01 = $10.00 | H, K, N, U, Z | 8:30–1:15 | First Friday of month preceding contract month |
| Coffee | CSC | 01 = $3.75 | H, K, N, U, Z | 8:15–12:50 | First Friday of month preceding contract month |
| Wheat (Hard, Red, Winter) | KCBT | 1/8 = $6.25 | H, K, N, U, Z | 9:35–1:15 | Friday which precedes contract month by at least 10 business days |
| Corn | CBT | 1/8 = $6.25 | H, K, N, U, Z | 9:30–1:15 | Friday (12:00 CST) preceding contract month by 6 business days |
| Soybeans | CBT | 1/8 = $6.25 | F, H, K, N, Q, U, X | 9:30–1:15 | Friday (12:00 CST) preceding contract month by 6 business days |
| Live Cattle | CME | 2.5 = $10.00 | G, J, M, N, Q, V, Z | 9:05–1:00 | First Friday of contract month |
| Feeder Cattle | CME | 2.5 = $10.00 | F, H, J, K, Q, U, V, X | 9:05–1:00 | First Friday of contract month |
| Live Hogs | CME | 2.5 = $7.50 | G, J, M, N, Q, V, Z | 9:10–1:00 | First Friday of contract month |
| Pork Bellies | CME | 01 = $2.50 | G, H, K, N, Q | 9:10–1:00 | Friday which precedes contract month by at least 3 business days |

Source: David L. Caplan. Reprinted with permission.

# Most Common Option Strategies for All Markets/ How To Calculate Margins

## Most Common Option Strategies for All Markets

| Option Spread Strategy | Position | Characteristics | Best Time To Use |
|---|---|---|---|
| **Neutral Strategies** | | | |
| Strangle | Sell out-of-money put and call. | Maximum use of time value decay. | Trading range market with volatility peaking. |
| Guts | Sell in-the-money put and call. | Receive large premium. | Options have time value premium and market in trading range. |
| Arbitrage | Purchase and sell similar options simultaneously. | Profit likely if done at credit. | Any time credit received. |
| Conversion | Buy futures, buy at-the-money put and sell out-of-the-money call. | Profit certain if done at credit. | Any time credit received. |
| Box | Sell calls and puts of same strike prices. | Profit certain if done at credit. | Any time credit received. |
| Butterfly | Buy at-money call (put), sell 2 out-of-money calls (puts) and buy out-of-money call (put). | Profit certain if done at credit. | Any time credit received. |

## Most Common Option Strategies for All Markets (cont.)

| Option Spread Strategy | Position | Characteristics | Best Time To Use |
|---|---|---|---|
| Calendar | Sell near month, buy far month, same strike price. | Near month time value will decay faster. | Small debit, trading range market. |
| **Mixed Strategies** | | | |
| Ratio Call | Buy call, sell calls of higher strike price. | Neutral to slightly bullish. | Large credit and difference between strike prices of options bought and sold. |
| Ratio Put | Buy put, sell puts of lower strike price. | Neutral to slightly bearish. | Large credit and difference between strike prices of options bought and sold. |
| Straddle Purchase | Buy put and call. | Options will lose time value premium quickly. | Options undervalued and market likely to make a big move. |
| Covered Call | Buy future, sell call. | Collect premium on calls sold. | Neutral to slightly bullish. |
| Covered Put | Sell future, sell put. | Collect premium on puts sold. | Neutral to slightly bearish. |
| **Bullish Strategies** | | | |
| Buy Call | Most bullish option position. | Loss limited to premium. | Undervalued option with volatility increasing. |
| Sell Put | Neutral to bullish option position. | Profit limited to premium. | Option overvalued, market flat to bullish. |
| Vertical Bull-Calls | Buy call, sell call of higher strike price. | Loss limited to debit. | Small debit, bullish market. |
| Vertical Bull-Puts | Sell put, buy put of lower strike price. | Loss limited to price difference. | Large credit, bullish market. |
| **Bearish Strategies** | | | |
| Buy Put | Most bearish option position. | Loss limited to premium. | Undervalued option with volatility increasing. |
| Sell Call | Neutral to bearish option position. | Profit limited to premium. | Option overvalued, market flat to bearish. |

## Most Common Option Strategies for All Markets (cont.)

| Option Spread Strategy | Position | Characteristics | Best Time To Use |
|---|---|---|---|
| Vertical Bear-Puts | Buy at-money put, sell out-of-money put. | Loss limited to debit. | Small debit, bearish market. |
| Vertical Bear-Calls | Sell call, buy call of higher stike price. | Loss limited to strike price difference minus credit. | Large credit, bearish market. |

## How To Calculate Options Margins

| Positions | Margin |
|---|---|
| **Outright Positions** | |
| Long Option | Premium paid in full. No margin. |
| Short Option (in-the-money) | Premium marked to market, plus original futures margin marked to market. |
| Short Option (out-of-the-money) | Premium marked to market, plus the greater of futures margin minus one-half the amount that the option is out-of-the-money or one-half of the futures margin. (CME has lower minimums.) |
| **Spread Positions** | |
| Guts Short Call/Short Put (in-the-money) | Both premiums marked to market, plus one of the original futures margins marked to market. |
| Strangle Short Call/Short Put (out-of-the-money) | The greater of the margin requirements of one of the two short options (not to exceed futures margin) plus the premium marked to market of the other short option. (CME has lower minimums.) |
| **Ratio** (long call/put short calls/puts) | Difference in premiums marked to market plus one of the two short options plus the premium marked to market of the other short option. |
| **Long Option Futures** (long call v. short future) (long put v. long future) | Premium paid in full plus original futures margin marked to market. |
| **Short Option Futures** (short call v. long future) (short put v. short future) | Premium marked to market, plus the greater of (1) original futures margin minus one-half the intrinsic value or (2) spread futures margin |

**Long Call (Put)**
**Short Call (Put)**
(Same expiration date)
Where the long call (put) strike price is equal to or less (greater) than the short call (put) strike price

Pay the difference in the options' premiums. No margin required.

Where the long call (put) strike price is greater (less) than the short call (put) strike price

Receive the difference in the options' premiums. Margin equals the difference between strike prices not to exceed the margin requirements for the naked short option.

**Calendar Spread**
Long Call (Put)/Short Call (Put)
(Different expiration date)
Where the long call (put) strike price is equal to or less (greater) than the short call (put) strike price

Pay or receive the difference in the options' premiums. Margin equals the short option premium marked to market minus the long option premium marked to market. If the long option expires before the short option, add futures margin.

Some firms or exchanges may have different requirements for these positions. We have listed the most commonly used margin requirements.

Source: David L. Caplan. Reprinted with permission.

# APPENDIX C

# Option Action Chart

| Market Direction | Option Volatility | Strategy | Advantages | Disadvantages |
|---|---|---|---|---|
| Up | Low-Average | Buy Call (To initiate free trade) | Risk limited to amount of premium paid; profit/loss ratio usually exceeds 10-1; no margin required or loss potential when free trade is completed. | Premium decay of time value. |
| Up | Average-High | Sell Put | Can profit if market moves sideways, lower or even slightly higher; can buy commodity at lower price. (Not recommended except to complete free trade.) | Unlimited loss potential. |
| Up | High | Ratio Spread (Buy call, sell 2 or more higher calls) | No loss if market remains stable or moves against you. | Can lose if market continues to move substantially higher. |
| Up | Average | In-the-Money Debit Call Spread | Risk limited to amount of premium paid; no margin; can take advantage of market trend, time decay and price disparities of options. | Loss occurs if market moves opposite of predicted direction. |

| Market Direction | Option Volatility | Strategy | Advantages | Disadvantages |
|---|---|---|---|---|
| Sideways-Neutral | Average-High | Neutral Option Position | Only strategy that can profit in flat or choppy markets; can be successful without having to determine market direction; has high probability of profit; decay of time value for both options works in your favor. | Limited profit but unlimited loss potential. |
| Sideways-Neutral | Average | Reverse Ratio Spread | Can be successful without having to determine market direction. | Loss occurs unless market moves in either direction. |
| Down | Low-Average | Buy Put (To initiate free trade) | Risk limited to amount of premium paid; profit/loss ratio usually exceeds 10–1; no margin required or loss potential when free trade is completed. | Premium decay of time value. |
| Down | Average-High | Sell Call | Can profit if market moves sideways, higher or even slightly lower. (Not recommended except to complete free trade.) | Limited profit but unlimited loss potential. |
| Down | High | Ratio Spread (Buy put, sell 2 or more lower puts) | No loss if market remains stable or moves against you. | Can lose if market continues to move substantially lower. |
| Down | Average | In-the-Money Debit Put Spread | Risk limited to amount of premium paid; no margin; can take advantage of market trend, time decay and price disparities of options. | Loss occurs if market moves opposite of predicted direction. |

Source: David L. Caplan. Reprinted with permission.

# APPENDIX D

# Obtaining Fills on Option Orders

| Contract | Usual Bid-Ask (ticks) | | | | Comments |
|---|---|---|---|---|---|
| | *Single Option— Front Month* | *Single Option— Back Month* | *Two Option Spread— Front Month* | *Two Option Spread— Back Month* | |
| British Pound | 2–3 | 3–4 | 3–4 | 6–12 | With the British pound you can usually get filled a little better than market. Back months are difficult to trade, and you must be prepared to pay on a hasty exit. |
| Cattle | 5 | 10 | 10 | 20 | On spreads, you can frequently do better by doing legs individually. |
| Copper | 2–5 | 3–10 | 3–10 | 4–20 | Most of the action occurs in front months. |
| Corn | 2 | 3–4 | 2–4 | 4–5 | You can usually get filled 2–6 ticks better than the market. |
| Crude Oil | 1–3 | 2–5 | 2–5 | 3–9 | You can usually get 1 tick better than market. Do spreads as spreads. Prices do not get too out of line due to good volume. |
| Eurodollar | 1–2 | 2–3 | 4–6 | 4–6 | Do spreads as spreads. If quotes are 2–3 ticks wide, you can usually get 1 better than market; at 5–6 wide you might be able to get 2 ticks better than market. |

| Contract | Usual Bid-Ask (ticks) | | | | Comments |
|----------|-------------------------------------|------------------------------------|--------------------------------------------|-------------------------------------------|----------|
| | *Single Option— Front Month* | *Single Option— Back Month* | *Two Option Spread— Front Month* | *Two Option Spread— Back Month* | |
| German Mark | 2–3 | 4–10 | 3–5 | 6–20 | Front months are liquid. Back months are not. |
| Gold (COMEX) | 2–3 | 4–10 | 3–5 | 6–20 | You can almost always do better than market, unlike silver. Place single-option orders a tick off round numbers to facilitate fills. |
| Hogs | 4–6 | 6–10 | 6–10 | 8–12 | Like cattle, but harder to trade. |
| J-Yen | 2–3 | 4–10 | 3–5 | 6–20 | Similar to German mark, volume has increased, making options easier to trade than in the past. |
| Silver (COMEX) | 2–4 | 3–6 | 3–6 | 4–8 | Difficult to get filled better than market. Back months are difficult to trade; spreads can often be done better individually. |
| Soybeans | 4 | 4–8 | 6–10 | 6–12 | Like corn, orders can usually be done 2–6 ticks better than market. |
| S&P500 | 2–3 | 4–5 | 2–4 | 4–8 | Expect 1–2 ticks slippage in and out. |
| Sugar | 3–6 | 4–8 | 5–10 | 10–15 | Volume has increased, making options easier to trade than in the past. |
| Swiss Franc | 2–4 | 4–10 | 4–7 | 6–20 | Less liquid than the mark, but front months not a problem. Sometimes can get better than market. |
| Treasury Bond | 1–2 | 2–4 | 2–5 | 3–10 | The best option trading market. Fills can be had up to halfway across bid-ask. |
| Treasury Notes | 2–4 | 3–6 | 4–8 | 5–15 | Front month is liquid, but back months do not trade much. Tough to get filled better than market. Bond options are superior for option strategies. |

Source: David L. Caplan. Reprinted with permission.

# G L O S S A R Y

# Glossary of Options, Futures and Stocks Definitions

The following organizations and exchanges have granted permission for the compilation of the glossary for this book. We express our thanks for the use of selected materials. The editor has picked the best definition from among the possible choices from different organizations.

Chicago Board of Trade (CBOT)
Chicago Mercantile Exchange (CME)
Chicago Board Options Exchange (CBOE)
Commodity Exchange of New York (COMEX)
Financial Exchange (FINEX)
International Stock Exchange of London (ISE)
Kansas City Board of Trade (KCBT)
London Financial Futures Exchange
MidAmerica Commodity Exchange
Montreal Exchange
Morgan Stanley Foreign Exchange
National Futures Association (NFA)
New Zealand Futures & Options Exchange
New York Futures Exchange
New York Stock Exchange (NYSE)
Pacific Stock Exchange
Philadelphia Stock Exchange
Swiss Options & Financial Futures Exchange, Ltd. (SOFFEX)
The Options Clearing Corporation (OCC)

**abandon**   An option that is not exercised or liquidated on the market is abandoned. Purchasers usually abandon their options position when it has no value at expiration. (Montreal Exchange)

**accountant's opinion**    See **auditor's report**. (NYSE)

**accrued interest**    The interest due on a bond since the last interest payment was made. The buyer of the bond pays the market price plus accrued interest. (NYSE)

**acquisition**    The acquisition of control of one corporation by another. In unfriendly takeover attempts, the potential buying company could offer a price well above current market values, new securities and other inducements to stockholders. The management of the subject company might ask for a better price or try to join up with a third company. See **merger, proxy**. (NYSE)

**actuals**    The physical commodity underlying a futures contract. Also referred to as spot or cash commodity, or physicals. (COMEX)

**adjusted futures price**    The cash-price equivalent reflected in the current futures price. This is calculated by multiplying the futures price by the conversion factor for the particular financial instruments (e.g., bond or note) being delivered. (CBOT)

**adjusted strike price**    The strike price of an option, which results from a special event such as a stock split or a stock dividend. The adjusted strike price can differ from the regular intervals prescribed for strike prices. (CBOE)

**adjusting**    A dynamic trading process by which a floor trader with a spread position buys or sells options or stocks to maintain the delta neutrality of the position. (CBOE)

**adjustment**    The many changes, or adjustments, such as capital distribution payments, dividend payments, rights and bonus issues, stock splits or consolidations, to which physical shares are subject. (New Zealand Futures & Options Exchange)

**affiliate member**    Non–share-holding members of the New Zealand Futures Exchange. Orders placed with affiliate members must then be placed with trading members. Clients of affiliate members are protected by the exchange's fidelity fund. (New Zealand Futures & Options Exchange)

**afloat**    A physical commodity in harbor or in transit in a vessel. (CBOT)

**against actuals**    See **exchange for physicals**. (CBOT)

**aggregate exercise price**    The total dollar value transferred in settlement of an exercised option. (CBOE)

**aggregation**    The policy under which all futures positions owned or controlled by one trader or a group of traders are combined to determine reporting status and speculative limit compliance. (NFA)

**American depository receipt (ADR)**    A security issued by a U.S. bank in place of the foreign shares held in trust by that bank, thereby facilitating the trading of foreign shares in U.S. markets. (NYSE)

**American option**   1. An option that can be exercised at any time up until the expiration date. (Morgan Stanley Foreign Exchange) 2. An option that can be exercised any time during the life of the option up to and including the last trading day. (Montreal Exchange)

**American Stock Exchange (AMEX)**   The second largest stock exchange in the United States, located in the financial district of New York City. (Formerly known as the Curb Exchange from its origin on a Manhattan street.) (NYSE)

**amortization**   Expenses or charges as applicable rather than as paid; includes such practices as depreciation, depletion, write-off of intangibles, prepaid expenses and deferred charges. (NYSE)

**annual report**   The formal financial statement issued yearly by a corporation. The annual report shows assets, liabilities, revenues, expenses, earnings—how the company stood at the close of the business year, how it fared profit-wise during the year and other information of interest to shareowners. (NYSE)

**appreciation**   The rise in a currency's value against other currencies. Opposite of **depreciation**. (FINEX)

**arbitrage**   1. The holding of more than one position at the same time in similar commodities, financial instruments or indexes in the cash, forward or futures markets to take advantage of existing or expected disparities in their pricing relationship. (FINEX) 2. A technique employed to take advantage of differences in price; if, for example, ABC stock can be bought in New York for $10 a share and sold in London at $10.50, an arbitrageur may simultaneously purchase ABC stock here and sell the same amount in London, making a profit of 50 cents a share, less expenses. Arbitrage may also involve the purchase of rights to subscribe to a security, or the purchase of a convertible security—and the sale at or about the same time of the security obtainable through exercise of the rights or of the security obtainable through conversion. See **convertible, rights**. (NYSE)

**arbitrageur**   One who attempts to profit by taking advantage of futures and physical prices being temporarily out of line with each other. The arbitrageur buys in the relatively cheap market and sells in the relatively dear one when the gap between prices in the two is greater than the cost of transferring the relevant commodity or instrument between them. The activity of arbitrageurs ensures that futures and physical prices are kept in line with each other most of the time. (New Zealand Futures & Options Exchange)

**arbitration**   The process of settling disputes between members or between members and customers. National Futures Association's arbitration program provides a forum for resolving futures-related disputes. (NFA)

**Articles of association and bylaws** Regulations that are the basis of the day-to-day and long-term running of the exchange. The bylaws contain specifications for each contract traded on the exchange. (New Zealand Futures & Options Exchange)

**ask** An expression of willingness to sell at a given price. Opposite of **bid**. (FINEX)

**assets** Everything a corporation owns or that is due to it. Cash, investments, money due it, materials and inventories are called current assets; buildings and machinery are called fixed assets; and patents and goodwill are called intangible assets. See **liabilities**. (NYSE)

**assignment** 1. Notification of the clearinghouse to a broker-dealer that an option written by one of its clients has been exercised. (New Zealand Futures & Options Exchange) 2. The random selection of a short option position holder to fulfill the delivery requirements of the contract when a long position in the same series is exercised. (SOFFEX)

**assignment of hedging account** The establishment of first lien by the lender who provided credit to the borrower for purposes of hedging (margin money). (CME)

**associated person** An individual who solicits orders, customers or customer funds on behalf of a futures commission merchant, introducing broker, commodity trading advisor, commodity pool operator or leverage transaction merchant and who is registered with the Commodity Futures Trading Commission. (NFA)

**at-the-money option** An option with a strike price equal to the market price of the underlying. (SOFFEX)

**auction market** The system of trading securities through brokers or agents on an exchange such as the New York Stock Exchange. Buyers compete with other buyers, while sellers compete with other sellers for the most advantageous price. (NYSE)

**auditor's report** An accounting firm's statement of work and its opinion of a corporation's financial statements, especially if they conform to the normal and generally accepted practices of accountancy. Often called the accountant's opinion. (NYSE)

**Automated Trading System (ATS)** The computerized trading facility operated by the New Zealand Futures Exchange. All offering and bidding is conducted through the ATS. The ATS also generates the trading documentation for brokers and provides continuously updated information on trading. (New Zealand Futures & Options Exchange)

**automatic exercise** See **exercise by exception**. (CBOE)

**averages** Various ways of measuring the trend of securities prices, one of the most popular of which is the Dow Jones 30 industrial stocks, listed on the New York Stock Exchange. The prices of the 30 stocks are totaled and then divided by a divisor that is intended to compensate for past stock splits and stock dividends and that is changed from time to time. As a result, point changes in the average have only the vaguest relationship to dollar price changes in stocks included in the average. See **NYSE Composite Index**. (NYSE)

**averaging**    See **dollar cost averaging**. (NYSE)

**averaging down**    Buying more of a stock or an option at a lower price than the original purchase price in order to reduce the average cost. (CBOE)

**backspread**    A delta-neutral spread consisting of more long options than short options on the same underlying stock. This position generally profits from a large movement in either direction in the underlying stock. (CBOE)

**backwardation**    A market condition in which futures prices are lower in the distant market. A profit can be realized from the difference in prices. (COMEX)

**balance of payment**    A summary of the international transactions of a country over a period of time, including commodity and service transactions, capital transactions and gold movements. (CBOT)

**balance sheet**    A condensed financial statement showing the nature and amount of a company's assets, liabilities and capital on a given date. In dollar amounts the balance sheet shows what the company owned, what it owed and its stockholders' ownership interest. See **assets, earnings report**. (NYSE)

**bar chart**    A chart that graphs the high, low and settlement prices for a specific trading session over a given period of time. (CBOT)

**basis**    The difference between the price of a cash commodity at a specific location and the price of a futures contract for that commodity. Basis reflects factors such as transportation costs between the location and the futures delivery point, local supply and demand conditions and local storage availability. (KCBT)

**basis point**    1. One gradation on a 100-point scale representing 1 percent, it is used especially in expressing variations in the yields of bonds. Fixed income yields vary often and slightly within 1 percent, and the basis point scale easily expresses these changes in hundredths of 1 percent; for example, the difference between 12.83 percent and 12.88 percent is five basis points. (NYSE) 2. The smallest increment of price measurement. (London Financial Futures Exchange)

**basis point value (BPV)**    The absolute price change of a specific security given a one basis point (0.01) change in the security's yield. (Montreal Exchange)

**basis risk**    The risk that the value of a future position taken to hedge a physical market position will not move dollar for dollar inversely with the physical market position. (New Zealand Futures & Options Exchange)

**bear, bear market, bearish**   A bear is someone who expects prices to decline; the price trend is downwards in a bear market; information that will tend to depress prices is bearish news. The opposite of bear is **bull**. (New Zealand Futures & Options Exchange)

**bearer bond**   A bond that does not have the owner's name registered on the books of the issuer. Interest and principal, when due, are payable to the holder. See **coupon bond, registered bond**. (NYSE)

**bear spread**   1. A limited risk/limited profit option strategy, involving the purchase of an option and the sale of another at a lower strike but with the same expiration date, which allows the investor to profit from the depreciation of the underlying currency. (Morgan Stanley Foreign Exchange) 2. In most commodities and financial instruments, the term refers to selling the nearby contract month and buying the deferred contract to profit from a change in the price relationship. (CBOT)

**bear spread (call)**   The sale of one call option with a lower strike price and the simultaneous purchase of another call option with a higher strike price. (CBOE)

**bear spread (put)**   The purchase of one put option with a higher strike price and the simultaneous sale of another put option with a lower strike price. (CBOE)

**beta**   A quantitative measure of the sensitivity of a particular stock or portfolio to price movements of the overall stock market. A beta of greater than one means the stock moves faster than the market. A beta of less than one means the stock moves more slowly than the market. (New Zealand Futures & Options Exchange)

**beta analysis**   A technique of statistical analysis that estimates the relationship between the movement in the returns or price of a particular share and the movements in the share market as a whole. (New Zealand Futures & Options Exchange)

**bid**   An expression of willingness to buy at a particular price. Opposite of **ask**. (FINEX)

**bid and asked**   Often referred to as a quotation or quote. The bid is the highest price anyone wants to pay for a security at a given time, and the asked is the lowest price anyone will take at the same time. See **quote**. (NYSE)

**Black-Scholes model**   A mathematical formula used to calculate an option's theoretical value from the following inputs: stock price, strike price, interest rates, dividends, time to expiration and volatility. (CBOE)

**block**   A large holding or transaction of stock; popularly considered to be 10,000 shares or more. (NYSE)

**blue chip**    A company known nationally for the quality and wide acceptance of its products or services and for its ability to make money and pay dividends. (NYSE)

**blue-sky laws**    A popular name for laws various states have enacted to protect the public against securities frauds. The term is believed to have originated when a judge ruled that a particular stock had about the same value as a patch of blue sky. (NYSE)

**board of trade**    See **contract market**. (NFA)

**bond**    Basically an IOU or promissory note of a corporation, usually issued in multiples of $1,000 or $5,000, although $100 and $500 denominations are not unknown. A bond is evidence of a debt on which the issuing company usually promises to pay the bondholders a specified amount of interest for a specified length of time and to repay the loan on the expiration date. In every case a bond represents debt; its holder is a creditor of the corporation and not a part owner, as is the shareholder. See **collateral, convertible, debenture, general mortgage bond, income bond**. (NYSE)

**bonus issue**    A free issue of shares to existing shareholders, usually in a predetermined ratio. (New Zealand Futures & Options Exchange)

**book**    See **public order book**. (CBOE)

**book entry securities**    Electronically recorded securities that include each creditor's name, address, Social Security or tax identification number and dollar amount loaned (i.e., no certificates are issued to bondholders; instead, the transfer agent electronically credits interest payments to each creditor's bank account on a designated date). (CBOT)

**book value**    An accounting term. Book value of a stock is determined from a company's records, by adding all assets then deducting all debts, other liabilities and the liquidation price of any preferred issues. When this total is divided by the number of common shares outstanding, the result is book value per common share. Book value of the assets of a company or a security may have little relationship to market value. (NYSE)

**box spread**    A four-sided option spread that involves a long call and short put at one strike price as well as a short call and long put at another strike price. In other words, this is a synthetic long stock position at one strike price and a synthetic short stock position at another strike price. (CBOE)

**break-even cost**    If a business operation breaks even on average for each unit of production, the operator is doing as well as he or she could by investing money and time in other less risky ventures. One who is breaking even is being paid a wage and interest on any money invested. If the enterprise earns more than the break-even costs, then the operator's management and risk taking have been rewarded with returns greater than he or she would have had by investing in something less risky. (CME)

**break-even point**  The price of the underlying product at which a particular options strategy neither makes nor loses any money. (Montreal Exchange)

**broker**  An individual who is paid a commission for executing customer orders. Either a floor broker, who executes orders on the floor of the exchange, or an upstairs broker who handles retail customers and their orders. (COMEX)

**brokerage**  The commissions brokers charge either at a fixed rate or on a percentage basis. (New Zealand Futures & Options Exchange)

**brokerage firm**  1. Any futures commission merchant as licensed by the CFTC. 2. A firm or person engaged in soliciting or accepting and handling orders for the purchase or sale of futures contracts, subject to the rules of a futures exchange and who, in connection with such solicitation or acceptance or orders, accepts any resulting trades or contracts. (CME)

**brokers' loans**  Money borrowed by brokers from banks or other brokers for a variety of uses. It may be used by specialists to help finance inventories of stock they deal in; by brokerage firms to finance the underwriting of new issues of corporate and municipal securities; to help finance a firm's own investments; and to help finance the purchase of securities for customers who prefer to use the broker's credit when they buy securities. See **margins**. (NYSE)

**bull, bull market, bullish**  A bull is someone who expects prices to rise. The price trend is upwards in a bull market. Bullish news is information that will tend to raise prices. The opposite of bull is **bear**. (New Zealand Futures & Options Exchange)

**bullion**  Gold or silver in bar or ingot form. (COMEX)

**bull spread**  1. A limited risk/limited profit option strategy involving the purchase of an option and the sale of another at a higher strike but with the same expiration date, which allows the investor to profit from appreciation of the underlying currency. (Morgan Stanley's Foreign Exchange) 2. In most commodities and financial instruments, the term refers to buying the nearby month and selling the deferred month to profit from the change in the price relationship. (CBOT)

**bull spread (call)**  The purchase of one call option with a lower strike price and the simultaneous sale of another call option with a higher strike price. (CBOE)

**bull spread (put)**  The sale of one put option with a higher strike price and the simultaneous purchase of another put option with a lower strike price. (CBOE)

**butterfly spread**   1. A strategy in which two interdelivery futures spreads are placed in opposite directions, with the center of delivery month common to both spreads. (CBOT) 2. A strategy involving four options and three strike prices that has both limited risk and limited profit potential. A long call butterfly is established by buying one call at the lowest strike price, selling two calls at the middle strike price and buying one call at the highest strike price. A long put butterfly is established by buying one put at the highest strike price, selling two puts at the middle strike price and buying one put at the lowest strike price. (CBOE)

**buyer**   A market participant who takes a long futures position or buys an option. An option buyer is also called a taker, a holder or an owner. (FINEX)

**buy in**   An option writer who does not hold enough assets to deliver to the option buyer at exercise will buy in the assets at the market. (ISE)

**buying hedge**   Buying a futures contract to hedge against the possibility of a rise in the price of a commodity or instrument which has to be purchased some time in the future. Also known as a long hedge or going long. (New Zealand Futures & Options Exchange)

**buy on close**   To buy a futures contract at the end of the trading day at a price within the closing range. (FINEX)

**buy on the opening**   To buy a futures contract at the start of the trading day at a price within the trading range. (FINEX)

**buy-write**   Same as **covered call option writing**. (CBOE)

**calendar spread**   A neutral calendar spread is a limited risk/limited profit option strategy, involving the sale of a short-term option and the purchase of a longer-term option at the same strike, which allows the investor to exploit the differential time decay effects of options with different maturities. (Morgan Stanley Foreign Exchange)

**call**   An options contract that gives the buyer of the option the right but not the obligation to buy a specific quantity of shares at a fixed price on or before a specific future date. The seller of the option has the obligation to sell a specific quantity of shares at a fixed price on or before a specific future date should he/she be exercised against. (New Zealand Futures & Options Exchange)

**callable**   A bond issue, all or part of which may be redeemed by the issuing corporation under specified conditions before maturity. The term also applies to preferred shares that may be redeemed by the issuing corporation. (NYSE)

**Canadian Depository for Securities Limited (CDS)**   CDS is owned by six Canadian chartered banks, five Canadian trust companies and the members of the Montreal Exchange, The Toronto Stock Exchange and the Investment Dealers Association. CDS provides both computer-based security clearing and depository services in major Canadian cities as well as through international links to U.S. and European markets. (Montreal Exchange)

**cancel former order**   Directions to cancel or change the quantity or price of a previously entered order. (CME)

**canceling order**   An order that deletes a customer's previous order. (CBOT)

**capital gain or capital loss**   Profit or loss from the sale of a capital asset. The capital gains provisions of the tax law are complicated. Consult a tax adviser for specific information. (NYSE)

**capital intensive**   A description applied to any process requiring large expenditures or financial investment for production. (CME)

**capitalization**   Total amount of the various securities issued by a corporation. Capitalization may include bonds, debentures, preferred and common stock and surplus. Bonds and debentures are usually carried on the books of the issuing company in terms of their par or face value. Preferred and common shares may be carried in terms of par or stated value. Stated value may be an arbitrary figure decided upon by the directors or may represent the amount received by the company from the sale of the securities at the time of issuance. See **par**. (NYSE)

**capital stock**   All shares representing ownership of a business, including preferred and common. See **common stock, preferred stock**. (NYSE)

**carrying broker**   A member of a commodity exchange, usually a clearinghouse member, through whom another broker or customer chooses to clear all or some trades. (NFA)

**carrying charges**   The costs involved in owning commodities over a period of time, such as storage, insurance and any interest charges. (COMEX)

**carryover**   Grain and oilseed commodities not consumed during the marketing year and remaining in storage at year's end. These stocks are carried over into the next marketing year and added to the stocks produced during the crop year. (CBOT)

**cash and carry**   An arbitrage transaction involving the purchase of a Government of Canada bond in the cash market with borrowed funds and the simultaneous sale of a Government of Canada bond futures contract, held until delivery. (Montreal Exchange)

**cash commodity**   The physical commodity or underlying instrument as distinguished from the futures. Sometimes called spot commodity or actuals. (FINEX)

**cash contract**   A sales agreement for either immediate or future delivery of the actual product. (CBOT)

**cash flow**    Reported net income of a corporation plus amounts charged off for depreciation, depletion, amortization or extraordinary charges to reserves, which are bookkeeping deductions and not paid out in actual dollars and cents. See **amortization, depreciation**. (NYSE)

**cash market**    1. A place where people buy and sell the actual commodities, i.e., grain elevator, bank, etc. See **spot market** and **forward contract**. (CBOT) 2. The market in the actual financial instrument on which a futures or options contract is based. (London Financial Futures Exchange).

**cash price**    The price in the marketplace for the actual cash commodity. The cash price of the U.S. Dollar Index is the current value of the index multiplied by $500. (FINEX)

**cash sale**    A transaction on the floor of the stock exchange that calls for delivery of the securities on the same day. In regular way trades, the seller is to deliver on the fifth business day, except for bonds, which are to be delivered on the next business day. See **regular way delivery**. (NYSE)

**cash settlement**    The settlement of a contract through payment or receipt of the cash equivalent of the profit or loss of the contract. In the case of option contracts, the profit or loss of the contract is determined by the difference between the exercise price of the option contract and the settlement price of the underlying instrument. In the case of financial futures contracts, the cash settlement is determined by the difference between the final settlement price and the settlement price from the previous trading day. (SOFFEX)

**cash settlement contract**    A futures contract that cannot be settled by delivery of a commodity or financial instrument, but must be settled by the payment of accumulated profits and losses in cash. Also called a nondeliverable contract. (New Zealand Futures & Options Exchange)

**cash settlement month**    The month in which trading ceases and cash settlement takes place for a specific futures contract. Also known as the contract month or delivery month. (New Zealand Futures & Options Exchange)

**central bank**    A financial institution that has official or semiofficial status in a federal government. Central banks are the instruments used by governments to expand, contract or stabilize the supply of money and credit. They hold reserves of other banks, act as fiscal agents for their governments, and can issue paper money. (FINEX)

**certificate**    The actual piece of paper that is evidence of ownership of stock in a corporation. Watermarked paper is finely engraved with delicate etchings to discourage forgery. (NYSE)

**certificate of deposit (CD)**   A money market instrument issued by banks. The time CD is characterized by its set date of maturity and interest rate and its wide acceptance among investors, companies and institutions as a highly negotiable short-term investment vehicle. (NYSE)

**charting**   The use of graphs and charts in the technical analysis of futures markets to plot price movements, volume, open interest or other statistical indicators of price movement. (NFA)

**cheap**   Colloquialism implying that a commodity is underpriced. (CBOT)

**cheapest to deliver**   A method to determine which particular cash debt instrument is most profitable to deliver against a futures contract. (CBOT)

**cheapest-to-deliver bond**   The deliverable Government of Canada issue that will create the maximum profit or the minimum loss for a short Canadian Government bond futures position holder who makes delivery. (Montreal Exchange)

**Chicago Board Options Exchange (CBOE)**   The oldest and largest listed options exchange, opened in April 1973. (CBOE)

**Christmas tree spread**   A strategy involving six options and four strike prices that has both limited risk and limited profit potential. For example, a long call Christmas tree spread is established by buying one call at the lowest strike, skipping the second strike, selling three calls at the third strike and buying two calls at the fourth strike. (CBOE)

**churning**   Excessive trading that results in the broker deriving a profit from commissions while disregarding the best interests of the customer. (NFA)

**class**   All options contracts of the same type (put or call), referring to the same underlying instrument. (SOFFEX)

**clearing**   The process of matching all trades by the clearinghouse. Because there must be a buyer for every seller, all transactions on a futures exchange for a given day must match up. Each buy order must be matched by a sell order for the same number of contracts, price, time and contract month. A trade that does not match up is an outtrade and must be reconciled by the beginning of trading the next day. (CME)

**clearing corporation**   An agency, connected with an exchange, through which all futures contracts are reconciled, settled and guaranteed and through which financial settlement is made. (Montreal Exchange)

**clearinghouse**   1. An organization associated with a futures exchange, usually operating autonomously, that clears trading activity to make sure buyers' and sellers' records agree and that contracts are honored; at the Kansas City Board of Trade, this function occurs at the

Kansas City Board of Trade Clearing Corporation. (Kansas City Board of Trade) 2. An independent body that sets the initial and maintenance margin, collects the relevant funds and maintains the records of the market. (New Zealand Futures & Options Exchange) 3. An adjunct to a commodity exchange through which transactions executed on the floor of the exchange are settled; also charged with assuring the proper conduct of the exchange's delivery procedures and the adequate financing of the trading. (FINEX)

**clearing margin**    Financial safeguards to ensure that clearing members (usually companies or corporations) perform on their customer's open futures and options contracts. (Clearing margins are distinct from customer margins that individual buyers and sellers of futures and options contracts are required to deposit with brokers.) See **customer margin**. (CBOT)

**clearing member**    A member of the clearinghouse or association. All trades of a non-clearing member must be registered and eventually settled through a clearing member. (FINEX)

**client fund regulations**    See **Futures Industry (Client Fund) Regulations 1990**. (New Zealand Futures & Options Exchange)

**close, the**    The period at the end of the trading session, officially designated by the exchange, during which all transactions are considered made at the close. (NFA)

**closed-end investment company**    See **investment company**. (NYSE)

**close out**    Taking out a position in the futures market equal and opposite to that already held—i.e., a bought if a sold is held. Also to liquidate. (New Zealand Futures & Options Exchange)

**closing out**    Liquidating an existing long or short futures or option's position with an equal and opposite transaction. Sometimes called **offset**. (FINEX)

**closing purchase**    1. A transaction in which the purchaser's intention is to reduce or eliminate a short position in a given series of options. (The Options Clearing Corporation) 2. Buying an option with the same terms as the option originally sold (written); this results in the liquidation of the writer's position. (New York Futures Exchange)

**closing range**    The range between the highest and lowest priced trades during the final minutes of a trading session. (COMEX)

**closing rotation**    See **trading rotation**. (CBOE)

**closing sale**    Selling an option with the same terms as the option originally bought. This results in the liquidation of the buyer's position. (New York Futures Exchange)

**closing trade**    A trade that reduces or eliminates a short or long position in a contract. (SOFFEX)

**collateral**    Securities or other property pledged by a borrower to secure repayment of a loan. (NYSE)

**combination**    1. Strategies using options of the same class but different series and/or types: selling one at-the-money call and one at-the-money put is a combination used in an anticipated neutral market. (Montreal Exchange) 2. Also known as synthetic positions; any position involving the purchase or sale of more than one option to create a desired result; for example, buy call/buy put, sell call/sell put. (New York Futures Exchange)

**commercial paper**    Debt instruments issued by companies to meet short-term financing needs. (NYSE)

**commission**    1. The broker's basic fee for purchasing or selling securities or property as an agent. (NYSE) 2. The fee charged by a broker for carrying out instructions. It is usually charged on a *round turn* basis, i.e., for the buying and selling of a contract. (New Zealand Futures & Options Exchange)

**commission broker**    An agent who executes the public's orders for the purchase or sale of securities or commodities. (NYSE)

**commission house**    A concern that buys and sells actual commodities or futures contracts for the accounts of customers. (FINEX)

**Commodity Credit Corporation**    A branch of the U.S. Department of Agriculture established in 1933 to supervise the government's farm loan and subsidy programs. (CBOT)

**Commodity Exchange Act**    The act that provides for federal regulation of futures trading. (NFA)

**Commodity Futures Trading Commission (CFTC)**    An independent federal regulatory agency established in 1974 to oversee futures trading and the operation of organized futures exchanges in the United States. (FINEX)

**commodity pool**    An enterprise in which funds contributed by a number of persons are combined for the purpose of trading futures contracts or commodity options. (NFA)

**commodity pool operator**    An individual or organization that operates or solicits funds for a commodity pool; that is, an enterprise in which funds contributed by a number of persons are combined for the purpose of trading futures contracts or commodity options. Registration with the Commodity Futures Trading Commission is generally required. (NFA)

**commodity trading advisor**    A person who, for compensation or profit, directly or indirectly advises others as to the value of, or the advisability of, buying or selling futures contracts or commodity options. Providing advice indirectly includes exercising trading authority over a customer's account. Registration with the Commodity Futures Trading Commission is generally required. (NFA)

**common stock**    Securities that represent an ownership interest in a corporation. If the company has also issued preferred stock, both common and preferred have ownership rights. Common stockholders assume the greater risk, but generally exercise the greater control and may gain the greater award in the form of dividends and capital appreciation. The terms *common stock* and *capital stock* are often used interchangeably when the company has no preferred stock. (NYSE)

**competitive trader**   A member of the exchange who trades in stocks on the floor for an account in which there is an interest. Also known as a registered trader. (NYSE)

**complements**   Products that are used together for economic benefit (e.g., corn and feeder cattle). (CME)

**computerized trading reconstruction**   A Chicago Board of Trade computerized surveillance program that pinpoints in any trade the traders, the contract, the quantity, the price and the time of execution to the nearest minute. (CBOT)

**condor spread**   A strategy involving four options and four strike prices that has both limited risk and limited profit potential. A long call condor spread is established by buying one call at the lowest strike, selling one call at the second strike, selling another call at the third strike and buying one call at the fourth strike. This spread is also referred to as a flat-top butterfly or a top hat spread. (CBOE)

**confirmation statement**   A statement sent by a futures commission merchant to a customer when a futures or options position has been initiated. The statement shows the number of contracts bought or sold and the transaction prices. Sometimes combined with a **purchase and sale statement**. (NFA)

**conglomerate**   A corporation that has diversified its operations, usually by acquiring enterprises in widely varied industries. (NYSE)

**consolidated balance sheet**   A balance sheet that shows the financial condition of a corporation and its subsidiaries. See **balance sheet**. (NYSE)

**Consolidated Tape**   The ticker tape reporting transactions in NYSE listed securities that take place on the NYSE or any of the participating regional stock exchanges and other markets. Transactions in AMEX listed securities, and certain other securities listed on regional stock exchanges, are reported on a separate tape. (NYSE)

**Consumer Price Index**   A major inflation measure computed by the U.S. Department of Commerce. It measures the change in prices of a fixed market basket of some 385 goods and services in the previous month. (CBOT)

**contango**   A market condition in which futures prices are higher in the distant delivery months. (COMEX)

**contingency order**   An order to conduct one transaction in one security that depends on the price of another instrument. An example might be: Sell the XYZ Jan 50 call at 2, contingent upon XYZ being at or below $49½. (CBOE)

**contract**    The unit of trading in commodity futures. A futures contract specifies the exact grade, amount and month of delivery of the commodity. (COMEX)

**contract grades**    The various grades of a commodity that are stipulated in the rules of an exchange as being deliverable against a futures contract. (COMEX)

**contract market**    A board of trade designated by the Commodity Futures Trading Commission to trade futures or option contracts on a particular commodity. Commonly used to mean any exchange on which futures are traded. (NFA)

**contract month**    1. The month in which trading ceases and cash settlement takes place for a specific futures contract. Also known as the cash settlement or delivery month. (New Zealand Futures & Options Exchange) 2. The month in which delivery is to be made in accordance with the futures contract. Sometimes called delivery month. (FINEX)

**contract unit**    The actual amount of a commodity stipulated for delivery against a given futures contract. (COMEX)

**convergence**    The process whereby cash and futures prices converge as delivery approaches. (Montreal Exchange)

**conversion**    1. Creation of a synthetic futures short position by writing calls and buying puts with the same strike price and simultaneously entering a genuine futures long position. (SOFFEX) 2. A position of buying 1,000 shares, selling a call and buying a put is an arbitrage process whereby an investor may be able to lock in a profit at little or no risk. (New Zealand Futures & Options Exchange)

**conversion factor**    1. Factor used in the calculation of the price of a particular deliverable issue of Government of Canada bond when it is delivered; the conversion factor is the price per $1 nominal value at which a specific Government of Canada bond will yield 9 percent. (Montreal Exchange) 2. A factor used to equate the price of a T-bond and T-note futures contract with the various cash T-bonds and T-notes eligible for delivery; this factor is based on a static relationship of various coupons to an 8 percent bond, the coupon underlying the contract of the same first call date. (CBOT)

**convertible**    A bond, debenture or preferred share that may be exchanged by the owner for common stock or another security, usually of the same company, in accordance with the terms of the issue. (NYSE)

**corporate bond**    A financial instrument evidencing indebtedness of a corporation. (CBOT)

332 *correspondent / covered strangle*

**correspondent**   A securities firm, bank or other financial organization that regularly performs services for another in a place or market to which the other does not have direct access. Securities firms may have correspondents in foreign countries or on exchanges of which they are not members. Correspondents are frequently linked by private wires. Member organizations of the NYSE with offices in New York City may also act as correspondents for out-of-town member organizations that do not maintain New York City offices. (NYSE)

**cost of carry**   1. The interest forgone when establishing a position at a debit, i.e., the cost of financing a position. 2. The cost of financing a futures position now. (ISE)

**cost-of-delivery basis**   The costs—transportation, yardage, inspection fees—of delivering livestock that fulfill the contract specifications of a CME futures contract to a CME-approved delivery point. (CME)

**coupon**   The interest rate on a debt instrument expressed in terms of a percent on an annualized basis that the issuer guarantees to pay the holder until maturity. (CBOT)

**coupon bond**   Bond with interest coupons attached. The coupons are clipped as they come due and presented by the holder for payments of interest. See **bearer bond, registered bond**. (NYSE)

**cover**   The purchase or sale of a contract to offset a previously established position. (COMEX)

**covered call option writing**   A short call option position in which the writer owns the number of shares of the underlying stock represented by his or her option contracts. (OCC)

**covered combination**   See **covered strangle**. (CBOE)

**covered option**   An option position that is offset by an equal and opposite position in the underlying security. (NYSE)

**covered put option writing**   A short put option position in which the writer also is short the corresponding stock or has deposited, in a cash account, cash or cash equivalents equal to the exercise value of the option. (OCC)

**covered straddle**   An option strategy in which one call and one put with the same strike price and expiration are written against 100 shares of the underlying stock. In actuality, this is not a covered strategy because assignment on the short put would require purchase of stock on margin. (CBOE)

**covered strangle**   A strategy in which one call and one put with the same expiration, but different strike prices, are written against 100 shares of the underlying stock. In actuality, this is not a covered strategy because assignment on the short put would require purchase of stock on margin. This method is also called a covered combination. (CBOE)

**covered write**   Writing an option on a currency already owned, assuring that the potential obligation to deliver the currency can be met. (Morgan Stanley Foreign Exchange)

**credit**   Money received in an account either from a deposit or a transaction that results in increasing the account's cash balance. (CBOE)

**credit spread**   A spread strategy that increases the account's cash balance when it is established. A bull spread with puts and a bear spread with calls are examples of credit spreads. (CBOE)

**crop marketing year**   The time span from harvest to harvest for agricultural commodities. The crop marketing year varies slightly with each agricultural commodity, but it tends to begin at harvest and end before the next year's harvest (e.g., the marketing year for soybeans begins September 1 and ends August 31). The futures contract month of November represents the first major new-crop marketing month, and the contract month of July represents the last major old-crop marketing month for soybeans. (CBOT)

**crop reports**   Reports compiled by the U.S. Department of Agriculture on various agricultural commodities that are released throughout the year. Information in the reports includes estimates on planted acreage, yield and expected production, as well as comparison of production from previous years. (CBOT)

**cross-hedge**   The hedging of a cash market risk in a futures contract for a different but price-related commodity. (FINEX)

**cross order (CRO)**   An order entered into the system to buy and sell an equal number of lots at the same price at the same time, and for which the buyer and seller will always involve the same principal. A prerequisite is the existence of at least one existing offer and bid in the system for that contract and delivery month. If the order price is between the best price and best offer, a deal will be generated. (New Zealand Futures & Options Exchange)

**crush**   The purchase of soybean futures (or cash soybeans) and the simultaneous sale of soybean oil and meal futures (or cash soybean oil and meal). This spread is used to minimize the financial risks of sudden increases in soybean costs and/or declining values of finished soybean oil and meal. (CBOT)

**cum-dividend**   Shares that are sold with the right to the current dividend. (New Zealand Futures & Options Exchange)

**cumulative preferred**   A stock having a provision that if one or more dividends are omitted, the omitted dividends must be paid before dividends may be paid on the company's common stock. (NYSE)

**cumulative voting**   A method of voting for corporate directors that enables the shareholders to multiply the number of their shares by the number of directorships being voted on and to cast the total for one director or a selected group of directors. A ten-share holder normally casts ten votes for each, say, 12 nominees to the board of directors. Under the cumulative voting principle, the shareholder has 120 votes ($10 \times 12$) that can be cast for only one nominee, 60 for two, 40 for three, or any other distribution he or she chooses. Cumulative voting is required under the corporate laws of some states and is permitted in most others. (NYSE)

**current assets**   Those assets of a company that are reasonably expected to be realized in cash, sold or consumed during one year. These include cash, U.S. government bonds, receivables and money due (usually within one year) and inventories. (NYSE)

**current liabilities**   Money owed and payable by a company, usually within one year. (NYSE)

**current return**   See **yield**. (NYSE)

**current yield**   The amount of money currently received divided by the instrument purchase price. (CBOT)

**curvature**   See **gamma**.

**customer margin**   Within the futures industry, financial guarantees required of both buyers and sellers of futures contracts and sellers of options contracts to ensure fulfillment of contract obligations. Futures commission merchants are responsible for overseeing customer margin accounts. Margins are determined on the basis of market risk and contract value. Also referred to as performance-bond margin. See **clearing margin**. (CBOT)

**customer segregated funds**   See **segregated account**. (NFA)

**cycle**   The expiration dates applicable to the different series of options. Traditionally, there were three cycles: January/April/July/October, February/May/August/November, and March/June/September/December. Today, equity options expire on a sequential cycle that involves a total of four option series: two near-term months and two far-term months. For example, on January 1, a stock traditionally in the January cycle will be trading options expiring in January, February, April and July. Index options, however, expire on a consecutive cycle that involves the four near-term months. For example, on January 1, index options will be trading options expiring in January, February, March and April. (CBOE)

**daily settlement price**   The price of a futures contract set by SOFFEX after the close of trading. (SOFFEX)

**daily trading limit**   The maximum price range set by the exchange each day for a contract. (CBOT)

**day order**   Orders that expire at the close of a day's trading. If not filled during that trading day, they are withdrawn. (COMEX)

**day trader**   A commodity trader who takes market positions and liquidates them prior to the close of the same trading day. (COMEX)

**day trading**   The practice of taking a position and liquidating it within a single day's trading. (FINEX)

**dealer**   An individual or firm in the securities business who buys and sells stocks and bonds as a principal rather than as an agent. The dealer's profit or loss is the difference between the price paid and the price received for the same security. The dealer's confirmation must disclose to the customer that the principal has been acted upon. The same individual or firm may function, at different times, either as broker or dealer. See **National Association of Securities Dealers, specialist**. (NYSE)

**dealer option**   A put or call on a physical commodity, not originating on or subject to the rules of an exchange, written by a firm that deals in the underlying cash commodity. (NFA)

**debenture**   A promissory note backed by the general credit of a company and usually not secured by a mortgage or lien on any specific property. See **bond**. (NYSE)

**debit**   Money paid out from an account either from a withdrawal or a transaction that decreases a cash balance. (CBOE)

**debit balance**   In a customer's margin account, that portion of the purchase price of stock, bonds or commodities that is covered by credit extended by the broker to the margin customer. (NYSE)

**debit spread**   A spread strategy that decreases the account's cash balance when it is established. A bull spread with calls and a bear spread with puts are examples of debit spreads. (CBOE)

**decay**   See **time decay**. (CBOE)

**default**   The failure to perform on a futures contract as required by exchange rules, such as a failure to meet a margin call or to make or take delivery. (NFA)

**deferred delivery**   The distant delivery months in which futures trading is taking place, as distinguished from the nearby futures delivery month. (NFA)

**delayed opening**   The postponement of trading of an issue of stock exchange beyond the normal opening of a day's trading because of market conditions that have been judged by exchange officials to warrant such a delay. Reasons for the delay might be an influx of either buy or sell orders, an imbalance of buyers and sellers or pending corporate news that requires time for dissemination. (NYSE)

**deliverable**   A futures contract that is settled by making or taking delivery of the commodity or instrument named in the contract. (New Zealand Futures & Options Exchange)

**deliverable grades**   The standard grades of commodities or instruments listed in the rules of the exchanges that must be met when delivering cash commodities against futures contracts. Grades are often accompanied by a schedule of discounts and premiums allowable for delivery of commodities of lesser or greater quality than the standard called for by the exchange. (CBOT)

**delivery**    1. The making and taking delivery of either a commodity or financial instrument for a deliverable contract or a cash settlement for a nondeliverable contract. (New Zealand Futures & Options Exchange) 2. The transfer of ownership of the actual commodity in the form of a warehouse receipt. (COMEX)

**delivery date**    The day when fulfillment of the contractual obligations of a financial futures contract occurs. See **delivery, cash settlement**. (SOFFEX)

**delivery month**    Also known as contract or cash settlement month. The month in which trading ceases and cash settlement takes place for a specific futures contract. (New Zealand Futures & Options Exchange)

**delivery points**    Livestock auction yards that are approved by the CME to accept deliveries of livestock as fulfillment of CME contract obligations. Selection of these points and par or discount status are made by the CME Board of Governors. (CME)

**delivery settlement price**    Price to be paid upon delivery of the deliverable bonds, based on the futures contract settlement price on the day the delivery notice was tendered to the clearing corporation, adjusted by the conversion factor of the issue being delivered, plus accrued interest up to the delivery date. (Montreal Exchange)

**delta**    1. The amount by which an option's price will change for a unitary change in price of the underlying instrument. An option with a delta of 0.5 will move 0.5 in price for every 1.00 movement of the underlying instrument. Delta is an instantaneous measure; therefore in practice, if the underlying instrument moves 1.00, the premium value will not move exactly equal to the delta. (Montreal Exchange) 2. The delta factor describes the change of the option price if the price of the underlying instrument changes by one point. (SOFFEX) 3. The net exposure of an option position, measured by the change in value of the position resulting from a change in the spot rate. (Morgan Stanley Foreign Exchange)

**delta-neutral spread**    A trading strategy, sometimes used by professional market makers, that matches the total long deltas of a position (long stock, long calls, short puts) with the total short deltas (short stock, short calls, long puts). (CBOE)

**demand, law of**    The relationship between product demand and price. (CBOT)

**depletion accounting**    Natural resources, such as metals, oil, gas and timber, which conceivably can be reduced to zero over the years, present a special problem in capital management. Depletion is an accounting practice consisting of charges against earnings based upon the amount of the asset taken out of the total reserves in the period for which accounting is made. A bookkeeping entry, it does not represent any cash outlay nor are any funds earmarked for the purpose. (NYSE)

**deposit**  The amount of money futures traders are required to lodge with their broker when they open a position in the market. The minimum deposit is set by the clearinghouse. (New Zealand Futures & Options Exchange)

**Depository Trust Company (DTC)**  A central securities certificate depository through which members effect security deliveries between each other via computerized bookkeeping entries, thereby reducing the physical movement of stock certificates. (NYSE)

**depreciation**  1. The decline in a currency's value against other currencies; opposite of **appreciation**. (FINEX) 2. Normally, charges against earnings to write off the cost, less salvage value, of an asset over its estimated useful life. It is a bookkeeping entry and does not represent any cash outlay nor are any funds earmarked for the purpose. (NYSE)

**derivative security**  A financial security whose value is derived in part from the value and characteristics of another security, the underlying security. (OCC)

**devaluation**  A formal, official decrease in the exchange rate or price of currency made unilateral by a country. (FINEX)

**diagonal spread**  A strategy involving the simultaneous purchase and sale of two options of the same type that have different strike prices and different expiration dates; e.g., buy 1 May 45 call and sell 1 March 50 call. (CBOE)

**differentials**  Price differences between classes, grades and delivery locations of various stocks of the same commodity. (CBOT)

**director**  Person elected by shareholders to serve on the board of directors. The directors appoint the president, vice presidents and all other operating officers. Directors decide, among other matters, if and when dividends will be paid. See **proxy**. (NYSE)

**disclosure document**  The document that must be provided to and signed by prospective customers and that describes fees, performance, etc. (NFA)

**disclosure statement**  The statement required by the CFTC that enumerates the risks involved in trading futures and/or options on futures. (NFA)

**discount**  1. The amount a price would be reduced to purchase a commodity of lesser grade. 2. Sometimes used to refer to the price differences between futures of different delivery months, as in the phrase "July is trading at a discount to May," indicating that the price of the July future is lower than that of May. 3. Applied to cash grain prices that are below the future. See **option premium**. (NFA) 4. The amount by which a preferred stock or bond may sell below its par value; also used as a verb to mean "takes into account," as the price of the stock has discounted the expected dividend cut. See **premium**. (NYSE)

**discount basis**   A method of quoting securities wherein the price is expressed as an annualized discount from maturity value. (CBOT)

**discount delivery**   The quality, quantity, time or location of delivery deviate slightly from par, but are still within the allowances of the CME contract. The seller delivering to fulfill his or her contract commitment will receive the futures price at which he or she sold, less appropriate discounts for deviations from par and less commissions and grading fees. (CME)

**discount rate**   The interest rate charged on loans by the Federal Reserve to member banks. (CBOT)

**discretion**   Freedom given to the floor broker by an investor to use judgment regarding the execution of an order. Discretion can be limited, as in the case of a limit order that gives the floor broker $1/8$ or $1/4$ point from the stated limit price to use his or her judgment in executing the order. Discretion can also be unlimited, as in the case of a market-not-held order. See **market-not-held order**. (CBOE)

**discretionary account**   An arrangement by which the owner of the account gives written power of attorney to someone else, usually the broker or a commodity trading advisor, to buy and sell without prior approval of the account owner. Often referred to as a managed account in futures and futures options. (NFA)

**diversification**   Spreading investments among different types of securities and various companies in different fields. (NYSE)

**dividend**   The payment designated by the board of directors to be distributed pro rata among the shares outstanding. On preferred shares, it is generally a fixed amount. On common shares, the dividend varies with the fortunes of the company and the amount of cash on hand, and may be omitted if business is poor or the directors determine to withhold earnings to invest in plant and equipment. Sometimes a company will pay a dividend out of past earnings even if it is not currently operating at a profit. (NYSE)

**dollar cost averaging**   A system of buying securities at regular intervals with a fixed dollar amount. Under this system investors buy by the dollars' worth rather than by the number of shares. If each investment is of the same number of dollars, payments buy more shares when the price is low and fewer when it rises; thus, temporary downswings in price benefit investors if they continue periodic purchases in both good times and bad and if the price at which the shares are sold is more than their average cost. See **formula invest-ing**. (NYSE)

**Dow theory** A theory of market analysis based on the performance of the Dow Jones industrial and transportation stock price averages. The theory says that the market is in a basic upward trend if one of these averages advances above a previous important high, accompanied or followed by a similar advance in the other. When the averages both dip below previous important lows, this is regarded as confirmation of a downward trend. The Dow Jones is one type of market index. See **NYSE Composite Index**. (NYSE)

**downtick** See **uptick**. (NYSE)

**duration** A measure of the volatility of a Government of Canada bond price to changes in its yield to maturity. (Montreal Exchange)

**dynamic hedging** A short-term trading strategy generally using index options in which the delta of an index option is taken into consideration so that the total price movement of the index options used will approximate the total dollar value change in an equity portfolio. See **delta**. (CBOE)

**early exercise** The option buyer has the right to exercise an option before the expiration date. (New Zealand Futures & Options Exchange)

**earnings report** A statement—also called an income statement—issued by a company showing its earnings or losses over a given period. The earnings report lists the income earned, expenses and the net result. See **balance sheet**. (NYSE)

**econometrics** The application of statistical and mathematical methods in the field of economics to test and quantify economic theories and the solutions to economic problems. (CBOT)

**edge** 1. The spread between the bid and ask price. This is called the trader's edge. 2. The difference between the market price of an option and its theoretical value, using an option pricing model. This is called the theoretical edge. (CBOE)

**elasticity** A characteristic of commodities that describes the interaction of the supply, demand and price of a commodity. A commodity is said to be elastic in demand when a price change creates an increase or decrease in consumption; the supply of a commodity is said to be elastic when a change in price creates change in the production of the commodity. (NFA)

**equilibrium price** The market price at which the quantity supplied of a commodity equals the quantity demanded. (CBOT)

**equipment trust certificate** A type of security, generally issued by a railroad, to pay for new equipment. Title to the equipment, such as a locomotive, is held by a trustee until the notes are paid off. An equipment trust certificate is usually secured by a first claim on the equipment. (NYSE)

**equity**    1. The ownership interest of common and preferred stockholders in a company. 2. Also refers to excess of value of securities over the debit balance in a margin account. (NYSE) 3. The dollar value of a futures trading account if all open positions were offset at the going market price. (NFA)

**equity options**    Options on shares of stock. (OCC)

**Eurodollars**    U.S. dollars on deposit with a bank outside of the United States and, consequently, outside the jurisdiction of the United States. The bank could be either a foreign bank or a subsidiary of a U.S. bank. (CBOT)

**European Currency Unit (ECU)**    A basket containing fixed amounts of currency from each of the member countries of the European Economic Community (EEC). (FINEX)

**European-style options**    1. Options that are exercisable only at expiration. (New Zealand Futures & Options Exchange) 2. An option that ·may be exercised only on the last trading day before expiration. (SOFFEX)

**exchange for physicals (EFP)**    A transaction generally used by two hedgers who want to exchange futures for cash positions. Also referred to as against actuals or versus cash. (NFA)

**exchange rate**    The cost of one currency in terms of another. (FINEX)

**Exchange Rate Mechanism of the European Monetary System (EMS)**    An agreement among most countries in the European Economic Community (EEC) to limit their currencies' movements against one another to preestablished ranges. (FINEX)

**exchange-traded option**    An organized marketplace over which options trading takes place. (Morgan Stanley Foreign Exchange)

**ex-dividend**    A synonym for "without dividend." The buyer of a stock selling ex-dividend does not receive the recently declared dividend. Every dividend is payable on a fixed date to all shareholders recorded on the books of the company as of a previous date of record. For example, a dividend may be declared as payable to holders of record on the books of the company on a given Friday. Since five business days are allowed for delivery of stock in a regular way transaction on the New York Stock Exchange, the exchange would declare the stock ex-dividend as of the opening of the market on the preceding Monday. That means anyone who bought it on or after that Monday would not be entitled to that dividend. When stocks go ex-dividend, the stock tables include the symbol "x" following the name. See **cash sale, net change, transfer.** (NYSE)

**exercise**    1. Declaration by an option holder that he or she wishes to buy or sell the underlying values under the agreed-upon conditions of the option contract. (SOFFEX) 2. To elect to buy or sell, taking advantage of the right (but not the obligation) conferred by an option contract. (FINEX)

**exercise by exception**  A procedure used by the Options Clearing Corporation to exercise in-the-money options, unless specifically instructed by the holder of the option not to do so. This procedure protects the holder from losing the intrinsic value of the option because of failure to exercise. Unless instructed to do so, the OCC will exercise all equity options of 75 cents or more in the money in customer accounts, and 25 cents or more in firm and market maker accounts. For index options subject to cash settlements, the OCC, unless instructed to do so, will exercise all index options 25 cents or more in the money in customer accounts, and a penny or more in firm and market maker accounts. (CBOE)

**exercise cut-off date**  The final date on which an option contract may be executed. (SOFFEX)

**exercise cycle**  See **cycle**. (CBOE)

**exercise limits**  The total number of puts and/or calls that a holder is allowed to exercise during any five consecutive trading days. (CBOE)

**exercise (or strike) price**  The price specified in the option contract at which the buyer of a call can purchase the commodity during the life of the option, and the price specified in the option contract at which the buyer of a put can sell the commodity during the life of the option. (FINEX)

**expanded trading hours**  Additional trading hours of specific futures and options contracts at the CBOT that overlap with business hours in other time zones. (CBOT)

**expiration cycle**  An expiration cycle relates to the dates on which options on a particular underlying security expire. A given option will be placed in one of three cycles, the January cycle, the February cycle or the March cycle. At any point in time, an option will have contracts with four expiration dates outstanding, two in near-term months and two in far-term months. (OCC)

**expiration date**  The date on which an option contract automatically expires; the last day an option can be exercised. (FINEX)

**expiry**  See **expiration date**. (New Zealand Futures & Options Exchange)

**ex-rights**  Without rights. Corporations raising additional money may do so by offering their stockholders the right to subscribe to new or additional stock, usually at a discount from the prevailing market price. The buyer of a stock selling ex-rights is not entitled to the rights. See **ex-dividend, rights**. (NYSE)

**extra**   The short form of "extra dividend." A dividend in the form of stock or cash in addition to the regular or usual dividend the company has been paying. (NYSE)

**extrinsic value**   See **time value**. (NFA)

**face value**   The value of a bond as it appears on its face, unless the value is otherwise specified by the issuing company. Face value is ordinarily the amount the issuing company promises to pay at maturity. Face value is not an indication of market value. Sometimes referred to as par value. See **par**. (NYSE)

**fair value**   A price that favors neither buyer nor seller. In the case of options, this term is often used to describe the theoretical price of an option derived from a mathematical formula. (CBOE)

**federal funds**   Member bank deposits held by the Federal Reserve; these funds are loaned by the Federal Reserve to other member banks. (CBOT)

**federal funds rate**   The rate of interest charged for the use of federal funds. (CBOT)

**Federal Housing Administration**   A division of the U.S. Department of Housing and Urban Development that insures residential mortgage loans and sets construction standards. (CBOT)

**Federal Reserve System**   A central banking system in the United States, created by the Federal Reserve Act in 1913, designed to assist the nation in attaining its economic and financial goals. The structure of the Federal Reserve System includes a Board of Governors, the Federal Open Market Committee and 12 Federal Reserve Banks. (CBOT)

**feed ratio**   A ratio used to express the relationship of feeding costs to the dollar value of livestock. See **hog/corn ratio** and **steer/corn ratio**. (CBOT)

**fees**   Variable amounts charged by the exchange and clearinghouse for each options contract entered into. (New Zealand Futures & Options Exchange)

**fence**   A strategy involving a long call and a short put, or a short call and long put at different strike prices with the same expiration date. When this strategy is established in conjunction with the underlying stock, the three-sided tactic is called a risk conversion (long stock) or a risk reversal (short stock). This strategy is also called a combination. See **conversion** and **reverse conversion**. (CBOE)

**fidelity fund**   A fund operated by New Zealand Futures Exchange to assist in the protection of the exchange members' clients against such things as fraud. (New Zealand Futures & Options Exchange)

**fill**   The price at which an order is executed. (COMEX)

**fill or kill**   A designation added to an order indicating that if the order is not filled immediately, it is cancelled. (CME)

**final settlement value**   Settlement value fixed by the exchange on the last trading day. (SOFFEX)

**Financial Analysis Auditing Compliance Tracking System**   The National Futures Association's computerized system of maintaining financial records of its member firms and monitoring their financial conditions. (CBOT)

**financial futures contract**   A standardized contract to purchase or deliver a fixed quantity of a defined financial instrument at a set price in the future. (SOFFEX Strategies)

**financial instruments**   The generic name for securities, such as bills, bonds, debentures and shares, currencies and financial market indexes. (New Zealand Futures & Options Exchange)

**first notice day**   The first day on which notice of intent to deliver a commodity in fulfillment of an expiring futures contract can be given to the clearinghouse by a seller and assigned by the clearinghouse to a buyer. Varies from contract to contract. (NFA)

**fiscal year**   A corporation's accounting year. Due to the nature of their particular business, some companies do not use the calendar year for their bookkeeping. A typical example is the department store that finds December 31 too early a date to close its books after the Christmas rush. For that reason many stores wind up their accounting year January 31. Their fiscal year, therefore, runs from February 1 of one year through January 31 of the next. The fiscal year of other companies may run from July 1 through the following June 30. Most companies, though, operate on a calendar-year basis. (NYSE)

**fixed charges**   A company's fixed expenses, such as bond interest, which it has agreed to pay, whether or not earned, and which are deducted from income before earnings on equity capital are computed. (NYSE)

**fixed costs**   Costs incurred for resources that do not change as output is increased or decreased (i.e., can't be changed during the short run—usually one year). (CME)

**fixed exchange rate system**   A system in which the values of various countries' currencies are tied, or pegged, to one currency. Prior to 1973, most nations' currencies were pegged to the U.S. dollar, which was in turn pegged to gold. (FINEX)

**fixed investment**   An investment that, once made, cannot be converted to another use during the production period or short run; a fixed cost, i.e., farrowing house. (CME)

**flat income bond**   The price at which a bond is traded includes consideration for all unpaid accruals of interest. Bonds that are in default of interest or principal are traded flat, income bonds that pay interest only to the extent earned are usually traded flat. All other bonds are usually dealt in and interest, which means that the buyer pays to the seller the market price plus interest accrued since the last payment date. (NYSE)

**floating exchange rate system**    The current international monetary system, in which each currency's value in terms of other currencies is determined by market forces. It contrasts with a fixed rate system such as existed prior to 1973. (FINEX)

**floor**    The huge trading area—about the size of a football field—where stocks, bonds and options are bought and sold on the New York Stock Exchange. (NYSE)

**floor broker**    Any person who, in or surrounding any pit, ring, post or other place provided by a contract market for the meeting of persons similarly engaged, executes for another any orders for the purchase or sale of any commodity for future delivery. (FINEX)

**floor trader**    An exchange member who usually executes his or her own trades by being present in the pit or place for futures trading; sometimes called a local. (FINEX)

**foreign exchange**    Foreign currency. In the foreign exchange market, foreign currency is bought or sold for immediate or future delivery. (FINEX)

**formula investing**    An investment technique. One formula calls for the shifting of funds from common shares to preferred shares or bonds as a selected market indicator rises above a certain predetermined point, and the return of funds to common share investments as the market average declines. See **dollar cost averaging**. (NYSE)

**forward (cash) contract**    A contract on which a seller agrees to deliver a specified cash commodity to a buyer sometime in the future. In contrast to futures contracts, the terms of forward contracts are not standardized. Forward contracts are not traded on federally designated exchanges. (NFA)

**forward exchange rate**    Price of foreign currency for delivery at some date in the future, the value date. Forward value dates must be longer than two business days. (FINEX)

**forward market**    A market where foreign currencies are traded for future delivery. Unlike futures, trading in forward markets does not take place on organized exchanges, but through individual financial institutions. Forward currency contracts are not transferable and are generally expected to be settled through actual delivery of currencies. (FINEX)

**free and open market**    A market in which supply and demand are freely expressed in terms of price. Contrasts with a controlled market in which supply, demand and price may be regulated. (NYSE)

**front-running**    An illegal securities transaction based on prior non-public knowledge of a forthcoming transaction that will affect the price of a stock. (CBOE)

**fulfillment date**   See **delivery date**. (SOFFEX)

**full carrying charge market**   A futures market in which the price difference between delivery months reflects the total costs of interest, insurance and storage. (CBOT)

**fully disclosed**   An account carried by the futures commission merchant in the name of the individual customer; opposite of an **omnibus account**. (NFA)

**fundamental research**   Analysis of industries and companies based on such factors as sales, assets, earnings, products or services, markets and management. As applied to the economy, fundamental research includes consideration of gross national product, interest rates, unemployment, inventories, savings, etc. See **technical research**. (NYSE)

**funded debt**   Usually interest-bearing bonds or debentures of a company. Could include long-term bank loans. Does not include short-term loans, preferred or common stock. (NYSE)

**fungibility**   Interchangeability resulting from standardization. Options listed on national exchanges are fungible, while over-the-counter options generally are not. (CBOE)

**futures**   See **futures contract**.

**futures commission merchant (FCM)**   An individual or organization that solicits or accepts orders to buy or sell futures contracts or commodity options and accepts money or other assets from customers in connection with such orders. Must be registered with the CFTC. (NFA)

**futures contract**   1. A legally binding agreement to buy and sell a specified quantity of a specific commodity or financial instrument at a specific date in the future. Futures contracts are only traded through futures exchanges. (New Zealand Futures & Options Exchange) 2. A firm commitment to deliver or to receive a specified quantity of a commodity or cash payment during a designated month. The commodity price or cash payment is determined by a public auction among exchange members. (FINEX)

**Futures Industry Association (FIA)**   The national trade association for the futures industry. (NFA)

**Futures Industry (Client Fund) Regulations 1990**   Regulations that reinforce the exchange's requirements for the separation of client funds from a broker's house funds and require all client funds to be immediately paid into client bank accounts with registered banks. (New Zealand Futures & Options Exchange)

**gamma**   The rate of change of the delta relative to the asset price is called the gamma of the option. It measures how much the delta will change if the market price of the underlying instrument changes; it also corresponds to the acceleration of the option premium. Also known as curvature. (New Zealand Futures & Options Exchange)

**general mortgage bond**   A bond that is secured by a blanket mortgage on the company's property but may be outranked by one or more other mortgages. (NYSE)

**gilt-edged**   High-grade bond issued by a company that has demonstrated its ability to earn a comfortable profit over a period of years and pay its bondholders their interest without interruption. (NYSE)

**give up**   A term with many different meanings. It is used when a member of the exchange on the floor acts for a second member by executing an order for him with a third member. The first member tells the third member that he is acting on behalf of the second member and gives up the second member's name rather than his own. (NYSE)

**gold fix**   The setting of the price of gold by dealers (especially in a twice-daily London meeting at the central bank); the fix is the fundamental worldwide price for setting prices of gold bullion and gold-related contracts and products. (NYSE)

**good delivery**   Certain basic qualifications that must be met before a security sold on the exchange may be delivered. The security must be in proper form to comply with the contract of sale and to transfer title to the purchaser. (NYSE)

**good-for-the-day order (GFD)**   An order that remains in the system until either fully matched or canceled. It is automatically canceled at the close of business on the day in which it was entered. (New Zealand Futures & Options Exchange)

**good-till-canceled order (GTC)**   An order that remains in the system indefinitely until it is either canceled or fully matched. (New Zealand Futures & Options Exchange)

**good-till-over order (GTO)**   An order that remains in the system for as long as it remains the best bid or ask price. It is automatically canceled at the end of the day. (New Zealand Futures & Options Exchange)

**government bonds**   Obligations of the U.S. government, regarded as the highest-grade securities issues. (NYSE)

**grade, quality and deviation**   The allowable limits outside of par that may be delivered, but at a discount specified by CME rules. (CME)

**grain terminal**   Large grain elevator facility with the capacity to ship grain by rail or barge to domestic or foreign markets. (CBOT)

**grantor**   A person who sells an option and assumes the obligation but not the right to sell (in the case of a call) or buy (in the case of a put) the underlying futures contract at the exercise price. (NFA)

**gross national product**   The total value of final goods and services produced in the United States over a specific time period. (CBOT)

**gross processing margin**    The difference between the cost of soybeans and the combined sales income of the processed soybean oil and meal. (CBOT)

**growth stock**    Stock of a company with a record of growth in earnings at a relatively rapid rate. (NYSE)

**guided account**    A customer account that is part of a program directed by a commodity trading advisor or futures commission merchant. Such programs usually require a minimum initial investment and may include a trading strategy that will utilize only a part of the investment at any given time. (NFA)

**guts**    The purchase (or sale) of both an in-the-money call and an in-the-money put. A box spread can be viewed as a combination of an in-the-money strangle and an out-of-the-money strangle. To differentiate between these two strangles, the term *guts* refers to the in-the-money strangle. See **box spread** and **strangle**. (CBOE)

**haircut**    Similar to the margin required of public customers, this term refers to the equity required of floor traders on equity option exchanges. Generally, one of the advantages of being a floor trader is that the haircut is less than margin requirements for public customers. (CBOE)

**hedge**    The sale of futures against ownership of a cash commodity to protect against a decline in the commodity's value; conversely, the purchase of futures against anticipated need for a cash commodity to protect against an increase in the commodity's value. (KCBT)

**hedge ratio**    A tool for assessing volatility, given a constant basis and applying it as a ratio of hedging contracts per physical position. (New Zealand Futures & Options Exchange)

**hedging**    Taking a position in a futures market opposite to a position held in the cash market to minimize the risk of financial loss from an adverse price change; a purchase or sale of futures as a temporary substitute for a cash transaction that will occur later. (FINEX)

**high**    The top price at which a contract was traded during a given period. (New Zealand Futures & Options Exchange)

**historical basis**    The historical difference between the cash market price and the futures market price for a particular time of the year. (CME)

**historical volatility**    A statistical measurement of past price movements. Historical volatility is the standard deviation of price movements observed in the past, expressed in an annualized percentage. A standard deviation has a confidence level of 66 percent; therefore, a historical volatility expressed in this manner evaluates the probable movement of the underlying, with a probability of $2/3$, at the end of one year. (Montreal Exchange)

**hog/corn ratio**    The relationship of feeding costs to the dollar value of hogs. It is measured by dividing the price of hogs ($/hundredweight) by the price of corn ($/bushel). When corn prices are high relative to pork prices, fewer units of corn equal the dollar value of 100 pounds of pork. Conversely, when corn prices are low in relation to pork prices, more units of corn are required to equal the value of 100 pounds of pork. See **feed ratio**. (CBOT)

**holder**    The purchaser of an option. (OCC)

**holding company**    A corporation that owns the securities of another, in most cases with voting control. (NYSE)

**horizontal spread**    See **calendar spread**. (CBOT)

**hypothecation**    The pledging of securities as collateral—for example, to secure the debit balance in a margin account. (NYSE)

**immediate at best (IAB)**    An order that is met immediately either exactly as requested or at the best price obtainable in the market. (New Zealand Futures & Options Exchange)

**immediate or cancel (IOC)**    If an IOC order remains unmatched or partially matched after the entry, the unmatched portion of the order is immediately canceled. (New Zealand Futures & Options Exchange)

**implied volatility**    A mathematical calculation made using one of the option evaluation models, which includes the option premium observed on the market, as well as other important factors to help determine the option's volatility. (Montreal Exchange)

**income bond**    Generally, income bonds promise to repay principal but to pay interest only when earned. In some cases unpaid interest on an income bond may accumulate as a claim against the corporation when the bond becomes due. An income bond may also be issued in lieu of preferred stock. (NYSE)

**indenture**    A written agreement under which bonds and debentures are issued, setting forth maturity date, interest rate and other specifications. (NYSE)

**independent broker**    Member on the floor of the NYSE who executes orders for other brokers having more business at the time than they can handle themselves, or for firms who do not have their exchange member on the floor. Formerly known as two-dollar brokers from the time when these independent brokers received $2 per hundred shares for executing such orders. Their fees are paid by the commission brokers. See **commission broker**. (NYSE)

**index**    A statistical yardstick expressed in terms of percentages of base year or years. For instance, the NYSE Composite Index of all NYSE common stock is based on 1965 as 50. An index is not an average. See **averages, NYSE Composite Index**. (NYSE)

**index multiplier**　The dollar value of each index unit, generally $100. (Pacific Stock Exchange)

**index option**　An option whose underlying entity is an index. Generally, index options are cash-settled. (CBOE)

**indicative market prices (IMP)**　Indicative market prices enable principals in the market to enter prices on the Automated Trading System (ATS) for information purposes only in inactive contracts, delivery months or exercise prices. They are considered indicative and cannot be traded, although they are identified as belonging to a particular market principal, enabling communication to take place. IMPs only stay live if there are no other firm orders quoted. If a firm order is entered, then the IMP is immediately canceled. (New Zealand Futures & Options Exchange)

**Individual Retirement Account (IRA)**　A pension plan with tax advantages. IRAs permit investment through intermediaries like mutual funds, insurance companies and banks or directly in stocks and bonds through stockbrokers. See **Keogh Plan**. (NYSE)

**inelasticity**　A characteristic that describes the interdependence of the supply, demand and price of a commodity. A commodity is inelastic when a price change does not create an increase or decrease in consumption; inelasticity exists when supply and demand are relatively unresponsive to change in price. (NFA)

**initial margin**　Security that must be paid by both the seller and the purchaser for opening futures positions. (SOFFEX)

**institution**　A professional investment management company. Typically, this term is used to describe large money managers such as banks, pension funds, mutual funds and insurance companies. (CBOE)

**institutional investor**　An organization whose primary purpose is to invest its own assets or those it holds in trust for others; includes pension funds, investment companies, insurance companies, universities and banks. (NYSE)

**intercommodity spread**　The purchase of a given delivery month of one futures market and the simultaneous sale of the same delivery month of a different, but related, futures market. (CBOT)

**interdelivery spread**　The purchase of one delivery month of a given futures contract and the simultaneous sale of another delivery month of the same commodity on the same exchange. Also referred to as an **intramarket spread**. (CBOT)

**interest**　Payments borrowers pay lenders for the use of their money. A corporation pays interest on its bonds to its bondholders. See **bond, dividend**. (NYSE)

**interest rate**　The prevailing risk-free interest rate that affects the option price. (New Zealand Futures & Options Exchange)

**interest rate differential**    The difference between the interest rates of two countries. (FINEX)

**intermarket spread**    The sale of a given delivery month of a futures contract on one exchange and the simultaneous purchase of the same delivery month and futures contract on another exchange. (CBOT)

**Intermarket Trading System (ITS)**    An electronic communications network now linking the trading floors of seven registered exchanges and the NASD to foster competition among them in stocks listed on either the NYSE or AMEX and one or more regional exchanges. Through ITS, any broker or market maker on the floor of any participating market can reach out to other participants for an execution whenever the nationwide quote shows a better price is available. (NYSE)

**international spread**    A spread that allows a trader to take advantage of changes in the spread in interest rates in two different countries. (Montreal Exchange)

**interrogation device**    A computer terminal that provides market information—last sale price, quotes, volume, etc.—on screen or paper tape. (NYSE)

**in-the-money option**    An option with intrinsic value. For calls, the strike price must be below the current market price of the underlying futures contract. For puts, the strike price must exceed it. (FINEX)

**intramarket spread**    The purchase of one delivery month of a given futures contract and the simultaneous sale of another delivery month in the same contract on the same exchange. (Montreal Exchange)

**intrinsic value**    1. The value of an option if it were to be exercised immediately with the underlying at its current price; the amount by which an option is in the money. For call options, this is the difference between the stock price and strike price, if that difference is a positive number, or zero otherwise. For put options, it is the difference between the strike price and the stock price if that difference is positive, or zero otherwise. (Montreal Exchange) 2. A measure of the value of an option or a warrant if immediately exercised. The amount by which the current futures price for a commodity is above the strike price of a call option or below the strike price of a put option for the commodity. (FINEX)

**introducing broker (IB)**    A firm or individual that solicits and accepts commodity futures orders from customers but does not accept money, securities or property from the customer. An IB must be registered with the CFTC and must carry all of its accounts through a futures commission merchant on a fully disclosed basis. (NFA)

**inverse conversion (reversal)**    Creation of a synthetic futures long position through the purchase of calls and the writing of puts with the

same strike price at the same time that a "genuine" futures short position is entered. (SOFFEX)

**inverted market**　A futures market in which the nearer months are
selling at premiums over the more distant months; characteristically,
a market in which supplies are currently in shortage. (NFA)

**investment**　The use of money for the purpose of making more money,
to gain income or increase capital, or both. (NYSE)

**investment banker**　Also known as an underwriter. The middleman
between the corporation issuing new securities and the public. The
usual practice is for one or more investment bankers to buy outright
from a corporation a new issue of stocks or bonds. The group forms
a syndicate to sell the securities to individuals and institutions. Investment bankers also distribute very large blocks of stocks or bonds
(perhaps those held by an estate). See **primary distribution, syndicate**. (NYSE)

**investment company**　A company or trust that uses its capital to invest
in other companies. There are two principal types. (1) The *closed-end*
investment companies, some of which are listed on the New York
Stock Exchange, are readily transferable in the open market and are
bought and sold like other shares. Capitalization of these companies
remains the same unless action is taken to change, which is seldom.
(2) *Open-end* funds sell their own new shares to investors, stand ready
to buy back their old shares, and are not listed. Open-end funds are
so called because their capitalization is not fixed; they issue more
shares as people want them. (NYSE)

**investment counsel**　One whose principal business consists of acting as
as investment advisor and rendering investment supervisory services. (NYSE)

**invisible supply**　Uncounted stocks of a commodity in the hands of
wholesalers, manufacturers and producers that cannot be identified
accurately; stocks outside commercial channels but theoretically
available to the market. (CBOT)

**iota**　The rate of change of an option premium with respect to interest
rate. (New Zealand Futures & Options Exchange)

**iron butterfly**　An option strategy with limited risk and limited profit
potential that involves both a long (or short) straddle, and a short (or
long) strangle. (CBOE)

**issue**　Any of a company's securities, or the act of distributing such securities. (NYSE)

**jelly roll spread**　A long call and a short put with the same strike price
in one month, and a short call and long put with the identical strike
in another month. This is the combination of synthetic long and
short positions in different months. Generally only floor traders use
this spread. (CBOE)

**kappa**    1. The change in option value caused by a percentage change in volatility. (Morgan Stanley Foreign Exchange) 2. See **vega**. (CBOE)

**Keogh Plan**    Tax advantaged personal retirement program that can be established by a self-employed individual. See **Individual Retirement Account**. (NYSE)

**lagging indicators**    An index that shows the general direction of the economy and confirms or denies the trend implied by the leading indicators. (CBOT)

**last day of trading**    1. The last day of trading in options is at the close of business on the second to the last business day of the option's expiration month. (New Zealand Futures & Options Exchange) 2. Day on which trading ceases for the maturing (current) delivery month. See **expiration date**. (FINEX)

**leading indicators**    Market indicators that signal the state of the economy for the coming months. Some of the leading indicators include: average manufacturing workweek, layoff rate of manufacturing workers, inflation-adjusted new orders for consumer goods and materials, speed of delivery of new goods, rate of net business formation, contracts for plant and equipment, change in inventories on hand, change in crude material prices, prices of stocks, change in total liquid assets and change in money supply. (CBOT)

**leg**    A term describing one side of a position with two or more sides. A trader who legs into a spread establishes one side first, hoping for a favorable price movement so the other side can be executed at a better price. This is, of course, a risk-oriented method of establishing a spread position. (CBOE)

**legal list**    A list of investments selected by various states in which certain institutions and fiduciaries, such as insurance companies and banks, may invest. Legal lists are often restricted to high-quality securities meeting certain specifications. See **prudent man rule**. (NYSE)

**leverage**    1. The effect on a company when it has bonds, preferred stock or both outstanding. If the earnings of a company with 1,000,000 common shares increases from $1,000,000 to $1,500,000, earnings per share would go from $1 to $1.50, or an increase of 50 percent; but if earnings of a company that had to pay $500,000 in bond interest increased that much, earnings per common share would jump from 50 cents to $1 a share, or 100 percent. (NYSE) 2. The ratio of the percentage change in the option premium to the percentage change in the underlying value. (SOFFEX)

**leverage contract**    A standardized agreement calling for the delivery of a commodity with payments against the total cost spread out over a period of time. Principal characteristics include: standard units and quality of a commodity and of terms and conditions of the contract;

payment and maintenance of margin; closeout by offset or delivery (after payment in full); and no right to or interest in a specific lot of the commodity. Leverage contracts are not traded on exchanges. (NFA)

**leverage effect**    The leverage effect enables participants on the forward market with modest capital to enter a much higher position in relation to the underlying value. The leverage effect causes the percentile win or loss on options or futures positions to be higher than the relevant change of the underlying value. (SOFFEX)

**leverage transaction merchant (LTM)**    The firm or individual through whom leverage contracts are entered. LTMs must be registered with the Commodity Futures Trading Commission. (Commodity Futures Trading Commission)

**liabilities**    All claims against a corporation. Liabilities include accounts, wages and salaries payable; dividends declared payable; accrued taxes payable; fixed or long-term liabilities, such as mortgage bonds, debentures and bank loans. See **assets, balance sheet**. (NYSE)

**limit, limited order or limited price order**    An order to buy or sell a stated amount of a security at a specified price, or at a better price, if obtainable after the order is represented in the trading crowd. (NYSE)

**limit move**    A price that has advanced or declined the limit permitted during one trading session as fixed by the rules of a contract market. (NFA)

**line of credit**    A commitment by the lender to provide short-term credit to a borrower as needed. (CME)

**linkage**    The ability to buy (sell) contracts on one exchange (such as the CME) and later sell (buy) them on another exchange (such as the Singapore International Monetary Exchange). (CBOT)

**liquidation**    1. The process of converting securities or other property into cash; in the dissolution of a company, after the sale of its assets and the payment of all of its indebtedness, the remaining cash is distributed to the shareholders. (NYSE) 2. A transaction that offsets or closes out a long or short position. (FINEX)

**liquidity**    The ability of the market in a particular security to absorb a reasonable amount of buying or selling at reasonable price changes. Liquidity is one of the most important characteristics of a good market. (NYSE)

**liquidity data bank**    A computerized profile of Chicago Board of Trade market activity, used by technical traders to analyze price trends and develop trading strategies. There is a specialized display of daily volume data and time distribution of prices for every commodity traded on the Chicago Board of Trade. (CBOT)

**liquid market**    A market characterized by the ability to buy and sell with relative ease. (COMEX)

**listed option**    A put or call traded on a national option exchange with standardized terms. In contrast, over-the-counter options usually have nonstandard or negotiated terms. (CBOE)

**listed stock**    The stock of a company that is traded on a securities exchange. The various stock exchanges have different standards for listing. Some of the guides used by the NYSE for an original listing are national interest in the company and a minimum of 11 million shares publicly held among not less than 2,000 round-lot stockholders. The publicly held common shares should have a minimum aggregate market value of $18 million. The company should have net income in the latest year of over $2.5 million before federal income tax and $2 million in each of the two preceding years. (NYSE)

**load**    The portion of the offering price of shares of open-end investment companies in excess of the value of the underlying assets; it covers sales commissions and all other costs of distribution. The load is usually incurred only on purchases, there being, in most cases, no charge when the shares are sold (redeemed). See **investment company**. (NYSE)

**loan program**    A federal program in which the government lends money at preannounced rates to farmers and allows them to use the crops they plant for the upcoming crop year as collateral. Default on these loans is the primary method by which the government acquires agricultural commodity stocks. (CBOT)

**loan rate**    The amount lent per unit of a commodity to farmers. (CBOT)

**local**    1. A floor trader who executes transactions for his or her own account only. (COMEX) 2. A floor trader on a futures exchange who buys and sells for his or her own account, fulfilling the same role as a market maker on an options exchange. (CBOE)

**localized futures price**    The futures market price for the contract month nearest, but in front of, the time one will be marketing one's livestock plus or minus one's estimated basis. (CME)

**locked in**    Investors are said to be locked in when they have profit on a security they own but do not sell because their profit would immediately become subject to the capital gains tax. (NYSE)

**long**    A trader who has purchased physical commodities, financial instruments or futures contracts and has not yet offset that transaction with a sale. *Long* can also be used as an adjective to describe such an option position. In the foreign exchange markets, long means buying or owning more of a currency than one has sold. Opposite of **short**. (FINEX)

**long hedge**   The purchase of a futures contract in anticipation of a cash market purchase. It is generally used to protect against a rise in the cash price. (FINEX)

**long position**   An investor with a long call (long put) option has the right to purchase (to sell) a futures contract at a predetermined price within a specified period of time. Purchasing an option does not automatically oblige the investor to assume all risks associated with the futures contract, but the investor must be prepared to assume responsibility when he or she exercises the option and holds the contract until delivery. (Montreal Exchange)

**long-run**   A time period long enough that all factors of production can be varied (i.e., cropland converted to feedlot or vice versa). (CME)

**low**   The lowest price at which a contract was traded during a given period. (New Zealand Futures & Options Exchange)

**maintenance margin**   Margin to facilitate the settlement of credits or debits of the variation margin determined daily. With the existence of a maintenance margin, the variation margin can be debited or credited against the originally deposited margin until the stipulated minimum margin is reached. A margin payment that reestablishes the level of the original margin deposited then becomes due. (SOFFEX)

**managed account**   See **discretionary account**. (NFA)

**manipulation**   An illegal operation. Buying or selling a security for the purpose of creating a false or misleading appearance of active trading or for the purpose of raising or depressing the price to induce purchase or sale by others. (NYSE)

**margin**   1. The amount of money or collateral deposited by a client with a broker, or by a broker with a clearinghouse, for the purpose of insuring the broker or clearinghouse against loss on open futures contracts; the margin is not a partial payment on a purchase. (1) Original or initial margin is the total amount of margin per contract required by the broker when a futures position is opened. (2) Maintenance margin is a sum that must be maintained on deposit at all times; if a customer's equity in any futures position drops to or under the level because of adverse price action, the broker must issue a margin call to restore the customer's equity. (FINEX) 2. The amount paid by the customer when using a broker's credit to buy or sell a security; under Federal Reserve regulations, the initial margin required since 1945 has ranged from the current rate of 50 percent of the purchase price up to 100 percent. See **brokers' loans, equity**. (NYSE)

**margin call**   1. A request from a brokerage firm to a customer to bring margin deposits up to minimum levels. 2. A request by the clearinghouse to a clearing member to bring clearing margins back to minimum levels required by the clearinghouse rules. (FINEX)

**margin requirement for options**   The amount an uncovered (naked) option writer is required to deposit and maintain to cover his or her daily position valuation and reasonably foreseeable intraday price changes. (OCC)

**market basket**   A group of common stocks whose price movement is expected to closely correlate with an index. (CBOE)

**market-if-touched order**   An order that specifies a price that when touched, the order becomes a market order. (CME)

**market maker**   An exchange member on the trading floor who buys and sells for his or her own account and who has the responsibility of making bids and offers and maintaining a fair and orderly market. (CBOE)

**market maker system**   A method of supplying liquidity in options markets by having market makers in competition with one another. (CBOE)

**market-not-held order**   A type of market order that allows the investor to give discretion to the floor broker regarding the time and price at which a trade is executed. (CBOE)

**market on close**   A designation added to an order specifying that it is to be executed as a market order within the closing range. (CME)

**market order**   An order to buy or sell a stated amount of a security at the most advantageous price obtainable after the order is represented in the trading crowd. See **good-till-canceled order, limited order, stop limited order.** (NYSE)

**market price**   The last reported price at which a stock or bond sold or the current quote. See **quote.** (NYSE)

**market quote**   A trading instruction from an investor to a broker to buy or sell a security immediately at the best available price. (CBOE)

**market reporter**   A person employed by the exchange and located in or near the trading pit who records prices as they occur during trading. (CBOT)

**market risk**   The possibility of price decline for the owner of a commodity or producer and the possibility of price increase for a person who is required to purchase the commodity. (CME)

**mark to market**   Daily cash flow system used by U.S. futures exchanges to maintain a minimum level of margin equity for a given futures or option contract position. This is done by calculating the gain or loss in each contract position resulting from changes in the price of the futures or option contracts at the end of the trading day. (FINEX)

**married put strategy**   The simultaneous purchase of stock and the corresponding number of put options. This is a limited risk strategy during the life of the puts because the stock can be sold at the strike price of the puts. (CBOE)

**matching**   The aligning of purchases with corresponding sales as trades are processed. (COMEX)

**matching volatility**   The process of adjusting the number of futures contracts taken in a hedge so as to reduce basis risk. (New Zealand Futures & Options Exchange)

**maturity**   The date on which a loan or bond comes due and is to be paid off. (NYSE)

**maturity date**   See **expiration date**. (Morgan Stanley Foreign Exchange)

**member corporation**   A securities brokerage firm, organized as a corporation, with at least one member of the NYSE. (NYSE)

**member organization**   This term includes NYSE member firms and member corporations. (NYSE)

**merger**   Combination of two or more corporations. (NYSE)

**minimum fluctuation**   The premium of an option as quoted in New Zealand cents per share of the underlying security, in minimum fluctuations of 0.1 cent. (New Zealand Futures & Options Exchange)

**minimum price fluctuation**   Smallest allowable increment of price movement in a given contract. See **tick**. (FINEX)

**mixed spread**   A term used loosely to describe a trading position that does not fit neatly into a standard spread category. (CBOE)

**model**   A mathematical formula used to calculate the theoretical value of an option. See **Black-Scholes model**. (CBOE)

**modified duration**   A more precise measure of volatility than duration. In mathematical terms, modified duration is equal to duration (as per McCauley formula) divided by $(1 + \text{Yield}/n)$ where n is the number of coupons paid annually. (Montreal Exchange)

**money market fund**   A mutual fund whose investments are in high-yield money market instruments such as federal securities, CDs and commercial paper. Its intent is to make such instruments, normally purchased in large denominations by institutions, available indirectly to individuals. See **certificate of deposit, commercial paper**. (NYSE)

**money supply**   The amount of money in the economy, consisting primarily of currency in circulation plus deposits in banks: M-1 is the U.S. money supply consisting of currency in circulation, traveler's checks, checking account funds, NOW and super NOW accounts, automotive transfer service accounts and balances in credit unions. M-2 is the U.S. money supply consisting of M-1 plus savings and small time deposits (less than $100,000) at depository institutions, overnight repurchase agreements at commercial banks and money market mutual fund accounts. M-3 consists of the U.S. money supply of M-2 plus large time deposits ($100,000 or more) at depository institutions, repurchase agreements with maturities longer than one day at commercial banks and institutional money market accounts. (CBOT)

**mortgage bond**    A bond secured by a mortgage on a property. The value of the property may or may not be equal to the value of the bonds issued against it. See **bond, debenture**. (NYSE)

**moving-average charts**    A statistical price analysis method of recognizing different price trends. A moving average is calculated by adding the prices for a predetermined number of days and then dividing by the number of days. (CBOT)

**municipal bond**    A bond issued by a state or a political subdivision, such as county, city, town or village. The term also designates bonds issued by state agencies and authorities. In general, interest paid on municipal bonds is exempt from federal income taxes and state and local income taxes within the state of issue. (NYSE)

**mutual fund**    See **investment company**. (NYSE)

**naked option**    The sale of a call or put option without holding an offset position in the underlying commodity. (FINEX)

**naked position**    Unprotected long or short position in a cash or futures market. (FINEX)

**naked writer**    See **uncovered call writing** and **uncovered put writing**. (OCC)

**National Association of Futures Trading Advisors**    The national trade association of commodity pool operators and commodity trading advisors and related industry participants. (NFA)

**National Association of Securities Dealers (NASD)**    An association of brokers and dealers in the over-the-counter securities business. (NYSE)

**National Association of Securities Dealers Automated Quotations (NASDAQ)**    An automated information network that provides brokers and dealers with price quotations on securities traded over the counter. (NYSE)

**National Futures Association**    Authorized by Congress in 1974 and designated by the CFTC in 1982 as a registered futures association, National Futures Association is the industrywide self-regulatory organization of the futures industry. (NFA)

**nearby**    The nearest listed trading month of a futures market. (FINEX)

**negative carry**    The net cost incurred when the cost of finance is greater than the return on the asset being held. (CBOT)

**negative yield curve**    See **yield curve**. (CBOT)

**negotiable**   In reference to a security, the title is transferable by delivery. (NYSE)

**net asset value**   1. Usually used in connection with investment companies to mean net asset value per share; an investment company computes its assets daily, or even twice daily, by totaling the market value of all securities owned; all liabilities are deducted, and the balance divided by the number of shares outstanding; the resulting figure is the net asset value per share. See **assets, investment company.** (NYSE) 2. The value of each unit of participation in a commodity pool; basically a calculation of assets minus liabilities plus or minus the value of open positions when marked to the market, divided by the number of units. (NFA)

**net change**   The change in the price of a security from the closing price on one day to the closing price on the next day on which the stock is traded. The net change is ordinarily the last figure in the newspaper stock price list. The mark + $1^{1}/_{8}$, means up $1.125 a share from the last sale on the previous day the stock traded. (NYSE)

**net farm income**   Commonly used in farm and ranch accounting, it measures the return to operator labor, capital, management and unpaid family labor. This is after all costs including depreciation changes in inventory are taken into account. (CME)

**net margin requirement**   The equity required in a margin account to support an option position after deducting the premium received from sold options. (CBOE)

**net order**   See **contingency order.** (CBOE)

**net performance**   An increase or decrease in net asset value exclusive of additions, withdrawals and redemptions. (NFA)

**neutral**   An adjective used to describe the belief that a stock or the market in general will neither rise nor decline significantly. (CBOE)

**new issue**   A stock or bond sold by a corporation for the first time. Proceeds may be used to retire outstanding securities of the company, for a new plant or equipment, for additional working capital or to acquire a public ownership interest in the company for private owners. (NYSE)

**ninety/ten strategy**   An option strategy in which an investor buys Treasury bills (or other liquid assets) with 90 percent of his or her funds and call options with the balance. (CBOE)

**noncumulative**   A type of preferred stock on which unpaid dividends do not accrue. Omitted dividends are, as a rule, gone forever. See **cumulative preferred.** (NYSE)

**nondeliverable**   A future contract that is settled by cash rather than delivery of a commodity or financial instrument. All contracts currently available on the New Zealand Futures & Options Exchange are nondeliverable. (New Zealand Futures & Options Exchange)

**nonequity option**    Any option that does not have common stock as the underlying asset. Nonequity options include options on futures, indexes, interest rate composites, physicals and so on. (CBOE)

**nonsystematic risk**    The portion of total risk that can be attributed to the particular firm. See **systematic risk**. (CBOE)

**not-held order**    An order that allows the investor to release the floor broker from the normal obligations implied by the other terms of the order. For example, a limit order designated as not-held allows the floor broker to use discretion in filling the order when the market trades at the limit price of the order. In this case, the floor broker is not obligated to provide the customer with an execution if the market trades through the limit price on the order. See **discretion, market-not-held order**. (CBOE)

**notice day**    Any day on which notices of intent to deliver on futures contracts may be issued. (NFA)

**notice of exercise**    The notice originated by an option holder and assigned to an option writer stating that an option is being exercised. There are three important points to remember in connection with option exercise: (1) Only an option holder may exercise an option. (2) The holder of an American-style option may exercise the option, and the option writer may be assigned a notice of exercise at any time prior to expiration of the option. (3) An automatic exercise feature does not exist in the currency option market. Customers who wish to exercise positions must notify their brokers, regardless of how far in the money the position may be. (Philadelphia Stock Exchange)

**novation**    The process by which the clearinghouse effectively substitutes one contracting party to a futures contract for another party. Novation permits holders of futures positions to close out even though they may do the offsetting trade with a different party than was on the other side when the position was opened. (New Zealand Futures & Options Exchange)

**NYSE Composite Index**    The composite index covering price movements of all common stocks listed on the NYSE. It is based on the close of the market December 31, 1965 as 50.00 and is weighted according to the number of shares listed for each issue. The index is computed continuously and printed on the stock ticker tape. Point changes in the index are converted to dollars and cents to provide a meaningful measure of changes in the average price of listed stocks. The composite index is supplemented by separate indexes for four industry groups: industrials, transportation, utility and finance. See **averages**. (NYSE)

**odd lot**    An amount of stock less than the established 100 share unit. See **round lot**. (NYSE)

**off-board**   Refers to transactions over the counter in unlisted securities or to transactions of listed shares not executed on a national securities exchange. (NYSE)

**offer**   A proposal to sell at a specified price. (COMEX)

**offset**   To liquidate a futures position with a transaction that is equal to and opposite the original transaction. A futures purchase is offset by a later sale of the same quantity and delivery month, and a futures sale is offset by a later purchase of the same quantity and delivery month. (KCBT)

**offset the hedge**   A short hedger would buy the futures and sell the cash product. A long hedger would sell the futures and buy the cash product. Sometimes called liquidate or unwind. (CME)

**omega**   See **vega**. (CBOE)

**omnibus account**   An account in which the transactions of two or more persons are combined and carried in the name of the originating futures commission merchant rather than of the individual customers. (NFA)

**OPEC (Organization of Petroleum Exporting Countries)**   Emerged as the major petroleum pricing power in 1973, when the ownership of oil production in the Middle East transferred from the operating companies to the governments of the producing countries or to their national oil companies. Members are: Algeria, Ecuador, Gabon, Indonesia, Iran, Iraq, Kuwait, Libya, Nigeria, Qatar, Saudi Arabia, the United Arab Emirates and Venezuela. (CBOT)

**open, the**   The period at the beginning of the trading session, officially designated by the exchange, during which all transactions are considered made at the open. (NFA)

**open-end investment company**   See **investment company**. (NYSE)

**opening only order**   An order to be executed at a price within the opening range of prices. (CME)

**opening purchase**   A transaction in which an option is bought that establishes a long position for the buyer. (New York Futures Exchange)

**opening range**   The range of prices at which buy and sell transactions took place during the opening of the market. (NFA)

**opening rotation**   See **trading rotation**. (CBOE)

**opening sale**   A transaction in which an option is sold that establishes a short position for the writer (grantor). (New York Futures Exchange)

**opening transaction**   Purchase or sale through which a long or short position is established. (FINEX)

**open interest**   The sum of futures contracts to one delivery month or one market that have been entered into and not yet liquidated by an offsetting transaction or fulfilled by delivery. (FINEX)

**open market system**   The buying and selling of government securities (Treasury bills, notes and bonds) by the Federal Reserve. (CBOT)

**open order**   See **good-till-canceled order**. (NYSE)

**open outcry**   The method of trading that is an auction without an auctioneer.   The members of the pit, whether trading for themselves or customers, announce the number of contracts they want to buy or sell and the price they want in the transaction. (CME)

**open position**   A long position that has not been exercised or a short position that has not been assigned. (SOFFEX)

**open trade equity**   The unrealized gain or loss on open positions. (NFA)

**option**   A right to buy (call) or to sell (put) a fixed amount of a given stock at a specified price within a limited period of time. The purchaser hopes that the stock's price will go up (a call) or down (a put) by an amount sufficient to provide a profit when the option is sold. If the stock price holds steady or moves in the opposite direction, the price paid for the option is lost entirely. There are several other types of options available to the public but these are basically combinations of puts and calls. Individuals may write (sell) as well as purchase options. Options are also traded on stock indexes, futures and debt instruments. (NYSE)

**optionable stock**   A stock on which options are traded. (CBOE)

**option period**   The time from when an option contract is created to the expiration date. (CBOE)

**option premium**   See **premium**. (NFA)

**option price**   Price to be paid for the right represented by the option. (SOFFEX)

**option pricing curve**   A graphical representation of the estimated theoretical value of an option at one point in time, at various prices of the underlying asset. (CBOE)

**options class**   Options that all have the same underlying instrument. The ten-year Government of Canada bond futures options are one options class because they all have the ten-year government of Canada bond futures contract as their underlying value. (Montreal Exchange)

**Options Clearing Corporation (OCC)**   A corporation owned by the exchanges that trade listed stock options, OCC is an intermediary between option buyers and sellers. OCC issues and guarantees all option contracts. (CBOE)

**options series**   Options that have the same class, the same type (calls or puts), the same expiration date and the same exercise price. For example, all ten-year Government of Canada bond futures March call options, with an exercise price of $98, are of the same options series. (Montreal Exchange)

**options type**   There are two types: call options and put options. (Montreal Exchange)

**option valuation model**    See **model**. (CBOE)

**option writer**    The option buyer's counterparty who is obligated to supply (call) or to accept (put) the underlying value, for which he or she receives the option price. (SOFFEX)

**order book official (OBO)**    An exchange employee in charge of keeping the public order book and executing the orders therein. (CBOE)

**original margin**    The total amount of margin per contract required when a futures position is opened. (FINEX)

**out-of-the-money options**    In the case of call options, when the exercise price is greater than the market price of the underlying and, in the case of put options, when the exercise price is below the market price of the underlying. (Montreal Exchange)

**overbought**    A technical opinion that the market price has risen too steeply and too fast in relation to underlying fundamental factors. (NFA)

**overline loan**    A loan that exceeds the legal lending limit of a lender made to a customer by a larger lending institution that has an agreement with the smaller lender to service its needs. (CME)

**oversold**    A technical opinion that the market price has declined too steeply and too fast in relation to underlying fundamental factors. (NFA)

**over-the-counter market**    A market for securities made up of securities dealers who may or may not be members of a securities exchange. The over-the-counter market is conducted over the telephone and deals mainly with stocks of companies without sufficient shares, stockholders or earnings to warrant listing on an exchange. Over-the-counter dealers may act either as principals or as brokers for customers. The over-the-counter market is the principal market for bonds of all types. See **National Association of Securities Dealers, National Association of Securities Dealers Automated Quotations**. (NYSE)

**over-the-counter option**    An option that is traded in the over-the-counter market. OTC options are not usually listed on an options exchange and generally do not have standardized terms. (CBOE)

**overvalued**    An adjective used to describe an option that is trading at a price higher than its theoretical value. It must be remembered that this is a subjective evaluation, because theoretical value depends on one subjective input—the volatility estimate. (CBOE)

**overwrite**    An option strategy involving the sale of a call option against an existing long position. This is different from the covered write strategy that involves the purchase of stock and simultaneous sale of a call. (CBOE)

**P&S statement**    See **purchase and sale statement**. (CBOT)

**paper profit (loss)**    An unrealized profit or loss on a security still held. Paper profits and losses become realized only when the security is sold. See **profit taking**. (NYSE)

**par**    In the case of a common share, par means a dollar amount assigned to the share by the company's charter. Par value may also be used to compute the dollar amount of common shares on the balance sheet. Par value has little relationship to the market value of the common stock. Many companies issue no-par stock but give a stated per share value on the balance sheet. In the case of preferred stocks, it signifies the dollar value upon which dividends are figured. With bonds, par value is the face amount, usually $1,000. (NYSE)

**par delivery**    The quality, quantity, time and location of delivery of livestock to fulfill the commitment of a CME contract are such that there are no discounts. The seller will receive the futures price at which he or she sold the contract, less commissions and grading fees. (CME)

**parity**    An adjective used to describe the difference between the stock price and the strike price of an in-the-money option. When an option is trading at its intrinsic value, it is said to be trading at parity. (CBOE)

**participating preferred**    A preferred stock that is entitled to its stated dividend and also to additional dividends on a specified basis, upon payment of dividends on the common stock. (NYSE)

**passed dividend**    Omission of a regular or scheduled dividend. (NYSE)

**payment-in-kind program (PIK)**    A government program in which farmers who comply with a voluntary acreage-control program and set aside an additional percentage of acreage specified by the government receive certificates that can be redeemed for government-owned stocks of grain. (CBOT)

**payoff diagram**    Options can be illustrated by the use of payoff diagrams that are derived from the profit and loss profile of the share. (New Zealand Futures & Options Exchange)

**penny stock**    Low-priced issues, often highly speculative, selling at less than $1 per share. Frequently used as a term of disparagement, although some penny stocks have developed into investment-caliber issues. (NYSE)

**perfect competition**    A market with a homogenous product (uniform quality and quantity), large numbers of buyers and sellers who are all free to enter and exit the market, information equally available to all and participants who are risk-neutral. (CME)

**performance bond margin**    The amount of money deposited by both buyer and seller of a futures contract or an options seller to ensure performance of the term of the contract. Margin in commodities is not a payment of equity or down payment on the commodity itself, but rather it is a security deposit. (CBOT)

**physical option**    An option whose underlying entity is a physical good or commodity. For example, currency options traded at the Philadelphia Exchange and many OTC currency options are options on the currency itself, rather than on futures contracts. (CBOE)

**physicals**    The underlying commodity or financial instrument. (New Zealand Futures & Options Exchange)

**pin risk**    The risk to a floor trader with a conversion or reversal position is that the stock price will exactly equal the strike price at option expiration. The trader will not know how many long options to exercise because he or she will not know how many of the short options will be assigned. The risk is that on the following Monday the trader will have a long or short stock position and thus be subject to the risk of an adverse price move. (CBOE)

**pit**    The area on the trading floor of some exchanges where trading in futures or options on futures is conducted by open outcry. (NFA)

**point**    In shares of stock, a point means $1. If ABC shares rise three points, each share has risen $3. In bonds, a point means $10, because a bond is quoted as a percentage of $1,000. A bond that rises three points gains 3 percent of $1,000, or $30 in value. An advance from 87 to 90 would mean an advance in dollar value from $870 to $900. In market averages, the word *point* means merely that and no more. If, for example, the NYSE Composite Index rises from 90.25 to 91.25, it has risen a point. A point in this index, however, is not equivalent to $1. See **indexes**.

**point-and-figure chart**    Charts that show price changes of a minimum amount regardless of the time period involved. (CBOT)

**pool**    See **commodity pool**. (NFA)

**portfolio**    A collection of financial securities/instruments. (New Zealand Futures & Options Exchange)

**position**    A market commitment; the number of contracts bought or sold for which no offsetting transaction has been entered into. The buyer of a commodity is said to have a long position and the seller of a commodity is said to have a short position. (COMEX)

**position day**    According to the Chicago Board of Trade rules, the first day in the process of making or taking delivery of the actual commodity on a futures contract. The clearing firm representing the seller notifies the Board of Trade Clearing Corporation that its short customers want to deliver on a futures contract. (CBOT)

**position limit**    A maximum number of contracts of an underlying instrument that may be held as a position by a customer or a group of customers acting in concert. (SOFFEX)

**position trading**    The establishment of a position in the market with the expectation of profiting from a fundamental change in price level. It usually requires a position lasting more than one day. (CME)

**positive carry**    See **carrying charges**. (CBOT)

**positive yield curve**    See **yield curve**. (CBOT)

**preferred stock**    A class of stock with a claim on the company's earnings before payment may be made on the common stock. It is usually entitled to priority over common stock if the company liquidates. It is also usually entitled to dividends at a specified rate when declared by the board of directors and before payment of a dividend on the common stock, depending upon the terms of the issue. See **cumulative preferred, participating preferred**. (NYSE)

**premium**    1. The purchase price of an option; the premium is the amount the buyer pays the option writer for the opportunity to be long or short the underlying futures contract; the premium is the option buyer's maximum risk. (KCBT) 2. A premium paid that does not constitute a down payment on an eventual purchase of the underlying. (Montreal Exchange) 3. The amount by which a bond or preferred stock can sell above its par value; can also refer to the redemption price of a bond or preferred stock if it is higher than face value. See **discount**. (NYSE)

**price discovery**    The determination of a fair market value for a commodity. (COMEX)

**price/earnings ratio**    A popular way to compare stocks selling at various price levels. The P/E ratio is the price of a share of stock divided by earnings per share for a 12-month period. For example, a stock selling for $50 a share and earning $5 a share is said to be selling at a price/earnings ratio of 10. (NYSE)

**price limit**    The maximum advance or decline from the previous day's settlement price permitted for a futures contract in one trading session. (NFA)

**primary distribution**    Also called primary or public offering. The original sale of a company's securities. See **investment banker**. (NYSE)

**primary market**    1. For securities that are traded in more than one market, the primary market is usually the exchange where the most volume is traded. 2. The initial sale of securities to public investors. See **secondary market**. (CBOE)

**prime rate**    The lowest interest rate charged by commercial banks to their most creditworthy and largest corporate customers. Personal, automobile, commercial and financing loans are often pegged to the prime. (NYSE)

**principal**   1. (1) A sole proprietor, general partner, officer or director, or person occupying a similar status or performing similar functions, having the power to exercise a controlling influence over the activities of the entity; (2) any holder or any beneficial owner of 10 percent or more of the outstanding shares of any class of stock of the entity; or (3) any person who has contributed 10 percent or more of the capital of the entity. (NFA) 2. The person for whom a broker executes an order or dealers buying or selling for their own accounts; the term *principal* may also refer to a person's capital or to the face amount of a bond. (NYSE) 3. Approved market trader with direct access to the Automated Trading System. (New Zealand Futures & Options Exchange)

**Producer Price Index**   An index that shows the cost of resources needed to produce manufactured goods during the previous month. (CBOT)

**profit graph**   A graphical presentation of the profit and loss possibilities of an investment strategy at one point in time (usually option expiration), at various stock prices. (CBOE)

**profit taking**   Selling stock that has appreciated in value since purchase in order to realize the profit. The term is often used to explain a downturn in the market following a period of rising prices. See **paper profit**. (NYSE)

**prospectus**   The official selling circular that must be given to purchasers of new securities registered with the Securities and Exchange Commission. It highlights the much longer registration statement filed with the commission. (NYSE)

**proxy**   Written authorization given by a shareholder to someone else to represent him or her and vote his or her shares at a shareholders' meeting. (NYSE)

**proxy statement**   Information given to stockholders in conjunction with the solicitation of proxies. (NYSE)

**prudent man rule**   An investment standard. In some states, the law requires that a fiduciary, such as a trustee, may invest the fund's money only in securities designated by the state on the so-called legal list. In other states, the trustee may invest in a security if it is one that would be bought by a prudent person of discretion and intelligence, who is seeking a reasonable income and preservation of capital. (NYSE)

**public offering**   See **primary distribution**. (NYSE)

**public order book**   The limit buy and limit sell orders from public customers that are away from the current market price and are managed by the order book official or specialist. If the market price moves so that an order in the public order book is the best bid or offer, that order has priority and must be the first one filled at that price. (CBOE)

**pulpit**    A raised structure adjacent to, or in the center of, the pit or ring at a futures exchange where market reporters, employed by the exchange, record price changes as they occur in the trading pit. (CBOT)

**purchase and sale statement (P&S)**    A statement sent by a futures commission merchant to a customer when a futures or options position has been liquidated or offset. The statement shows the number of contracts bought or sold, the prices at which the contracts were bought or sold, the gross profit or loss, the commission charges and the net profit or loss on the transaction. Sometimes combined with a **confirmation statement**. (NFA)

**put-call parity**    The value of a call at a certain strike price and expiration date can be deduced from the value of a put with the same strike price and expiration date. (New Zealand Futures & Options Exchange)

**put option**    1. An option to sell a specified amount of a commodity at an agreed price and at any time until the expiration of the option; a put option is purchased to protect against a fall in price; the buyer pays a premium to the seller/grantor of this option; the buyer has the right to sell the commodity or enter into a short position in the futures markets if the option is exercised. See **call**. (FINEX) 2. An option contract that gives the holder the right to sell a specified quantity of the underlying instrument for a specified price at or before a specified date (physical delivery), or the right to receive the exercise price of an option less the settlement price of the underlying value at or before a specified date (cash settlement). (SOFFEX).

**pyramiding**    The use of unrealized profits on existing futures positions as margin to increase the size of the position, normally in successively smaller increments. (NFA)

**quotation**    The actual price or the bid or ask price of either cash commodities or futures or options contracts at a particular time. Often called **quote**. (NFA)

**quote**    The highest bid to buy and the lowest offer to sell a security in a given market at a given time. If you ask your broker for a quote on a stock, he or she may come back with something like "45¼ to 45½." This means that $45.25 is the highest price any buyer wanted to pay at the time the quote was given on the floor of the exchange, and that $45.50 was the lowest price that any seller would take at the same time. See **bid and asked**. (NYSE)

**rally**    An upward movement of prices. (COMEX)

**range**    The difference between the high and low price of a commodity during a given trading session, week, month, year, etc. (NFA)

**ratio backspread**    A limited risk/unlimited profit option strategy, involving the sale of fewer options than the investor holds long. It is used to exploit expectations regarding the future exchange rate direction or volatility. (Morgan Stanley Foreign Exchange)

**ratio calendar combination**   A term used loosely to describe any variation of an investment strategy that involves both puts and calls in unequal quantities and at least two different strike prices and two different expirations. (CBOE)

**ratio calendar spread**   An investment strategy in which more short-term options are sold than longer-term strike prices and that has two different expirations. (CBOE)

**ratio spread**   An unlimited risk/limited profit option strategy, involving the sale of more options than the investor holds long. It is used to exploit expectations regarding future exchange rate direction or volatility. (Morgan Stanley Foreign Exchange)

**ratio write**   An investment strategy in which stock is purchased and call options are sold on a greater than one-for-one basis. (CBOE)

**Real Estate Investment Trust (REIT)**   An organization similar to an investment company in some respects but concentrating its holdings in real estate investments. The yield is generally liberal since REITs are required to distribute as much as 90 percent of their income. See **investment company**. (NYSE)

**realized gains and losses**   The net amount received or paid when a closing transaction is made and matched together with an opening transaction. (CBOE)

**Recognized Investment Exchange (RIE)**   An exchange that is authorized by the Securities and Investments Board and conforms to Schedule 4 of the Financial Services Act (1986). (ISE)

**record date**   The date on which one must be registered as a shareholder of a company in order to receive a declared dividend or, among other things, to vote on company affairs. See **ex-dividend, transfer**. (NYSE)

**redemption price**   The price at which a bond may be redeemed before maturity, at the option of the issuing company. Redemption value also applies to the price the company must pay to call in certain types of preferred stock. See **callable**. (NYSE)

**refinancing**   A process in which new securities are sold by a company, and the money is used to retire existing securities. The object may be to save interest costs, extend the maturity of the loan, or both. Same as refunding. (NYSE)

**registered bond**   A bond that is registered on the books of the issuing company in the name of the owner. It can be transferred only when endorsed by the registered owner. See **bearer bond, coupon bond**. (NYSE)

**registered commodity representative**   See **broker, associated person**. (NFA)

**registered competitive market maker**    Members of the New York Stock Exchange who trade on the floor for their own account and who have an obligation, when called upon by an exchange official, to narrow a quote or improve the depth of an existing quote by their own bid or offer. (NYSE)

**registered representative**    The man or woman who serves the investor customers of a broker/dealer. In a New York Stock Exchange member organization, a registered representative must meet the requirements of the exchange as to background and knowledge of the securities business. Also known as an account executive or customer's broker. (NYSE)

**registrar**    Usually a trust company or bank charged with the responsibility of keeping a record of the owners of a corporation's securities and preventing the issuance of more than the authorized amount. See **transfer**. (NYSE)

**registration**    Before a public offering of new securities can be made by a company, the securities must be registered under the Securities Act of 1933. A registration statement is filed with the SEC by the issuer. It must disclose pertinent information relating to the company's operations, securities, management and purpose of the public offering. Before a security may be admitted to dealings on a national securities exchange, it must be registered under the Securities Act of 1934. The application for registration must be filed with the exchange and the SEC by the company issuing the securities. (NYSE)

**regular way delivery**    Unless otherwise specified, securities sold on the New York Stock Exchange are to be delivered to the buying broker by the selling broker and payment made to the selling broker by the buying broker on the fifth business day after the transaction. Regular way delivery for bonds is the following business day. See **transfer**. (NYSE)

**Regulation T**    The federal regulation governing the amount of credit that may be advanced by brokers and dealers to customers for the purchase of securities. (NYSE)

**Regulation U**    The federal regulation governing the amount of credit that may be advanced by a bank to its customers for the purchase of listed stocks. See **margin**. (NYSE)

**repair strategy**    An investment strategy in which an existing long stock position is supplemented by buying one in-the-money call (or one at-the-money call) and selling two out-of-the-money calls, all calls having the same expiration. The effect of this strategy is to lower the break-even point of stock ownership without significantly increasing the risk of the total position. (CBOE)

**reparations**    Compensation payable to a wronged party in a futures or options transaction. The term is used in conjunction with the

CFTC's customer claims procedure for recovery of civil damages. (NFA)

**reportable position**   The number of open contracts specified by the Commodity Futures Trading Commission at which one must begin reporting total positions by delivery month to the authorized exchange and/or the CFTC. (NFA)

**repurchase agreement (REPO)**   An agreement between a seller and a buyer, usually concerning U.S. government securities, where the seller agrees to buy back the security at a later date. (CBOT)

**reserve currency**   One that central banks are willing to hold in reserve and that functions as an accepted vehicle for world trade and finance. Prior to World War II, the British pound served as the international reserve currency; in the postwar era, the U.S. dollar has filled that role. (FINEX)

**reserve requirements**   The minimum amount of cash and liquid assets as a percentage of demand deposits and time deposits that member banks of the Federal Reserve are required to maintain. (CBOT)

**resistance**   A level above which prices have had difficulty penetrating. (CBOT)

**resumption**   The reopening the following day of specific futures and options markets that also trade during the evening session at the Chicago Board of Trade. (CBOT)

**return to equity**   The sum that results when an operator includes all other costs (charge for labor and management as well as cash costs) in his or her break-even costs. This tells how well the money that has been invested in the enterprise has performed. (CME)

**revaluation**   A formal official increase in the exchange rate or price of currency, made unilaterally by a country. (FINEX)

**reversal**   A position in which the investor sells shares short, sells a put and buys a call with the same terms. (New Zealand Futures & Options Exchange)

**reverse conversion**   An investment strategy used by professional option traders in which a short put and long call with the same strike price and expiration are combined with short stock to lock in a nearly riskless profit. The process of executing these three-sided trades is sometimes called reversal arbitrage. (CBOE)

**rho**   A measure of the expected change in an option's theoretical value as a response to a 1 percent change in interest rate. (CBOE)

**rights**   When a company wants to raise more funds by issuing additional securities, it may give its stockholders the opportunity, ahead of others, to buy the new securities in proportion to the number of shares each owns. The piece of paper evidencing this privilege is called a right. Because the additional stock is usually offered to stockholders below the current market price, rights ordinarily have a market value of their own and are actively traded. In most cases they must be exercised within a relatively short period. Failure to exercise or sell rights may result in monetary loss to the holder. See **warrant**. (NYSE)

**ring method**   A method of settlement used by futures markets from the early 1900s until the 1920s, when the first formalized clearing operations were developed. Settlement clerks of brokerage houses maintained daily accounting records of customer transactions in ring notebooks. (CBOT)

**rings**   Trading arenas located on the floor of an exchange in which traders execute orders. Sometimes called pits. (COMEX)

**risk**   The possibility of adverse outcomes associated with an action or business decision. (CME)

**risk arbitrage**   Commonly used term to describe the purchase of a stock subject to takeover rumors with the hope of selling at a significant profit to a company effecting the takeover. The risk is present because there is never any guarantee that a takeover will materialize. (CBOE)

**risk-averse**   The businessperson or manager who seeks to treat risk conservatively whenever possible and desires a steady stream of profits versus the risk and reward associated with jumping in with both feet. (CME)

**risk conversion/reversal**   See **fence**. (CBOE)

**risk disclosure document**   See **disclosure document**. (CBOT)

**risk factors**   The factors (deltas) that are published daily by the exchange and indicate the risk of an option position relative to that of the related futures contract. These factors are used as the basis of the option margining system. (London Financial Futures Exchange)

**risk level**   Commonly used in agriculture to refer to equity or debt capital placed at risk as a result of committing those resources to production of a product with uncertain results. (CME)

**risk management**   The process of identifying the risk exposure of a company and hedging it to cover potential losses. (New Zealand Futures & Options Exchange)

**risk-neutral**   The businessperson who neither avoids all risks at all cost, nor seeks huge risks and opportunities. (CME)

**risk preference**   An individual may have a risk-averse, risk-neutral or risk-taking attitude toward business opportunities. (CME)

**risk transfer**   Removing the impact of price change from a market participant who is actually producing or processing the commodity to a participant willing to assume the risk. (CME)

**rolling**   A trading action in which the trader simultaneously closes an open option position and creates a new option position at a different strike price, different expiration or both. Variations of this include roll up, roll down and roll out. (CBOE)

**rolling over**   Establishing a new hedge to take over from one due to expire. (New Zealand Futures & Options Exchange)

**rotation**   See **trading rotation**. (CBOE)

**round lot**   A unit of trading or a multiple thereof. On the NYSE the unit of trading is generally 100 shares in stocks and $1,000 or $5,000 par value in the case of bonds. In some inactive stocks, the unit of trading is 10 shares. See **odd lot**. (NYSE)

**round trip**   Buying and selling of a futures or options contract. (London Financial Futures Exchange)

**round turn**   The completion of both a purchase and offsetting sale, or of a sale and offsetting purchase. (KCBT)

**runners**   Messengers who rush orders received by phone clerks to brokers for execution in the pit. (CBOT)

**scale order**   An order to buy or sell a security that specifies the total amount to be bought (or sold) at specified price variations. (NYSE)

**scalper**   Speculators, usually locals, who trade for small, short-term profits during the course of each trading session. (CME)

**scripophily**   A term coined in the mid-1970s to describe the hobby of collecting antique bonds, stocks and other financial instruments. Values are affected by beauty of the certificate and the issuer's role in world finance and economic development. (NYSE)

**seasonality of basis**   Variations in the difference between the cash market price and the futures price that historically occur during a certain season of the year. (CME)

**seat**   A traditional, familiar name for a membership on an exchange. (NYSE)

**secondary distribution**   Also known as a secondary offering. The redistribution of a block of stock some time after it has been sold by the issuing company. The sale is handled off the NYSE by a securities firm or group of firms and the shares are usually offered at a fixed price related to the current market price of the stock. Usually the block is a large one, such as might be involved in the settlement of an estate. The security may be listed or unlisted. See **investment banker, primary distribution**. (NYSE)

**secondary market**   1. A market that provides for the purchase or sale of previously sold or bought options through closing transactions. (OCC) 2. A market where securities are bought and sold after their initial purchase by public investors. (CBOE)

**Securities Amendment Act 1988**   An act that requires all principals acting in the market on behalf of other persons to be members of a recognized exchange. New Zealand Futures & Options Exchange

Limited is the only authorized futures and options exchange in this country. (New Zealand Futures & Options Exchange)

**Securities and Exchange Commission (SEC)**  1. The SEC is a federal government agency that regulates the securities industry. (CBOE) 2. It was established by Congress to help protect investors. The SEC administers the Securities Act of 1933, the Securities Exchange Act of 1934, the Securities Act Amendments of 1975, the Trust Indenture Act, the Investment Company Act, the Investment Adviser Act and the Public Utility Holding Company Act. (NYSE)

**Securities Industry Automation Corporation**  An independent organization established by the New York and American stock exchanges as a jointly owned subsidiary to provide automation, data processing, clearing and communications services. (NYSE)

**Securities Investor Protection Corporation**  A corporation that provides funds for use, if necessary, to protect customers' cash and securities that may be on deposit with a SIPC member firm in the event the firm fails and is liquidated under the provisions of the SIPC Act. SIPC is not a government agency. It is a nonprofit membership corporation created, however, by an act of Congress. (NYSE)

**security**  Common or preferred stock; a bond of a corporation, government or quasi-government body. (CBOT)

**security agreement**  A signed document, required by a lender of a borrower, that provides a guarantee to the lender that the borrowed funds will be repaid. (CME)

**segregated account**  An account that has only one customer's funds in it with no other customer funds commingled with those funds. (CME)

**seller/writer/grantor**  1. An individual who sells an option, establishing a short position. (FINEX) 2. The seller of an option; an option writer. The seller receives the buyer's money and is obligated to take an opposite futures position if the option is exercised. (KCBT)

**seller's option**  A special transaction on the NYSE that gives the seller the right to deliver the stock or bond at any time within a specified period, ranging from not less than two business days to not more than 60 days. (NYSE)

**sequential expiration cycle**  See **cycle**. (CBOE)

**serial bond**  An issue that matures in part at periodic stated intervals. (NYSE)

**series (of options)**  Options of the same type (i.e., either puts or calls, but not both), covering the same underlying futures contract or physical commodity, having the same strike price and expiration date. (FINEX)

**settlement**  Conclusion of a securities transaction when a customer pays a broker/dealer for securities purchased or delivers securities sold and receives from the broker the proceeds of a sale. See **regular way delivery, cash sale**. (NYSE)

**settlement price**   Daily price at which a clearinghouse clears all trades. It is based on the closing range of that day's trading and is the basis for both margin calls and the next day's price limits. (FINEX)

**settlement-to-market**   The process whereby the profits or losses determined under the mark-to-market basis are received/paid in cash by way of variation margin as the contracts are deemed to be closed out at the closing market price at the same price. (ISE)

**short**   A trader who has sold physical commodities, financial instruments or futures contracts and has not yet offset that transaction with a purchase. Short can also be used as an adjective to describe such an open position. In the foreign exchange markets, short means selling more of a currency than one has bought. Opposite of **long**. (FINEX)

**short covering**   1. The offsetting of an existing short position by purchasing futures contracts. See **liquidation** (COMEX) 2. Buying stock to return stock previously borrowed to make delivery on a short sale. (NYSE)

**short hedge**   A cash market participant who needs to sell the cash commodity in the future and is at a risk if prices decline. The hedger would sell a futures contract to offset that risk. (CME)

**short option position**   The position of an option writer that represents an obligation to meet the terms of the option if it is assigned. (CBOE)

**short position**   Stocks, options or futures contracts sold short and not covered as of a particular date. On the NYSE, a tabulation is issued once a month listing all issues on the exchange in which there was a short position of 5,000 or more shares and issues in which the short position had changed by 2,000 or more shares in the preceding month. Short position also means the total amount of stock an individual has sold short and has not covered, as of a particular date. (NYSE)

**short-run**   A time period where one or more of the units for production are fixed or cannot be converted to another use (e.g., feedlot converted to hog production). (CME)

**short sale**   A transaction by a person who believes a security will decline and sells it, though the person does not own any. For instance: A person instructs a broker to sell short 100 shares of XYZ stock. The broker borrows the stock so delivery of the 100 shares can be made to the buyer. The money value of the shares borrowed is deposited by the broker with the lender. Sooner or later one must cover this short sale by buying the same amount of stock that was borrowed for return to the lender. If the person can buy XYZ at a lower price than it was sold for, the profit is the difference between the two prices, not counting commissions and taxes. But if one has to pay more than the price received, that is the amount of one's loss. Stock exchange and federal regulations govern and limit the conditions under which a short sale may be made on a national securities exchange. Sometimes people will sell short a stock they already own in order to protect a paper profit. This is known as selling short against the box. (NYSE)

**short stock position**    A strategy that profits from a stock price decline. It is initiated by borrowing stock from a broker-dealer and selling it in the open market. This strategy is closed out at a later date by buying back the stock. (CBOE)

**sinking fund**    Money regularly set aside by a company to redeem its bonds, debentures or preferred stock from time to time as specified in the indenture of the charter. (NYSE)

**specialist**    A member of the New York Stock Exchange who has two primary functions: (1) To maintain an orderly market in the securities registered to the specialist. In order to maintain an orderly market, the exchange expects the specialists to buy or sell for their own account, to a reasonable degree, when there is a temporary disparity between supply and demand; (2) the specialist acts as a broker's broker. When commission brokers on the exchange floor receive a limit order, say, to buy at $50 a stock then selling at $60, they cannot wait at the post where the stock is traded to see if the price reaches the specified level. They leave the order with a specialist, who will try to execute it in the market if and when the stock declines to the specified price. At all times the specialists must put their customers' interests above their own. See **limited order**. (NYSE)

**speculation**    The employment of funds by a speculator. Safety of principal is a secondary factor. See **investment**. (NYSE)

**speculator**    An investor who buys or sells for his or her own account, either as a day trader (initiates and offsets positions in one trading day) or a position trader (holds either a long or a short position over a period of time). (COMEX)

**spin off**    The separation of a subsidiary or division of a corporation from its parent by issuing shares in a new corporate entity. Shareowners in the parent receive shares in the new company in proportion to their original holding and the total value remains approximately the same. (NYSE)

**split**    The division of the outstanding shares of a corporation into a larger number of shares. A three-for-one split by a company with one million shares outstanding results in three million shares outstanding. Each holder of 100 shares before the three-for-one split would have 300 shares, although the proportionate equity in the company would remain the same; 100 parts of one million are the equivalent of 300 parts of three million. Ordinarily, splits must be voted by directors and approved by shareholders. See **stock dividends**. (NYSE)

**spot commodity**  A physical commodity, financial instrument or index that underlies a futures contract. The U.S. Dollar Index is the spot commodity for U.S. Dollar Index futures. Sometimes called cash commodity. (FINEX)

**spot exchange rate**  Price of foreign currency for delivery (value date) in two business days. (MidAmerica Commodity Exchange)

**spot market**  Also cash market and physical market. The market where trade for immediate delivery of the actual commodity or financial instrument takes place. (New Zealand Futures & Options Exchange)

**spot price**  1. The price of the item being traded on the cash market on that day. (New Zealand Futures & Options Exchange) 2. The price for a futures contract that will mature and become deliverable in the current month. (COMEX)

**spread**  Simultaneous positions in the same contract but in different months or simultaneous positions in related contracts for the same or a different month. See **arbitrage**. (FINEX)

**spreading**  The purchase of one futures contract and the sale of another in related commodities or different contract months of the same commodity. A spread is established in anticipation of a change in the price relationship between the futures contracts in such a way that a subsequent offsetting sale and purchase will yield a net profit. (KCBT)

**spreading contracts**  The simultaneous purchase or sale in one futures contract, and purchase or sale in another related futures contract, in anticipation that the difference between the prices, the spread, will change in a manner profitable to the position. Spreading is sometimes used to describe straddling. (New Zealand Futures & Options Exchange)

**standard deviation**  A statistical measure. One use of the standard deviation is to measure how stock price movements are distributed about the mean. (CBOE)

**standardized**  All contracts traded on futures exchanges are standardized to facilitate trading, that is, all details of the contract are defined in the contract specifications: the contract unit, delivery month, cash settlement price calculations and contract price. (New Zealand Futures & Options Exchange)

**steer/corn ratio**  The relationship of cattle prices to feeding costs. It is measured by dividing the price of cattle ($/hundredweight) by the price of corn ($/bushel). When corn prices are high relative to cattle prices, fewer units of corn equal the dollar value of 100 pounds of cattle. Conversely, when corn prices are low in relation to cattle prices, more units of corn are required to equal the value of 100 pounds of beef. See **feed ratio**. (CBOT)

**stock dividend**   A dividend paid in securities rather than cash. The dividend may be additional shares of the issuing company, or in shares of another company (usually a subsidiary) held by the company. (NYSE)

**stock exchange**   An organized marketplace for securities featured by the centralization of supply and demand for the transaction of orders by member brokers for institutional and individual investors. See **New York Stock Exchange**. (NYSE)

**stockholder of record**   A stockholder of record whose name is registered on the books of the issuing corporation. See **registrar**. (NYSE)

**stock index**   An indicator used to measure and report value changes in a selected group of stocks. How a particular stock index tracks the market depends on its composition—the sampling of stocks, the weighing of individual stocks and the method of averaging used to establish an index. (CBOT)

**stock index futures**   Futures contracts based on market indexes, e.g., NYSE Composite Index futures contracts. (NYSE)

**stock ticker symbols**   Every corporation whose transactions are reported on the NYSE and the AMEX ticker or on NASDAQ has been given a unique identification symbol of up to four letters. These symbols abbreviate the complete corporate name and facilitate trading and ticker reporting. Some of the most famous symbols are: T (American Telephone & Telegraph), XON (Exxon), GM (General Motors), IBM (International Business Machines), S (Sears Roebuck) and XRX (Xerox). (NYSE)

**stop limited order (SLM)**   An SLM is entered with two prices: a trigger price and a limit price. When the market trades at or beyond the trigger price the system attempts to complete the order but only up to (or down to) the limit price. An unmatched portion of the SLM order remains in the system as a GTC order at the limit price. (New Zealand Futures & Options Exchange)

**stop loss order**   An STP is entered with a price known as the trigger price. When the market trades at or beyond the trigger price the system immediately completes the order at the best price available. (New Zealand Futures & Options Exchange)

**straddle**   Position consisting of both a long (short) put and a long (short) call option on the same underlying instrument and having the same exercise price and expiration date. (SOFFEX)

**straddle order (STR)**   The broker selects two different delivery months, and the order will be traded at a premium or discount differential between the two. To be effective, both the buy and sell executions must be successful. If the range set cannot be matched immediately, the entire straddle will be canceled. (New Zealand Futures & Options Exchange)

**strangle**  Position consisting of both a long (short) put and a long (short) call option on the same underlying instrument and having the same expiration date but different exercise prices. (SOFFEX)

**strap**  A strategy involving two calls and one put. All options have the same strike price, expiration and underlying stock. (CBOE)

**street name**  Securities held in the name of a broker instead of a customer's name are said to be carried in street name. This occurs when the securities have been bought on margin or when the customer wishes the security to be held by the broker. (NYSE)

**strike price**  A predetermined price at which the buyer of an option can choose to take a long or short position in the underlying futures contract. Several different strike prices of a particular option are traded at the same time. (KCBT)

**strike price increments**  Intervals established by the exchange between exercise prices on options. (FINEX)

**strike price interval**  The normal price difference between option exercise prices. Equity options generally have $2.50 strike price intervals (if the underlying security price ranges from $10 to $25), $5 intervals (from $25 to $200), and $10 intervals above $200. Index options generally have $5 strike price intervals at all price levels. See **adjusted strike price**. (CBOE)

**strip**  1. A sequence of bought or sold 90-day or three-month interest rate futures in successive quarterly contract months forming a continuous investment or borrowing. (New Zealand Futures & Options Exchange) 2. A strategy involving two puts and one call. All options have the same strike price, expiration, and underlying stock. (CBOE)

**substitutes**  Products that can replace each other or serve the same economic purpose (e.g., beef and pork as meat products). (CME)

**suitability**  A requirement that any investing strategy fall within the financial means and investment objectives of an investor. (CBOE)

**supply, law of**  The relationship between product supply and its price. (CBOT)

**support**  The place on a chart where the buying of futures contracts is sufficient to halt a price decline. (CBOT)

**suspension**  The end of the evening session for specific futures and options markets traded at the Chicago Board of Trade. (CBOT)

**swapping**  Selling one security and buying a similar one almost at the same time to take a loss, usually for tax purposes. (NYSE)

**Swiss Market Index**  The Swiss Market Index (SMI) is he the capitalization-weighted stock index based on a basket of permanently traded securities on the Basel, Geneva and Zurich stock exchanges. (SOFFEX)

**syndicate**   A group of investment bankers who together underwrite and distribute a new issue of securities or a large block of an outstanding issue. (NYSE)

**synthetic futures contract**   Reproduction of the profit and loss characteristics of a futures contract while using options. The simultaneous purchase of a ten-year Government of Canada bond futures call option and the sale of a ten-year Government of Canada bond futures put option with the same strike price create a synthetic product that will closely monitor the movements of a futures contract. (Montreal Exchange)

**synthetic long call**   A long stock position combined with a long put. (CBOE)

**synthetic long put**   A short stock position combined with a long call. (CBOE)

**synthetic long stock**   A long call position combined with a short put. (CBOE)

**synthetic options**   Call options can be created by combining shares with puts and put options can be created by combining shares with calls. (New Zealand Futures & Options Exchange)

**synthetic short call**   A short stock position combined with a short put. (CBOE)

**synthetic short put**   A long stock position combined with a short call. (CBOE)

**synthetic short stock**   A short call position combined with a long put. (CBOE)

**systematic risk**   A form of risk dependent on factors that influence the whole market and cannot be reduced or excluded by portfolio diversification. (SOFFEX)

**technical analysis**   An approach to analysis of futures markets that examines patterns of price change, rates of change and changes in volume of trading, open interest and other statistical indicators. This data is often charted. (NFA)

**tender offer**   A public offer to buy shares from existing stockholders of one public corporation by another company or organization under specified terms good for a certain time period. Stockholders are asked to "tender" (surrender) their holdings for stated value, usually at a premium above current market price, subject to the tendering of a minimum and a maximum number of shares. (NYSE)

**theoretical value**   An estimated fair value of an option derived from a mathematical model. (CBOE)

**theta**   The rate of change of an option premium with respect to time. A portfolio of options with a positive theta will gain in value as time elapses (and nothing else changes); whereas a portfolio with a negative theta will lose value as time elapses. (New Zealand Futures & Options Exchange)

**third market**  Trading of stock exchange listed securities in the over-the-counter market by nonexchange member brokers. (NYSE)

**tick**  See **minimum price fluctuation**. (FINEX)

**ticker**  A telegraphic system that continuously provides the last sale prices and volume of securities transactions on exchanges. Information is either printed or displayed on a moving tape after each trade. (NYSE)

**time decay**  The time premium is a wasting asset in the hands of the option buyer or holder. (New Zealand Futures & Options Exchange)

**time limit order**  A customer order that designates the time during which it can be executed. (CBOT)

**time spread**  An option strategy most commonly used by floor traders that involves options with the same strike price but different expiration dates. (CBOE)

**time value**  1. The amount by which the option premium exceeds its intrinsic value; time value is a function of time to expiration, volatility and interest rate. (Morgan Stanley Foreign Exchange) 2. One of two major components of the premium of an option; the time value is equal to the difference between the premium and the intrinsic value. (Montreal Exchange) 3. The time value of an option reflects the probability that the option will move into the money. Therefore, the longer the time remaining until expiration of the option, the greater its time value. Sometimes called **extrinsic value**. (FINEX)

**trade balance**  The difference between a nation's imports and exports of merchandise. (CBOT)

**trade house**  A firm that deals in actual commodities. (COMEX)

**trader**  Individuals who buy and sell for their own accounts for short-term profit. Also, an employee of a broker-dealer or financial institution that specializes in handling purchases and sales of securities for the firm or its client. See **investor, speculator**. (NYSE)

**trading halt**  A complete interruption of trading and/or application possibilities at SOFFEX for an individual or for several contracts in one or more accounts of one or several exchange members. (SOFFEX)

**trading post**  The structure on the floor of the New York Stock Exchange at which stocks or options are bought and sold. (NYSE)

**trading rotation**  A trading procedure on exchange floors in which bids and offers are made on specific options in a sequential order. Opening trading rotations are conducted to guarantee all entitled public orders an execution. At times of extreme market activity, a closing trading rotation can also be conducted. (CBOE)

**traditional expiration cycle**    See **cycle**. (CBOE)

**transaction costs**    All of the charges associated with executing a trade and maintaining a position. These include brokerage commissions, exchange fees and margin interest. The spread between bid and ask is sometimes taken into account as a transaction cost. (CBOE)

**transfer**    A term that refers to two different operations: (1) The delivery of a stock certificate from the seller's broker to the buyer's broker and the legal change of ownership, normally accomplished within a few days; (2) To record the change of ownership on the books of the corporation by the transfer agent. When the purchaser's name is recorded, dividends, notices of meetings, proxies, financial reports and all pertinent literature sent by the issuer to its securities holders are mailed directly to the new owner. See **registrar, street name**. (NYSE)

**transfer agent**    An agent who keeps a record of the name and address of each registered shareowner and the number of shares owned. The transfer agent sees that certificates presented for transfer are properly canceled and new certificates issued in the name of the new owner. See **registrar**. (NYSE)

**Treasury bill option strategy**    See **ninety/ten strategy**. (CBOE)

**treasury stock**    Stock issued by a company but later reacquired. It may be held in the company's treasury indefinitely, reissued to the public or retired. Treasury stock receives no dividends and has no vote while held by the company. (NYSE)

**turnover rate**    The volume of shares traded in a year as a percentage of total shares listed on an exchange, outstanding for an individual issue or held in an institutional portfolio. (NYSE)

**type**    The classification of an option contract as either a put or a call. (OCC)

**uncovered call option writing**    A short call option position in which the writer does not own the shares of underlying stocks represented by his or her option contracts. (OCC)

**uncovered put option writing**    A short put option position in which the writer does not have a corresponding short stock position or has not deposited in a cash account cash or cash equivalents equal to the exercise value of the put. (OCC)

**underlying**    The merchandise that can be purchased (in the case of a call option) or sold (in the case of a put option) when the option is exercised. (Montreal Exchange)

**underlying commodity**    The commodity or futures contract on which a commodity option is based, and which must be accepted or delivered if the option is exercised. (FINEX)

**underlying instrument**    The security, index or other financial instrument that a contract refers to. (SOFFEX)

**undervalued**  An adjective used to describe an option that is trading at a price lower than its theoretical value. It must be remembered that this is a subjective evaluation because theoretical value depends on one subjective input—the volatility estimate. (CBOE)

**underwriter**  See **investment banker**. (NYSE)

**unit of trading**  The minimum quantity or amount allowed when trading a security. The normal minimum for common stock is one round lot or 100 shares. The normal minimum for options is one contract (which covers 100 shares of stock). (CBOE)

**unlisted stock**  A security not listed on a stock exchange. See **over-the-counter market**. (NYSE)

**upstairs trader**  A professional trader who makes trading decisions away from the exchange floor and communicates instructions to the floor for execution by the floor broker. (CBOE)

**uptick**  A term used to designate a transaction made at a price higher than the preceding transaction. Also called a *plus tick*. A *zero-plus* tick is a term used for a transaction at the same price as the preceding trade, but higher than the preceding different price. Conversely, a *downtick*, or *minus tick*, is a term used to designate a transaction made at a price lower than the preceding trade. A plus sign, or a minus sign, is displayed throughout the day next to the last price of each stock at the trading post on the floor of the New York Stock Exchange. (NYSE)

**variable annuity**  A life insurance policy where the annuity premium (a set amount of dollars) is immediately turned into units of a portfolio of stocks. Upon retirement, the policyholder is paid according to accumulated units, the dollar value of which varies according to the performance of the stock portfolio. Its objective is to preserve, through stock investment, the purchasing value of the annuity which otherwise is subject to erosion through inflation. (NYSE)

**variable limit**  A price system that allows for larger than normally allowable price movements under certain conditions. In periods of extreme volatility, some exchanges permit trading at price levels that exceed regular daily limits. (NFA)

**variation margin**  Profits or losses on open futures positions that are paid or collected daily. (Montreal Exchange)

**vega**  The rate of change of an options premium with respect to volatility. A portfolio with a positive vega implies that it will gain in value if volatility rises but will decline in value if volatility falls. (New Zealand Futures & Options Exchange)

**versus cash**  See **exchange for physicals**. (CBOT)

**vertical spreads**  Buying and selling puts or calls of the same expiration month but different strike prices. (CBOT)

**volatility**    The extent of the actual or anticipated price fluctuation of a share. The measured volatility for an instrument can be different according to the life span to which it relates. It may be rated as either historical or implied volatility. (SOFFEX)

**volatility test**    A procedure in which a multisided option position is evaluated, assuming several different volatilities for the purpose of judging the risk of the position. (CBOE)

**volume**    The number of shares or contracts traded in a security or an entire market during a given period. Volume is usually considered on a daily basis and a daily average is computed for longer periods. (NYSE)

**volume of trading**    The number of contracts traded during a specified period of time. It can be quoted as the number of contracts traded or in terms of the total physical units, such as bales or bushels, pounds or dozens. (FINEX)

**voting right**    The common stockholders' right to vote their stock in the affairs of a company. Preferred stock usually has the right to vote when preferred dividends are in default for a specified period. The right to vote may be delegated by the stockholder to another person. See **cumulative voting, proxy**. (NYSE)

**warehouse receipt**    A document issued by an exchange-approved storage facility showing possession of the commodity named. (COMEX)

**warrant**    A certificate giving the holder the right to purchase securities at a stipulated price within a specified time limit or perpetually. Sometimes a warrant is offered with securities as an inducement to buy. See **rights**. (NYSE)

**wasting asset**    An asset that has a limited life and tends to decrease in value over time. (OCC)

**when issued**    A short form of "when, as and if issued." The term indicates a conditional transaction in a security authorized for issuance but not as yet actually issued. All when-issued transactions are on an "if" basis, to be settled if and when the actual security is issued and the exchange or National Association of Securities Dealers rules the transactions are to be settled. (NYSE)

**wirehouse**    See **futures commission merchant**. (NFA)

**working control**    Theoretically, ownership of 51 percent of a company's voting stock is necessary to exercise control. In practice—and this is particularly true in the case of a large corporation—effective control sometimes can be exerted through ownership, individually or by a group acting in concert, of less than 50 percent. (NYSE)

**writing options**    Selling options. (Morgan Stanley Foreign Exchange)

**yield**    The dividends or interest paid by a company expressed as a percentage of the current price. A stock with a current market value of $40 a share paying dividends at the rate of $3.20 is said to return 8 percent ($3.20/$40). The current yield on a bond is figured the same way. Also known as return. (NYSE)

**yield curve**   A chart in which yield level is plotted on the vertical axis and the term to maturity of debt instruments of similar creditworthiness is plotted on the horizontal axis. (NFA)

**yield to maturity**   The yield of a bond to maturity takes into account the price discount from or premium over the face amount. It is greater than the current yield when the bond is selling at a discount and less than the current yield when the bond is selling at a premium. (NYSE)

**zero coupon bond**   A bond that pays no interest but is priced, at issue, at a discount from its redemption price. (NYSE)

# INDEX